CRIME THROUGH TIME

Stephen Richards

Mirage Publishing

A *Mirage Publishing Book*

Publishers of Investigative authors
Investigative authors welcome to submit manuscripts

New Hardback

Published in Great Britain
By Mirage Publishing 2003

Copyright © Stephen Richards 2003

A CIP catalogue record for this book
is available from the British Library.

ISBN 1 902578 17 1

Mirage Publishing
PO Box 161
Gateshead
NE8 4WW
Great Britain

Printed and bound in Great Britain by
C P Print Ltd, Dunston, Tyne & Wear NE11 9EL

© Cover design and layout Sharon Anderson - Artistic Director

We have endeavoured to contact copyright holders.
Any that were untraceable – please contact us.

CONTENTS

For Ray,

I hope that one day you find your pot of gold, but even so, it wouldn't be as valuable as your business acumen has been to me, thanks.

FOREWORD
by
John Blake

Scandals have long been the food of the media, without the daily serving of front page headlines that grab our attention we might be served a diet of boring mish-mash. Having worked in the newspaper industry before entering the world of book publishing I helped manufacture some of those appealing headlines.

Within the features offering an insight in to the scandalous behavour of the famous and not so famous there are often some keywords that get overlooked. On closer examination a story, for instance, relating to a sexual scandal might contain elements of blackmail, betrayal, infidelity, murder, fear of exposure by the media and desperate measures that only add to the depth of the scandal.

The ingredients that make up a scandal can either make it worthy of front page news or a full scale international incident. Eventually, when the news of such a scandal dies down we are left with questions that need answered. Those questions are often answered in the form of a book such as a biography, autobiography or an investigative review, such as in the instance of the death of Lady Diana.

By reading this book I hope it is able to help you understand the frailties and weaknesses of mankind by virtue of it touching upon some of the more sensitive stories.

John Blake

Blake Publishing a comprehensive catalogue of true crime titles.
The Official web site of Blake Publishing - Unrivalled Publishers
http://www.blake.co.uk

X

Introduction

HISTORY IN THE MAKING!!!
IS THIS THE P T BARNUM OF THE 20th CENTURY???

Andy Jones ... seen here in the early 1980's as moody-like, dark and sinister looking bassist of Gloucester's cult rock band *Kiss The Blade.* Prior to this, Andy played a key role in performing in the earlier formed infamous punk rock band *Demob.*

The metamorphosis from punk rocker to survivalist businessman has catapulted Andy through various stages of transition to become the foremost authority on what he collects. Born 19 November 1961, the streetwise upbringing on a council estate firmly embedded Andy with a pride in his roots.

A one time wild-child of heavy metal, plasterer, builder, doorman and personal protection operative has paved the way to reveal a man of deep integrity and trusted confidante of many well-known figures.

Andy, since the age of 15, is an obsessive collector of all sorts. Here, within, is a brief insight for you, the reader, into the largest privately owned True Crime collection of its kind in the world.

Nicholson House, Newent in the 1880's. Formerly the town's Police Station and Courthouse

Andy is the curator and owner of the ever-controversial Crime Through Time Museum based in Newent, Gloucestershire.

www.crimethroughtime.com

The infamous Crime Through Time Museum at the haunted property Nicholson House is prominently situated in the historical market town in the centre of Newent, Gloucestershire. Already steeped in local history and notoriety this late Victorian building is exceptionally unique in that it is the town's former magistrates' court, police station and police house complete with its very own small, but chilling, cell block. It was the areas only 'lock up' provision in bygone times for those in need of punishment or restraint - the perfect property to house a crime museum.

The grounds of Nicholson House and the grounds of their immediate surrounds formerly being the land owned by the monks of the old priory has its very roots established in the realms of medieval justice. Prior to this property forming an essential part of the Victorian correctional system within the region the land had sacrificed itself with a bizarre, sinister and sadistic past. **1298:** Records show that a medieval tithe barn stood here.

Crime Through Time

1558: Crowds of onlookers gathered and stood here to witness the horrific death of Edward Horne a controversial protestant martyr who was tried, condemned and then horrifically burnt to death close to the lawn in front of Nicholson House.

1660: During the reign of Charles II there was a witch's ducking stool housed at the museum where upon unfortunate wretches were tried and drowned as alleged witches into Peacocks brook. The brook still to this day runs alongside the rear of this property. Some say the lost souls of these poor drowned wretches can be seen when the reflection of a full moon shines off the brook!

Nicholson House is regarded as being one of the towns most haunted properties and allegedly still occupied by one of the witches drowned at the time. Rest assured there is certainly something odd going on here. It is claimed by locals that a headless monk still haunts the land and walks the adjoining lake at night.

1882: The original police house was extended to provide the town with its very own historically important magistrates' court and police station. During this period many infamous local characters and rogues were held there and charged at the court. One character in particular held at the original police station being the notorious local solicitor Edmund Edmunds. His wife had died in mysterious circumstances in 1867, the body was later exhumed in Newent some five years after her death and this resulted in him being charged with manslaughter and was brought before the Newent magistrates. After hearing a brief summary of the evidence and deliberating for some 30 minutes they returned a verdict of wilful murder. He was later to be tried by a jury in Gloucester and was acquitted in just 16 minutes.

1975: Used as such until its controversial closure. Another notorious person to be held in the cells and charged at Newent magistrates' court in his petty criminal days was local infamous character Fred West, one of Britain's worst serial killers who later cheated justice by hanging himself in his prison cell in January

Introduction

1995 whilst on remand awaiting trial with his wife Rose West for the now infamous 25 Cromwell Street murders that took place in Gloucester.

The property was later sold to the National Federation of 18 Plus Group hence the property title name of Nicholson House, being named and retained after its founder member. It had become their national headquarters as well as being a residential hostel and meeting place for organisations in and around Newent.

1998 May: Nicholson House was acquired by new owners subsequently to become, in part, a family home and in the main to house the astonishing private collection and legacy of the, some say, controversial and infamous figure Andy Jones. A new era begins and its bizarre, sinister and sadistic past is reborn.

1998 1st August: The doors to the museum officially opened attracting a great deal of celebrity, media and public interest. Let's face it, we all have skeletons in our cupboard and many are on show at the museum. By no means a particularly large museum it is pleasantly proportioned retaining its simple design layout, as was originally built and later extended in 1882. The police cells and courtroom on their own are of great historical significance to the town of Newent and have been retained and preserved by owners past and present. For the first time in its history these features and much, much, more are open for public viewing providing a simple and chilling reminder of times past and present.

There are a great many places of interest in and around this small historic market town of Newent. Regarded by many as the Black Museum of Gloucestershire, Crime Through Time at the haunted property of Nicholson House is an unrestrained repository crammed full of disturbing and bizarre crimes and events to provide stark and blunt reminders of genocide, tabloid sensationalism, fetishism, sadism, titillation and fantasies that appear to derive from them in past and present time a diverse collection to say the least.

HUMAN SKIN TABLE LAMP

Crime Through Time

A carnival of carnage is explored and revealed to the onlooker, mesmerising them with an uncanny connection to the past. Many visitors have been painfully awakened from their sedate and ordinary lives by the revelations awaiting them. Some of the most bizarre exhibits await you – the table lamp made from human skin, soap bars made from human fat are a legacy from the holocaust, sure to send shivers up your spine!

The unique private collection has and will continue to be the focus of much media attention attracting visitors from all over the world to the only museum of its kind throughout the world. For visitors with vivid imaginations and an open mind, rest assured Crime Through Time will inevitably be regarded as housing one of the world's finest and, certainly in many ways, shocking and chilling collections ever exhibited on public display. Arguably offensive in parts but what do you honestly expect to see in a crime museum anyway, if easily offended and of a sensitive nature, sadly the best option is not to come in. New pieces are being constantly added to the collection.

Displays include the Grim Reaper, guillotine and body cages, instruments of punishment and torture, a seriously sad and disturbing exhibition relating to the Nazi Holocaust years including genuine death camp and Nazi SS uniforms, insignia, etc.

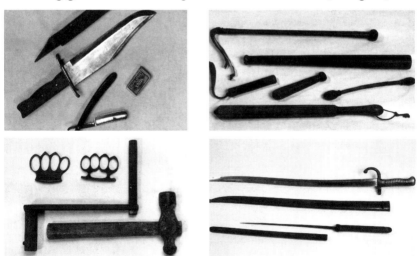

'TOOLS OF THE TRADE'
ONCE OWNED, USED AND CARRIED BY THE KRAY TWINS AND THE FIRM

Introduction

Oswald Mosley's Blackshirts/fascism in Britain, Ku Klux Klan uniform insignia, etc. Cons to Icons insight including personal exhibit items. The works and personal exhibits by the man the press have described as Britain's maddest, baddest, hardest and most dangerous prisoner in the UK, Charles Bronson. Tools and weapons used by the criminal underworld, an impressive collection of British and foreign police items including police weapons, uniforms and insignias. Bizarre fetishes, titillation and fantasies - an interesting collection of, the so say, tools of the trade.

Indonesian fertility statue, dare you touch the forbidden fruit? (Pregnancy is not guaranteed.) An impressive pictorial history of crime including a large collection of autographed material from world-renowned infamous real life alleged criminals and popular fiction TV, cinema screen characters and glamour queens and a small collectors souvenir curiosity shop.

INDONESIAN FERTILITY STATUE - DARE YOU TOUCH IT ??

Crime Through Time

Museum: *Gibbets 'break advertising rules'*

Cameras to roll at crime museum

by Julia Etherington

Cages rattle plans bosses

by Ron Gardiner

THE CITIZEN . MONDAY OCTOBER 19TH 1998

'Torture and terror' in former police station

INSTRUMENTS of torture and terror are packed into a former police station in Newent — bringing people from across the country to gaze on death and destruction.

The small town has become host to a rather unusual museum dedicated to crime and punishment which opened its doors to the public last month.

'Crime through Time' features such delights as mass murderer Denis Neilson's police uniform and a display dedicated to the Cray brothers.

Examples of French and English guillotines are on offer alongside stocks, knives and knuckledusters.

The collection is housed in Newent's former police station and court building, which itself dates from 1878, and is the brainchild of Andy Jones who has moved with his family into the adjoining police house.

Mr Jones, who runs an architectural business, has been collecting crime memorabilia for 15 years.

The museum has attracted a pleasing number of visitors in its first four weeks of opening, despite one lady who left with an experience to remember.

"We had a young woman who ran out screaming because she thought she'd been touched by a ghost," said museum volunteer Mel Davies who donated his own police memorabilia collection to the display.

"I haven't seen anything in the building but there is a definite atmosphere down by the cells.

"There is also a strong smell of cigarettes even though nobody here smokes," he said.

The building is undoubtedly full of history are protestant martyrs were

THE cameras are rolling once more at Newent's controversial but increasingly popular Crime Through Time museum.

The tourist attraction, a magnet for publicity since it was first opened in October 1998, has once caught the eyes of HTV bosses and will feature on their Crime Holidays programme currently being filmed.

The museum has more under fire from townsfolk and visitors.

Set up by owner Andy Jones, Crime Through Time records the deeds of many of Britain's most infamous villains and has already featured on Channel Four's Cutting Edge programme.

Mr Jones said: "HTV have chosen Newent and the Forest of Dean as one of the more attractive places to visit, which is great.

"They're filming parts of the museum and I think they want to show how intriguing it is for many people, but at the same time show that it's not everybody's cup of tea and let viewers make up their own minds.

"They don't want to film too many of the pieces inside because they feel it might be too gruesome, which I think is sensible."

The museum's information and exhibits relate to the crimes of notorious characters like Mr Jones's personal friend, the prisoner Charles Bronson, Dr Crippen and London's Kray twins, as well as others in the pipeline.

Crime Through Time has brought Newent much publicity, and Mr Jones claims despite offers to move his museum to London, he remains committed to bringing it back to Newent.

"The number of visitors is increasing all the time and it will hopefully continue to boost the economy of Newent and of the Forest of Dean generally."

CRIME museum boss has been told he is breaking the law himself and could be taken to court for using macabre iron body cages in public display.

Andy Jones, owner of the new Crime Through Time museum at Newent, said it was "daft" for Forest of Dean District Council officials to insist they want advertisements which required planning permission.

"I suppose I could stick a tulip in them and call them hanging baskets," he said Andy.

The gibbets were used centuries ago to shame and deter low offenders — or display dead ones as a warning.

Mr Jones is refusing to take them down from the entrance to his museum in the former police station and court, which is already attracting visitors from all over the country.

On Saturday he put a grotesque dummy he had made in one cage, purporting to be a punishment victim who had been hanging for five years with parts of his body picked away by birds...

"The enforcement officer from the council said they were going to take me to court but I told him if he wasn't careful I would hang him up in one of the cages to embarrass him," said Mr Jones.

He is already in trouble with planners for taking down an old iron brick wall around his property and putting up a higher natural stone wall which they say was done without permission. It has been dubbed the Great Wall of Newent.

"Everybody tells me it's a nicer attraction on the way to the lake and there would be uproar if I was forced to take it down," said Mr Jones.

Martin Hillier, planning officer for Newent, said: "We are pursuing enforcement action against Mr Jones for a breach of the advertising regulations because of the body cages and the planning regulations for the wall."

He said it was a means of drawing attention to the size of the property so it has an advertisement.

"If a Sainsbury hung up a fish outside his shop that would be advertising his business and this is the same," he said.

...me memorabilia: a guillotine and pair of handcuffs on show at a new museum of crime and punishment in Newent

'Slap me in irons'

Torture for tourists

by Andrew Morrell

ANDY JONES had a problem. He had nowhere to keep his growing collection of knives, knuckledusters and an original French Revolution guillotine. So he bought a former police station and magistrates' court — dating from the 1800s — in Newent, Gloucestershire. He has amused his...

Mr Jones, who runs an architectural business that specialises in reclaim...

Museum in clash over Nazi scenes

by Andrew Morrell

A NEWENT museum owner defended his popular tourist attraction after a family complained their six-year-old son had become hysterical after a visit.

In their letter of complaint, the family and the Crime Through Time Museum in the centre of the market town was discussed with the Nazis and featured images of bondage.

The family, who do not want to be named, said when they visited the attraction at the end of August they found the displays offensive and left Newent feeling depressed, calling the museum an evil place and sending never to return to the town.

Andy Jones, who manages the

emotions, said the Forest of Dean District Council had passed on the letter to him.

He said he found the suggestion that he had an obsession with the Nazis and the death of Jews primarily offensive.

"Crime Through Time is not passed together to create a pleasant type of visitor attraction," he said. "Crime itself is not pleasant, and neither should it be presented in such a way.

"There are simple signs both outside and inside the museum, as well as in the museum brochure, pointing out that there is a fairly accurate insight into what to expect.

"It was never the intention of the material on display would be found shocking by some.

That was why there were a number of signs clearly evident before anyone entered the museum, warning visitors not to enter if they were easily offended.

Signs also stated clearly, said Mr Jones, that children were welcome at their premises.

Rachel Lewis, of tourism and marketing services at the Forest of Dean District Council, said the council had received the family's letter and automatically acknowledged it.

Mr Jones as they would with any other business.

She said: "Writing to Mr Jones was standard procedure.

When we receive a complaint we forward the contents to the establishment and that is what we did in this case. Obviously it is a person's point of view by the family and everyone has an individual viewpoint."

Museum set for the TV spotlight

by Andrew Morrell

CRIME may be one of the public's biggest enemies — but it seems the appetite for information on its most notorious exponents is as great as ever...

...led to Dean town chiefly evident before making anyone entered the museum, warning...changing visitors not to enter if they were easily offended.

...rough amount to planning...

...ewent, ...re part

...said: ...is case. ...rs are ...used to

around the town to attract people to the museum and the irons are part of the display.

"There is not a chance I will take them down. If it goes to court I will win the case

and I will sue for costs for wasting time."

Mr Jones, who opened the museum July after spending 15 years amassing collection, added that he had a mass guillotine on the front lawn with a Reaper figure next to it, but these were regarded as advertising by the planne...

The museum is in a former police tion and magistrates' court in Newen contains criminal and police paraph lia from all over the world.

Yesterday Andrew Grenyar, a Fore Dean district council planning officer responsibility for enforcement, said: have pointed out to him that these tures are advertisements and that would like to see an application for th

"If push comes to shove I would re mend to have court action taken alth we don't want to if we can avoid it Jones is being stubborn shall we say..."

CONTROVERSIAL...NAH!!!!!!!!

No Action on Hitler advert

Andy Jones with the offending 'A' board

Crown prosecutors (CPS) decided that there was no action to take against the Crime Through Time museum's 'A' board bearing a near naked Hitler being crucified to a Swastika. Police in Gloucester had received a number of complaints and passed it on to the CPS.

Hitler is shown contorted over the Swastika with the Jewish Star of David behind it. Andy Jones was visited by police in August 2001 and told no further action would be taken. Andy Jones says: "For me the sign symbolises the Nazi Holocaust years for which Hitler sacrificed himself in the end." The sign was used as a warning of what lay ahead on display in the museum in order to forewarn potential visitors of the emotive exhibits within.

The cover of this book bears a more graphic composition of the sign, which signifies the Star of David shining through all adversity and that Hitler had created his own downfall – good overcoming evil. Although at first glance it may seem offensive by those reading evil into it, that was never the intention when first designed.

Crime Through Time

Together with his father, Ron, and brother Darren Andy Jones helps run Ronsons Architectural Salvage based at Norton Village, Gloucestershire.

RON and ANDY JONES...2001

Ronsons operates from Norton Barns, Wainlodes Lane, Norton, Gloucestershire. The picturesque entrance to Ronsons and Norton Barns is rather misleading, pass through the gateway and you enter a tract of organised chaos – an, apparently, haphazard jumble of aged artefacts and materials rescued from demolished buildings of every age.

Incredibly some 30,000+ visitors per year come to this pioneering company to marvel at a treasure trove of architectural salvage, often buying an original piece of history to install in their own home or to provide a romantic reminder of the past in their garden.

Ronsons Reclamation & Restoration offers a unique and comprehensive display of reclaimed and recycled building materials and artefacts complete with their own original and venerable 'lyching' – dirt grime and woodworm to you and me.

You may have to rummage around to find what you want, but it's almost certainly there. Church pews, oak and elm timbers, bricks, slates, flagstones, roof tiles, chimney pots, cast iron roll top baths, suits of armour and just about everything else including the kitchen sink (Victorian or Edwardian naturally).

Popular with architects, landscapers and builders, interior designers, local authorities, breweries and theme parks Norton Barns is an important and valuable educational resource not only in supply terms but also allowing both adults and children to experience a visual and hands on encounter with the past.

Introduction

If you feel that the world of reclamation, restoration and recycling is not quite your thing then just go and watch the craftsmen at work using traditional methods that have changed little throughout the centuries reusing reclaimed and recycled materials.

No action on Hitler advert

by Britta Priebe

"This sign is a warning to give visitors the opportunity to choose whether they want to go in or not."

Andy Jones

Crime museum stays locked up

by Ron Gardiner

Rattled: Andy Jones with the body cage at the centre of a planning row

Nicholson House: Planning row

Wall battle at new museum

by Ron Gardiner

ANDY Jones is ready to defy the planners over the new stone wall outside the law and order museum he is opening in Newent at the end of the month.

The controversial wall of reclaimed Forest stone which has replaced the red brick wall outside Nicholson House.

Norton: Planning dispute

'I'll go to jail if necessary' says recycler

by Hugh Worsnip

Ronsons will run the risk of prison sentence

Could Ron and son, Andy, be the Steptoe & Son of the Architectural Salvage Industry – In the salvage industry there is no such thing as rubbish!!

Andy Jones on his father:

"He's a great power of strength to me."

How on earth my Mother tolerates his overwhelming adrenalin and get up and go is astonishing.

"Without a big wad of cash in his pocket for wheeling and dealing - it wouldn't be Ron."

"A true old-school character."

"I owe a great deal to my old man for giving me the benefit of a streetwise upbringing...dragged up!!"

Behind every great man is a great woman...and that's my Mother for him.

"His East End (Wormwood Scrubs) background gave him a head start... am I a chip off the old block - guilty m'lord."

"All in all a great guy."

Introduction

Andy Jones – Background Dossier

PLASTERED: Served a plastering apprenticeship at Brunel Technical College, Bristol. Ex-plastering, building, demolition and reclamation contractor. Had the bailiffs hammering at his door more than once during the course of running these businesses, but always managed to overcome 'cash flow' problems by using the robbing Peter to pay Paul scenario although was once on the brink of bankruptcy and voluntary liquidation. Tax and VAT problems have been overcome along with the usual 'death threats.' Was once quoted as saying, *"You haven't lived until you've experienced similar problems."* It's rumoured that Andy has a wardrobe full of T-shirts with the motto 'I've been there' emblazoned on the front.

ANGELS WITH DIRTY FACES: Had the benefit of a turbulent streetwise upbringing alongside the wild and raunchy punk and heavy rock days all of which Andy attributes to having been "great times" in his life. Lack of confidence has been overcome by using the experiences from difficult times. Although not a man to back down from conflicts he believes in the Winston Churchill ethos of 'jaw, jaw before war, war.' Another Jones quote: *"In my view at the end of the day even if you're stinking rich, financially stable or poor, we are still all equals. We came into the world naked, with nothing and we go out in the same way."*

MAKE MY DAY, PUNK: Punk and heavy rock days are lost in the mists of time when marriage changes his previous desires and values. Was a member and bass guitar player in various punk bands. Almost became a pro footballer but opted for punk rock bands instead. Supports Chelsea even though he says: *"It's like supporting a foreign football club."* Played in bands 'Demob', 'Focal Point' and 'Kiss The Blade'.

MUSIC: Always loved the more controversial raunchy bands and for his sins he thought the band Bay City Rollers was great – plenty of girl followers to tag on to. Sweet, Gary Glitter, Alice Cooper, Slade, Marc Bolan and T-Rex musically influenced the young Andy Jones. When having drifted into the punk and heavy rock days his favourite bands included singer Billy Idol and Generation X, UK Subs, Sex Pistols, Siouxsie and the Banshees,

The Stranglers, 999, Angelic Upstarts, Skrewdriver, The Clash, Sham 69 and The Ruts. Also likes Ska bands - The Specials, The Beat and Madness. Heavy Rock: Motorhead, Iron Maiden & Ozzy Osbourne

SHAGGED AND FAGGED OUT: Andy has been identified as having toured the country watching great bands, having great fights and great shags...great times. In spite of this he has never been to prison as an inmate but has been locked up plenty of times for D & D (Drunk and Disorderly) and fighting. Spent many a night sleeping in old sheds, cardboard boxes and on park benches, etc. Has, believe or not, never touched drugs or even smoked a cigarette – always acquainted with alleged rough and ready characters, drug dealers, hookers, racketeers, etc but he couldn't be bothered with all that nonsense...preferred to do his own thing and always seemed to have a great time. Loads of drink consumed and when the heat was on could be relied on.

SKELETONS IN THE CUPBOARD: Fatal attractions have been plentiful along with three and four in a bed sex sessions and massage parlour visits has broadened his horizons – had hopes of one day owning and running a brothel or massage parlour (called chicken farms in USA). As a punk rocker he took part in some very odd antics i.e. a game called 'pain' to see how many $1\frac{1}{2}$ inch long safety pins could be put through your arm, he once managed forty...blood everywhere and the pain!!!!!!! Had tattoos applied with the pin ends of matches by rubbing them deep into the skin. Once performed a 'love bite' session on a young lady at a party and created a large letter 'A' all over the girl's chest, starting at the bottom of her neck to the waist. The cross member of the 'A' being right across her tits!

GOOD TIME GIRLS: Associated with a good friend, Shaun Thompson - both Jones and Thompson were punk rockers and regularly picked up girls. On one occasion Jones took Thompson over to Cheltenham to lose his virginity with a friend of the girl Jones was with. Jones having done the business with his girl was kept waiting for hours by Thompson. The girl was up for up it when Thompson went running up to his friend Andy and said, "I haven't got any fucking condoms and she's laid down waiting for it?" Andy replied, "Shaun, no problem just be careful, pull it out when you're ready to shoot your load and unload all over her tits." Thompson failed to pull out and shot his load right inside her and then went down on her to give her a muff dive and then said to Andy, "Shit! I think I've made her pregnant?" Andy and Shaun then called into a Fish & Chip shop; Shaun munched into a meat pie and then with all the juice and sauce dripping down his chin asked Andy if he wanted a bite! Andy resented this and told Shaun that he didn't fancy a load of Shaun's cum in his chops. Another incident involving Andy and his friend, they ended up in a four in bed session and Shaun puked over all of them…Andy still classes Shaun as a great guy.

One of Andy's past punk rock stories relates to the time Billy Idol was performing with Generation X in Gloucester at a venue called the 'Jamaica Club'. Andy went there and met up with a young lady, Alison West. An hour later a friend of Andy's went up to him and said, "Andy, guess what, your bird's down there in Billy Idol's changing room giving him a blow job." Jones was intent on revenge and thought about rushing in on Idol but soon changed his mind when the attentions of another lady were on him and ten minutes later Andy was having his own blow job outside…wild, wet and raunchy!

FAIRGROUND BOOTHS: Jones had a few rough and ready punch ups boxing in the famous Taylor booths in Gloucester having to bang ten tons of shite out of each other for three X three-minute rounds for a shitty couple of quid – found it to be good fun. Was unbeaten in the few fights he had, didn't pretend to be a good boxer although he seemed to love 'having a go'. Was more of a street fighter than a boxer so ended up going in with a few head butts and elbows although he never used Tyson's technique of boxing with his teeth! By trying to outbox them he may never have won.

Andy Jones, left, with Mel Smith lookalike, friend, Andy Greenhorn in the late 1970s

Crime Through Time

Surveillance over the years on Andy Jones

Jones loitering in the park with his mother

Looks a bit like Andy now at present time

Andy at Finlay Rd. Infants School
Gloucester

Andy and son Dean

Andy with Jeremy Beadle

Andy with Billy Murray

Foreword to Planning Battleground
Adapted from letters by
Albert Dryden

See further on chapter for fuller explanation
I know how you feel mate!! Almost shot one <u>myself??</u>

After the shooting the police asked all the witnesses to report to the police station at 5pm. Among the witnesses were Mr Cameron, Mr Graham and Mr Armstrong. Sergeant Campbell said to them, "All you had to do was sit down in front of the digger on Albert's side of the fence. The driver would have stopped the job and put the digger back on the low loader." Mr Cameron asked the sergeant why he had not told them that. The sergeant said that Mr Collinson (the deceased) had told him not to help Dryden's friends or Dryden in any way. Mr Graham, Mr Armstrong and the digger driver were not called to give evidence at my trial.

I don't know how to explain it but when I made preparations to defend myself I was whistling in the dark.

I have since sent nine letters to the Home Office with proof of posting but I have not received a single Certificate of Posting. Either my letters are not leaving the prison or the Home Office has ordered that I do not have proof of posting.

They all hate me because of what I did. No wonder... they keep me in a remand prison and 200 miles from home. It is further away from home - 178 miles. So I will get no visitors - 18 of my friends wrote to the Home Office to try to get me nearer home. So they are moving me 40 miles further away!

Planning Battleground

The probation people say that I talk about guns and have a violent temper and will still be a danger to the public 100 years from now.

When I saw the television crews, the newspaper reporters, the police, the mob and the bulldozer and thought of my animals I, sadly, killed a man. Women acting under far less provocation have killed their partners and have not been imprisoned. I think the Home Office is trying to get me to top myself. I am in my cell 22 hours a day. My head is going.

Best wishes, Albert Dryden

Albert Dryden, 62, is serving a life sentence, imposed in April 1992, for the shooting of the chief planning officer of Derwentside District Council (England), Harry Collinson. Mr Collinson was shot at point blank range while serving a demolition notice at Dryden's illegally erected bungalow, in countryside at Butsfield, near Consett, County Durham, in June 1991. Two others were injured - PC Stephen Campbell was shot in the buttocks and a BBC television reporter was hit in the arm by another bullet when the planning dispute ended in tragedy.

Claims by supporters of Mr Dryden say that one prisoner had tried to strangle him with a towel while he was incarcerated in Durham's top security Frankland Prison - a warder rescued him.

Dryden claims Collinson befriended him and guided him on every part of the development of his land with a view to transferring the ownership to a Judge who lived nearby. Mr Dryden invested his life savings in his land and thousands of hours of his labour.

Mr Dryden wrote to the Home Office Tariff Department between August 1994 and December 1996 and was ignored.

Finally in July 1997 the Secretary of State (Straw) wrote: Having recently considered your representations and those submitted on your behalf your tariff has been set afresh at thirteen years in line with the recommendation of the Lord Chief Justice. (Increased from 10 to 13 years!)

http://www.vomituk.com

Crime Through Time
A Family At War (with the planners) - The Jones's

| Lee | Vince | Dave | and Andy Jones |

(A nice head of hair then)

Once there were four brothers ↑
Four became five ↓

From left to right Lee, Darren, Ron, Dave, Andy looking over them all and Vince

The year, 2001. A night out with the old man 'Ron' -
The Guv'nor and four brothers

Andy Jones: "I remember once when I was at primary school...Saintbridge School, Gloucester...me and my brothers nicked a bit of small change from the old man's coat pocket to buy a dripping cake at break time. Before we knew it...the old man came barging into school...dragged us in front of the Headmaster...made us empty our pockets, take off our shoes and socks...holy shit, there was the cash...hidden in my socks! Bloody embarassing or what!! Had to take the wrap...better than grassing anyone up, even then!"

Planning Battleground

Would any of these rebels have tolerated planning constraints?

REBEL WITHOUT A CAUSE
Signed Photo of James Dean, left, and an Andy Jones look-a-like, right

Above signed photo of infamous and notorious libyan leader Colonel Gadaffi - Very Scarce

Above signed award document from Che Guevara the Marxist guerrilla - exceptionally rare

All above items can be seen in original format in the museum

1

Planning Battleground

Find out how these two black magic voodoo dolls were used to bring down two power-hungry officials to the size of ordinary mortals…turn the page to find out.

What goes around comes around???

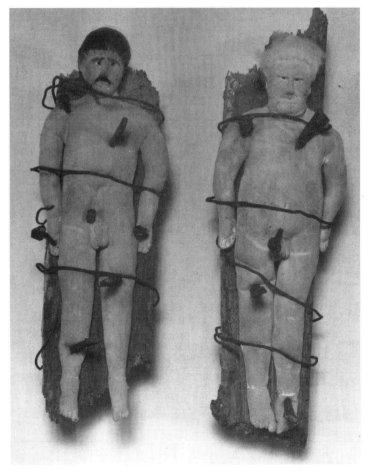

Cor Blimey!!! These geezers look familiar???

Planning Battleground

Alan Martin - Ex-Ass. Planning Officer
Tewkesbury Borough Council

Derek Davies - Ex leader of Tewkesbury
Borough Council

Battles have been fought and lost over land for thousands of years.
An Englishman's home, they say, is his castle (not if you're called
Tony Martin) and land rights have existed and been fought over to
the death, in many cases this still goes on today.

Albert Dryden takes down a planning official

Crime Through Time

In 1991 Albert Dryden was ordered by the courts to demolish a bungalow built below ground level at his Derwentside, County Durham smallholding, which he'd built for his aging mother. Dryden gunned down planning official Harry Collinson in full view of police officers and news teams. Collinson had arrived with the full backing of the law with a demolition order and a demolition team in a jack assed decision that resulted in the death of Collinson and a life prison term for Dryden. Such is life and they say what goes around comes around.

In 1988, using the analogy of Albert Dryden we will see how a planning officer, Alan Martin, eventually got right up the nose of the Jones family…and it was war!!!!!!!!!!!!!

Ronsons Reclamation is a small traditional family run business and as such you would expect the local council to support such enterprises run in the rural community, after all HRH The Prince of Wales, Prince Charles, also runs a similar business – The Duchy of Cornwall. Tewkesbury Borough Council had taken a disliking to the Jones family and compared them akin to gypsies, which could be taken as a compliment or an insult whichever way you looked at it.

Show business entered the lives of the small village of Norton, Tewkesbury, when in October 1992 an auction was held at Ronsons Reclamation and under the hammer fell props from films as diverse as 'Live and Let Die' (James Bond) to 'Indiana Jones'. Madonna's bath, as used in the film 'Shanghai Surprise', and the Tardis used in the 1963 series of Doctor Who were up for grabs in this film props auction. It would seem that such headline grabbing business acumen might have been seen as cockiness by the local elder statesmen on Tewkesbury Borough Council.

1993, 3rd April: The Norton Barns Trust was set up by Andy Jones to promote recycling of building materials and to help provide an educational resource for schools. Primary school teacher, Karen Pritchard, was employed by Andy Jones to set up the project and link it in with the then National Curriculum. Rumours though threatened to bring this project to an end when it was thought that Jones was intending to open a nightclub at the scenic Norton Barns. Private parties were held at the premises and it is thought that this had helped spread the Chinese whispers.

Jones quote: *"...I understand planners will recommend refusals of my proposals, but I feel this would be most unfortunate, as the project is worthwhile and of extreme educational value. I remain optimistic and I mean to pursue this project."*

Tewkesbury Borough Council had received an application from the Trust to change the use of part of the building to an exhibition and display centre. A Planning Committee meeting recommended refusing the change of use. The refusal was based on a narrow country lane not being able to handle increased traffic.

1994 May: On appeal, after a six day hearing permission was granted for the country's first Architectural Heritage Centre, but Ron Jones, Andy's father, was still unhappy about the earlier decision disallowing the project and intended to take Tewkesbury Borough Council (TBC) to court to recover the £80,000 accrued in costs by the Heritage Centre. Norton Barn Trust, a subsidiary of Ronsons Reclamation, was set up with the aim of reclaiming tons of reclaimed items from old buildings in order to form an Architectural Heritage Centre, which would be of use to educational establishments such as schools and colleges. Two enforcement notices placed on the barn by the council were rejected and it would seem a battle had been won, but not the war!

1994 December: The gloves were off and TBC had a nosebleed from the last round, which was won by the Jones family. Now it would seem that TBC were considering asking a judge to step in and enforce their bidding by stopping a proposed Christmas party bash that was planned to be held at the Norton Barns complex.

Council officials tried all sorts of ploys included securing the report from the local Fire Brigade Viz. that there was insufficient means of escape in case of a fire, etc. A council official, Peter Eccleshare, said that there was evidence that public safety was at risk if such a party went ahead. TBC solicitor, Sarah Freckleton, recommended that an injunction be served to stop retailing activities at the Barns, which she claimed was excluded by a government inspector who heard the planning appeal. Call TBC spoilsports or call them pillars of the community in stopping such projects, but it would seem that personal vendettas were being funded by TBC.

1995 April: At a council meeting Andy Jones showered copies of letters down from the public gallery onto the heads of councillors what he deemed was proof of a clash of roles alleging that TBC planning officer Alan Martin had a conflict of interests by also being the Principal of **The Robert Lindsay Planning Consultancy**.

Committee chairman, Councillor Derek Davies said:

> *"During the time of Ronsons planning dispute with the council Mr Jones had conducted a campaign of personal harassment against a senior officer* (**Alan Martin – Planning Officer**). *This involved making written allegations of professional misconduct. The claims have been found to be completely unfounded. I think it very wrong for one of our employees to be harassed in this way, if any evidence could be produced that had any truth in it I would be the first to take action."*

It was at this point that Andy Jones showered the committee with paperwork, shouting: "Here's your evidence." Councillor Davies said afterwards: "There was nothing new in the paperwork Mr Jones threw at us."

The paperwork in question was leaked to Andy Jones by colleagues of Alan Martin from within the TBC Planning Dept…it would seem that Alan Martin had enemies within his department!

Included here is an actual letter that Jones threw down to the committee and you will see it clearly bears the signature of Alan Martin in his role as Principal of The Robert Lindsay Planning Consultancy, during this time Mr Martin was also senior Planning Officer for TBC – was it a conflict of interests…decide for yourselves?

Planning Battleground

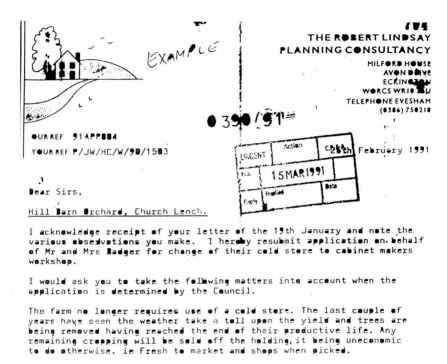

EXAMPLE

**THE ROBERT LINDSAY
PLANNING CONSULTANCY**

MILFORD HOUSE
AVON DRIVE
ECKINGTON
WORCS WR10 3DU
TELEPHONE EVESHAM
(0386) 750218

OUR REF 91APP004

YOUR REF P/JW/HC/W/90/1503

Dear Sirs,

Hill Barn Orchard, Church Lench.

I acknowledge receipt of your letter of the 19th January and note the various observations you make. I hereby resubmit application on behalf of Mr and Mrs Badger for change of their cold store to cabinet makers workshop.

I would ask you to take the following matters into account when the application is determined by the Council.

The farm no longer requires use of a cold store. The last couple of years have seen the weather take a toll upon the yield and trees are being removed having reached the end of their productive life. Any remaining cropping will be sold off the holding, it being uneconomic to do otherwise. ie Fresh to market and shops when picked.

I emphasise my belief that the proposal falls within the terms set out in PPG 4 and draw attention to Para 18 therein. The PPG advises that Conditions should be used where objections arise that can thus be met. In that regard I made reference in my earlier letter to the access and hours of work as well as landscaping and refurbishment for the building.

I have not applied for a temporary permission since some certainty is sought for the prospective tenant. I must leave the Council to decide whether it feels it must seek a time limitation by Condition. If you are able to grant my client a consent but subject to a time limit I should welcome a clear statement as to these matters which will need attention if a renewal is to be successful (or not). This will enable me to adequately advise my client and prospective tenant.

On the question of storage requirements my client does not have a need for 1700sqft but may require a small store. If so he intends to re-erect the small building which you will see is shown on the survey map just to the west of the store.

I stress that there is a genuine need for my client to seek additional support for the holding and this appears to represent the circumstances envisaged by Governmental advice. I hope, therefore, that the Council will feel able to add their support and grant as free a permission as possible.

Yours faithfully,

PRINCIPAL A. MARTIN FRICS. MRTPI

The letter that Andy Jones threw down to the committee - Note signature of Alan Martin

10

1997 June: TBC had their decision that making replica suits of armour was not a craft endorsed by Gloucester County Court. An injunction was granted to TBC in order to have the trade carried on at Ronsons Reclamation stopped, saying they were in breach of planning permission. Because the men making the armour used modern machinery to make the armour it was deemed not to be a craft?

Jones quote: *"I'm going to take Tewkesbury Borough Council (TBC) for a judicial review. If they can't even define what a craft workshop is then they shouldn't be able to decide what's on this site. Under planning permission granted in 1995 the site was reserved for craftsmen."*

It would seem that the daggers were out for the Jones family and that TBC were misusing the public purse to pursue frivolous actions against Ronsons Reclamation purely on an eye for an eye basis! "At no personal cost to themselves !!!"

1997 late June: Rather than back down to the injunction Andy Jones said he was prepared to go to prison.

Deputy District Judge, Clive Major, sitting at Gloucester County Court said, " Mr Jones has been involved in running battles with the council for years about development of his land at Norton Barns."

Jones quote: "...I do not accept that I am in breach of planning laws. If they send me to prison I will have to go. I am doing work to comply with the orders but there are some business principles which I am not prepared to compromise. Tewkesbury Borough Council do not understand the recycling and reclamation industry."

1997 October: The threat of prison loomed over Andy Jones as he was warned he faced prison if he did not comply with planning regulations. Solicitor for TBC, Sarah Freckleton, said, "...We'll be going back to the county court to ask for Mr Jones to be committed to prison." It would seem that TBC were all heart when it came to understanding the requirements of such a business. Although one man who stood alone and applauded what Mr Jones was doing was Councillor Sean Connors who said, "This is an outstanding business and reclamation is only to be applauded."

1998 May: Norton councillors pressed for Andy Jones to be thrown into prison and will brief a barrister to pursue this action because Jones was alleged to have failed to comply with a court injunction. Standing in the public gallery whilst this was being decided was Andy Jones who shouted down to the committee: "You've tried that before and it didn't work." This was the ninth year in which Jones and his father, Ron, had fought a planning battle over their reclamation business.

Councillor Derek Davies, TBC planning chairman quote:

"This man has been the bane of this council. More time and taxpayers money has been spent on this case than any other. This man has done it again. He is a pain in the behind of this council"

Andy Jones: *"I've done everything they've asked of me... I would go to prison over this."*

1998 July: Andy Jones acquires Newent's Nicholson House and was granted planning permission for change of use to become a 'Law & Order' museum and for residential use...maybe things were looking up for Andy – that was until a new stone wall replaced the old red brick wall around the premises and the war was on once again.

A planning contravention notice was served at an early stage and Jones was told to stop work on the wall...the notice was tore up and discarded because Jones claimed permission had already been obtained to build the replacement wall. Councillor David Blick said, "...The new wall is not at all in keeping with the area." Councillor Sheila Smith said, "Now it's finished I think it looks quite nice and is in keeping with the building. Jones was asked to put a retrospective planning application in for the wall.

Crime Through Time

1999 January: Andy Jones faced further action when he was charged with erecting hanging steel torture body cages outside of the museum that contravened advertising regulations!!!!!!!!!! Forest of Dean District Council prosecuted Jones for breach of advertising regulations and the case was brought before Coleford magistrates' court – Jones entered a not guilty plea and the case was adjourned. A complaint was lodged with the Local Government Ombudsman alleging maladminstration by the council and Andy Jones was considering taking civil action for intrusion of privacy because of pictures taken of his property.

> **Andy Jones:** *"I am not going to give in to this at all, it is a point of principal. The Forest of Dean planners lack entrepreneurial skills and don't support the tourism of Newent."*

2001 August: Andy Jones faced criminal charges when an 'A' board outside of the museum advertising the Holocaust Exhibition displays graphic details of Hitler crucified to a Swastika. The advertising board gave rise to complaints from certain alleged members of the public, but as previously mentioned in the introduction the Crown Prosecution Service discontinued their intended action.

Newent Town Council branded the 'Swastika' logo as 'deplorable' and was condemned as a 'celebration of Adolf Hitler' at a meeting of the Recreation, Environment & Planning Committee. The committee expressing disapproval and disgust at the museum issued a statement, the resolution to do so was passed by Councillor Peter Moore. Against the proposal to issue such a statement was level headed Councillor Len Lawton saying, "You can see exactly the same if you visit the London Dungeon."

> **Andy Jones:** *"I have already got full planning consent, which I gained from democratic channels. The reason why the council complains so much now is because they missed the chance to stop it, and the fact they have slipped up is entirely down to them. The museum will carry on with even more signs and exhibitions that will be displayed in the entrance area. To be honest, I am not really bothered about what they have been saying."*

Call Andy Jones a fighter if you want, but in reality he was just doing what has been natural to the citizens of an island that has been fighting off the foe for centuries. Since the year dot the UK has been like a used car, changing hands quite a few times.

Andy Jones beat them all including the Forest of Dean Planning Officer Philip Manser, chief Andrew Grenyer and his sidekick Norman Hale. Local parish Councillor Jeremy Phelps has also become involved in ensuring Ronsons Reclamation is continuously under his eagle eye and, some say, Councillor Phelps is power crazy in his stance against the Norton Barns complex...not surprisingly he has a farm next to Ronsons.

After Ronsons had every bit of ammunition thrown at them at a cost in excess of £300,000 to the local taxpayers they're still standing, TBC failed in their tactical ploys to put an end to a family just looking to make a living and return something to the community. Local councils are supposed to support growing businesses yet in this case it seems to be a flagrant breach of policy in trying to suppress a growing concern that is fast adding culture to the Gloucestershire countryside.

Since first crossing swords with Andy Jones at a planning committee meeting in 1991 when he branded the Jones family as 'Gypsies', Councillor Derek Davies has put a drain on the public purse to pursue what seems like frivolous actions against Andy Jones' business interests in and around the controlled area of TBC and has lost most of the battles along the way. Councillor Davies, nicknamed Henry V111, said he supported local business yet he preferred to set up a business in Cardiff as opposed to his own ward area or even Gloucester.

As Andy Jones once said, *"We all have skeletons in our cupboard,"* so does Councillor Davies, he once stripped down to his underpants at a TBC Christmas party in 1998 and made a fool of himself in front of other councillor colleagues. **(See drawing by Charles Bronson at end of Chapter.)**

The tale of Assistant Borough Planning Officer Alan Martin goes that one day whilst at work the fire alarm went off…all the staff marched out to the car park in an orderly manner for a role check. What they saw on exiting to the car park was the embittered wife of Martin caught red-handed…painting his car as revenge for finding out that he had an affair with one of his colleagues from his office – just a tad embarrassing for Mr Martin. **(See drawing by Charles Bronson at end of Chapter.)**

It would seem that the voodoo dolls had worked their black magic…there doesn't seem to be a modern day law against using such witch craft – so long as you've got planning permission to put the dolls on display (in the museum)! The final coup de grace being in May 2000 when Councillor Derek Davies was ousted from his position as leader of TBC when Conservative and Labour groups joined forces to vote 22 to 10 in favour of scrapping the roles of leader and deputy leader of the council.

> **Councillor Davies:** *"The first time I heard about this was last night. It's pure discourtesy. If we don't need a leader then why do we need a mayor?"*

Andy Jones:

"We beat them all in the end."
"No Gain without Pain."
"Against All The Odd's!!!!"

May 2002… Ronsons is granted planning consent for change of use at it's reclamation site at Norton for residential development… this being despite planning officers recommending refusal. Councillors voted overwhelmingly, in support of Ronsons proposals, even Derek Davies.

Planning Battleground

UK prisoner Charles Bronson gives his opinion

Crime Through Time

UK prisoner Charles Bronson gives his opinion

GARY MILLS

TONY POOLE

2

Mills & Poole - Gloucester's Forgotten Two

On 26th January 1990 Gary Mills and Tony Poole were convicted of the murder of Hensley Hendrix Wiltshire who died in mysterious circumstances whilst in police custody on 6th January 1989. Although Wiltshire was declared dead when taken to hospital there are doubts that he actually died in the hospital.

About midnight 5th/6th January 1989, Hensley Wiltshire is taken to Gloucester Royal Hospital from outside Conduit St by an ambulance.

For over three hours he refuses to tell hospital staff or the police, who attend, how he came about his injuries. He is aggressive in his response to questions, repeatedly telling officers to "fuck off", and "leave me alone". At about four O'clock in the morning, (6th January), Wiltshire is arrested for a serious sexual assault and a murder, due to

information received from the Met. Soon after this he is conveyed to Gloucester Police Station.

Sgt Worrallo, the custody officer, is not happy about Wiltshire's condition and calls in the Police Surgeon. Around 5am Dr Chaudhuri arrives and examines the prisoner. Sgt Worrallo, Dr Chaudhuri and, indeed, Wiltshire himself all agree that he should be in hospital, so the doctor orders him to be returned to GRH.

Just after 5.30am, Wiltshire arrives back at GRH. This time he is much more co-operative and is again fully examined and found to have no internal injuries. Some X-rays are taken but these are clear. Wiltshire is now walking around unaided in the treatment room.

At 6am the Police Surgeon, Dr Chaudhuri receives a telephone call from the Casualty doctor, Dr Fletcher, to say returned to the Police Station as treatment has been concluded.

Dr Chaudhuri tells Dr Fletcher that he is not happy about Wiltshire being returned to the cells and that he thinks he should be admitted to hospital. Dr Fletcher's response to this is to tell the Police Surgeon that Wiltshire has been fully treated, and is much improved since his last visit to GRH. Dr Fletcher also says that Wiltshire has only superficial injuries and hasn't any broken bones, and is probably faking. This was the general consensus of opinion by most of the hospital staff and police officers that came into contact with Wiltshire.

Wiltshire arrives back at the station around 6.30am. At one point during transit he says to a police officer, "...don't do me over, I couldn't take it". This is rather a strange comment to make if one has not been threatened, and has been treated as compassionately as the police claim. Over the next few hours, Wiltshire is heard moaning and asking for help.

At approximately 10am, two prisoners, Mark Singh and John Osmond, arrive from Gloucester prison and are taken to the cells whilst waiting to be produced at magistrates' court. They hear moaning and loud noises coming from the female cell area. They look in on the cell and see Wiltshire lying on the mattress clearly in distress with blood all over his face.

Two other prisoners, Dave Bolton and Tim Lordan, also hear banging and shouts for help during the morning, and the police respond by shouting, "Shut up, you black bastard."

At 11.30am DC Geenty along with Sgt Norgate and DS Turley arrest Wiltshire for possession of an offensive weapon. Then at 11.54am DC Geenty, DS Turiey, Sgt Norgate and PC Easter enter the cell to dress Wiltshire in a paper boiler suit so that he can be questioned in the presence of a solicitor.

All these police officers except Geenty clearly remember and record in statements that Wiltshire's head "makes contact with the wall".

The attempt to dress Wiltshire in the boiler suit was unsuccessful so the officers left the cell.

Just after this, PC Easter takes Paul Griffin, the duty solicitor, to Wiltshire's cell where DC Geenty is waiting for him.

When Mr Griffin arrives everything is quiet, and there is no sign of any emergency in the cell area, until he enters the cell and sees "blood everywhere." Geenty nudges Wiltshire to let him know his solicitor has arrived, Wiltshire's head goes back and from his throat he emits what Mr Griffin could only describe as "a death rattle". Geenty begins mouth to mouth and calls for assistance. Supt. Bennet arrives and gives heart massage.

> "IT'S PROBABLY ONE OF THE WORST NEGLECTS OF DUTY I'VE SEEN IN THE FIVE YEARS I'VE BEEN LOOKING AT CUSTODY RECORDS"
> - ex-police Sergeant Michael Kitson

At 12.20pm the ambulance crew arrive and also try to resuscitate Wiltshire for a time. During this period Dr Chaudhuri arrives and administers an injection. At 12.50pm Wiltshire is taken to Gloucester Royal Hospital where more attempts are made to revive him, but at 3.30pm on the 6th January 1989 Wiltshire is officially declared dead.

On the 10th anniversary, 2000, of the conviction of Gary Mills and Tony Poole Bristol supporters of the two men decided to inform the public about this miscarriage of justice by hanging a banner across a motorway bridge.

Another action took place in Cheltenham where activists rallied and released 574 balloons to symbolize each week Gary and Tony had spent in prison. They then went to police headquarters to demand that criminal charges be brought against D.I. Gladding.

A High Court ruled that Gladding had perjured himself and perverted the course of justice when he threatened a key witness not to attend court – the police have taken no action against this man, why? Fabricated police evidence has been proven and payments being made to a witness and evidence withheld, the CCRC (Criminal Case Review Commission) has still not referred the case back to the court of appeal.

The CCRC is, in my opinion, an arm of the law that acts for the prosecution and should be abolished. Two cases I have been working on very recently warrant a referral back to the courts – one case was turned down flat whilst the CCRC refuse to become involved in a clear breach of the law by HM Prison Service in not allowing a prisoner, Morgan Duffy, access to a journalist – an act of perverting the course of justice.

Under the Symms & O'Brien ruling made by the House of Lords a prisoner has a right to a meeting with any member of the media he so elects to speak to about his claim for injustice or prison conditions. Both HM Prison Service and the government, assisted by an

MP, have abused legal rights to two UK prisoners other than the ones this chapter relates to. What chance has Mills and Poole to a bite at freedom?

Both Mills and Poole refuse to accept the guilt placed upon them and are refusing to apply for parole and therefore cannot win their freedom. Accepting parole is an acknowledgement of guilt and neither is prepared to compromise their 'innocent' status by taking the offer of parole, which of course the authorities would like to have happened in order to gag the pair of them including their loyal supporters.

Legal Aid is not an option available to the pair therefore all legal lawyers acting on their behalf have done work on a pro bono basis.

The Court of Appeal clearly felt deep unease at the actions of DI Gladding. Indeed, the appeal judges described his course of action as "most unwise" and "reprehensible" yet they claim that no unfairness occurred. With respect, that is ridiculous. In *Hui*

Chi Ming v Regina (1992) an abuse of process was defined as: "something so unfair and wrong that the court should not allow a prosecutor to proceed with what is in all other respects a regular proceeding." In the recent case of former Detective Inspector Trevor Gladding v Channel Four, David Jessel and Headline Publications, the jury unanimously decided 11-0 (one juror had been dismissed) that the defendants had justifiably accused Gladding of perverting the course of justice with respect to his taped conversation with Juice, which included threats of arrest if he turned up at the magistrates' court for the committal hearing in the Mills and Poole's case and perjury by lying about that conversation at Mills' and Poole's trial.

KIMBERLY STADDEN

Gave evidence as the opening witness for the Crown at the trial in Bristol Crown Court, in January 1990. She confidently told the jury that she had arrived at 34 Conduit Street to obtain drugs (amphetamines) from Tony Poole. She then gave a vivid account of how Gary Mills had had a fistfight with Wiltshire, and beat him with a crowbar. She told the jury, in graphic terms, of the horror of watching Poole systematically stabbing Wiltshire several times in the back of the thighs and buttocks as he tried to crawl away on all fours.

Her evidence was as follows, when she arrived outside the door of the room she heard shouting inside the room and it stopped when she entered the room. Some time later she was sitting on the settee in the room mixing amphetamine in a glass prior to injecting herself with the drug.

Wiltshire and Mills were sitting on the settee next to her talking about which of them was better at fighting, when Wiltshire got up and jogged her arm and a fight then broke out between Mills and Wiltshire. The fighting was initially punching and kicking but she then saw Mills with a crowbar, which he used to strike Wiltshire, who was unarmed, several times to the legs and head. Poole joined in the fight and kicked Wiltshire twice and also used a knife on Wiltshire's arm.

Wiltshire then tried to get out of the room through a window but failed to do so and fell back onto a settee and then onto the floor. Mills, says Kimberly Stadden, punched him and Poole kicked him before stabbing him in the buttocks with the knife four or five times.

Duke (Ian Christopher Duke) then tried to intervene to stop the violence and then stopped her from seeing any more of the violence by pushing her head into his shoulder so that she could not see. While her head was turned away she heard "a sort of squishing noise."

She then saw Duke drag Wiltshire out of the room and onto the pavement of the street outside. She then walked to her flat in Gloucester which was a little under a quarter of a mile away.

She met both Gary Mills and Tony Poole just outside her flat and they had a conversation about using a telephone to get a taxi. She noticed that they had blood on their clothing and hands.

> All told, the account given by Stadden to the jury was strong and uncompromising. It was of two armed men, one with a crowbar (Mills) and one with a knife (Poole), taking part in unwarranted attacks on a defenceless man (Wiltshire).

PAUL WHITE

White was not nearly so confident or as graphic as Stadden in his evidence, but nevertheless, his evidence was equally damning. White said that on the evening in question he called at 34 Conduit Street at 9pm, to purchase speed (amphetamines) from Poole. He said that Poole told him to call back later.

White then went to a friend's house, where he remained until just before midnight He borrowed his friend's car and went alone to Conduit Street.

On arrival, he approached the door and heard raised voices arguing. White became apprehensive, descended the steps in front of the house and positioned himself on the pavement, by the garden fence, directly in front of the window of the room where the argument was taking place.

White told the jury how he looked through a gap in the curtains and saw the head and raised arms of a man on the floor, pleading, saying, "No Tony, no," while Poole struck down at this man. He also thought Mills was in the room, as he saw a shadow and heard Mills' voice.

White became frightened, left the scene and returned to the house of the friend from whom he had borrowed the car. About half an hour later, White and his friend returned again, to Conduit Street where they were stopped by police and gave their details.

Although White was not a confident witness his evidence was crucial to the prosecution case, as it corroborated Stadden's evidence and made Tony Poole an equally active party in the alleged assault on Wiltshire.

> **Given then what you have read about Wiltshire having two thorough check ups at hospital and each time he was returned to police custody he was deemed fit to do so, doesn't it seem rather strange that he somehow, and mysteriously, obtained horrendous injuries sufficient enough to bring his life to an end whilst in police custody?????? After Wiltshire's death, the police said that the hospital must have missed his injuries whilst examining him!**

IAN CHRISTOPHER DUKE

On 23 March 1989 the Senior Crown Prosecutor wrote to Mr Gadd, the solicitor representing Mills and Poole, and stated:

'As per our discussion at Court on the 21 March I informed you that the view of the prosecution was that we are not prepared to disclose the statement of Ian

Christopher Duke at this stage. You are aware of his identity, there is no property in a witness and if you wish to obtain a statement from him you are at liberty to do so.'

On 2 May 1989 Mr Gadd interviewed Duke. Mr Gadd recorded the interview on a tape recorder and the interview was then typed out and consisted of twelve pages.

The interview was a careful one in which Mr Gadd asked Duke about what had happened in the room when Wiltshire was injured and about what he had said to the police in his statements, and Duke gave detailed answers to Mr Gadd.

In the interview Juke stated clearly that Wiltshire was picking a fight and was the aggressor, and that Mills acted in self-defence. At one stage Mr Gadd asked Duke if Poole had taken part in an attack on Wiltshire:

CG: Now, let me ask you this question. During the attack did Tony Poole have anything to do with it? Did he strike a blow, help Gary in any way?

Duke: *During the attack?*

CG: At any time during that evening was he part and parcel of that assault?

Duke: *Not as far as I can see.*

CG: Right. Now the girl says that he was. She says that he was involved in cutting him, kicking him, stabbing him in the arse when he was on his knees. Do you remember that?

Duke: *I think that was when I turned her head around, I saw Tony just get up and then I turned back when I had turned her head around. I thought she'd come down to see Tony not Willie.*

At a later stage in the interview Mr Gadd asked Juke what he had told the police that would implicate Mills and Poole. Duke gave a lengthy reply in which he said that the police had shown him statements, which said that Poole was involved.

The police asked him if he had seen Poole move and he replied that he had seen Poole move but he had not seen Poole stabbing. The police told him that Wiltshire had got stab wounds on the buttocks and asked him how they got there if Mills was in front of him. Duke's answer to Mr Gadd then continued:

I told them I wasn't looking at the time. I didn't want to see what was happening and I didn't want the girl to see what was happening, so I looked away . . . I am happy to say I didn't see Tony do anything to him, right. I saw Tony move but I turned my head away .

In his second statement to the police Duke told an entirely different story. He said that at one stage when Wiltshire and Mills were fighting together on the floor he saw Poole get up and crouch down behind Wiltshire and using a knife, stab Wiltshire in the buttocks about two or three times.

He had not mentioned this in his first statement because he did not wish to involve his friend Tony Poole, as he did not really play a very major role in events. He then described how he turned the young woman's head away, as he did not want her to see this and he lost sight of the three men.

When he turned around, again, he saw Wiltshire lying on his side with Poole standing away from him and Mills was standing over Wiltshire hitting him on the thigh and calves, mostly on the thighs, but not on the kneecaps. The statement continued:

Mills kept hitting him with the crowbar saying something each time between blows to Willie. I don't know what he was saying. Gary Mills was giving Willie a severe beating so I said, "Leave it out, leave it alone."

He then said that as he knew the ambulance was on its way he became panicky and, thinking he could do no more for Wiltshire, he ran off to his home in Gloucester, as he did not wish to be involved in another assault having been already involved in one incident before Christmas.

In this statement Duke then described how he dragged Wiltshire out of the room, into the corridor and eventually out into the street.

He realised that Willie had to get out of there. A short time later a friend of

Wiltshire arrived at his home and accused him of letting Wiltshire be beaten up by the others.

He was concerned about Mills and Poole and he gave a woman friend a bag of clothes to take to Poole. He then went to another house in Gloucester where he saw Mills and Poole and he noticed that they had both changed their clothing. He then went to Cheltenham to start work at 7.20am and Poole accompanied him to Cheltenham and Mills joined them in Cheltenham a short time later.

In a subsequent statement made after the trial to police officers who were conducting an inquiry into the circumstances relating to the death of Wiltshire, Duke said that the contents of his second statement of 10 January about Poole were untrue and had come about as a result of police pressure to implicate Poole, the police having taken a statement from Kimberley Stadden 'ing Poole, which ed Duke to cofirm. 'aid he was put ire by the police

to explain the injuries to Wiltshire's legs, the suggestion being made that if he did not implicate Poole the police might have to conclude that as he was the last person to be with Wiltshire at Conduit Street he might have had something to do with those injuries.

> "THE POLICE ARE THE ONLY EMPLOYEES WHO HAVE MORE RIGHTS THAN THEIR EMPLOYERS, THE PUBLIC."
> Paddy Hill. One of the Birmingham Six.

GARY MILLS

The evidence of Mills was that when Wiltshire came to Poole's room he was in an aggressive and argumenta- tive mood and wanted to start a fight.

At a later stage Wiltshire attacked him and pulled out a knife and started to slash at him. There was a crowbar on the wall so he hit Wiltshire with it a few times to get the knife off him.

There was then a pause, and then Wiltshire came at him again, and in the course of the struggle Mills got hold of the knife and Wiltshire the crowbar.

28

Wiltshire was on top of him with the crowbar striking at him, so he stabbed Wiltshire in the legs and buttocks. Mills said that he feared for his life and he used the crowbar and then the knife on Wiltshire in self-defence.

Defence counsel did not raise the defence of provocation on behalf of Mills, but in his summing up the learned trial judge referred to provocation as a possible defence, which the jury should consider. In his evidence Poole said that he had taken no part in the fight with Wiltshire and had inflicted no injuries on him.

Hensley Wiltshire decided to move to Gloucester to escape the ravages of London's Metropolitan Police Force – he had an official complaint lodged against them that they beat him up.

In moving out of his territory he was bound to meet up with the seedy side of life in Gloucester. Although both Mills and Poole have no convictions for drug dealing they certainly mixed with drug dealers and drug users by

virtue of being friendly with them. Somehow the meeting with Wiltshire was fated.

To date Gary Mills and Tony Poole deny their guilt. All of those who have become involved in this travesty of justice are now of firm belief that Mills and Poole are scapegoats in another sinister 'cell death' in order to keep the real guilty parties safe.

Former PM (Prime Minister) Edward Heath has solidly lent his support to their case, as has David Jessel.

Crime prevention needs to start in school just as 'sex education' was introduced to make children aware of 'safe sex' and the consequences of sexual activity so do they need to be made aware of the dangers of becoming involved in criminal activities.

These two websites relate to Gary Mills and Tony Poole.

http://www.number7.demon.co.uk/hol/reports/01/49.htm

http://www.squall.co.uk/millspool.html

A website relating to those claiming to be innocent.

http://www.innocent.org.uk

3

Crime Through Time

Willium - Town Crier of Newent - Public Hangings and floggings attended
Ex World War II - Dunkirk Veteran...a truly wonderful and sincere gentleman

Christianity WORLD'S BIGGEST religion
2 Billion plus believers

Has a satellite spotted the original Garden of Eden in eastern Turkey?

Tempted: Adam and Eve in the Garden of Eden

A BRITISH scholar claimed last night that he had located the original Garden of Eden in Eastern Turkey.

Michael Sanders said he made the discovery by analysing satellite photographs from Nasa, the U.S. space agency.

Mr Sanders, 60, who grew up in Leeds and now lives in Califor-

From **Matthew Kalman** in Jerusalem

nia, added that his research indicates that all the earliest Bible stories occurred in what is now Turkey, and not in the Persian Gulf as previously believed.

'The Garden of Eden, the Flood, the Tower of Babel, the story of Abraham – all took place in a relatively small area between the Black Sea in the North and

the Ararat range in the East,' he said.

According to the biblical story in Genesis, the Garden of Eden was an earthly paradise created by God as a home for Adam and Eve, the first man and woman.

They were exiled after disobeying God and eating an apple from the Tree of Knowledge.

The second chapter of Genesis describes a river which watered the Garden of Eden and then split into 'four heads.' The Bible

calls these Pison, Gihon, Hiddekel and the Euphrates.

Until now, scholars have identified these waterways with the head of the Tigris and Euphrates in the Persian Gulf.

Mr Sanders, director of the Mysteries of the Bible Research Foundation in Irvine, California, suggested they are hundreds of miles further north-west.

'We obtained a startling satellite image of a configuration of rivers which seemed to fit the above description much better than any other theory so far proposed,' he said.

'It is obvious from the biblical account, when you read about a river rising out of Eden, that rivers don't rise in the desert. With the satellite image, it is just remarkable that there are four rivers in this region in Turkey.'

Mr Sanders says the four rivers are the Murat, which runs through Samsun on the Black Sea coast, the Tigris, the Euphrates and a northern branch of the Euphrates.

'It is quite remarkable that one of the four rivers out of Eden runs

directly to the Ararat range,' said Mr Sanders. Ararat was the mountain top where, according to the Bible, Noah's Ark came to rest after the Flood.

'It is quite likely that the biblical account describes a situation that after the great catastrophe of the Flood where the survivors were at Ararat, they proceeded to 'go home', that is follow the river back to Eden,' added Mr Sanders.

In 1999, the biblical explorer led a submarine expedition to the Dead Sea to search for the lost cities of Sodom and Gomorrah, also using Nasa satellite photographs.

He said he discovered some unexplained forms at the bottom of the sea, which he believes are the cities destroyed by fire and brimstone for the sins of their inhabitants.

Why create such an ill-fated garden? Could Charlie Dimmock and Alan Titchmarsh give it a makeover?

If we are to believe Christianity, it all started in the Garden of Eden. God, supposedly, created Adam and Eve…but with some fatal flaws, indeed, all was not perfect. The Tree of Knowledge was a great temptation…an apple was eaten and it resulted in God exiling Adam and Eve from the Garden.

Ever been Tempted? Is it a Crime?

NO ENTRY

KEEP LEFT

NO PARKING

DO NOT TOUCH

NO BALL GAMES

NO NUDE BATHING

NO DOGS ALLOWED

KEEP OFF THE GRASS

WET PAINT - DO NOT TOUCH

A British man, Michael Sanders, says he's discovered the original Garden of Eden in Eastern Turkey by using satellite photographs from NASA. Mr Sanders is director of the Mysteries of the Bible Research Foundation, in Irvine, California, USA.

He points out that the second chapter of Genesis tells of a river that watered the Garden of Eden and eventually split into four heads. The four heads are called Gihon, Pison, Euphrates and the Hiddekel, which have been identified as the head of the Tigris and Euphrates situated in the Persian Gulf.

The satellite pictures showed an amazing image of rivers that fitted in with the descriptions of the four heads, but hundreds of miles further northwest.

One of the four rivers runs right into the Ararat range – the place where Moses got his Ark stuck on top of a mountain after the great flood. This is a startling discovery, if true, and could add some weight to the story of the Great Flood.

Written with the finger of God
THE TEN COMMANDMENTS

Was Moses the first Home Secretary of Israel or just a con man? Speaking on behalf of God, it was the job of Moses to transmit the Ten Commandments that he'd collected from Mount Sinai. But what other job did Moses do – he promised punishment for breaking any of the Commandments, so as well as being God's spokesman he was also a tool of fear.

Thunder and lightening were accompanied by fire and smoke when daybreak arrived at Sinai, and the odd trumpet blast. Moses went up the mountain and was told by God that he would reveal himself to the people. In reality the only person who ever gets to see God is Moses when his people ask him to mediate with the man of divine power. "Let no God speak to us, lest we die," they cried.

All agreed to follow the law of God, but a rebellion was to take place, which resulted in Moses spending more time up Mount Sinai (40 days) than Sir Chris Bonnington spent climbing mountain ranges in Nepal.

Moses brought down from Sinai the stone tablets and in his absence the people had made a golden calf to worship, this prompted Moses to smash the tablets in disgust.

In spite of this, Moses once again returned to Sinai and got new tablets for inscription where God revealed himself as a 'merciful' God abounding in love and faithfulness.

The Ten Commandments were called the 'Decalogue' or 'Ten words' spoken by God. In actual fact the manifesto of laws God decreed was some 613, which out of them 365 were prohibitions and 248 positive commands. It would most certainly have helped to be in the legal profession due to this mass of new laws that were supposed to show mankind how to live.

Social values and modern day laws can still be fundamentally traced back to these commandments. Both the Jewish and Christian religions use the commandments in their teachings.

MONOTHEISM = THE WORSHIP OF ONE GOD

It is believed that rather than one god being accepted that the Israelites may have practised monolatry – worshipping one god whilst not denying the existence of other gods.

God was asking his followers to ditch all other gods, which in itself was a new angle since people looked to many gods on a day-to-day basis. One god would control the weather whilst another would control the growing of food products. What God was saying to people, via Moses, was that all these other gods were obsolete.

By 539 B.C. the Jews were a monotheistic people. This tied in with the first commandment: *Thou shalt have no other gods before me.*

God was applying psychological pressure along with his fire and brimstone and even gave a curse or two, which sounds just a little far fetched considering that God was the all powerful and all seeing. Such a powerful being surely didn't need to threaten with the use of a curse?

Behold, I set before you this day a blessing and a curse;
A blessing, if ye obey the commandments of the LORD
your God, which I command you this day:
And a curse, if ye will not obey the commandments of the
LORD your God, but turn aside out of the way which I
command you this day, to go after other gods, which ye
have not known. I call heaven and earth to record this
day against you, that I have set before you life and death,
blessing and cursing: therefore choose life, that both
thou and thy seed may live.

God quote:
"I am the Lord your God, you shall have no other gods before me.

Whilst surfing the net I decided to do a search on the subject of God and I found a number of surprising results:

MEET GOD
http://www.god.net

AN INTERVIEW WITH GOD
http://www.god.info

SEND GOD AN EMAIL VIA THE WEB
AND CONFESS YOUR SINS

http://www.god.org

There is also a website where you can actually, if it is to be believed, send God an email. Wherever the email ends up isn't quite clear but for those wishing to make anonymous confessions this could be the way forward in dwindling congregation numbers. What, say, if a crime has been committed by a Christian, could he or she email a confession and accept being absolved from the crime?

Letters to God @ god.org

Who am I?

Where am I from?

My e-mail address

Letter to God:

DELIVER

Never the twain shall meet...yet as alike as two peas in a pod!

Moses collecting the laws of God
(Museum exhibit of signed photo of actor Charlton Heston, playing the role of Moses)
THE
TEN COMMANDMENTS

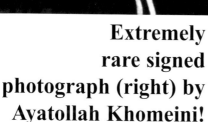

Extremely rare signed photograph (right) by Ayatollah Khomeini!

Iranian political and religious leader. A Shiite Muslim who was bitterly opposed to the pro-Western regime of Shah Mohammed Reza Pahlavi, he was exiled to Turkey and Iraq in 1964, and from Iraq to France in 1978. He returned to Iran amid great popular acclaim in 1979 after the collapse of the Shah's government, and became virtual head of state. Under his leadership, Iran underwent a turbulent "Islamic Revolution" in which a return was made to the strict observance of Muslim principles and traditions. In 1979, a new Islamic constitution was sanctioned, into which was incorporated his leadership concept of the Vilayet-i faqih (Trusteeship of the Jurisconsult). This supreme religious and political position was recognised as belonging to Khomeini, as was the title Rahbar (Leader).

THE TEN COMMANDMENTS

ONE: *Thou shalt have no other gods before me.*

TWO: *Thou shalt not make unto thee any graven image, or any likeness of any thing that is in heaven above, or that is in the earth beneath, or that is in the water under the earth: Thou shalt not bow down thyself to them, nor serve them: for I the LORD thy God am a jealous God, visiting the iniquity of the fathers upon the children unto the third and fourth generation of them that hate me; And showing mercy unto thousands of them that love me, and keep my commandments.*

THREE: *Thou shalt not take the name of the LORD thy God in vain; for the LORD will not hold him guiltless that taketh his name in vain.*

FOUR: *Remember the Sabbath day, to keep it holy. Six days shalt thou labour, and do all thy work: But the seventh day is the Sabbath of the LORD thy God: in it thou shalt not do any work, thou, nor thy son, nor thy daughter, thy manservant, nor thy maidservant, nor thy cattle, nor thy stranger that is within thy gates: For in six days the LORD made heaven and earth, the sea, and all that in them is, and rested the seventh day wherefore the LORD blessed the Sabbath day, and hallowed it.*

FIVE: *Honour thy father and thy mother: that thy days may be long upon the land which the LORD thy God giveth thee.*

SIX: *Thou shalt not kill.*

SEVEN: *Thou shalt not commit adultery.*

EIGHT: *Thou shalt not steal.*

NINE: *Thou shalt not bear false witness against thy neighbour.*

TEN: *Thou shalt not covet thy neighbour's house, thou shalt not covet thy neighbour's wife, nor his manservant, nor his maidservant, nor his ox, nor his ass, nor any thing that is thy neighbour's.*

The commandments were literally carved in stone by the finger of God, but did Moses steal the idea from someone else? Five centuries before Moses climbed Sinai to collect these commandments the Babylonian king Hammurabi (note the last four letters of the name Hammu**rabi**) had already done something similar.

King Hammurabi erected a black stone, eight feet high, which had inscriptions of laws for his kingdom. Carved at the top of the stone was a relief showing him standing before the god of justice. Amazingly this seems to be the forerunner of what subsequently happened to Moses.

The god of justice is seen, in the relief at the top of the stone, to be giving Hammurabi his sceptre as king and lawgiver, the exact same role (as lawgiver) as Moses claimed for himself! Some 282 laws were decreed by Hammurabi ranging from arson to homicide.

The actual pillar bearing Hammurabi's code was excavated in Iran in 1902 by French archaeologists. Although the laws were quite different to the law of Moses they still both had their roots in common law of the ancient Middle East. The Law of Moses was God's decree whilst that of Hammurabi's was royal law without the religious stamp of approval and therefore was not a covenant between God and the people.

A Palestinian baby is dressed to kill.
This is how far the Middle East
conflict has sunk!!!

WORLD'S BIGGEST
RELIGIOUS DEMONINATION
Roman Catholicism = 1.045 billion
Source Guinness

WORLD'S BIGGEST
NON-CHRISTIAN RELIGION
Islam = 1.16 billion
Source Guinness

"THOU SHALT NOT KILL"

In ancient Israel law the custom of blood vengeance meant that if one person killed another then the nearest kinsman of the victim had a right to kill the perpetrator. The *Avenger of Blood* did not need to think about whether the killing had been accidental but simply to know who did it. (An eye for an eye.) This code operated in most of the Middle East and could well be seen to be continuing in the feud between Israel and the Palestinians whereby revenge is sought under the *Avenger of Blood* code.

Crime Through Time

The death penalty in ancient Israeli law was brought into play for crimes against God and human life. Blasphemy against God, breaking the Sabbath, idolatry (worship of idols), sorcery and necromancy (communication with the dead) and violations of sacred property meant death. Other capital crimes included adultery, incest, sodomy and bestiality.

The particular act of necromancy seems an outdated law that would have been long forgotten but for a rather absurd criminal trial that took place in the UK in April 1944. The Witchcraft Act of 1735 was brought into force in a modern court of justice and prompted wartime leader, Winston Churchill, to angrily ask the Home Secretary in amazement why such an outdated law was used.

Winston and the witch hunt

Dangerous? Helen Duncan was jailed for nine months in 1944 under the Witchcraft Act of 1735

The trial of Helen Duncan was brought about as a result of a séance that took place on January 19, 1944, attended by a crowd including Stanley Worth and his friend, Rupert Goss, a War Reserve Constable.

Crime Through Time

During the séance, which took place in a dimly lit room, ghostly apparitions were seen to fly around the room only to be revealed as none other than Helen Duncan running around with several yards of white cloth about her.

The revelation happened when Worth switched on his torch and Goss pulled back the 'blackout' curtains (used in wartime). What was seen just before someone knocked Worth's torch out of his hand was Helen Duncan throwing the cloth into the audience.

From the darkness of the room Goss blew his policeman's whistle, which attracted more police. The sitters, including a woman with a large cloth bundle wrapped around her arm, were allowed to leave, but Mrs Duncan was remanded to prison. At her trial Duncan was sentenced to nine months imprisonment for fraud.

After her sentence she successfully went on to become a celebrated medium that was enthusiastically taken up by the serious spiritualist associations in London.

The Witchcraft Act was soon repealed – brought about by the case of Helen Duncan. Some say that the Government deliberately constructed her arrest in order to bring about her imprisonment. The reason being, if indeed so, was that Duncan had twice successfully predicted the sinking of a British Battleship in 1941.

The death penalty in ancient Israeli law could also be enforced for kidnapping a person for purposes of slavery. If that rule applied in Britain it would have meant slavery in the British colonies would not have existed.

On a modern day theme there was a real life plot by South Americans to kidnap Australia's movie heartthrob Russell Crowe. A ransom of $13 million was going to be the asking price for the safe return of the star and if the money wasn't forthcoming then the kidnappers planned to use torture on Crowe.

FBI sources revealed that a high-class source had informed them of the kidnap plan and they were working hand in hand with Scotland Yard detectives to ensure Mr Crowe's safety. Far from being worried Mr Crowe threw caution to the wind and went about his usual activities.

> **Crowe quote:**
> *"Bring it on home, baby, come and get me."*

R
U
S
S
E
L
L

C
R
O
W
E

THE PLOT TO KIDNAP AND TORTURE RUSSELL CROWE

"COME and get me, baby – that was the defiant challenge from screen tough guy Russell Crowe to the shadowy gangsters behind a $13 million kidnap and torture plot.

In an exclusive interview, Crowe said the threat – most likely, say sources, from South American revolutionaries – forced him 'to make some adjustments, but it's business as usual.'

The Oscar-nominated Gladiator star was worried at first when the FBI warned him about the kidnappers, and soon started traveling with a small army of bodyguards.

"The FBI have been very nice, professional chaps,' New Zealand-born Crowe says. 'They came to me at the beginning and said: 'All right now, Mr. Crowe, you realize you're going to have to change your lifestyle.' But they looked at

> 'The FBI had enough information to realize this wasn't a crank call!'

me and realized I'm not the type to change."

Asked if he was still concerned about the threat, Crowe laughed and motioned with his hands as if he was challenging the kidnappers. "Bring it on home, baby, come and get me," he says.

Ruthless gangsters in South America head the suspect list, especially since Crowe and then-lover Meg Ryan risked their lives to shoot the movie Proof of Life in Ecuador almost a year ago, say sources.

Ironically, Crowe played a hostage negotiator in the film. "The entire cast and crew were under threat from Ecuadorian terrorists whose specialty is kidnapping for ransom, and no one was allowed to venture out anywhere without armed guards to protect them at all times," says an insider.

The nightmare began with a sinister phone call to the FBI just before the Jan. 21 Golden Globe Awards, says a source.

An informant revealed that the actor was the target of a sophisticated kidnap plot – and the kidnappers wanted $13 million," says an insider.

"The informant stressed that the kidnappers didn't care about their own lives and would stop at nothing to get their money.

"It was made chillingly clear that they'd do anything – including torture – to persuade Crowe's friends, family and movie bosses to pay up."

FBI spokesman, Special Agent Matthew McLaughlin, confirms: "We were at the Golden Globes in tuxedos, conducting our investigation."

In classic Crowe style, the security precautions did not interfere with the Gladiator hunk's pursuit of romance that night when he brought Courtney Love back to the hotel with him.

Suburban to a Lincoln limo to throw off any pursuers. And security was just as tight the next night when he attended the Screen Actors Guild awards at the Shrine Auditorium. He arrived in the back of the Suburban and was surrounded by four bodyguards each wearing earpieces.

Crowe was also under special armed guard last month when he went first to England and then Italy for the European premieres of Proof of Life.

According to a Scotland Yard source, "Intelligence agents based at the American embassy in London were alerted several weeks ago after an informant told the FBI that a top Hollywood star was going to be kidnapped and held for ransom – but they were not given a name at that point.

"Days before he flew into London for his movie premiere Feb. 21, they were told the target was Russell Crowe and a ransom of $13 million was going to be asked. Scotland Yard was notified and met him when he arrived in London."

Another source added: "After questioning Crowe about whether he had any suspicions about who might want to kidnap him, he was assured that he would be under 24-hour guard at all times, with at least two men watching his every move.

"While he was in London plugging his film, he carried out his role like a man without a care on his mind," says the insider.

"But it was all an act. He was nervous and he knew every move he made was being watched by Scotland Yard."

In Italy, the actor was constantly followed by a pro-foot-

ball-sized bodyguard who tipped the scale at more than 260 pounds, as well as two Italian bodyguards from the Palazzi Protection Agency in Rome.

During the film's premiere, armed police and soldiers were also present.

And when Crowe made a surprise appearance at the San Remo Music Festival with his band, 30 Odd Foot of Grunts, he was accompanied by police, soldiers and festival heavies. One witness in Rome said: "Russell's muscular minder really looked the part.

"He was discreet, but you could see the guard was on high alert, looking for anything out of the ordinary."

FBI officials declined to say whether Crowe has continued to receive federal protection.

"They are worried because their informant made it clear that Russell Crowe's kidnap threat was very serious.

"The informant said the kidnappers had threatened the slow, sadistic torture of Crowe if they didn't get what they wanted."

Noted former FBI profiler Gregg McCrary said that the primary security force surrounding Crowe now is likely private.

"The FBI doesn't provide a bodyguard service to anyone, including celebrities.

"They will accompany someone under the threat of kidnapping, but their primary job is to catch the criminal."

Former White House Secret Service agent Joe Paolella, who now heads up a Los Angeles executive protection firm, adds: "If someone is looking for round-the-clock protection, as is Mr. Crowe, they're looking at four to eight bodyguards working three eight-hour shifts and with a total cost of nearly $10,000 a day."

–JOSE LAMBIET ★

THE GLADIATOR is raging mad at the kidnap threat.

HE REVEALS ALL IN EXCLUSIVE INTERVIEW

Why Gladiator should be scared

FEELING THE HEAT Crowe and then-love Meg Ryan filmed Proof of Life in dangerous Ecuador

RUSSELL CROWE has good reason to be worried about the threat from South American gangsters, says author William Prochnau.

The writer, whose Vanity Fair article Adventures in the Ransom Trade inspired the movie Proof of Life, worked closely with the actor in Ecuador.

"Kidnap and ransom is an epidemic that's worse than murder, because it can last for upward of six months or more," explains Prochnau. "And the last thing Russell Crowe would want is to be secreted away when he's about to win the Oscar for Gladiator.

"For the FBI to come to Crowe, they clearly had enough information to determine this wasn't simply the usual celebrity crank call.

> 'Kidnap and ransom is an epidemic that's worse than murder'

"In Ecuador during the filming of Proof of Life, the daughter of a wealthy local businessman was kidnapped on one of downtown's busiest streets, just three blocks from the hotel where the cast and crew were staying.

"That sent a chill up the spine of Russell and everyone else associated with the movie, because it drove home the point how easily something like that could happen to anyone.

"We were only 100 miles from the Colombian border, which is the prime region in South America for kidnappers. There was a lot of tension and even tighter security on the set after that kidnapping, but we never felt like there were enough bodyguards."

Author Prochnau also has this chilling warning: "Snatching a Hollywood celebrity off a street in Los Angeles would be no more difficult than doing it in South America. They'd come in fast and hard with overwhelming speed and firepower and be gone within 30 seconds.

"The driver and bodyguards either drop their weapons on command – or they drop dead."

–BOB MICHALS ★

ANGRY
YOUNG
MAN!!

Crime Through Time

If a killer reached a city of refuge (six cities – three on each side of the Jordan) in ancient Israel times they were entitled to a trial to discover if they had killed intentionally. If found guilty then not even the age old time honoured clinging to the horns of a sacred altar could save them from death. This fits in with the plea of "Sanctuary, sanctuary" by those who would cling to the door knockers of churches in medieval times in the UK when pursued by the king's men. The church was a powerful tool and not to be meddled with…not unless you were King Henry XIII. (More about this man further on.)

Even if the accidental death was confirmed by a hearing it didn't mean the killer was safe. The kinsman still had a right to kill, but so long as the perpetrator stayed within the confines of the city they continued to enjoy safe refuge.

Once human blood had been spilled it could not be overlooked. The *Book of Numbers* says: 'Blood pollutes the land, and no expiation can be made for the land, for the blood that is shed in it, except by him who shed it.' Could it be that the disease of AIDS was prophesised by the Book of Numbers when it states, 'Blood pollutes the land.'

The taking of someone's life by lawful means has been approved of for over two thousands years. So what was it about the hanging of Ruth Ellis, 28, the last woman to be hanged in Britain in 1955 for shooting her lover, David Blakely, outside the Magdala pub, in Hampstead, North London that even to this day causes an outrage?

Nightclub hostess Ruth shot Blakely whilst she was drunk and suffering from depression although these details and the fact that Blakely punched her causing her to have a miscarriage were never revealed at the trial.

The Sunday People newspaper was praised when solicitor Bernard De Maid said: *"The Sunday People has been instrumental in getting the case reviewed and should take a lot of credit."* Newly discovered evidence indicates that Ellis told a cellmate that the gun she used to kill Blakely with was given to her by another lover who had driven her to the scene. This was shown in a TV documentary some years prior to the case being reported on and it would now seem that a posthumous royal pardon could be granted.

Crime Through Time

TWINS WHO WENT TO THE GALLOWS

The Perreau twins were the only twins hanged in Britain

TWINS WHO STAYED IN THE TOWER

In the 1950s the Kray Twins spent the night in a cell in the Tower of
London after being absent without leave from their National Service.

LAW
MAKERS

LAW
BREAKERS

and then
there's hangmen

HANGED: Ruth Ellis

Ruth probe
thanks to
PEOPLE

Ruth Ellis-
The last woman to be
hanged in Britain

The letter on the facing page is a reply from the infamous and notorious British Hangman James Berry in reply to a request from a fan in the USA for his signature. The letter written Monday 28th January 1889 reads:

Dear Sir, This is the fifth application from America for my signature I said I would not answer any more but under the circumstances I have granted your request and in return I would like to beg a favour of you to send me a few photographic views of America as I would have them framed I take a great interest in views of different countries I have now a good collection of views of the continent included some very fine views of Russia. I would only be to (sic.) glad to make you a present of my photo if you kindly send me a few views of the United States. Here with (sic.) enclose card with my name written on also the date when I wrote it. Trusting this will meet with your requirements.

I am,

Yours faithfully,

James Berry

Crime Through Time

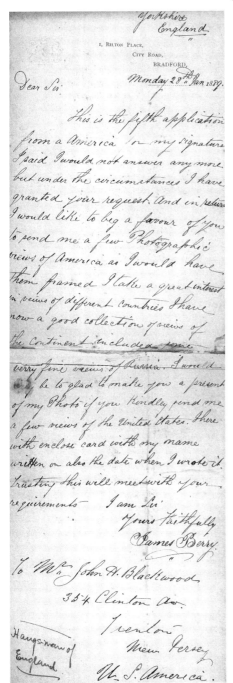

The penned letter, above, from notorious hangman James Berry As displayed in the museum along with many other thousands of exhibits

Above, Andy Jones holds the rope used by James Berry to hang the man who couldn't be hanged, John 'Babbacombe' Lee, bought at auction by Andy for £3,050. This item is on display in the museum.

Crime Through Time

Caught in the act – Eve picking the forbidden fruit
Atun cathedral, France

If we are to believe that Adam and Eve were the first lawbreakers then it can also be said that it was also the first sin committed by mankind when they ate the fruit from the Tree of Knowledge. Some have suggested that the sin was carnal knowledge between man and woman, but whatever the sin the consequences of such lawbreaking has lasted ever since.

God imposed the pain of childbirth on woman and on man he condemned to earn his keep by sweat alone. The final punishment for all mankind was kept until last, mankind was made out of dust and "to dust you shall return" and with this they were driven, like squatters, out of the Garden of Eden, God having exacted his punishment.

So there we have Adam and Eve, full of carnal knowledge and with plenty of spare time on their hands – Cain and Abel, two sons, are produced. On investigation it is pretty academic that for the whole of mankind to be descended from Adam and Eve that there must have been some incestuous activity in order to produce the billions of people now living all these thousands of years later.

An early Jewish commentary that is often called 'little Genesis' (the Torah) reveals two daughters of Adam and Eve – Awan and Azura. Cain takes the third born (after Cain and Abel) as his wife. Eve's third son was called Seth (Sheth) who takes Azura, born after him, for his wife. You can look through the Bible from start to finish and you will not find a mention of Cain's wife, Awan?

Crime Through Time

There are fatal flaws in the Bible and its layout between the book of Genesis and other books that were amalgamated as one. Albeit the Bible has sold billions of copies it surely would not have won a prize for fluent narratives. It's rather like watching your favourite soap on TV and then having one or two of the shows deleted at the crucial moment. Who killed 'JR' from the USA TV series 'Dallas'…what if it was never revealed?

Larry Hagman played 'JR' Ewing in Dallas
'Who Killed JR'

Crime Through Time

Adam became a farmer followed in his footsteps by Cain, Abel became a shepherd and as time went on each of the two sons prospered and decided to offer God a gift. Cain's gift was a portion of the crop he had grown whilst Abel's gift was some of the firstborn from his flock. The offerings were ascending, in smoke, and God took no notice of Cain's gift but did take notice of Abel's – resentment and jealousy took hold of Cain.

Soon after this God come across Cain in a field and asked him where Abel, his brother, was? Sarcasm came from Cain, *"I don't know, am I my brother's keeper."* For killing Abel God banished Cain to the land of Nod, east of Eden.

The picture, a 14th century German painting, depicts Cain bludgeoning Abel to death with the jawbone of an ass, yet the Bible does not mention a murder weapon?

The Bible gave us many legends, whether the facts have been distorted or whether they are true it seems strange that such events depicted in graphic narrative took place only in biblical times.

Crime Through Time

Take for instance the story of Samson and Delilah. (Book of Judges) Although Samson was not a judge in the sense of a military leader or a religious leader he was a great help in solidifying the Israelites hold on Canaan, which led to a united monarchy.

Stories of how he took on the Philistines single-handedly, slaying 1,000 of them, with the jawbone of an ass are legendary. Such a man as Samson had zero tolerance and often was motivated by nothing more than a personal grudge.

Ray Mallon – Happier days ahead of him…he hopes

Compare this to disgraced chief of detectives (CID), Detective Superintendent Ray Mallon of Cleveland Police Force, Teesside, UK. (Faced and admitted 14 disciplinary offences in Operation Lancet – Four-year investigation into police corruption.)

Mallon exercised complete zero tolerance towards crime, just like Samson. But the price paid by both Samson and Mallon, although from different time spans, for their success was to bring them both toppling down.

**SAMSON HAD A WEAKNESS FOR WOMEN
WHAT TYPE OF WOMAN WOULD TURN HIM ON?
TURN THE PAGE TO FIND OUT**

Brigitte Nielsen (The Body) – Would she have been Samson's 'Delilah'?

Samson had a weakness for women and this was to prove his downfall when he fell in love with Delilah. Samson was an Israelite hero – Mallon was the Citizens' hero.

Certain lords of the Philistines wanted to bring down Samson and bribed Delilah to find out the secret of his strength. Eventually after much persuasion and haranguing Samson told Delilah his secret of his Nazirite vow: *"If I be shaved, then my strength will leave me."*

During a deep sleep Delilah had a servant shave Samson's seven locks off his head. He awoke weak and his captors gouged out his eyes, making him grind grain, walking in circles.

During Operation Lancet Ray Mallon was having salt rubbed into his wounds when the inquiry team asked many witnesses what Mallon's weaknesses and strengths were and those that sought his downfall did all they could to bring it about. Mallon resisted all temptations to cop for what he was accused of and after a four-year investigation nothing criminal was proven against him. There were, however, some disciplinary charges to face!

Samson had his revenge when his hair started to grow back whilst in prison. The now blind Samson was led to a pagan sacrifice honouring the god Dagon. Samson was stood between two supporting pillars in the house of worship. Calling on God to restore his strength he successfully pushed down the pillars - those in the house were all killed including Samson.

Ray Mallon had intentions of running for the newly created position of Lord Mayor, but whilst he was in the employ of the police force he could not be in the running. Simple, he thought, I'll resign. His resignation was refused! So in order to expedite the disciplinary proceedings against him he opted to accept the disciplinary charges he faced. This he thought would expedite matters because the election deadline was closing in on him.

His resignation being refused earlier would now be a case of dismissal from the force because of his acceptance of the disciplinary charges. This game of chess between Mallon and those in high places seems to have been won by Mallon after he won the election and became Mayor, will it now see Mallon get his day of revenge just as Samson did?

Is divorce a crime?

Crime Through Time

> The law of Moses actually permitted an Israelite man to win a divorce from his wife if he didn't favour her because of some sort of indecency.

> The law of Hammurabi allowed a husband to divorce his wife simply by telling her, "Thou art not my wife."

Divorce laws are akin to criminal laws in many countries around the world, Britain must be one the few places where you can get a divorce without too many reprisals or raised eyebrows. Asking for a divorce in the Western world is becoming easier but in the Eastern countries it wouldn't be thought of for fear of death. One of the laws of marriage is 'Thou shalt not commit adultery.' Marital fidelity is not as strong as it used to be, the proverbs warn against "…the loose woman." Israelite law called for severely punishing harlots.

> Jesus speaking to priests and elders who questioned his authority:
>
> ## "…tax collectors and harlots go into the kingdom of God before you."

Harlots can get to heaven, says Jesus

Crime Through Time

Jesus says
PRIESTS GET INTO HEAVEN
AFTER HARLOTS AND TAX COLLECTORS

Parliamentary inquiry chief to help Catholic church end abuse scandal

MPs' watchdog is called in to target paedophile priests

By Steve Doughty
Social Affairs Correspondent

Archbishop ignored warnings over child molester

Catholics turned a blind eye to perverted priest

By Michael Seamark and Neil Sears

HUSH MONEY
Cardinal signed cheque for pervert monk's victim

Priest who preyed on boys to be freed early

By Rebecca English

By NICK PARKER

HUSH MONEY
Victims of perv priest paid off by Archbishop

Hill . . . priest's abuse left youngsters scarred

Shaken . . . Archbishop has denied negligence

53

Crime Through Time

The Bible does not condone prostitution, it tends to suggest that a 'blind eye' is given to their activities, as must happen on the streets in modern daytime. The Bible tells a story of the harlot Rahab who was spared destruction in Jericho because she helped conceal Joshua's' spies. Although Judaism strictly forbade ritual prostitution and fertility cults – people could not resist.

WHEN THE SHIT HITS THE FAN!!!

The church-going grandfather didn't dare tell his magistrate wife he was in trouble over a prostitute. But on the day of his court appearance he could hide the secret no longer ... she was the JP hearing his case

Why do we turn to God in times of need?

Why is it that, generally, families as a whole only appear to get together for weddings or funerals...then drift away from each other again?

Jesus Christ was found guilty of blasphemy, but it was put across to Pontius Pilate by the accusers in political terms that Jesus was 'perverting our nation.' Jewish officials said Jesus forbade them from giving tribute to Caesar.

When Pontius Pilate asked Jesus if he was the king of the Jews, Jesus' answer neither confirmed nor denied this.

RIPPER: I'M SANE

CAGED: Yorkshire Ripper Sutcliffe in 1981

Jesus was to be executed for political insurrection, but Pontius Pilate gave an option to the crowd of either saving Jesus or a man called Barabbas. In an anti-Roman insurrection in Jerusalem Barabbas had killed someone and since Jesus appeared to be a popular person Pilate had hoped they would select Jesus to go free. The chief priests had been working like spin doctors on the crowd, probably the first spin-doctors ever, whipping up support for Barabbas.

Jesus was crucified at 9.00am and when Pilate was told that Jesus had died at 3.00pm he was astonished that Jesus had only lasted six hours! Eventually Jesus was taken from the cross and custody of his body was requested from Pontius Pilate.

A dissenting member of Sanhedrin, Joseph of Arimathea, who was a secret disciple of Jesus, buried him in a tomb near Golgotha. A Pharisee called

Mass killer Sutcliffe claims he's cured of demon 'voices'

By GARY JONES, Chief Reporter

YORKSHIRE Ripper Peter Sutcliffe claims he is now sane – and that experts no longer consider him a threat to society.

Sutcliffe, 54, who murdered 13 women, says Broadmoor's consultant psychiatrist Andrew Horne has pronounced him sane 20 years after his arrest in Sheffield's red light district ended his reign of terror.

When Sutcliffe was sentenced in 1981, he was told he should serve at least 30 years. But, he now believes he has been cured of the "voices from God" he blamed for making him kill.

And the devout Jehovah's Witness – who reveals that ministers visit him twice a week to pray and read Bible passages – has been told that it is possible he will be freed one day.

In a revealing letter to a pen pal, Sutcliffe wrote from the Berkshire hospital: "At my last Mental Health Review Tribunal Dr Horne told them that he no longer considered me a danger to anyone!

"So I was pleased about that as he was so right. I now realise how ill I was all those years ago and I owe a lot to the doctors here for making me well."

Sutcliffe, a former grave digger and HGV driver, still receives injections of anti-psychosis drugs Stellazine and Depixol, but his medication has been levelling off in recent years.

His condition has recently improved considerably, according to hospital staff who regard him as a model inmate.

Sutcliffe, blinded in the left eye after inmate Ian Kay stabbed him with a pen in 1996, has a close relationship with Dr Horne, whom he praises for helping him accept and cope with his mental illness.

The mass killer listens intently to

EXCLUSIVE

everything the psychiatrist says, and has taken his advice to try to learn as much as possible about his medical state.

"Living quietly in solitude", reading the Bible and listening to the radio Sutcliffe still speaks warmly of ex-wife Sonia, who is credited with helping improve his mental well-being.

Sonia, who with her husband Michael Woodward treats illnesses and stresses with alternative medicines, still sees him regularly.

But the one person Sutcliffe is desperate to see one more time is his cancer-stricken father John, 76, who lives in Bingley, West Yorks.

Father and son have maintained telephone contact but have not met since 1993 and Sutcliffe fears his dad has little time left to live.

Last night Broadmoor declined to comment on Sutcliffe's condition.

A Home Office spokesman admitted it would take a "very brave" Home Secretary to agree that he was cured and should be freed.

Nicodemus and Joseph bound the body of Jesus in linen cloths with spices and rolled a stone across the tomb entrance.

The first person to see Jesus after his resurrection was Mary Magdalene – his mother. Call this an apparition or an illusion of the mind, but to Mary it was real. Such apparitions can seem very real even to the point of hearing voices in the head as happens with many schizophrenics like serial killer Peter Sutcliffe who is serving life for the murder of 13 women.

WHAT IF JESUS WAS A WOMAN?

Would she have been conspired against?

FUCK

CUNT

FUCKING

BASTARD

ARSEHOLE

FUCKING HELL

MOTHERFUCKER

JESUS FUCKING CHRIST

Has the use of expletives been abused by swearing an oath?

How did swearing on the Bible come about? The Old Testament – 'God is witness between you and me.' Jews would swear oaths when touching a sacred object such as the Torah. Oath taking, though, in the time of Jesus had been abused and Jesus greatly discouraged swearing. By the middle ages it was customary to swear by a cross or a copy of a scripture, placing a hand over it and kissing it. Modern day we see the Bible being used as a means of taking an oath for those who are Christians.

FRIDAY 13th has been embalmed in superstition since who knows when?

Don't walk under ladders
Don't pass on the stairs

King Philip the Fair
A raised relief-France

On Friday, October 13th, 1307 the French king, King Philip the Fair, planned to have every one of the 3,000 Templars (forerunners to the Masons) in France arrested in one fell swoop. This is the original 'Friday 13th' that has been swathed in superstition ever since!

What was it all about? To get an idea of what it was all about we have to go back to when the Templars were formed in 1118 in Jerusalem. The Christians had seized control of Jerusalem from the Muslims (the first Crusade), but even so some breakaway Muslim groups continued to attack visitors entering the area's shrines.

Nine founding Templars lived the lives of armed monks – protecting pilgrims from the Muslims. The Knights Templars took their name from the temple built by Solomon. The temple was an extravagance beyond comprehension, glittering with precious metals - the king of Babylon's soldiers eventually destroyed it. The contents of the temple have since disappeared without trace.

The founding Templars were said to have spent years digging for this lost treasure including searching for the Ark of the Covenant. A bizarre claim is that they discovered the embalmed head of Jesus!

Eventually the Knights Templars numbered 20,000, defending the Crusader states and every town in the Holy Land. The typical dress of the Knights Templars is what we're use to seeing in films when the Crusaders are depicted as wearing a white surcoat with a red cross on it. The code of conduct within the Templars was strict and every aspect of their life was regimented. Although personal possessions were outlawed the Knights soon amassed priceless stores of holy relics and treasures.

**VISIT THE HOLY LAND
TRAVEL WITH KNIGHTS TEMPLARS**

The Templars soon grew into a multi-national conglomerate to be reckoned with and controlled travel agencies, became bankers and were also diplomats. All good things come to an end and in 1187 Saladin recaptured Jerusalem for Islam and the Templars were kicked out of their HQ. Since then Jerusalem has never returned to Christian rule.

Pope's patronage exempted Templars from taxation!

The Templars had some 9,000 manors in Europe and because the Pope was a patron the Templars were exempt from taxes. At that time Paris was the centre of the world money market and it just so happened that the Templars had a place there to work from. The crowned heads of Europe, if needing money, were in no other position than to seek the loans they required from the Templars.

Soon such a set-up attracted resentment and jealousy from the King of France. King Philip was having none of it and decided to outlaw the Templars. On hearing this many Templars fled to safety but many hundreds were arrested and tortured beyond comprehension - they were accused of blasphemy and sexual perversion.

Was this the first religious cult?

Prince Charles
refused to join
the Masons...
is this why he
hasn't become
King??

A very rare chance to see the bizarre Initiation
Ceremony of a modern day Mason

The initiation ceremony of the Templars was said to involve urinating or spitting on an image of Christ on the cross. Worse still, accusations were that the Templars worshipped a severed head called Baphomet – said to have three faces and to glow in the dark! It would seem that the Templars had strayed far beyond conventional orthodox Christianity.

GNOSTICISM A RELIGIOUS MOVEMENMT BELIEVING IN INTUITIVE SPIRITUALIST KNOWLEDGE
A heresy of the Christian faith

Kidnapped and put on trial. Can one crime be overlooked just to get a conviction?

Slobodan Milosevic -
War Crimes Hearing

The secret rites of the Templars were steeped in Gnosticism. (Adherents can communicate with God without the use of a priest or even a church.) The King of France, with the support of the Pope, was doing exactly what   Slobodan Milosevic stood trial for war crimes over – he wanted the Templars snuffed out. Although it was not ethnic cleansing it would have certainly amounted to the ending of an entity...a living entity.

Philip the Fair (Philip IV) didn't manage to get his hands on the treasures of the Templars and far from being the end of the Knights Templars they had got wind of the King's plot and shifted their valuables via their own fleet of ships based at La Rochelle, In Brittany.

13th of March 1314:
Jacques de Molay and Geoffroy de Charnay on the Stake
(Please note, some records indicate 13th March whilst others 15th March)

November 28, 1309: Trial of Jacques de Molay,
Grand Master of the Templars (in Paris)

March 15th, 1314: Jacques de Molay, Templar grand master,
and Preceptor of Normandy burned at the stake in Paris
(Same year as the death of King Philip IV)

The Knights Templars were going underground and many merged with other orders. In Germany some joined the ranks of the Teutonic Knights – one of Hitler's inspirations! The main destination, though, was Scotland, to the Isle of May, in the Firth of Fourth. The Pope had excommunicated the Scottish king, Robert the Bruce; therefore it lends itself to the Templars seeking refuge in Scotland.

From the Templars was born the Masons and across Europe many Masonic lodges exist having been born from the pain and suffering meted out to the Templars.

Crime Through Time

The Teutonic Knights were established as an Order in 1199. (Founded in 1190) when it received papal confirmation by Pope Innocent III. Related website: http://www.dtorden.or.at/

A Teutonic Emblem (above) that influenced Hitler's use of a similar style logo around the swastika (right)

Germany's Nazi party adopted the swastika. Prior to the Nazis co-opting this symbol, it was known as a good luck symbol and was used by various religious groups. Hitler made the Nazi swastika unique to his party by reversing the normal direction of the symbol so that it appeared to spin clockwise. Today, it is widely used, in various incarnations, by neo-Nazis, racist skinheads and other supremacist groups. The Masonic movement has become an all powerful, all seeing machine - universal and worldwide animal with a membership that is thought to total quite a few million members. Most Masonic Lodges raise money for good causes, no one doubts that but there is an ulterior side to the Masonic movement that has been questioned.

Many of the world's civil service, military personnel, also many of the founders of the United States of America were Freemasons, many of the world's greatest composers, movie stars, and scientists also were and still are members of the Freemasons.

Freemasonry is the World's largest fraternity, having members in almost every town and village and country across the globe. From your schoolteacher, handyman, auto mechanic, stockbroker, appliance repairman, grocery stock clerk, gardener, the list goes on and on.

This is quite a total sum of people to cross swords with. For one man he has taken on the might of the Masonic fraternity and has set up a website to warn people of the dangers of Freemasonry.

Maurice Kellett quote:

FREEMASONRY IS... CORRUPTION IS... INJUSTICE IS... EVIL... IS FREEMASONRY...

http://www.mason-rule.bizhosting.com

"666"

According to certain interpretations of the Christian Bible, this is the mark that Satan gives to his allies so that they can avoid the punishment meted out to Christians who refuse to abandon their faith during the Tribualtion. This symbol is also used to symbolize Satan or evil.

Harry S. Trueman

"...which believes in justice and truth and honourable action in your community...men who are endeavouring to be better citizens...[and] to make a great country greater. This is the only institution in the world where we can meet on the level all sorts of people who want to live rightly."

Harry S. Trueman   President of the United States

HOW MANY PRESIDENTS HAVE BEEN OR ARE MASONS? TURN THE PAGE TO FIND OUT

14 Presidents of the United States of America

George Washington
James Monroe
Andrew Jackson
James Polk
James Garfield
James Buchanan
Andrew Johnson
William McKinley
Theodore Roosevelt
Howard Taft
Warren Harding
Franklin Roosevelt
Harry Trueman
Gerald Ford

Would a British policeman be allowed to wear such insignia?

Why are we so fascinated about the lives of the rich, powerful and famous, would you be as interested in a coalman from Ashington, in the north of England, if all on offer was his life story? What if that coalman had gone on and become the president of the United States of America, suddenly we want to know what his life was all about when he was down the pits! Crime Through Time Museum has exhibits that will help you understand the lives of the very people you read or hear about in everyday news – from coalmen to presidents.

Are you concerned at the amount of money being thrown away on staffing the secret service establishments that run on a blank chequebook? We all have to travel, and experience various modes of transport, we all pay taxes in order to help fund that travel (fuel tax, insurance tax, road tax) even if we're not responsible for paying tax directly we have to pay indirectly as passengers – where does all that money go?

Crime is one of the country's biggest industries, but for those of you who don't agree I would ask you to consider how many would be out of work if the crime world retired overnight? How many people make a living from crime? Police, private security firms, stewards, club doormen, probation officers, police support units from the Home Office, law courts, prisons, drug rehabilitation units, insurance companies, alarm installers, locksmiths, glaziers, etc, the list is endless.

Compare that to if everyone stopped eating peas overnight – would it hurt our economy? Modern day crime has moved on by leaps and bounds and now the police have an even bigger task in tackling and policing white collar and computer related crime. The police have a difficult task to meet the standards we have come to expect from them.

Politicians with a poor streetwise education fail to reason why the drug problem has spiralled – what is it coming to when MP's get 22 weeks holiday per year in the UK! MP's are the decision makers, but the whiz kids behind the computer keyboards make the country tick over.

Look at the millions of pounds these whiz-kids can make vanish in computer related frauds, look at the damage that can be done to computer systems by viruses created to cause chaos.

Crime enters your life on a daily basis:

Is the house door locked?
Is the car door locked?
Is the safe locked?
DO YOU THINK OF ALL THESE THINGS AND MORE?
Dare I pull my money out?
Dare I use my mobile cell phone?
Dare I walk down this dark alley?

Every day the newspapers are full of crime related incidents...full of contents with graphic displays of criminal behaviours makes us stop what we're doing and paying attention. Do we really need the fix? Do we seek sensationalism that the media feed us? Can we blame the media for spoon-feeding us a daily diet of crime news? Newspapers on the whole do a good job in opening up stories for us and are working round the clock to report news; we cannot blame them if it's not the type of news we want to hear. No one would have wanted to hear of the death of Lady Diana, but it had to be told...somehow.

NO NEWSPAPERS - NO NEWS

NEWS, GLORIOUS NEWS, NEWS, GLORIOUS NEWS

WAS HE SIMPLY TRYING TO BLAME ALI G?

CRIME NEWS - BIG BUSINESS

Amazing new revelations about Britain's top gangsters

KRAYS MADE £10M FROM INSIDE JAIL

- They ordered **30** murders from their cells
- They duped star Shane in charity con
- They paid for blinding the Ripper

EXCLUSIVE
By LUCY PANTON
Crime Reporter

> Ron & Reg Kray
> R.I.P.

JOHN STALKER on brutal truth behind underworld thugs who cash in on the public's hunger for true crime stories

MAJOR league criminals are more commonplace in your local bookshop than at the Old Bailey these days.

Men who once visited uninvited wearing balaclavas now arrive by limo wearing smiles.

We're mugs to buy these crook books

THE MOST WANTED LIST

CROOK BOOKS REVEAL CRIME NEWS IN DETAIL

Crime Through Time

Daily Mail

SATURDAY, MAY 20, 1536 · First choice of the Tudors · Still one farthing

Win a penny a day for life
● Trade up from your wattle and daub hovel
● Buy a horse of your own
● Go on that dream pilgrimage

Nice smile, but she's no oil painting
Femail on Italy's pin-up girl

IF NEWSPAPERS EXISTED WHEN IT HAPPENED!!

As the royal crisis worsens, a plea on behalf of England

MONARCH OR MONSTER?

With the execution of An...
VIII has enraged the re...
of sanity, Sire, stop chop...

Unkindest cut: Anne dies yesterday

INSIDE: Daily Harry II-III, galleons ...

Daily Mail

WEDNESDAY, DECEMBER 30, 1170 · Informative Parchment of the year · Still one groat

Should Eleanor of Aquitaine really be wearing this outfit at 58?

AT the Daily ...
ourselves on ...
King Henry.
So it is as faith...
treasonable varie...
plead urgently f...
restored to his re...
For all its superfici...
tion of the Queen at...
will be seen by ever...
The way the King...
second wife – the fa...
like – an unwelcome ch...
to base him a son is...
And the route with...
hurled to the new I...
only minutes after ...
decided so...
Although Henry's ...
ter by Anne, Princes...
he was said to have ...
boy was stillborn fo...
that sad event seele...

Fuel scandal
● Hay soars to a shilling a ton
● Now a farthing to fill a horse
● Angry carters blockade farms

Did furious King order knights to kill 'turbulent' archbishop?

BECKET SLAIN IN CATHEDRAL

the knights moved in to hack Thomas Becket to death

Daily Mail

SUNDAY, OCTOBER 15, 1066 · News scroll of the year · One groat

HISTORY BEHIND THE HEADLINES: A BRILLIANT NEW SERIES

■ Today Weekend brings you the first of a fantastic new 8-part, pull-out-and-keep partwork bringing 1,000 years of British history to life

■ Packed with Daily Mail-style front page news reports, compelling features and beautiful drawings, it can be treasured for years to come

■ PLUS over the eight weeks, every reader can claim FREE gifts worth over £30, win prizes and benefit from offers including 2-for-1 stately home visits

■ In this first part, we explore the gory era of conquests and crusades, starting with the year the Normans invaded and changed Britain forever

neddler' a martyr

...rd nor clothes
...ed a murderer —
...n weakness
...tter a word, nor
...t, or a sign
...Instead, he held
...ant towards the
...t that the
of Magna Carta and plague

CONQUERED

Harold is killed, Normans storm in and England demands – how did it happen?

ENGLAND writhes under the heel of Europe today after being conquered by the Normans.

By Orderic Vitalis
Warfare Chronicle

Our brave King Harold is dead – cut down as he tried to defend his realm against the massed ranks of the French invaders.

His brothers Earl Leofwine and Earl Gyrth and many elite beserker troops also perished in the slaughter yesterday.

A triumphant Duke William of Normandy is already on his way from the battlefield near Hastings, Sussex, to London to seize the throne he claims is rightfully his. Bishop Odo is ...

Battle of haste that left us open to invasion

The advice King Harold's astrologers gave him about the mysterious comet seen over England in April will now be ...

68

Crime Through Time

Daily Mail

SATURDAY, OCTOBER 26, 1415 · Continental Victory Edition · One franc

HISTORY BEHIND THE HEADLINES: OUR BRILLIANT SERIES

- Today Weekend presents the third section of our compelling 8-part, pull-out-and-keep partwork bringing 1,000 years of British history to life
- PLUS another chance to claim a superb free gift – a royal genealogy chart, one of over £30 worth of giveaways available for every reader over the series
- In part 3, we look at the era of Agincourt and adventure – from Henry V's triumph and the Wars of the Roses to Caxton and the discovery of the New World

MIRACLE AT AGINCOURT

10,000 French killed ... ... chers ... dds

Deadly: Our archers in action yesterday
Left: King Henry called his men 'We band of brothers'

Another string to our bow

YESTERDAY'S victory again shows the stupendous power of the longbow – especially in the expert hands of our troops. English archers can shoot six arrows a minute with uncanny accuracy. At 400 yards, they can wound, at 200 yards kill and at 100 yards pierce armour. Tactically, the French have learned nothing from similar defeats at the hands of our bowmen at Crecy 69 years ago and at Poitiers ten years later – recklessly sending knights and men-at-arms into the deadly arrow storm. As well as the longbow, morale won Agincourt. Our troops are well-trained and well-fed. The French mainly fielded a rabble of raw recruits.

Daily Mail

TUESDAY, APRIL 12, 1814 · Your Exile-ent Newspaper · Still one halfpenny

Income Tax

Fifteen years after it was brought in, it's time to end this 10 per cent robbery

He went from bad to verse

My passionate fling with star poet Lord Byron, by Lady Caroline Lamb

BONEY'S BONUS

After 20 years of war and millions dead, Bonaparte is finally defeated. So what is his punishment? A firing squad ... are letting him retire to his ow... island with a huge pension and ... us, a warship to use as a pleas... Has the world gone totally ma...

NAPOLEON Bonaparte is to be given his own luxurious island kingdom, the Daily Mail can reveal today.

Far from facing execution after more than 20 years of murder, terror and plunder, the defeated French dictator – who abdicated six days ago – will be 'exiled' to sun-kissed Elba in the Mediterranean to live in pomp and splendour.

Under an astonishing deal agreed by the main allied powers – Britain, Austria, Russia and Prussia – Bonaparte will become emperor of the Italian island, and his wife Maria Louise will be granted sovereignty of three Italian duchies.

WORLD EXCL...

From **Hector Ch...**
Diplomatic Editor, i...

Normally signed the abdi... up at Fontainebleau, he said he will agree to its... The agreement clears... Bourbon monarchy to... after King Louis XVI... Antoinette were execut... ing the revolution that... to power – and put Eur... Last night, news of... meant British military... belief', said one offic... Lord Wellington in the...

Daily Mail

THURSDAY, OCTOBER 26, 1854 · Valued by Victorians · No charge (...)

CALIFORNIA DREAMING

In search of the good life: why thousands are saddling up for the glitter of GOLD

Married 14 years, but only EIGHT children. Is Victoria setting a trend for small families?

INTO HELL

Light Brigade heroes sacrificed as blundering generals order them to charge Russian guns

Tennyson's Balaclava blockbuster

ALFRED, Lord Tennyson, is composing a sure-fire hit ode to the Light Brigade, it was revealed last night. His preliminary notes – obtained by the Mail – show it is certain to be another blockbuster for the Poet Laureate. It could even become bigger than his earlier hits, The Lady Of Shalott, The Lotos Eaters and In Memoriam. The new poem, in part, reads: Half a league, half a league / Half a league onward / All in the valley of Death / Rode the six hundred / 'Forward, the Light Brigade! / Charge for the guns!' he said / Into the valley of Death / Rode the six hundred. / 'Forward, the Light Brigade!'...

Warlords flee the jungle as two scared little boys

Tired, hungry and thirsty, guerilla leaders aged 12 give themselves up

IS NEWS TOO HARROWING OR REVEALING?

To 3 or not to 3

Was Shakespeare a druggie?

By ROSA PRINCE

FORSOOTH. 'Tis thought the great Bard relieth upon more than mere genius to pen his works.

Those famous lines of tragedy, comedy and romance may have been inspired by a whiff of halfobthecmperile drugs, say experts.

Scientists have found traces of cocaine and other substances on clay pipes found near the playwright's Stratford-Upon-Avon home. They say it adds weight to the theory that 'home of Shakespeare's texts were associated with the use of certain substances.'

Academics have long speculated that he was partial to narcotics.

In his Sonnet 76 he wrote of "noted weed" and "compounds strange". Sonnet 27 mentions "a journey in his head."

Traces of cocaine and myristin acid, derived from cannabis, were found on the 34 clay pipes tested by Dr Francis Thackeray of the Transvaal Museum in Pretoria, South Africa.

He still even if the Bard did not take drugs himself, the find proved for the first time that his 17th Century contemporaries may have.

Dr Thackeray added: "We do not claim the pipes belonged to Shakespeare himself. However, they were found in the area in which he lived."

But Ann Donnelly of Stratford Shakespeare Birthplace Trust Museum, which exhibits the pipes, said the find was "no proof" he used drugs.

PLAYS HE MIGHT HAVE WRITTEN

1. Smackbeth
2. The Hempest
3. Hash You Like It
4. Henry the Spliffed
5. Taming of the 'Shroom
6. Much Adope about nothing
7. Trip-us Andronicus
8. Romito and Juliht
9. Two Gentlemen of Colombia
10. Julius Seizure

Hash You Like It ... or did Shakespeare use drugs for inspiration?

Daily Mail Reporter

WAS Shakespeare partial to something rather more exotic than a pinch of tobacco while composing his plays and sonnets?

Was A Midsummer Night's Dream, in other words, the product of a Midsummer Night's trip?

That is the question set to occupy scholarly minds following a discovery at the Bard's home in Stratford-on-Avon.

Clay pipe fragments from the 17th century which were dug up there show conclusively that cocaine and myristic acid – a hallucinogen derived from plants, including nutmeg – were being smoked at that time.

They also show hints of residues of cannabis or marijuana.

The evidence was described as 'quite remarkable' by palaeontologist Dr Francis Thackeray, who examined 24 pipe fragments and found cocaine in two of them.

The find is certain to spark speculation that Shakespeare himself was working under the influence of substances more usually associated with Bohemian authors of the 20th century.

According to Dr Thackeray, based at the Transvaal Museum in

Pretoria, South Africa, there is some 'suggestive' literary evidence to that effect.

'In Sonnet 76 he refers to a "noted weed" which may have been a reference to cannabis,' he said. 'In the same sonnet, he refers to "compounds strange" and the word compounds is a known reference to drugs.'

But Dr Thackeray – who is descended from the 19th century author of the same name – was more excited about the fact that the drug was smoked at all that about who may have been doing it.

'Cocaine was recorded in Europe about 200 years ago, but to our knowledge never this early,' he said.

'The Spanish had access to it in the Americas, but the fact that it was smoked in England at this time is a first.'

Cannabis sativa, the plant from which marijuana is derived, was certainly accessible in Elizabethan England for paper, rope, garments and sails, he added.

The pipe fragments were lent to Dr Thackeray, who examined them with the help of a South African police forensic scientist, by the Shakespeare Birthplace Trust. But

$100 WILL BUY THIS CAR MUST HAVE CASH LOST ALL ON THE STOCK MARKET

Wall Street Crash of 1929. 20th-century US history is of key importance for the 21st century student

Does

Crime

Affect Your Life

USA

ASSASSINATION

September 6th, 1901: President William McKinley - an anarchist blasted the 58-year-old statesman with a .32 short-barrelled revolver.

ST. VALENTINES DAY MASSACRE

February 1929: Even today, the St. Valentine's Day Massacre is a household term.

LINDBERGH BABY

March 1932: Someone placed a ladder beneath the window of 20-month-old Charles Lindbergh Jr's room. The baby was spirited away, never to be seen alive again.

SPIES IN THE CAMP

1953: National Security Agency (NSA) documents show Julius Rosenberg passed the Soviets some secrets on the design of America's first nuclear bomb! Julius Rosenberg and his wife Ethel - whose share of the affair amounted to typing her husband's notes - were convicted of conspiracy to commit espionage in 1951. The USA government executed them in 1953.

1964: The Boston Strangler, Albert DeSalvo, claims his 13th victim.

ASSASSINATION

April 1968: Standing in the bathtub of a cheap Memphis rooming house, James Earl Ray raised a window and pushed open the screen. Across the street, the Rev Dr Martin Luther King stepped out of Room 306 at the Lorraine Motel to speak to aides waiting for him downstairs in the motel courtyard.

According to the most accepted version of events, on April 4, 1968, Ray raised his .30-06 hunting rifle at 6:01 pm and fired. The bullet struck King as he leaned over the second-floor balcony, smashing King's jawbone, tearing through his jugular vein, and severing his spinal cord. Doctors declared King dead an hour later.

Helter Skelter

1969: Charles Manson – Sharon Tate murder.

1972: Watergate: President Nixon.

1973: Ted Bundy serial killings.

Son of Sam

1977: A 24-year-old Jewish mailman, David Berkowitz, turns out to be the couples killer.

Assassination

1980: John Lennon – murdered in New York.

1990: Ted Bundy. Serial killer.

1995: OJ Simpson - High profile murder trial.

CAN YOU THINK WHAT FAMOUS CRIMES HAPPENED UP TO 2003?

September 11th, 2001: Osama Bin Laden is accused of Terrorism.

UK

1879: Charlie Peace – Legendary character, hung for murder.

The Whitechapel Murders

1888: Jack the Ripper is credited with five murders, but two others are thought to be his too. Not ever caught, much debate on his identity, over 200 books written on this ever fascinating subject. The closest anyone has ever come to revealing the real killer is author Martin Fido.

Doctor Death

1910: Dr Crippen hanged for murder.

1952: Craig and Bentley – celebrated British case of murder.

1953: Christie – killer.

1963: The Great Train Robbery.

1963-64: Moors Murders – Brady & Hindley.

1966: Harry Roberts – "He shoots coppers…"

1966/67: The Kray Twins.

Crime Through Time

1968: On the eve of her eleventh birthday, Mary Bell murdered a four-year-old boy. A few weeks later, she killed a three-year-old.

Catch me if you can

1974: Lord Lucan disappears forever after nanny is murdered.

Black Panther

1976: The man known as the 'Black Panther', Donald Nielsen, is caught.

1980: Jeremy Thorpe, leader of the Liberal Party, cleared of murder conspiracy.

Yorkshire Ripper

1981: The Hoax Tape! God's voice! Did he commit all the murders on his own?

Brinks-Matt

1983: £26 million robbery.

1985: Jeremy Bamber - farm murders.

Hungerford Massacre

1987: Michael Ryan goes berserk in a sleepy Berkshire town with licensed guns, blasting and killing 13, injuring 13 more before shooting himself.

1986: Suzy Lamplugh, the estate agent, abducted – her killer has not been caught, last appointment was with Mr Kipper.

1987: Gloucestershire rapist and killer John Cannon is questioned over possible Suzy Lamplugh abduction, his nickname in prison was 'Kipper'!

1991: Robert Maxwell, rumoured to still be alive and living in Israel?

1993: Beverley Allitt – nurse turned killer.

1993: Infant, James Bulger, murdered by two boys.

CAN YOU THINK WHAT FAMOUS CRIMES HAPPENED UP TO 2003?

2002: Domeraiders convicted of audacious plan to steal diamonds valued at between £200 million and £350 million from the Millennium Dome. http://www.domeraiders.co.uk

THE MUSEUM HAS THE WORLD'S LARGEST PRIVATE COLLECTION OF CRIME MEMORABILLIA ON DISPLAY TO THE PUBLIC

Crime Through Time

Some connections to the Black Museum of Gloucestershire

Major Herbert Rowse Armstrong the solicitor and clerk to the court at Hay-on-Wye, near Newent, was charged with murder and was tried at his own court with murder in 1921. Monies held in escrow for a client of a rival solicitor, Oswald Martin, was unable to be repaid. Anonymously whilst Mr Martin was pursuing the Major for the money a box of chocolates arrived through the post. A friend of Mr Martin's was sick after eating one of the chocolates, the rest were thrown away.

During a chat over tea and scones at the Major's home Mr Martin became sick after eating one the scones passed to him by the Major. Later when Mr Martin's doctor analysed his urine it was discovered that it contained traces of arsenic.

The police were informed of this poisoning and they were aware that the Major's wife, a woman prone to scolding and intimidating her fearful and diminutive husband...she died the year before. It was noted that she was ill at times but when away from her husband she would make a recovery. Orders were given to exhume her body and analyse the contents of Mrs Armstrong's remains. Not surprisingly Mr Martin declined multiple invitations to attend his home for tea!

On New Year's Eve the Major was arrested and it was discovered on his person that he had a small packet of arsenic and on further investigation a further nineteen similarly small packs of the poison were dotted around his home. The Major's excuse for having such a cache of poison was that he liked to sprinkle individual dandelions that appeared on his lawn with a serving of the deathly contents of each pack.

Harold Greenwood, another local solicitor, was acquitted of murder the year before and similarly had poisoned his wife too. This gave the Major the false hope that he too would be acquitted - the Major was found guilty and was hanged in 1922.

Joe Meek the murderer, Britain's first independent record producer, was born in Newent, Gloucestershire in 1929. He spent his first four years of childhood kept in dresses by a mother disappointed that he was not a daughter. Teased and chased by other boys in Newent for being dressed as a girl for the local pantomimes.

Aged just 16 he built the town's first television set before moving to London. Meek led a promiscuous sex life (homosexual), which was highlighted by an arrest for importuning in 1963. Had a fascination with the occult and was obsessed with his idol Buddy Holly and forecasted Holly's death on February 3rd 1958. On February 3rd 1967 he blew away his landlady, then himself in London.

The Joe Meek Appreciation Society still flock to the town to see his burial site in the local church graveyard - his family still live in Newent today.

He produced the No 1 hit 'Telstar' by The Tornados, 'Have I the Right' by the Honeycombs, 'Johnny Remember Me' by John Leyton, 'Just Like Eddie' by Heinz also produced for Rod Stewart, Tom Jones, Freddie Starr, David Bowie and Screaming Lord Sutch. He rejected the Beatle's audition tape – big costly mistake!

Eventually, in the face of lawsuits, lack of financial success, depression due to his sexual orientation, paranoia, strange voices and increasing doses of barbiturates, Joe Meek felt done for. On Feb 3rd 1967, eight years to the day after Buddy Holly's death, he killed his landlady, then himself. Joe's connection with the underworld was consolidated when he had a homosexual affair with Ronnie Kray:

During Andy Jones's prison visits with London gangster Reg Kray... Reg had told Andy that Joe Meek was a former lover of his brother Ron and that Joe had also supplied Ron with toyboy lovers.

Joe Meek, with being actively involved in a great many seedy and sordid activities also paid the Kray's protection money in fear of reprisals.

Was it the Kray's that ordered the gangland hit on Joe Meek??? Andy Jones say's that it would not surprise me, as he was heavily involved in importuning at young juveniles and was rumoured to have helped kill a young lad who was later to be found cut up into pieces and dumped. Joe Meek Appreciation Society: http://www.rgmsound.co.uk/ and www.joemeek.com

Dick Whittington – born in Gloucestershire in 1350. He really did go to London and went on to become Lord Mayor of London (four times). The Whittington family from 1311 to 1546 used St Nicholas House in Westgate Street, Gloucester as a town house, now a pub aptly named *Dick Whittington!*

WARNING

What follows in this chapter is of a very harrowing nature.

For those with a weak disposition or with a very sensitive nature, you may find certain graphic scenes to be emotionally disturbing.

Perhaps some might say that the images featured are of a gruesome nature...that is not the intention. It has been with great fortitude that such stills have been used.

As a mark of respect to the relevance this chapter may mean to you every page is framed in black.

Crime Through Time Museum

4

Genocide: murder of a nation

Who is this man?

Left school semi-literate

Faced trial for treason

Survived 17 assassination attempts

His father was called Alois Schicklgruber

Was elected leader of his party by one vote

Had his autobiography banned in many countries

Was raised as a Catholic and wanted to become an Abbot

Failed to take over the government of his country in a failed beer hall revolution

Once contemplated suicide and hid in his friends attic for two days evading the local police

Spent five years in prison as a result of a failed plot to take over the government of his country

Turn the page to find out

Adolf Hitler quotes

"Ayrian race" was the sole creative element of **mankind. The natural unit of mankind was the "volk", of which the German was the greatest ... and the state only existed to serve the "volk".**

"The Catholic Church has spilt more blood than any other religion."

"There is no such thing as coming to an understanding with the Jews. It must be the hard-and-fast 'Either-Or'."

"The Jews will be liquidated for at least a thousand years."

"The New Testament is also full of contradictions, but that hasn't prevented the spread of Christianity."

"If twelve or fifteen thousand of these Jews who were corrupting the nation had been forced to submit to poison-gas, just as hundreds of thousands of our best German workers from every social stratum and from every trade and calling had to face it in the field, then the millions of sacrifices made at the front would not have been in vain."

"If I had any inkling in 1924 that I should become Reich chancellor I would never have written *Mein Kampf*."

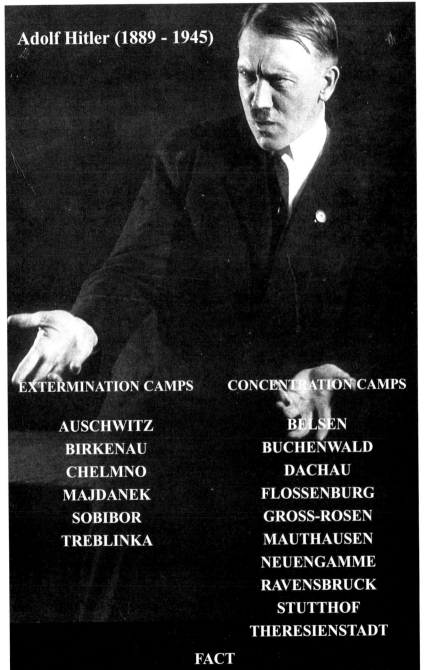

Adolf Hitler (1889 - 1945)

EXTERMINATION CAMPS	CONCENTRATION CAMPS
AUSCHWITZ	BELSEN
BIRKENAU	BUCHENWALD
CHELMNO	DACHAU
MAJDANEK	FLOSSENBURG
SOBIBOR	GROSS-ROSEN
TREBLINKA	MAUTHAUSEN
	NEUENGAMME
	RAVENSBRUCK
	STUTTHOF
	THERESIENSTADT

FACT

Some 56.4 million civilian and military lives were lost during
World War II - the bloodiest ever!

FOREWORD TO

Genocide: murder of a nation

Pictured above, Sir Winston seems to be giving the two fingers to the nation – Harvey Smith (show jumper) used the argument that he was only gesticulating in the same manner as Sir Winston when he was reprimanded in the 1970s for giving the 'V' sign to the crowd at an event.

PROFILE

Sir Winston, elder British statesman and military hero, gives his opinion in this frank foreword.

Sir Winston's career spanned both World War I and World War II. Winning the Nobel Peace Prize for literature in 1953 was not his finest hour…winning the war was. Awarded the Order of the Garter in 1953 he was to be honoured by the USA by being granted an honorary citizenship a few years before his death.

Overcoming a childhood stutter he went on to become one of history's greatest orators and is still quoted to this day with his 'Fight on the Beaches' speech.

Amazingly, Sir Winston was not the brightest of pupils at school and had great difficulty in learning to read and write.

In spite of this, Sir Winston Churchill served as Britain's Prime Minister twice, including during World War II.

Foreword
By the Rt. Hon. Winston S. Churchill
(1874 - 1965)

Sir Winston Churchill
1874 - 1965
British Statesman, Prime Minister, World War II Leader

Sir Winston giving the 'V' for 'Victory' sign...the right way round

A Struggle for the Soul of the Jewish People

SOME people like Jews and some do not; but no thoughtful man can doubt the fact that they are beyond all question the most formidable and the most remarkable race which has ever appeared in the world. And it may well be that this same astounding race may at the present time be in the actual process of producing another system of morals and philosophy, as malevolent as Christianity was benevolent, which, if not arrested would shatter irretrievably all that Christianity has rendered possible. It would almost seem as if the gospel of Christ and the gospel of Antichrist were destined to originate among the same people; and that this mystic and mysteri-

81

-ous race had been chosen for the supreme manifestations, both of the divine and the diabolical.

The National Russian Jews, in spite of the disabilities under which they have suffered, have managed to play an honourable and successful part in the national life even of Russia. As bankers and industrialists they have strenuously promoted the development of Russia's economic resources, and they were foremost in the creation of those remarkable organisations, the Russian Co-operative Societies. In politics their support has been given, for the most part, to liberal and progressive movements, and they have been among the staunchest upholders of friend-ship with France and Great Britain.

International Jews

In violent opposition to all this sphere of Jewish effort rise the schemes of the International Jews. The adherents of this sinister confederacy are mostly men reared up among the unhappy populations of countries where Jews are persecuted for their race. Most, if not all, of them have forsaken the faith of their forefathers, and divorced from their minds all spiritual hopes of the next world.

This movement among the Jews is not new. From the days of Spartacus-Weishaupt to those of Karl Marx, and down to Trotsky (Russia), Bela Kun (Hungary), Rosa Luxembourg (Germany), and Emma Goldman (United States), this worldwide conspiracy for the overthrow of civilisation and for the reconstitution of society on the basis of arrested development, of envious malevolence, and impossible equality, has been steadily growing.

It played, as a modern writer, Mrs Webster, has so ably shown, a definitely recognisable part in the tragedy of the French Revolution. It has been the mainspring of every subversive movement during the Nineteenth century; and now at last this band of extraordinary personalities from the underworld of the great cities of Europe and America have gripped the Russian people by the hair of their heads and have become practically the undisputed masters of that enormous empire.

Terrorist Jews

There is no need to exaggerate the part played in the creation of Bolshevism and the actual bringing about of the Russian Revolution: by these international and for the most part atheistical Jews. It is certainly a very great one; it probably outweighs all others. With the notable exception of Lenin, the majority of the leading figures are Jews.

Moreover, the principal inspiration and driving power comes from the Jewish leaders. Thus Tchitcherin, a pure Russian, is eclipsed by his nominal subordinate Litvinoff, and the influence of Russians like Bukharin or Lunacharski cannot be compared with the power of Trotsky, or of Zinovieff, the Dictator of the Red Citadel (Petrograd), or of Krassin or Radek - all Jews. In the Soviet institutions the predominance of Jews is even more astonish

ing. And the prominent, if not indeed the principal, part in the system of terrorism applied by the extraordinary Commissions for Combating Counter-Revolution has been taken by Jews, and in some notable cases by Jewesses.

The same evil prominence was obtained by Jews in the brief period of terror during which Bela Kun ruled in Hungary. The same phenomenon has been presented in Germany (especially in Bavaria), so far as this madness has been allowed to prey upon the temporary prostration of the German people. Although in all these countries there are many non-Jews every bit as bad as the worst of the Jewish revolutionaries, the part played by the latter in proportion to their numbers in the population is astonishing. "Protector of the Jews."

Needless to say, the most intense passions of revenge have been excited in the breasts of the Russian people. Wherever General Denikin's authority could reach, protection was always accorded to the Jewish population, and strenuous efforts were made by his officers to prevent reprisals and to punish those guilty of them. So much was this the case that the Petlurist propaganda against General Denikin denounced him as the Protector of the Jews.

The Misses Healy, nieces of Mr Tim Healy, relating their personal experiences in Kieff, have declared that to their knowledge on more than one occasion officers who committed offences against Jews were reduced to the ranks and sent out of the city to the front. But the hordes of brigands by whom the whole vast expanse of the Russian Empire is becoming infested do not hesitate to gratify their lust for blood and for revenge at the expense of the innocent Jewish population whenever an opportunity occurs.

The brigand Makhno, the hordes of Petlura and of Gregorieff, who signalised their every success by the most brutal massacres, everywhere found among the half-stupefied, half-infuriated population an eager response to anti-Semitism in its worst and foulest forms. The fact that in many cases Jewish interests and Jewish places of worship are excepted by the Bolsheviks from their universal hostility has tended more and more to associate the Jewish race in Russia with the villainies which are now being perpetrated.

A Home for the Jews

Zionism offers the third sphere to the political conceptions of the Jewish race. In violent contrast to international communism.

Zionism has already become a factor in the political convulsions of Russia, as a powerful competing influence in Bolshevik circles with the international communistic system. Nothing could be more significant than the fury with which Trotsky has attacked the Zionists generally, and Dr Weissmann in particular. The cruel penetration of his mind leaves him in no doubt that his schemes of a world-wide communistic State under Jewish domination are directly thwarted and hindered by this new ideal, which directs the energies and the hopes of Jews in every land towards a simpler, a truer, and a far more attainable goal. The struggle which is now beginning between the Zionist and Bolshevik Jews is little less than a struggle for the soul of the Jewish people

Sir Winston Churchill
1922

History howlers

The children who think Hitler was Britain's wartime leader

By **Tony Halpin**
Education Correspondent

Hitler: Whose side?

Henry VIII: How many wives?

Churchill: 16 per cent failed to name him as wartime premier

HE may have led Britain to victory in World War II, but his feats appear to have been lost on the children of today.

A survey of secondary school pupils published yesterday found that one in six could not identify **Winston Churchill** as our wartime prime minister.

Astonishingly, four per cent named Adolf Hitler and three per cent believed Margaret Thatcher guided us through our darkest days.

The findings led to calls last night for history to be re-established as an obligatory subject up to GCSE.

Among other gaffes uncovered in the survey of 200 youngsters, two out of three did not know when **World War I** was fought and nearly a quarter could not even place it in the right century.

Half had no idea that Oliver **Cromwell** was a key figure in the English Civil War. One in six, including a quarter of sixth formers, thought he was involved in the **Battle of Hastings**.

A third did not know who the English were fighting at Hastings, with one in eight saying Harold's men were repelling the Scots.

Forty per cent also did not

know how many wives Henry VIII had.

The survey, carried out for textbook publisher Osprey, concluded that history was being squeezed out of the curriculum. It called for the subject to be made compulsory for GCSE, alongside English, maths and science.

A quarter of those surveyed said they had dropped history at 14 because it clashed with other subjects on their timetables.

Two-thirds of them opted for geography instead, many because they regarded history as a more difficult subject.

A leading Oxford University

historian said many pupils dropped the subject without having gained an 'accurate knowledge of the main events of the past few hundred years'.

Professor Robert O'Neill said even students who went on to take history degrees lacked a broad understanding of the past.

'They have studied particular periods of history with great intensity but they don't have the breadth of knowledge students used to have 20 years ago,' he said.

'Children should at least know that it wasn't Oliver Cromwell on the beach at Hastings.'

Professor O'Neill, who is editor of a series of textbooks published by Osprey, said an 'awful lot' of students gained their knowledge of the past from films and television, often inaccurately.

'They go and watch Mel Gibson in The Patriot and come along with a very distorted picture of England's involvement in America,' he said.

His comments appeared to be borne out by the difficulty young-sters had distinguishing between historical and fictional characters - although the survey gave no estimate of the extent to which some may have been deliberately misleading interviewers.

One in seven believed that Rowan Atkinson's comic creation Blackadder was a real person, while 76 per cent thought Nell Gwynn was the product of a writer's imagination.

The findings shocked Shadow Education Secretary Theresa May, who said: 'What are we coming to when so many pupils don't know the dates of the world wars and don't know the basics of our country's history?'

t.halpin@dailymail.co.uk

IMPERIAL WAR MUSEUM AWARDED £17 MILLION GRANT FROM THE LOTTERY FUND FOR HOLOCAUST EXHIBITION

CRIME THROUGH TIME MUSEUM = £ZERO

The Times newspaper reported that tourism officials are considering taking action against the Crime Through Time museum because exhibits on display relating to the Holocaust are of questionable taste and are considered "offensive" and "voyeuristic".

The article went on to say, 'Most have been upset about seeing Nazi memorabilia, which includes Nazi helmets, badges, SS rings, swastika flags and a bust of Hitler.'

Such objections should also be directed at the Imperial War Museum, but it would seem their connections are in higher places when awarded an unbelievable £17 million for an exhibition which, although, is voyeuristic is by no means as comprehensive as that on display at the Crime Through Time museum, which receives no funding at all from any source other than the revenue of entry receipts.

Anger at Nazi exhibition

The Times - March 24, 200.

TOURISM officials are considering whether to take action following several complaints about a museum in Gloucestershire which displays Nazi memorabilia, Ku Klux Klan outfits and information about gangsters. Visitors to Crime Through Time, in Newent, say the museum exhibits are of questionable taste, with some saying they are "offensive and voyeuristic".

Most have been upset about seeing Nazi memorabilia, which includes Nazi helmets, badges, SS rings, swastika flags and a bust of Hitler, as well as references to "the legendary figure of Sir Oswald Mosley". A recently erected sign outside the museum, which shows a bare body stretched across a swastika, has drawn particular complaints from the public.

Further concern has been expressed about the museum website, which has profiles of former and current criminals, some of whom are still serving time, and has links to other websites devoted to criminals still in jail.

One link is to a website highlighting the life of Charles Bronson, who was sentenced to life in prison last year for taking a prison teacher hostage while serving time at Hull jail — and there is an Internet competition to win a

"unique piece of signed artwork from the legendary hard man himself", which was drawn in his cell.

A spokeswoman for the Newent Tourism Information Centre, which has passed complaints on to the Forest of Dea[n]
"Some people have said others have said that it i[s] children. People have fo[und it] offensive."

The Forest of Dean T[ourism] looking into the matter a[nd] the details of complaint[s].

The museum, which is [Vic]torian magistrates court [com]plete with its own cell blo[ck] for its fourth summer se[ason].

It is run by local bus[inessman] who is planning to hol[d an] October, with appearan[ces by] land members.

He says the museu[m is a] hobby gone mad", and [the posi]tion at the entrance to t[he] website, indicates that [it is] and not suitable for you[ng].

"Crime is not a pleasant subject," says Jones. "It's up to individuals to choose whether they come into the museum, or visit our website, and parents and guardians of children have to make decisions on their behalf. The exhibits here, in[...]

Museum owner Andy Jones with his controversial exhibition of Ku Klux Klan and Nazi costumes

Eicke - Wearing the
1942 Pattern Collar Insignia

The inventor of the concentration camp terror system was Theodor
Eicke - Joined the Nazis as an SA man in 1928 rising to command
an SS regiment. Himmler appointed him overlord of Concentration
Camps and head of the SS Totenkopfverbande (the 'Death's Head'
camp guards).

Poland 1939
Himmler, left, with Eicke

Eicke, right, controlled
SS Waffen Division

SS-Obergruppenfuhrer Theodor Eicke was awarded the Knights
Cross and then the Oakleaves by a grateful Hitler when the
Russians were unable to beat Eicke's Waffen-SS division that had
a ferocious fighting spirit.

Introduction

Phil Froom a highly respected Holocaust related collector, historian and researcher who first met Andy Jones whilst visiting the Auschwitz Death Camp in Poland.

For almost thirty years now I have been a collector of Militaria. My interest in the Holocaust came about when I had been visiting Krakow in Poland for a weekend and purely by chance saw an advertisement for a day trip to the Auschwitz death camp. With little more than a morbid curiosity I took the tour.

I have never before been so moved by a visit to anywhere in the world. Of Auschwitz I knew, but like most people I had not realised the true evil of the place — nor its size... *Auschwitz 1* is of a size I had expected, similar to a modest army camp. *Auschwitz 2* is massive and although most of the actual huts have been burned down, their locations can be clearly seen by the brick chimneys and steps. They go on as far as the eye could see...

I saw whole ends of huts filled with shoes, hand addressed suitcases and worse still - human hair. Then there was the saddest sight of all, a room dedicated to the children. Babies' everyday belongings filled the place. Young children's toys lay around with dummies and their clothes bringing the horror of it all to life. What use were these innocent children to the Reich - every one of them went straight to the gas chamber!

From this point on I came across ephemera and artifacts from the holocaust in my travels in Poland and the East, and my collection began. Eventually. I would spend my spare time and weekends actively seeking items for my collection and had some very interesting and poignant finds.

I have visited the "Crime Through Time" museum on many occasions, both to assist Andy Jones with research and also out of personal interest. The museum portrays all aspects of "Crime" and what greater crime can there have been but the Holocaust.

The museum has a fine and comprehensive collection of Holocaust related artifacts and ephemera and shows the Holocaust in all its aspects from the documentation to the much more graphic photographs taken by the shocked allies as they overran the camps.

What must be the best collection of concentration camp uniforms outside the actual camp museums themselves can be seen at Crime Through Time... I am told that the museum receives complaints about the graphic nature of the Holocaust section and the display of Nazi regalia and that "this type of thing" shouldn't be on display. However, it has to be remembered that no matter how terrible the Holocaust was and how graphic the pictures are — it is not a 'video nasty' — it is HISTORY.

The Holocaust happened and it must be remembered in order that nothing like it ever happens again. The Nazis existed and no matter what your personal views on them, they are irrevocably tied to German history and to the Holocaust and they too must be viewed in the same way — a case study from History.

When asked to write a little on the Holocaust and upon the museum's coverage of the subject I was happy to do so. I fully understand the reason Crime Through Time chose to portray the terrible events that took place in Europe between 1932 and 1945. I also hope that the following will give the reader a little of the black background which led to and resulted in the attempt by the Nazis to eradicate an entire race...

P.M. Froom
Holocaust collector and historian

Number 4 in Hitler's Nazi Party Manifesto:

Only those who are our fellow countrymen can become citizens. Only those who have German blood, regardless of creed, can be our countrymen. Hence no Jew can be a countryman.

An estimated 6 million Jews were murdered in the Holocaust. Over half were systematically exterminated by use of the gas chamber/crematorium system of the Nazi death camps between 1942 and 1945.

Treblinka, Auschwitz-Birkenau, Dachau, Chelmno, Sobibor, Belzek and Majdanek are names that will not be forgotten.

The Wannsee Conference, in Berlin, on 20th January 1942 the "Final Solution" was an official policy and a major obsession of the Nazi regime. From this point onwards camps were constructed for the express purpose of radical mass extermination, principally of Jews, but of other groups as well.

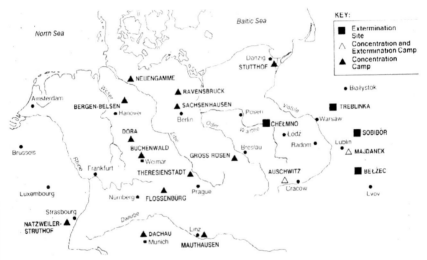

Map of Nazi Concentration and Death Camps

Almost immediately following his rise to power, Hitler began the creation of concentration camps. Initially these were designed to incarcerate political prisoners (enemies of the regime), criminals and security risks. While conditions were, predictably, horrible in these camps, and while the death rates were high, there is no evidence that they were used for extermination purposes. By the late 1930s there were literally hundreds of camps scattered throughout Germany and with the Nazi takeover of Czechoslovakia, Austria, Poland, Holland and France, camps were established throughout the Reich.

The death rates were so high from malnutrition, typhus and

Belsen - Nazi Horror Camp. In agony from mistreatment an inmate too weak even to walk sits within the enclosure waiting for aid.

exhaustion that the disposal of corpses became a serious problem. When the 11th Armoured Division of the British Second Army reached Belsen concentration camp at Hanover, Germany, in April 1945, about 60,000 helpless Jews and political prisoners were found dying from starvation, typhus, typhoid and dysentery. Some had never had water for more than six days.

The area was littered with decomposing bodies and investigation revealed that huts capable of sheltering 30 people were occupied by as many as 500. In many cases, prisoners had died of suffocation because they were too weak to struggle for a gasp of air. Allied Military Government officers immediately rushed medical aid to the area and ordered Nazi SS guards at the camp to bury the victims.

BELSEN - Located near the village of Bergen, was created as a model repatriation and transit centre. Never formally given the distinction of being a concentration camp it was known as a centre for the privileged. In 1943, Himmler had wanted Belsen to be a model camp that would withstand the rigours of inspection teams.

Belsen's purposes from the beginning were not very clear, so Himmler's aim was never achieved. In its first five months of existence, Belsen served as a small Russian POW camp, a convalescence camp, a transit centre, an exchange camp and a collection centre for the internal American citizens.

DEATH CAMPS

Two precedents for the death camps are the Nazi Euthanasia Project and the Aschaffenburg concentration camp.

An organisation created for the 'medical' killing of mental and physical defectives was under the guise of the T-4 organization also known as the Reich Work Group of Sanitoriums and Nursing Homes (Reichsarbeitsgemeinschaft Heil und Pflegeanstalten).

Operating from the Berlin Chancellery, at Tiergartenstrasse 4, the program was rationalized as the elimination of "life unworthy of life."

A dead baby and the body of other children lie in the mass grave dug by German civilians of Nordhausen

The T-4 programme paved the way for the Holocaust and had the effect of legitimising the Nazi killings and kept to the Nazi principle of racial purity, eugenics and health reasons.

Euthanasia was presented as a necessary program for eliminating those who carried defective genetic materials that might endanger the quality of the "Aryan" stock. The German medical profession was soon to become corrupted. The Nazi killing machine had, somehow, secured the services of doctors whose duty it was to heal the sick…not help kill them or carry out barbaric experiments on them.

The process of bastardising doctors was a gradual process but once on that slippery slope of euthanasia programmes headed as 'mercy killings' it soon resulted in the full scale involvement of some members of the medical profession in the mass extermination of Jews and others in the Nazi death camps.

The T-4 program was crucial in developing the technology that would later be applied to mass murder.

Euthanasia centres, like the ones at Hadamar and Brandenburg were equipped with gas chambers (using carbon monoxide) and crematoria.

Another development in the emergence of the death camps was a series of events that took place at the Aschaffenburg concentration camp, in Aschaffenburg, Bavaria.

Stutthof, November 1941: Himmler visits camp officers. (USHMM)

A group of SS men, in 1933, killed a number of Jews at the camp and were subsequently arrested by the local authorities. Of course SS officials insisted that their men were not subject to civil authority. Himmler demanded that no charges be brought against the men by the authorities. A precedent was now set for future mass murder in the concentration and extermination camps.

The Nazi Extermination Camps

There is a clear difference between death camps (killing centres) and concentration camps. Although there were many hundreds of concentration camps some could have been given the title of 'death camps' due to many thousands of inmates dying of starvation, dropping dead from hard work, dying because of the cold weather, dying from epidemics or executed for crimes or alleged crimes.

Early on in the Nazi regime many camps were established under the "Protective Custody" law of February 28, 1933, which authorized the police to make arrests on suspicion of criminal activity, and people were incarcerated without benefit of legal counsel or trial.

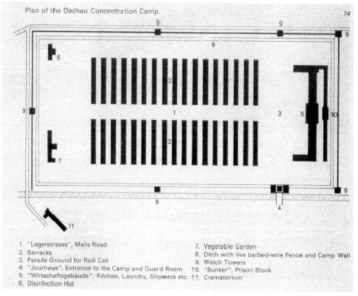

Plan of the Dachau Concentration Camp   74

1. "Lagerstrasse", Main Road
2. Barracks
3. Parade Ground for Roll Call
4. "Jourhaus", Entrance to the Camp and Guard Room
5. "Wirtschaftsgebäude", Kitchen, Laundry, Showers etc.
6. Disinfection Hut
7. Vegetable Garden
8. Ditch with live barbed-wire Fence and Camp Wall
9. Watch Towers
10. "Bunker", Prison Block
11. Crematorium

In 1933 the first camp to be created was Dachau, near Munich, in the south. Also in that same year, as the need for such camps increased, Buchenwald was established near Weimar in the central part of Germany and Sachsenhausen, near Berlin, in the north. Additional camps were constructed between 1934 and 1941. Communists, socialists, political criminals, homosexuals, democrats and Jews were the first inmates of these camps.

Genocide: Murder of a Nation

The beginning of mass extermination

(Kulmhof) Chelmno	Auschwitz Birkenau	Belzek	Sobibor	Treblinka	Majdanek	Stutthof
December 7 1941 Gas Vans	September 1941 Zyklon B	March 17 1942 Carbon Monoxide gas	March 1942 Carbon Monoxide gas	July 23 1942 Carbon Monoxide gas	October 1942 Carbon Monoxide & Zyklon B gas	June 1942 Zyklon B gas
Killed 320,000	Killed 1,500,000	Killed 600,000	Killed 250,000	Killed 700,000	Killed 1,380,000	Killed 65,000

"Most of you know what it means when 100 corpses are lying side by side, or 500, or 1,000.

This is a page of glory in our history which has never been written and is never to be written…!"

Himmler, on killing the Jews, in a speech to SS leaders – Poland, October 1943

Some camps were specifically equipped for mass killing by means of gas chambers and crematoria for disposing of the remains.

In the earlier camps some of the extermination methods were rather crude when exhaust fumes from truck engines or tank engines were pumped into sealed gassing vans, sealed railroad cars or specially constructed gas chambers.

In some of the later camps Zyklon-B pellets were used and in Stutthof lethal injections were used to kill sick prisoners. None of these methods made shootings, hangings and fatal beatings obsolete!

EXTERMINATION CAMPS

AUSCHWITZ-BIRKENAU - Easily the most notorious of the entire killing centres, Auschwitz-Birkenau had two function: being both a concentration camp, where inmates were used as forced labour, and an extermination centre.

The geographical location of Auschwitz (Polish: Oswiecim), the town, is some 37 miles west of Krakow, in Eastern Upper Silesia - annexed to Nazi Germany after the defeat of Poland, in September, 1939. Auschwitz was at the centre of several major Polish cities, and was ideal for the shipping of prisoners from German occupied Europe. Eventually there were three camps at Auschwitz. The first camp was built, on the orders of Heinrich Himmler, shortly after Poland's defeat, in a suburb of Oswiecim and was designed to hold about 10,000 political prisoners.

Above the main entrance were the words, "Arbeit Macht Frei" (work will make you free). Words that gave false hope that hard work would result in freedom. The camp, and later the "Buna" of Auschwitz III, made extensive use of slave labour, but the only hope of escape was death. The commandant's office and living quarters were on Auschwitz I which also held the administration building, kitchen, infirmary, the main guard station, one gas chamber and crematorium, the Gestapo camp, medical experiments centre and gallows. Criminals were housed in Barracks housed on the camp. These barracks also held the courtrooms where prisoners were tried and usually sentenced to death. Auschwitz I was surrounded by double barbed wire electric fences and nine watchtowers. Auschwitz was also a location for medical experiments - using humans as guinea pigs. Most notorious of the doctors of these experiments was Josef Mengele whose favourite experiments were on twins. Dwarfs were also used for experiments.

ALEXANDER KALAN – JEWISH DWARF

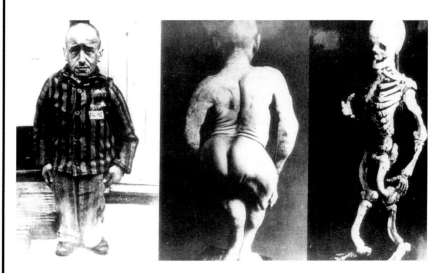

Above, the three photos of Kalan taken over a few days

Alexander Kalan was a Dutch Jew. He was born in 1899 and apart from being a dwarf he also suffered skeletal malformation (osteomalacia). This malformation didn't impinge his intelligence, however, and he was a highly skilled high school teacher. In 1941 the Germans were sending Jews from the Netherlands to labour camps. Kalan eventually arrived at Gusen – one of Mauthausen's labour camps. In 1943 he was transferred to the main camp of Mauthausen, where the camp doctors were extremely interested in him! The doctors ran a large programme of the usual ghoulish medical experiments. Kalan represented a very interesting chance to carry out an anatomical experiment on such an interesting specimen! A single knife thrust to his chest killed Kalan on 27th January 1943, his body was stripped of its flesh and his skeleton was mounted and used for research into bone malformation. It seems rather ironic that the Germans were looking to create a super race and iron out all the faults so why they would want to research bone malformation seems a waste of the little man's life.

The Angel of Death
Dr Josef Mengele
1911-1979?

Scarce photo of Mengele - many signed pieces are on display in the museum

Dr Josef Mengele cut a dashing figure in Nazi uniform. His horror experiments on inmates at Auschwitz earned him the sobriquet of "the Angel of Death".

Some female inmates at Auschwitz actually called him a "beautiful person" and others described him as "gorgeous".

His experiments on twins were notorious and he once had twin boys killed just so that he could settle an argument with another doctor and performed autopsies on them. He slipped away just before Auschwitz was liberated and escaped to South America, where he became a notorious legend.

A most bizarre act carried out by Mengele on the Jewish Day of Atonement, in 1943, happened when he roared up on his motorcycle at a soccer field where some 2,000 boys had been assembled. As per his instructions a plank was nailed to one of the goalposts, the boys were ordered to walk under it. Instinctively the boys knew what was going on. Anyone not measuring up to the marker would be selected for death!

One of the survivors said, "It was 100% clear to everyone what the purpose of the game was," "We all began stretching. Everyone wanted to get another half-inch, another centimeter."

Boys started stuffing stones and rags in their shoes to add height. Some boys who were too short hid amongst taller boys and somehow some managed to escape the test. Half the boys passed the test – the other half that failed were taken away to be gassed. Mengele, the Angel of Death, was literally playing God, he knew of the Jewish prayer, traditionally recited on Yom Kippur, that tells of the flock being led beneath the 'rod of the shepherd', the Lord who decides which of them will live.

Angel of Death

Mengele actually volunteered for Auschwitz in order to pursue research into biology of racial difference, one of Himmler's favourite topics! At Auschwitz Mengele selected about 1,500 sets of, mostly Jewish children, identical and fraternal twins. They would receive extra food and a (temporary) reprieve from the gas chambers for participating in his research.

He would use one twin for the control subject and would experiment with the other. The children would have to give blood, be injected with chemicals, and be exposed to radiation and, often, experimental surgery was performed on them. Often Mengele ordered that one or both twins were to be killed so that he could study them at autopsy.

Mengele, in attempting to demonstrate the purported genetic degeneracy of Jews, selected people with physical deformities, ordered them executed, and then had their flesh boiled away so that their skeletons could he studied.

Experiments were not just confined to Jews, he discovered a Gypsy family which included seven dwarfs – he subjected them to painful experiments, then would keep them for what was called his "private zoo" and forced them to perform nude before an audience of SS men.

In 1944, 3,000 Gypsies were sent to the gas chambers at Auschwitz after Berlin changed its Gypsy policy! Thousands of able-bodied Gypsy prisoners were sent to other camps as slave labourers. At Auschwitz two special sections were set up, one was the Gypsy camp, which housed 10,000 in thirty barracks of Block B2 at Birkenau. It had been established in February 1942, when Gypsies were first being deported from Germany and Western Europe. The Gypsies lived together as families, and few were put to work outside their compound.

Wounded on the Eastern Front in 1943, Mengele was given the position of SS garrison physician (Standortartz) of Auschwitz. In that capacity, he was responsible for the differentiation and selection of those fit to work and those destined for gassing.

Following the end of the war Mengele, after spending a short time in a British internment camp, went into hiding. Through a network of Vatican sympathizers, he was able to reach South America.

In the 1950s, Mengele's deeds at Auschwitz became known and prosecutors in West Germany sought him for arrest. A special court set up by Israel pronounced Mengele's guilt in 1985.

By the spring of that year investigators learned that Mengele had, in all likelihood, died in a swimming accident in Brazil in 1979. The Mengele family confirmed the story and the body was exhumed. After being examined by sixteen forensic experts, it was announced that "within a reasonable scientific certainty" that the body was that of the Angel of Death – Dr Josef Mengele

"Of course I am a doctor; to preserve a human life I would remove a gangrenous appendix. Well the Jew is the gangrenous appendix in the body of mankind."
Dr Fritz Klein – Concentration Camp Doctor

At times the death camps must have been like a cauldron of blood boiling over and spilling on to those inmates that were sickened by what they had seen or just could not contemplate what might happen to them. Sometimes inmates would revolt but as in this case an inmate at Mauthausen has elected to end his own life.

German newspapers and publications as on display at the museum

Hypothermia experiments were carried out using Gypsies as the primary subjects proving that the holocaust wasn't all about the Jews. Usually Jews or Gypsies were dumped naked into freezing cold baths of water or if it was winter they were left, naked, outside in sub-zero temperatures. Notes were taken of the subject's temperature, respiration and heartbeat as they deteriorated and died. The experiments were in aid of securing information in order to see if German pilots could survive if they ditched their planes in the freezing sea! More bizarre experiments beyond comprehension were carried out but in the face of saving human dignity these are withheld.

The second site, known as Auschwitz II, or Birkenau, was located 1.5 miles from the original camp. Construction began in October 1941. Rudolf Hoess was named the commandant of the camp. Under his command, the main goal of the camp was the extermination and elimination of all the prisoners. Auschwitz III, also known as Monoschwitz, consisted of a small area that contained the sub camp and the "buna." The main function of this sector was the production of synthetic fuel and rubber. As a result of expansion of the main Auschwitz camp in October 1942, Auschwitz III also was utilized for holding prisoners.

More than any of the killing centres in the Nazi system, Auschwitz exemplifies the rationalization of murder. It was the most efficient camp established by the Nazi regime for carrying out the "Final Solution." The total number of Jewish dead in Auschwitz-Birkenau will never be known for certain for most were not registered. Estimates vary between one and two and a half million. The crematories and gas chamber equipments, constructed by Hoch und Tiefbau AG Kattowitz, were delivered by the Erfurt firm J.A. Topf & sons. At its peak, more than 20,000 people could be murdered and their bodies burned in a single day. In fact, the single day highest output was 24,000. Jews comprised the largest number of victims; at least one-third of the estimated 5 million to 6 million Jews killed by the Nazis during World War II died there. For this reason, Auschwitz has come to symbolise the holocaust more vividly than any other symbol. In addition to the Jews, however, large numbers of Poles, Soviet prisoners of war, gypsies, and homosexuals also died at Auschwitz.

During peak operation from March 1942 until November 1944, trains arrived almost daily with transports of Jews from all over occupied Europe. On the unloading ramp, new arrivals would undergo selection (*selektion*) by SS officers. Most women, children and those that looked unfit to work were sent to the left; while most young men and others that were fit would be sent to the right. The left line meant immediate death at the gas chambers and the right meant probable death from hard forced labour. The selection split families - mothers from their children, husbands and wives, brothers and sisters.

Those selected for forced labour were sent to a part of the camp called the "quarantine," where their heads were shaved and they were issued prison uniforms before being sent to one of the labour camps nearby. These prisoners were registered and received numbers tattooed on their left arm. Initially the numbers were tattooed on the left side of the chest. Approximately 405,000 prisoners were registered in this way. The vast majority of the Auschwitz victims were not registered at all, those men and women who, upon arrival at Auschwitz II, were led to the gas chambers and killed there immediately. Only about 65,000 of the tattooed inmates survived the camp experience.

Arrivals at the complex were separated into three groups. One group went to the gas chambers within a few hours; these people were sent to the Birkenau camp, where more than 20,000 people could be gassed and cremated each day. Before the bodies were burned the victim's hair was cut off and gold fillings and false teeth made of precious metals were removed. The hair was used for making haircloth, and the metals were melted into bars and sent to Berlin. After the liberation, tons of hair were found in camp warehouses. Laboratory analysis of the hair conducted by The Kracow Institute of Judicial Expertise found traces of prussic acid, a poisonous component typical of Zyklon - proof that the victims were gassed! A second group of prisoners were used as slave labour at large industrial factories for such companies as I. G. Farben and Krupp.

> **Schindler's List**
> Some prisoners survived through the help of German industrialist Oskar Schindler, who diverted them from Auschwitz to his factory near Krakow and later at a factory in what is now the Czech Republic.

At the Auschwitz complex 405,000 prisoners were recorded as labourers between 1940 and 1945. Of these about 340,000 perished through executions, beatings, starvation, and sickness.

When the SS realised that the end of the war was near, they attempted to remove all evidence of the atrocities committed there. They dismantled the gas chambers, crematories and other buildings. They burned documents and evacuated all the prisoners who could walk to the interior of Germany. When the Soviet army marched into Auschwitz to liberate the camp on 27 January 1945, they found about 7,600 survivors abandoned there. More than 58,000 prisoners had already been evacuated by the Nazis and sent on a final death march to Germany.

In 1946, Poland founded a museum at the site of the Auschwitz concentration camp in remembrance of its victims. By 1994, about 22 million visitors 700,000 annually-had passed through the iron gates that bear the cynical motto previously mentioned "Arbeit macht frei" (Work makes one free).

> **Adolf Hitler**
> "I believe to-day that my conduct is in accordance with the will of the Almighty Creator. In standing guard against the Jew I am defending the handiwork of the Lord."

BELZEC – Founded by Odilo Globocnik, Belzec was located in the Lublin district of Poland. There was no industrial activity at Belzec; the Germans built the camp for the sole purpose of exterminating the Jews of south-eastern Poland. Belzec was the only killing centre that was not well hidden. There were no crematoria in the camp, so after people were gassed, their bodies were burned in open pits which had been dug in the ground. Since the camp was so small, prisoners had to be burned quickly and immediately upon arrival in order to make room for new transports.

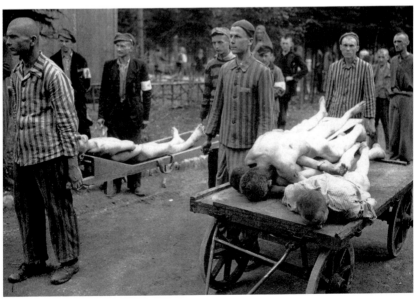

By mid-March 1942 the decision was made to convert the camp into a killing centre under the command of Odilo Globocnic, the police commander of Lublin. Globocnic also established the killing centres at Majdanek and Sobibor.. The Nazis began deporting Jews from Poland and later from the German Reich, Czechoslovakia, and Romania. For the first few months, extermination was accomplished by using diesel fumes; by August 1942 Zyklon-B (hydrocyanic acid fumes) gas was used experimentally. The gas proved to be so effective that it was also used at other death camps.

The corpses of the victims were stripped of any valuables (rings, gold fillings, etc.) and buried in nearby mass graves. Extermination ceased in late 1942, and early the next year the bodies were exhumed and cremated and the camp was closed. Germans were re-settled to the site for agricultural work. It is estimated that more than six hundred thousand persons died at Belzec, including two thousand non-Jews.

CHELMNO – Was a Nazi extermination camp in Poland on the river Ner, 37 miles (60 Km) from Lodz. The Germans called it Kulmhof. The village of Chelmno in the district of Kolo is situated 8 miles (14 Km) from the town of Kolo. A railway line from Lodz to Poznan runs through this town and is connected with the village of Chelmno with a branch line.

This was the first of the killing centres. Set up in 1942 in the middle of the Warta River region, this camp was geographically isolated. Because of its seclusion, the camp's existence remained a secret. Chelmno had no need for housing accommodations; prisoners were immediately gassed in large trucks and then taken to immense graves in nearby forests or to the crematoria. Ninety-nine percent of the people exterminated at Chelmno were Jews, including most of the population of the Lodz Ghetto. The camp was constructed there for the mass extermination of Jews from the Western Polish provinces that had been annexed by the Third Reich.

Under the command of Hauptsturmfuhrerer Herbert Lange, Jews transported to Chelmno were forced, or enticed, into vans, the doors were closed and latched and the motors were started. A hose carried the carbon monoxide fumes into the van. It usually required

10 or 15 minutes to murder all who were in the van. The driver then drove the bodies to the pre-dug graves in the forest where Jewish workers unloaded the bodies into the graves. The van then returned to the camp and the operation was repeated.

The estimated number of people killed at Chelmno varies from 170,000 to 360,000 men, women and children, virtually all Jews. Most authorities agree on the higher estimate. Despite this large number, few people in Poland or abroad ever knew of its existence, or were aware of the hundreds of thousands of victims it claimed. The camp was closed in 1943 but reopened in April 1944. Late in 1944 there were plans to shut down the camp; however, Soviet troops arrived before these plans could be implemented. As the Soviet troops advanced, SS guards liquidated the remaining prisoners.

Adolf Hitler – A rare signed photo dedicated by Hitler to Theodor Eicke, the inventor of the concentration camp terror system.

(This and many hundreds more of originals on display at the museum)

http://www.crimethroughtime.com

MAJDANEK - Was located two miles from Lublin. Although the camp had complete facilities for extermination and a very high death rate, Majdanek was not intended to be an extermination camp. Majdanek was the Nazi's second largest camp, and it had a very large inmate population. Eventually, the camp's purpose turned more toward execution than labour and methods of gassing, shooting, and hanging were used to kill hundreds or thousands of people at a time. This German extermination camp was originally constructed in 1941 as a prisoner-of-war camp. The camp was built using prison labour - mostly Polish and Soviet prisoners of war. In its first year of operation the camp housed mostly Jewish inmates. Unlike Belzek and Sobibor, there was some industrial activity at the camp and some non-Jewish inmates were housed there.

A 'gassing' facility was installed In October 1942, consisting of crude wooden barracks. Later, more sophisticated concrete chambers were constructed with airtight steel doors. Initially, carbon monoxide gas was utilized; later, after their successful use at Belzek, Zyklon-B gas canisters were brought in for use. Jews were transported to Majdanek from Germany and the Netherlands. Upon their arrival, a *selektion* was carried out. Those able to work were assigned to agricultural and forestry work details. Those too sick, too weak, too young or too old to work were sent directly to the gas chambers! By the fall of 1943, 200,000 had been gassed. Many thousands of others died from exposure, beatings, epidemics and starvation.

In late 1943, plans were made to dismantle the camp. At that time there were several thousand Jews still in the camp. 17,000 were shot as part of a larger programme, referred to euphemistically as the *Erntefest*, or Fall Harvest. Majdanek was evacuated in April 1944 in advance of the Soviet capture of Lublin.

The world… " would be eternally grateful to me and to national socialism for having exterminated the Jews in Germany and central Europe." – Adolf Hitler

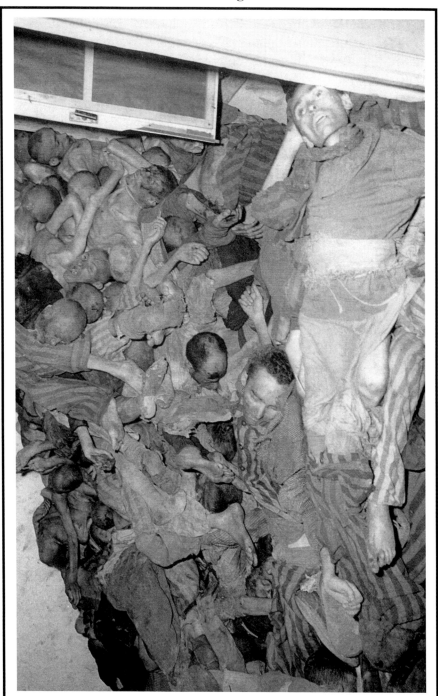

"Piles of dead bodies amassed during the Nazi Holocaust years."

SOBIBOR – This Nazi extermination camp was built in March 1942, in a forest near the village of Sobibór in eastern Poland, on the Bug River. Initially, the camp was assigned to SS-Obersturmfuhrer, Richard Thomella.

Franz Stangl
note the Horsewhip, a favourite status symbol

In April Obersturmfuhrer Franz Stangl replaced him. With the assistance of Christian Wirth, Stangl expanded the camp and its killing capacity.

In August, Stangl was transferred to Treblinka and was replaced by SS-Hauptsturmfuhrer Franz Reichleitner.

The Nazis built Sobibor as an advanced killing centre. Most of the prisoners brought to the camp were exterminated immediately upon arrival; only a few hundred remained in the camp as workers.

The camp operated from May 1942 until an uprising in October 1943. After the revolt in which 300 Jews escaped, Himmler ordered the camp to be liquidated because the witnesses who escaped posed a threat to the camp's secrecy.

Its five gas chambers killed an approximate total of two hundred and fifty thousand Jews. Most came from Poland and from the occupied areas of the Soviet Union, Slovakia and Western Europe.

Himmler with Hitler

STUTTHOF – Was an interment camp and later converted to a concentration camp and labour camp. In September 1939, the Nazis built the Stutthof concentration camp east of Danzig in the extreme northeast of Germany.

Heinrich Himmler inspects honour guard at Stutthoff , November 1941

Originally, the camp was under the jurisdiction of the Danzig chief of police; however, in 1941, it was reassigned as an SS camp. In 1943, the camp was enlarged and surrounded by electrified barbed wire fences.

Stutthof Commandant
Max Pauly 1941

While most of the prisoners at Stutthof were non-Jews, there were some Polish Jews interned in the camp. Stutthof was primarily a forced labour camp. The DAW (German Armament Works) installed a factory just outside the camp and in 1944 a Focke-Wulf aircraft factory was constructed there. Estimated victims are between 65,000 and 85,000.

TREBLINKA - Was located between the Polish towns of Siedlce and Malkinia, 62 miles northeast of Warsaw, Poland. Construction on the camp began in late May 1942 and was ready for operation in July 1942 as the third death camp in the River Bug chain, along with Sobibor and Belzec. The construction was carried out by Jewish and Polish slave labour under the direction of the SS. It was located about one and a half miles from the railway station. Heinrich Himmler chose Treblinka as the site for the extermination of the Jewish population of the Warsaw Ghetto because of its location northeast of Warsaw. Treblinka was the most efficient of all the killing centres. An estimated 1,000,000 people perished here! In just a little over a year, Jews from Poland, Germany, Austria, Czechoslovakia, Holland, Belgium, and Greece were exterminated at the rate of 25,000 to 35,000 a day.

From July 1942 to September 1942, three hundred thousand Jews were transported from Warsaw to Treblinka. Later, in May of 1943, the entire population of the Warsaw ghetto was liquidated and most were transported to Treblinka. By 11 July 1945, when Soviet troops entered Warsaw, more than 700,000 Jewish men, women, and children had been murdered at Treblinka. Under the command of Franz Stangl, who was also at the Sobibor concentration camp, the killing process was very similar to that of Belzek and Sobibor. Upon their arrival by railway freight cars, the victims at Treblinka II were separated according to sex and adults from children.

They were told that they were being transported to other work camps but first they had to bathe and be disinfected. They were stripped of their clothing and other possessions, marched into buildings containing "bathhouses," and gassed with carbon monoxide poison produced by the usual method of using diesel engines and pumped in through ceiling pipes camouflaged as showerheads. The route from the selection area to the gas chambers passed through a narrow fenced-in passage known as "the tube." Many realized that they were going to their death and, when they resisted, were beaten, clubbed with rifle butts and whips by the camp staff. In September 1942, several new and larger gas chambers were constructed!

The staff at both Treblinka camps was made up of about 40 SS officers and 150 Ukrainian guards. Extensive use was made of Jewish prisoners called *Sonderkommandos* - special work units. When they became too weak to do their work they were killed and replaced by younger and stronger inmates. Their job included the removal of gold teeth, dentures, and other valuables from the corpses. They were forced to transport the corpses to mass graves for burial, and later, when the bodies were exhumed, were used to burn the victims' bodies on iron grates.

On 2nd August, 1943 a planned rebellion by a *Sonderkommando* group occurred. Several Ukrainian guards and one SS officer were killed and more than 200 inmates escaped. Most were hunted down and killed or recaptured. Despite its failure, the rebellion and subsequent escape from Treblinka is a testimonial to the courage of the inmates and their resistance accelerated the closure of the camp. The facilities at Treblinka were closed at the end of November 1943. In 1967, Franz Stangl, commandant of Treblinka, was arrested in Brazil and extradited to the Germany. In December 1970, he was sentenced to life imprisonment for his part in the murder of 400,000 people. Stangl died in prison the following June.

"Christianity is the hardest blow that ever hit humanity. Bolshevism is the bastard son of Christianity; both are the monstrous issue of the Jews."

Adolf Hitler - 194

Genocide: Murder of a Nation

Nazi SS murder camp at Ohrdruf uncovered, photo shows evidence of
malnutrition to the point of slow starvation just before the Nazis fled

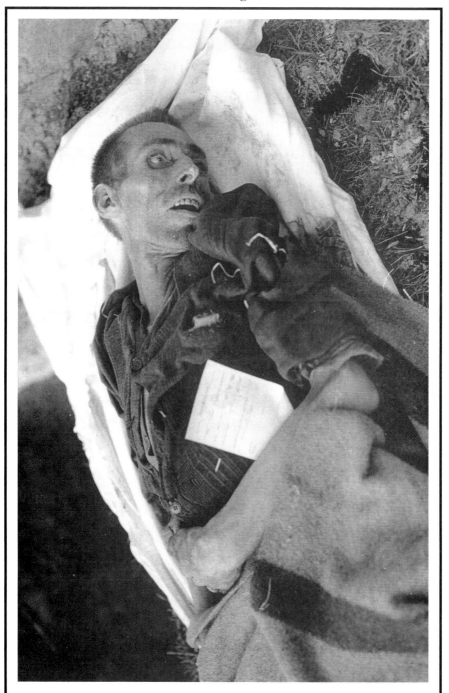

How can one human do this to another?

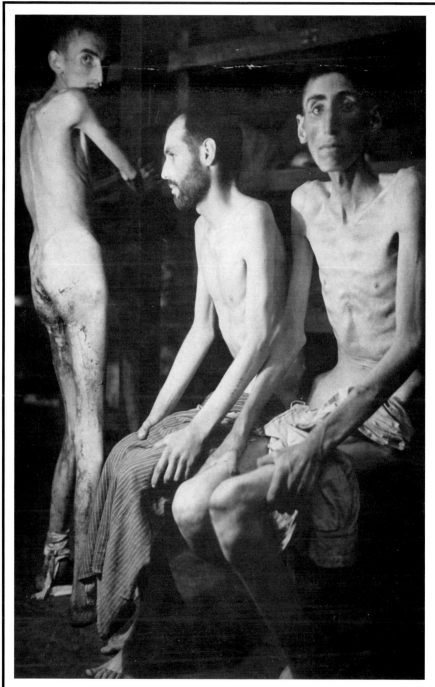

What can words say?

"When I think about it I realise I'm extraordinarily humane. ...if they (the Jews) refuse to go voluntarily, I see no other solution but extermination. Why should I look at a Jew through other eyes than if he were a Russian prisoner of war?"

Hitler discussing the Jews, Table Talk, 23rd January 1942 and 11th April 1942

CONCENTRATION CAMP REGIMES

BUCHENWALD – Located in central Germany, Buchenwald was one of the major concentration camps set up in 1933. Buchenwald was not, however, an extermination camp. Prisoners did die there, but they were not directly mass-murdered. The inmates of the camp consisted of communists, criminals, political prisoners, Jews and homosexuals. The latter two were considered the lowest. Buchenwald was one of the four infamous pre-war camps (Dachau, Ravensbruck, and Sachsenhausen were the others) and was actually a series of internal sub camps.

German prisoners of war are forced to exhume bodies of slave labourers. Here are some 800 bodies exhumed from a mass grave on the orders of American military authorities. When they were unable to complete a forced march from Buchenwald concentration camp they were murdered by SS troops. Location: five miles west of Passau, Germany. Date 15th May 1945.

American soldiers look on in horror before a pile of human ashes outside the crematorium at the notorious Buchenwald prison camp

'The Buchenwald Bitch'
Or 'The Red Witch of Buchenwald' 1917-1971

Ilse Koch was born and bred in Dresden, Germany and at the age of fifteen she worked in a cigarette factory. Two years later she worked in a bookshop. Blonde, blue-eyed and voluptuous she was enthralled by Hitler's storm troopers and had joined the Nazi Youth Party. The bookstore was a branch of the Nazi Party and soon the elderly owner, who pandered to the racist tastes of the Nazis, had Ilse reading obscene books so as to fuel her libido and heighten her passions for the young storm troopers. Eventually, after Ilse had many affairs, Heinrich Himmler (leader of the SS and Gestapo) spotted her in the shop and singled her out for marriage to his top aide at that time, Karl Koch.

Koch had the manners of a pig and soon he was given command of the new Buchenwald concentration camp outside of Weimar. Soon the blushing bride, Ilse, was taken to a fantastic villa near the camp and Koch promptly forgot about her – except to produce two children. Koch was entertaining himself at wild orgy parties and sex feasts with women at Weimar and left Ilse to her own devices!

The Buchenwald Bitch had an insatiable appetite for sex and soon she was staging her own wild orgies and bedded several junior officers, at once! Her desire for perversion and sadistic behaviour was increasing. Often she would sunbath naked and would tantalise her potential SS lovers. She would greet all incoming trains and trucks whilst standing semi naked.

Whilst fondling her breasts and wiggling her hips she would seek to distract lines of prisoners, mostly Jews, and if one dared to look up at her from the ground, he was beaten senseless! Three prisoners who glanced up at her on one occasion were beaten senseless, with clubs! Ilse filled out a report that these men had been executed for giving her 'lascivious looks'.

Random mass slayings were a turn on for Ilse and she encouraged the guards to carry these out. Another occasion, at her urging, guards opened up with guns firing indiscriminately on prisoners and Ilse was ecstatic, she grabbed a pistol and joined in murdering many of the 24 prisoners murdered that day.

Orgies were often arranged for Ilse by a female servant who would watch out for good -looking young officers arriving at the camp. Ilse's servant was also forced to join in with orgies. Ilse spotted two male prisoners working without their shirts on, but it wasn't their bodies she was interested in but rather their vivid tattoos! Ilse ordered that the prisoners be killed immediately, that night they were taken to the camp hospital and murdered by lethal injection. The skins bearing the tattoos were prepared and brought to her.

A lampshade made from human skin can be seen at the museum

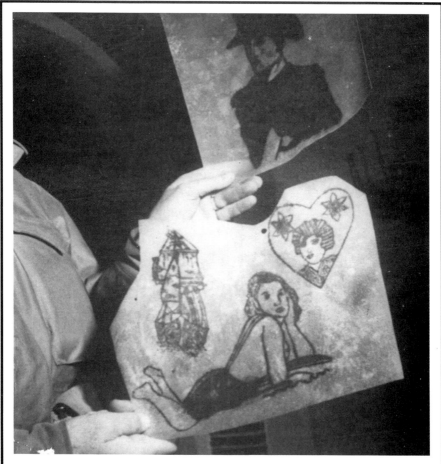

The actual tattooed skin that the Bitch of Buchenwald had prisoners killed for and then it was stripped from their bodies, cured and presented to her – macabre!

SKIN - BIGGEST ORGAN OF YOUR BODY

Lampshades made from human skin were soon adorning Ilse's home, the base of the lamp was made from human bones; even gloves and purses were being made for her...out of human skin! In an even more macabre twist Ilse had the heads of executed prisoners severed and on her instructions they were shrunk down to grapefruit size and put in jars on her sideboard. The sideboard had dozens of these voodoo creations and all in sight of her dining table where she sat with her children during mealtimes – looking at the ghastly sight!

Genocide: Murder of a Nation

After the war, Ilse Koch was tried at Nuremberg, in 1947, as a war criminal, which had people in an uproar, as she was a civilian. After two years in prison the Military Governor of the US Zone, General Clay, ordered her to be released. President Truman ordered an investigation but authorities declared that offences by a civilian against other civilians could not be considered a war crime.

Ilse Koch was tried as a war criminal

The German people themselves placed Ilse on trial in 1950-51 in Augsburg, Bavaria charged with murdering 45 prisoners and being involved as a willing accomplice in 135 concentration camp homicides. All of the good looks Ilse previously had about her had deserted her, the Titian coloured hair was now a straggly dirty blonde, her features no longer chiselled and her body was now like a lumpy bag of flour. Ilse blamed her husband, Karl Koch, but he was no longer around to defend himself, having been executed for embezzling party funds to pay for his orgy feasts.

The angry crowd outside of the court chanted, "Kill her, kill her." Ilse declared, "I was merely a housewife bringing up my children, I never saw anything which was against humanity."

When shown photos of mounds of corpses at Buchenwald she screamed, "LIES, ALL LIES!" She said that the dozens of camp survivors testifying against her were "actors" and "impostors" playing out roles assigned to them by the allies.

Midway through the proceedings it all became too much for Ilse and she forced her body to twitch uncontrollably with a blank stare masking her emotions. Eventually after many theatricals of her pretending to have epileptic fits she was examined by doctors and was said to be in perfect health, but stayed in her cell cajoling the doctor and asking him if he was enjoying her first class comedy act?

Her pretence continued and it was in her cell that she was told of the 'guilty' verdict, and that she was to be imprisoned for life, on hearing this she just let out an eerie cackle. Ilse died in prison in 1971 – the Buchenwald Bitch leaves behind a ghoulish relic or two in the form of human skin lampshades that is sure to set the hairs on your neck standing on end when viewing the exhibits at the museum.

THE PRISONER

Eugeniusz Polanski No 71475 born in Warsaw was arrested in August 1944 and sent to Buchenwald concentration camp, then to Dora (Nordhausen) and then finally to the infamous Bergen-Belsen. He was eventually liberated by British troops in April 1945.

Membership card for the Polish Association of former political prisoners in Nazi Concentration Camps.

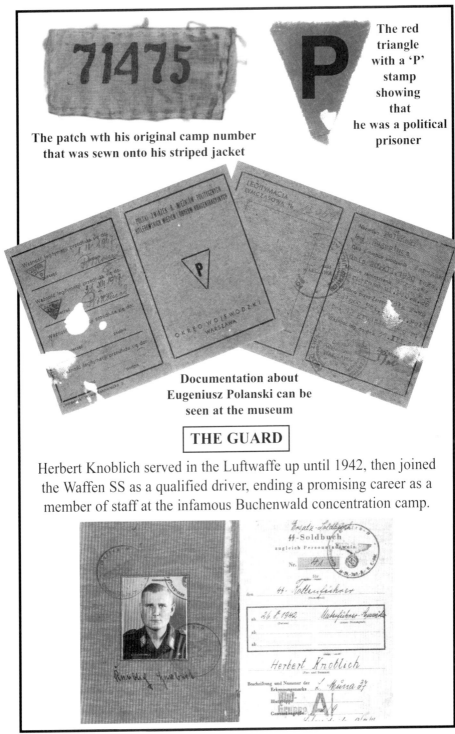

The patch wth his original camp number that was sewn onto his striped jacket

The red triangle with a 'P' stamp showing that he was a political prisoner

Documentation about Eugeniusz Polanski can be seen at the museum

THE GUARD

Herbert Knoblich served in the Luftwaffe up until 1942, then joined the Waffen SS as a qualified driver, ending a promising career as a member of staff at the infamous Buchenwald concentration camp.

Herbert Knoblich's original documents amongst many others which are on display in the museum

Buchenwald horror camp 1945. For benefit of visiting German people, the stripped uniform of one of the prisoners has been hung to resemble a man. In the background is one of the inmates.

DACHAU – Located in Bavaria, ten miles north of Munich opened in March 1933. In many ways this was small: its number of inmates, its percentage of Jewish prisoners, its crematoria and its number of deaths (compared to the other camps). Dachau was not intended to be an extermination camp. It was supposed to be a labour camp for the prisoners who could do only light work.

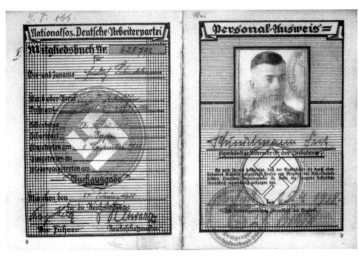

NSDAP PARTY BOOK

Belonging to Friedrich Schindelmann who, during this period, was a SS-Unterscharfuhrer and block Fuhrer at Dachau concentration camp. This book is an extremely rare find along with his Kepi, pictured below. Items are on display in the museum in original format.

Medical experiments on humans took place at this camp, where the Nazis developed the science of producing death. Medical experiments involved high altitudes, malaria, tuberculosis and hypothermia were carried out on inmates.

Alex Piorkowski

The commandant of Dachau Nazi death camp was Alex Piorkowski and amazingly his signature from his hands of death appears on an official access pass for SS-Oberscharfuhrer D R Fritz Fries dated 18th December 1940. Coincidentally, Alex Piorkowski was eventually executed by hanging!

From the hands of death - Signed Alex Piorkowski

In Dachau, one of the largest camps in Germany proper, crematoria were constructed for disposal of corpses. There was also a gas chamber constructed at Dachau; however, there is no evidence to this point that they were ever used for extermination. Presumably, the crematoria were used for disposing of the corpses of those who perished from other causes. There were other execution devices, such as a gallows, and presumably prisoners were executed and disposed of there.

Genocide: Murder of a Nation

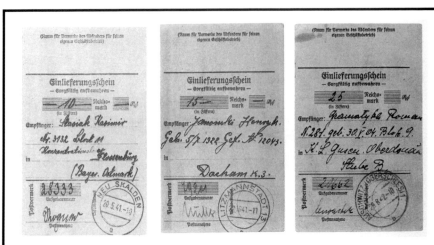

Tokens used at Dachau death camp

Dachau - Piles of starved bodies lying in goods wagons. They had been evacuated from other camps and were consigned to the crematorium.

The cost of World War II was $1.5 trillion US dollars - the costliest war ever!

Dachau The Last Train

Dachau – A liberated prisoner holds one of the savage dogs, which he has just clubbed to death. Prisoners lived in filth and squalor while the dogs were housed in scrubbed kennels. Imagine being jealous of a dog's kennel!

Similar to above, two prisoners brought a swift end to this killer dog's life.

Dachau – Liberation for prisoners from the horror camp of the Nazis, some wearing the characteristic striped dress of the concentration camp. They wildly cheer troops of the Seventh US Army. Note the Jewish pork 'pie hats' being thrown/waived in the air.

"It makes no difference whether they laugh at us or revile us, whether they represent us as clowns or criminals; the main thing is that they mention us, that they concern themselves with us again and again. " Hitler, 1920

Genocide: Murder of a Nation

SS Camp guard's peak cap and Jewish 'Pork Pie' hat, both worn at Nazi Death Camps as on display at the museum

Concentration camp uniforms can be seen in the museum

Various Nazi head wear can also be seen in the museum

Guns on display in the museum as used at Nazi Death Camps

Close up of various SS rings

An invaluable resource in the collecting field of Nazi, SS and Holocaust related material...Keith Beaumont.

Various patches as worn on prisoners' uniforms at Nazi Death Camps

NAZI USE OF THIS EMBLEM SINGLED OUT JEWS

WOULD I.D. CARDS IN UK SINGLE OUT AND IDENTIFY IN THE SAME WAY???

Jewish Star of David

The Star of David is an internationally recognised symbol and has, at times, caused more controversy than the Nazi swastika by virtue of its misuse by the media. At times it would seem that the Jewish community have overreacted in the use of the Star of David, but given that the use of such a symbol was meant to mark them out in their own communities, their reactions were not surprising.

Jews had risen to high political and social status in the majority of Western countries. In most cases they had fully assimilated into the local culture. The brutish systematic identification and segregation of Jews, as happened in Poland during the Second World War was deemed too uncivilised to be accepted in Western countries.

In the Netherlands on 10 January 1941, people deemed to be wholly or largely of Jewish blood were required to register. Dutch Jews were slowly stripped of their ability to function in Dutch society. Jewish professionals – doctors, estate agents, lawyers, etc - were not allowed to provide services for non-Jews.

The Nuremburg laws were introduced into the Netherlands in March of 1942, stripping Jews of any remaining rights or privileges. Hitler approved of the wearing of Jewish Stars on 27 April 1942. Three days later the head of Department IVB4 (Gestapo), Willi Zopf, enforced these laws.

The modern day UK government has been pressing for identification cards; this has been vigorously opposed by human rights and civil liberty groups so you can imagine the field day these groups would have if the laws of Hitler were used today! Maybe you can see why they so vigorously oppose such identification methods, what if you didn't have a card, would they throw you in prison?

In France, the German military commander issued an order dated 29 May 1942, implemented 1st June 1942, that required all Jews (including those of the Reich, Polish, Dutch, French, Croatian, Belgian, Romanian and Slovakian) over the age of six years to wear a yellow, palm sized, 'sexagram' cloth badge, which was a six pointed star, on the left side of the chest! Local police stations distributed the cloth badges.

Denmark, though, gave resistance to implementing the wearing of these badges. King Christian X said that he would be the first to wear the Jewish Star, which negated the German efforts to have Jews 'visibly' marked in this country.

Belgium was rather less brave than Denmark and a yellow star with a Hebraic looking 'J' in the centre was worn on the left breast of clothing. Jews were also required to carry identity cards displaying the word 'Jew' in them stamped in French and Flemish.

Left, Jewish Star of David cloth badge worn by Jews in the Netherlands

Right, Jewish Star worn by the Jews in France

Genocide: Murder of a Nation

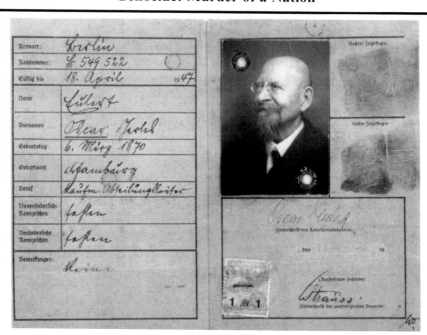

A very rare Jewish civilian identity pass complete with fingerprints. Signed
by the Berlin police, dated 18th April 1942 & again after liberation.

Above, Death Camp correspondence sent out from KL Sachsenhausen,
dated August 1949. Many like this on display in the museum.

CONCENTRATION CAMP LISTING

Germany:

Bergen-Belsen (probably 2 sub-camps but location is unknown)

Börgermoor (no sub-camp known)

Buchenwald (174 sub-camps and external kommandos)

Dachau (123 sub-camps and external kommandos)

Dieburg (no sub camp known)

Esterwegan (1 sub-camp)

Flossenburg (94 sub-camps and external kommandos)

Gundelsheim (no sub-camp known)

Neuengamme (96 sub-camps and external kommandos)

Papenburg (no sub-camp known)

Ravensbruck (31 sub-camps and external kommandos)

Sachsenhausen (44 sub-camps and external kommandos)

Sachsenburg (no sub-camp known)

Austria:

Mauthausen (49 sub-camps and external kommandos)

Belgium:

Breendonck (no sub-camp known)

Czechoslovakia:

Theresientadt (9 external kommandos)

Estonia:

Vivara

Finland:

Kangasjarvi

Koveri

France:

Argeles

Aurigny

Brens

Drancy

Gurs

Les Milles

Le Vernet

Noe

Recebedou

Rieucros

Rivesaltes

Suresnes

Thill

Work camps created by the Government of Vichy in Morocco and Algeria. Thousands of Jews sent to these camps by the French pro-Nazi government of Petain.

Abadla

Ain el Ourak

Bechar

Berguent

Bogari

Bouarfa

Djelfa

Kenadsa

Meridja
Missour
Tendrara
Holland:
Amersfoort
Ommen
Vught
Arnhem
Breda
Eindhoven
Gilze-Rijen
Gravenhage (The Hague)
Haaren par Tilburg
Leeuwarden
Moerdijk
Rozendaal
Sint Michielsgestel
Valkenburg par Leiden
Venlo (Luftwaffe airfield)
Westerbork (transit camp)
Italy:
Bolzano
Fossoli
Risiera di San Sabba (no sub-camp known)
Latvia:
Riga
Riga-Kaiserwald
Dundaga
Eleje-Meitenes
Jungfernhof
Lenta
Spilwe
Lithuania:
Kaunas
Aleksotaskowno
Palemonas
Pravieniskès

Volary
Norway:
Baerum
Berg
Bredtvet
Falstadt
Tromsdalen
Ulven
Poland:
 Auschwitz-Birkenau - Oswiecim-Brzezinka (extermination camp - 51 sub-camps and external kommandos)
Belzec (extermination camp - 1 sub-camp)
Bierznow
Biesiadka
Dzierzazna & Litzmannstadt (These two camps were children camps, "Jugenverwahrlage". Hundreds of children and teenagers considered as not good enough to be "Germanised" were transferred to these and later sent to the extermination centres)
Gross-Rosen- Rogoznica (77 sub-camps and external kommandos)
Huta-Komarowska
Janowska
Krakow
Kulmhof-Chelmo (extermination camp - no sub-camp known)

Lublin (prison - no sub-camp known)

Lwow (Lemberg)
Czwartaki
Lemberg

Maidanek (extermination camp - 3 sub-camps)

Mielec

Pawiak (prison - no sub-camp known)

Plaszow (work camp but became later sub-camp of Maidanek)

Poniatowa

Pustkow (work camp - no sub-camp known)

Radogosz (prison - no sub-camp known)

Radom

Schmolz

Schokken

Sobibor (extermination camp - no sub-camp known)

Stutthof - Sztutowo (40 subcamps and external kommandos)

Treblinka (extermination camp - no sub-camp known)

Wieliczka

Zabiwoko (work camp - no sub-camp known)

Zakopane

Russia: (The real number of concentration and extermina-tion camps established in occupied Soviet Union by the Nazis is unknown. The following list contains the name of the major camps. Some of these camps were under Romanian control; e.g. Akmétchetka or Bogdanovka where 54,000 were executed between 21 December and 31 December, 1941)

Akmétchetka

Balanowka

Bar

Bisjumujsje

Bogdanovka

"Citadelle" (The real name of this camp is unknown. The camp was located near Lvov. Thousands of Russians POW were killed in this camp)

Czwartaki

Daugavpils

Domanievka

Edineti

Kielbasin (or **Kelbassino**)

Khorol

Klooga

Lemberg

Mezjapark

Ponary

Rawa-Russkaja

Salapils

Strazdumujsje

Yanowski

Vertugen
(for all these camps, no sub-camp known).

Yugoslavia:

Banjica

Brocice

Chabatz	Jastrebarsko
Danica	Kragujevac
Dakovo	Krapje
Gornja reka	Kruscica
Gradiska	Lepoglava
Jadovno	Loborgrad
Jasenovac	

A conservative estimate of those who were murdered in the Nazi death camps stands at about 3.5 million. Most were European Jews who were killed for no other reason than the fact that they were Jews. The process was rationalised, however, by the Nazi ideology of racial superiority/inferiority. These ideas were given official legal sanction in the Nuremberg Laws (1935). Combined with Hitler's quest for lebensraum, "living space," and his goals of world domination, and with World War II as a cover, the Nazi regime was able to carry out the greatest crime in human history.

Lest we forget

Landsberg Death Camp - Lieutenant Colonel Ed F Soillor of the US Army stands amongst hundreds of Jewish prisoners burnt alive and speaks to the German civilians he ordered to tour the ghastly camp.

CONTRARY TO POPULAR BELIEF MOST OF THE CIVILIAN GERMAN NATION HATED HITLER

Between December 1939 and August 1941, about 50,000 to 60,000 Germans - children and adults - were secretly killed by lethal injections or in gassing installations designed to look like shower stalls. It was a foretaste of what was to come at Auschwitz. The victims were taken from the medical institution and put to death...Never to Forget.

The euthanasia programme proved to be a valuable precursor to the atrocities that were to come in connection with the "Final Solution." SS Major Christian Wirth was transferred from his duties at a euthanasia centre to take over the supervision of Chelmo, the first of six extermination camps in Poland to become operational. His expertise in mass extermination seems to have been a major consideration. Wirth later served at Belzek, Treblinka and Sobibor. In 1942, Franz Stangl was transferred from one of the euthanasia centres to Sobibor extermination camp where he served as camp commander. He performed so well there that he was transferred in the summer of 1942 to Treblinka. (Many years later, in 1970, Stangl was extradited from Brazil to West Germany to stand trial. He was found guilty of joint responsibility for the murder of 900,000 Jews.) After the Wannsee Conference in 1942, the staff of Euthanasie Programme was transferred to Operation Reinhard.

6 million Jews who were the targets of a complete annihilation policy in the Nazi Holocaust

5.5 million "enemies of the German State" were murdered under equally inhumane circumstances - Criminals, Asocials - (prostitutes, etc), Insane, Homosexuals, Jehovah's Witnesses, Political, Communists, Socialists and Gypsies

Estimates of the number of Gypsies murdered run from a high of 500,000 to 600,000

Genocide: Murder of a Nation

Himmler favoured sparing a couple of Gypsy tribes that had been defined as "pure Gypsies." However, by December 16, 1942, he ordered all Gypsies in Germany deported to Auschwitz.

The deportation of Gypsies was placed under Himmler's authority in 1942 and he ordered their extermination.
Who Are the Gypsies?

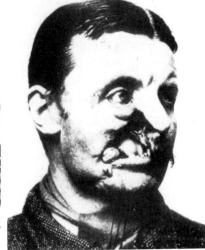

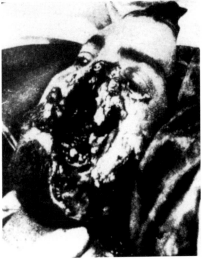

Above, Himmler, left, with Hitler watching manoeuvres just so their men can end up blown to bits...
The Price of War!!!

Crime Through Time

A very scarce, genuine, signature of the notorious Nazi SS Chief and ruthless practitioner of Nazi terrorism, Heinrich Himmler. This official one page Third Reich document can be seen in original format at the museum. With stamp and embossed seal, dated Berlin 27th November 1940 promoting Anton Vogler to the rank of SS Oberfuehrer (Brigadier General) who later went on to be promoted to SS Brigadefuehrer.

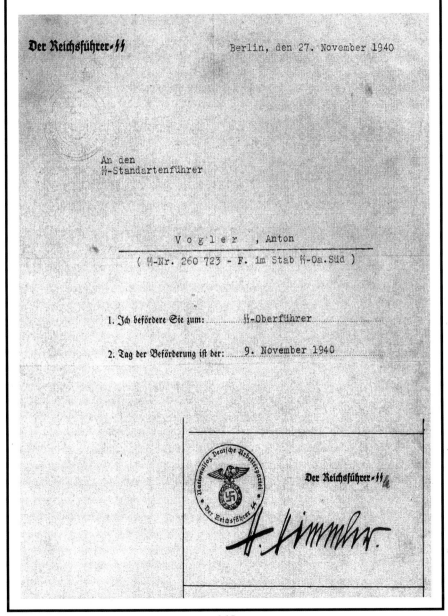

Genocide: Murder of a Nation

SS identity card belonging to Leo Kmietsch that appears to have a genuine signature on it from Heinrich Himmler – 1934.

Crime Through Time

Some very rare SS passes, service records and other documents that can all be seen at the museum with full explanations for each.

Some more very rare SS passes, service records and other documents that can all be seen at the museum with full explanations for each.

Crime Through Time

Commemorative stamp issued
after the death of assassinated
Heydrich showing his death mask

Commemorative stamp issued
after the fatal appointment of
Hitler as head of state, 1933

Stamp showing Waffen-SS
Mortar crew in action

Reinhard Tristan Eugen Heydrich
(1904—1942)

Chief of the Reich Security Head Office and Protector of Bohemia and Moravia, Reinhard Heydrich was born in Halle, Saxony, the son of the founder of the Halle Conservatory.

Among his many skills he numbered among his many talents the ability to play the violin at concert level.

Heydrich had inherited more than the musical ability of his father. In a contemporary *Lexicon of Music and Musicians* the elder Heydrich's name is accompanied by the note 'real name Süss'.

The clear implication is that Heydrich senior was Jewish, and throughout his life Reinhard Heydrich sought to suppress details of his Jewish ancestry! From his mother's gravestone he is said to have erased the suggestive forename Sarah.

As a young man, Heydrich served as an officer in the German

navy - in 1931 he was dismissed by an Honour Court (presided over by Admiral Canaris) for dishonourable conduct towards a young woman.

Heinrich Himmler found many elements of Reinhard Heydrich appealing: his considerable organisational abilities, his Nordic appearance, his total ruthlessness, the intensity of his anti-Semitism and, finally and ironically, the fact that he was himself either Jewish, partly Jewish or in fear of being considered Jewish. Perhaps Himmler saw in this fact the means by which he would control his talented associate. Certainly from 1931 he was prepared to promote Heydrich until he became the second most powerful man in the RSHA.

In July 1941, Goering ordered Heydrich to submit a comprehensive draft for the achievement of the 'final solution to the Jewish problem'; the Wannsee Conference was clearly part-result of this Goering instruction. It is certain that Heydrich organised the machinery of genocide in which Eichmann played an executive role. In September 1941 Heydrich was appointed to succeed Neurath as Protector of Bohemia and Moravia.

In the early months of 1942 the decision was made in London to attempt the assassination of Heydrich and is to this day still shrouded in mystery. The only Nazi leader the allies attempted to assassinate was Reinhard Heydrich. Historians have asked why Heydrich, when it was certain that his death would result in massive reprisals against the Czech people. A member of the British government at the time claims that this was precisely the object of the assassination.

In late spring 1942, a section of Czech soldiers flew from London and were parachuted into Czechoslovakia, outside Prague. The Czech resistance, hearing of the murder plan, urgently request-ed the Czech government in London to persuade the British government to abandon the assassination attempt – the British were unmoved.

The assassination squad struck in Prague on 27 May 1942 – Heydrich rode unprotected and unescorted in his car and was machine-gunned on the Kirchmayer Boulevard. Heydrich, injured, pulled his pistol and was about to pursue the Czech soldiers, a grenade was hurled towards him. The horsehair stuffing and pieces of the metal springs of the car penetrated the Reich Protector's body and he died on 4 June in a Prague hospital. The reprisals were as were feared, or possibly hoped for.

A commemorative memorial book produced by the SS in honour of Reinhard Heydrich and signed photograph can be seen in the museum.

> "When people are very curious in Britain and ask 'yes but why doesn't he come?' we reply: 'calm yourselves! Calm yourselves! He is coming! He is coming!'"
>
> **Hitler - 1940**

Gypsy Genocide

In September 1939, Reinhard Heydrich organised an official conference of racial policy. The conference was held in Berlin on September 21st. While the primary concern of the meeting was to plan the systematic deportation of Jews to Poland, it was also decided to relocate 30,000 German Gypsies. In preparation for that deportation, the conference called for the segregation of Gypsies in special camps. While the deportation of Gypsies took a back seat to the deportation of Jews and the desired 30,000 was not immediately achieved, several thousand were deported.

The 1937 Laws against Crime later labelled Gypsies as asocials, regardless of whether they had been charged with any unlawful acts. Two hundred Gypsy men were then selected by quota and incarcerated in Buchenwald concentration camp. By May 1938, SS Reichsfuehrer Himmler established the Central Office for Fighting the Gypsy Menace, which defined the question as 'a matter of race,' discriminating pure Gypsies from part Gypsies as Jews were discriminated, and ordering their registration. In 1939, resettlement of Gypsies was put under Eichmann's jurisdiction along with that of the Jews.

It is not known how many [Gypsies] were killed by the Einsatzgruppen charged with speedy extermination by shooting. For the sake of efficiency Gypsies were also shot naked, facing their pre-dug graves. According to the Nazi experts, shooting Jews was easier, they stood still, while the Gypsies cry out, howl, and move constantly, even when they are already standing on the shooting ground. Some of them even jumped into the ditch before the volley and pretended to be dead.

In 1939, resettlement of Gypsies was put under Eichmann's jurisdiction along with that of the Jews. Gypsies were forbidden to move freely and were concentrated in encampments with Germany in 1939, later (1941) transformed into fenced ghettos, from which they would be seized for transport by the criminal police (aided by dogs) and dispatched to Auschwitz in February 1943. During May 1940, about 3,100 were sent to Jewish ghettos in the Government-General: others may have been added to Jewish transports from Berlin, Vienna and Prague to Nisko, Poland (the sight of an aborted reservation to which Jews were deported). These measures were taken against Gypsies who had no claim to exemption because of having an Aryan spouse or having been regularly employed for five years.

On 16 December 1942, Himmler ordered the deportation of all Gypsies to Auschwitz. This is the official beginning of a "Final Solution" to the Gypsy Nuisance.

Many were used in Joseph Mengele's medical experimentation, others were used in the German Air Force tests on reactions to extreme freezing temperatures, and thousands were sent to the gas chambers. Similar fates for Gypsies are reported at Treblinka, Chelmo and other extermination centres.

The 'H' Word

Why is it whenever the word 'Holocaust' is mentioned by the media that people automatically say the right words and the right sounds, yet some people do not even know what the word Holocaust means? To some people the Holocaust could be a flame shooting from a hole in the ground. Many have become accustomed to seeing war veterans interviewed and little old ladies having TV microphones poked into their faces whilst the 'H' word is used and the interviewer just makes the right noises. Maybe now you know what the 'H' word really stands for.

What about Hiroshima, the other 'H' word, no one makes the right sounds when Hiroshima is mentioned. The USA murdered people in cold blood; do people accuse the United States of genocide? Hiroshima and the Holocaust is a double 'H' word, which one of the two words though conjure up horror thoughts in your head, maybe spare a moment for the Japanese victims.

The atom bomb dropped on Hiroshima, Japan by the USA on 6th August 1945 killed 155,200 people!

The rise and fall and rise and fall of Adolf Hitler

In 1923 the Nazis had 55,000 followers, the German state of Bavaria where the Nazis were based was a hotbed of groups opposed to the democratic government in Berlin. Nazi members demanded action; Hitler knew he had to act or risk losing the leadership of his party.

Hitler and the Nazis hatched a plot - kidnap the leaders of the Bavarian government and force them at gunpoint to accept Hitler as their leader. They put a plan into action when they learned there was going to be a large gathering of businessmen in a Munich beer hall and the guests of honour were scheduled to be the Bavarian leaders they now wanted to kidnap. On 8 November, 1923, SA troops under the direction of Hermann Göring surrounded the place. At 8:30 pm, Hitler and his storm troopers burst into the beer hall causing instant panic.

Hitler fired a pistol shot into the ceiling. "Silence," he yelled at the stunned crowd. Hitler and Göring forced their way to the podium as armed SA men continued to file into the hall. State Commissioner Gustav von Kahr, whose speech had been interrupted by all this, yielded the podium to Hitler.

"The National Revolution has begun!" Hitler shouted. "...No one may leave the hall. Unless there is immediate quiet I shall have a machine gun posted in the gallery. The Bavarian and Reich governments have been removed and a provisional national government formed. The barracks of the Reichswehr and police are occupied. The Army and the police are marching on the city under the swastika banner!" None of that was true, but those in the beer hall could not know otherwise.

To Hitler's great surprise, his three captives simply glared at him and, at first, even refused to talk to him. Hitler responded by waving his pistol at them, yelling: "I have four shots in my pistol! Three for you, gentlemen. The last bullet for myself!"

An emotional Hitler spoke to the crowd: "I am going to fulfil the vow I made to myself five years ago when I was a blind cripple in the military hospital - to know neither rest nor peace until the November criminals had been overthrown, until on the ruins of the wretched Germany of today there should have arisen once more a Germany of power and greatness, of freedom and splendour." The crowd in the beer hall roared their approval and sang "Deutschland über Alles." Hitler was euphoric. This was turning into a night of triumph for him. Tomorrow he might actually be the new leader of Germany. Hitler left the beer hall to sort out a tiny problem, German soldiers were not surrendering. His storm troopers had no luck in getting the soldiers who were holding out in barracks to surrender. Having failed at that, he went back to the beer hall.

When he arrived back at the beer hall he was aghast to find his revolution fizzling. There were no plans for tomorrow's march on Berlin. Munich wasn't even being occupied. Nothing was happening.

General Lossow had abandoned Hitler and ordered German Army reinforcements into Munich to put down the Nazi putsch. Troops were rushed in and by dawn the War Ministry building containing Röhm and his SA troops was surrounded. Hitler was up all night frantically trying to decide what to do. General Ludendorff then gave him an idea. The Nazis would simply march into the middle of Munich and take it over. Because of his World War I fame, Ludendorff reasoned, no one would dare fire on him. He even assured Hitler the police and the Army would likely join them. The now-desperate Hitler went for the idea.

Around 11am on the morning of November 9, a column of 3,000 Nazis, led by Hitler, Göring and Ludendorff marched toward the centre of Munich. Carrying one of the flags was a young party member named Heinrich Himmler.

After reaching the centre of Munich, the Nazis headed toward the War Ministry building but they encountered a police blockade. As they stood face to face with about a hundred armed policemen, Hitler yelled out to them to surrender. They didn't. Shots rang out. Both sides fired. It lasted about a minute. Sixteen Nazis and three police were killed. Göring was hit in the groin. Hitler suffered a dislocated shoulder when the man he had locked arms with was shot and pulled him down onto the pavement.

Hitler's bodyguard, Ulrich Graf, jumped onto Hitler to shield him and took several bullets, probably saving Hitler's life. Hitler then crawled along the sidewalk out of the line of fire and scooted away into a waiting car, leaving his comrades behind. The rest of the Nazis scattered or were arrested. Ludendorff, true to his heroic form, walked right through the line of fire to the police and was then arrested.

Hitler wound up at the home of his friends, the Hanfstaengls, where he was reportedly talked out of suicide. He had become deeply despondent and expected to be shot by the authorities. He spent two nights hiding in the Hanfstaengl's attic. On the third night, police arrived and arrested him. He was taken to the prison at Landsberg where his spirits lifted somewhat after he was told he was going to get a public trial. The court's verdict - guilty. Possible sentence - life. Hitler's sentence - five years, eligible for parole in six months. On 1st April 1924, Hitler was taken to the old fortress at Landsberg and given a spacious private cell with a fine view. He got gifts, was allowed to receive visitors whenever he liked and had his own private secretary, Rudolf Hess.

The Nazi party, after the Putsch, became fragmented and disorganised, but Hitler had gained national influence by taking advantage of the press to make his ideas known. Now, although behind bars, Hitler was not about to stop communicating.

Pacing back and forth in his cell, he continued expressing his ideas, while Hess took down every word. The result would be the first volume of a book, Mein Kampf, outlining Hitler's political and racial ideas in brutally intricate detail, serving both as a blueprint for future actions and as a warning to the world.

Hitler's Boy Soldiers
1939 – 1945

**Nazi child's SA (Sturmabteilung – Storm Detachment) tunic and helmet
As on display in the museum**

At the onset of war, the Hitler Youth totalled 8.8 million. But the war brought immediate, drastic changes as over a million Hitler Youth leaders of draft age and regional adult leaders were immediately called up into the army. This resulted in a severe shortage of local and district leaders. The problem was resolved by lowering the age of local Hitler Youth leaders to 16 and 17. The average age had been 24. These 16 and 17-year-olds would now be responsible for as many as 500 or more boys. Another big change was the elimination of the strict division between the Jungvolk (boys 10 to 14) and the actual HJ (Hitler Youth 14 to 18).

The younger boys were assigned to operate searchlights and assist with communications, often riding their bicycles as dispatch riders. In October 1943, a search light battery received a direct bomb hit, killing the entire crew of boys, all aged 14 and under.

Following each bombing raid, Hitler Youths assisted in neighbourhood cleanups and helped relocate bombed out civilians. They knocked on doors looking for unused rooms in undamaged houses or apartments. Occupants refusing to let in the new 'tenants' were reported to the local police and could likely expect a visit from the Gestapo.

Life inside the boys' camp was harsh, featuring a dreary routine of roll calls, para-military field exercises, hikes, marches, recitation of Nazi slogans and propaganda, along with endless singing of Hitler Youth songs and Nazi anthems.

Kill Hitler

After Colonel Henning von Tresckow's 13 March 1943 attempt to kill Hitler in Smolensk fails, another opportunity surfaces. Tresckow immediately seizes the chance when it becomes known that Hitler is to visit the Berlin Armoury Museum on March 21. The fuehrer's visit will include a short speech, an exhibition of Soviet weapons captured by Army Group Centre, a visit with war-wounded veterans, the laying of the memorial wreath, and the review of a military parade - all in honour of Hero's Memorial Day.

March 20, 1943 - Gersdorff accompanies Field Marshal Walter Model (who has been selected to guide Hitler on the tour of the captured weapons exhibit) to a meeting with Hitler's Wehrmacht adjutant, Lt-General Rudolph Schmundt. At the meeting, Model who wishes to visit his wife beforehand, and is totally oblivious to Gersdorff's real mission, demands to know the exact time of the ceremony. Schmundt initially refuses to disclose the information on the grounds of high secrecy and penalty of death for revealing such information.

Inside the museum's entrance hall, Hitler takes his place at the podium and delivers a 14-minute speech commemorating the heroism of the armed forces fighting on the Eastern Front and in North Africa. With the words "the danger has now been averted". Meanwhile, Gersdorff is standing by the entrance to the exhibit dressed in his army coat. Inside the left and right front pockets of his coat are two small 10-minute time bombs. Amidst the thunder of applause that follows Hitler's speech, Gersdorff discreetly slides his left hand into his left coat pocket to set off the fuse of one of the 10-minute bombs. Because Field Marshal Walter Model and the museum director are standing nearby along with the ever-vigilant SS guards, Gersdorff does not attempt to arm the bomb in his other pocket. This additional action would look too conspicuous.

As the Fuehrer's tour of the exhibit begins, Gersdorff positions himself as close as possible to Hitler, but not too close to avoid rousing suspicion. During this time, the fuse inside Gersdorff's time bomb is gradually eating its way towards the detonator.

Hitler then does something wholly unprecedented which startles everyone in the room. Instead of pausing to hear Gersdorff explain each piece of the arms exhibit, he suddenly picks up his heels and walks swiftly through the entire exhibit without once pausing to ask questions – did he have a sixth sense? Fate or Hitler's legendary sixth sense was to blame yet again for another well planned but ill-fated assassination plot.

Hitler's own generals tried to assassinate him on 20 July 1944, to end Nazi Germany's all-out commitment to a war that was now clearly lost. But the assassination attempt failed. Hitler took revenge by purging the General Staff of anyone deemed suspicious or exhibiting defeatist behaviour. Nearly 200 officers and others were killed, in some cases, slowly hanged from meat hooks.

Homosexuals and the Holocaust

Homosexuality in Hebrew culture was expressly prohibited in the Law of Moses. The New Testament writers retained the Mosaic prohibitions. Throughout the medieval and early modern periods, these definitions were retained and punishments for violators became increasingly harsh, including the death penalty.

Despite the Nazi laws and the resulting harassment, an identifiable homosexual community emerged in Germany, particularly in urban areas. Nazi deputies in the Assembly voiced the conviction that it was the Jews who were leading this movement in an attempt to undermine the morality of the German people. The racial theme in their position also emerged in their argument that homosexuality has a detrimental impact on desired Aryan family size and population. Therefore, homosexuality was incompatible with racial purity. This was later to be one of Himmler's major arguments.

PORTILLO'S 'GLAD GAY SECRET IS NOW OUT'

Claim by Aids lover No2

EXCLUSIVE from
ANTONELLA LAZZERI, in Madrid

A SECOND gay lover of Michael Portillo to get Aids said last night the Shadow Chancellor would be glad their secret was out.

Dying Jean Francois Kervran, 42, revealed yesterday how he and the top Tory began an affair in 1980.

And the frail ex-ballet dancer told The Sun at his home in Madrid, Spain: "It is better that people know. Michael feels that way too.

"I have not spoken to him today but I am sure he will be glad that news of our relationship is out.

"It is not something that either of us have thought to hide.

"We have always remained friends and kept in touch constantly. I have very fond memories of our time together, as close as we..."

Sexual

Kervran has been given only weeks to live and had to be steadied by a friend outside his apartment.

He said of his relationship with Mr Portillo: "It was private, a nice memory. But we have done nothing wrong. It was not a sordid affair."

Smiling whenever married Portillo's name was mentioned, he added: "I will be speaking to Michael today."

Kervran broke his 20-year silence yesterday in the News of the World.

He revealed he was introduced to Mr Portillo by the MP's former boyfriend Nigel Hart, who died of Aids last December, aged 52.

French-born Kervran, who went on to be an internationally-famous dancer, was teaching at a language school in London. Portillo was working at Tory Central Office.

Kervran admitted: "It was a sexual affair. I cannot deny it took place.

"Portillo, 47, confessed last September to gay flings while he was a student at Cambridge.

Yesterday he refused to comment on the new revelations.

But friends said his wife of 18 years, Carolyn, 47, will be furious more of his gay past has emerged.

Gay fling . . . Jean Francois Kervran

New shock . . . Portillo and Carolyn

How would Portillo have faired in Nazi Germany?

The leadership of the Nazi party included at least one avowed homosexual, Ernst Roehm. He was a member of Hirschfeld's League for Human Rights and openly attended homosexual meeting places. Between 1933 and 1934, Roehm was the leader of the SA (Stormtroopers) and, before the death of Hindenberg in 1934; he was a potential challenger to Hitler's supremacy. With the Nazis' rise to power came an attack from Germany's political left. Attempts were made to discredit Hitler and the Nazis. One of their arguments was the charge of homosexuality in the Nazi ranks. Hitler's old friend Roehm, just as happened with Portillo, was one of their main targets.

Heinrich Himmler defended Roehm. He expressed the belief that accusations against Roehm were the work of Jews who feared the SS and were trying to discredit the movement. The mood of the party, and of Himmler, changed, however, when Hitler decided in 1934 that Roehm was a threat to his authority. Specifically, Hitler feared that Roehm was attempting to turn the SA (at this time, over 2 million strong) into a militia and was planning a military challenge to Hitler. While there is no evidence that such a plan existed, Hitler ordered a purge. On 30 June 1934, Roehm, many of his supporters, and over 1,000 of Hitler's political and personal enemies, were murdered in the famous "Night of the Long Knives." While the purge was politically motivated, the justification given for it was the homosexuality of Roehm and several of his associates in the SS command.

Himmler now assumed leadership of the SS and, in the process, also assumed the role of ridding the movement and Germany of homosexuals. In the wake of the Roehm execution, Hitler ordered the registration of homosexuals and the Gestapo was charged with the responsibility of creating dossiers on homosexuals and other "asocials" in the Third Reich.

The following year, in 1935, the Reichstag amended Paragraph 175 of the Criminal Code to close what were seen as loopholes in the current law. The new law had three parts:

Paragraph 175: A male who commits a sex offence with another male or allows himself to be used by another male for a sex offence shall be punished with imprisonment.

Where a party was not yet twenty-one years of age at the time of the act, the court may in especially minor cases refrain from punishment.

Paragraph 175a: Penal servitude up to 10 years or, where there are mitigating circumstances, imprisonment of not less than three months shall apply to: (1) a male who, with violence or the threat of violence to body and soul or life, compels another male to commit a sex offence with him or to allow himself to be abused for a sex offence; (2) a male who, by abusing a relationship of dependence based upon service, employment or subordination, induces another male to commit a sex offence with him or to allow himself to be abused for a sex offence; (3) a male over 21 years of age who seduces a male person under twenty-one years to commit a sex offence with him or to allow himself to be abused for a sex offence; (4) a male who publicly commits a sex offence with males or allows himself to be abused by males for a sex offence or offers himself for the same.

Paragraph 175b: An unnatural sex act committed by humans with animals is punishable by imprisonment; the loss of civil rights might also be imposed.

Paragraph 174 of the penal code forbad incest and other sexual offences with dependents, while paragraph 176 outlawed paedophilia. Persons convicted under these laws also wore the pink triangle.

Compulsory Castrations!

The Nazi's passed other laws that targeted sex offenders. In 1933, they enacted the Law Against Dangerous Habitual Criminals and Measures for Protection and Recovery. This law gave German judges the power to order compulsory castrations in cases involving rape, defilement, illicit sex acts with children (Paragraph 176), coercion to commit sex offences (paragraph 177), the committing of indecent acts in public including homosexual acts (paragraph 183), murder or manslaughter of a victim (paragraphs 223-226), if they were committed to arouse or gratify the sex drive, or homosexual acts with boys under 14.

The Amendment to the Law for the Prevention of Offspring with Hereditary Diseases dated 26 June 1935, allowed castration indicated by reason of crime for men convicted under paragraph 175 if the men consented. These new laws defined homosexuals as "asocials" who were a threat to the Reich and the moral purity of Germany. The punishment for "chronic homosexuals" was incarceration in a concentration camp. A 20 May 1939 memo from Himmler allows concentration camp prisoners to be blackmailed into castration.

"The New Testament is also full of contradictions, but that hasn't prevented the spread of Christianity." Hitler

Genocide: Murder of a Nation

Order to make someone unfruitbearing

A chilling piece of Holocaust history. On 15th December 1937 at Dachau Concentration Camp Josef Kammennier was castrated. This is the original order to carry out this operation, original on show in museum.

16 XIII *975* / *37*

Antrag auf Unfruchtbarmachung

Auf Grund der §§ 1 bis 3 des Gesetzes zur Verhütung erbkranken Nachwuchses vom 14. Juli 1933 (Reichsgesetzbl. I S. 529) beantrage ich — meine Unfruchtbarmachung —[1]

die Unfruchtbarmachung — des — der — *Kammermeier Josef.*

zur Zeit wohnhaft in *Konzentr. Lager Dachau*

Ich — Der — Die — Genannte leide(t) an *angeborenem Schwachsinn*

Zur Glaubhaftmachung der vorstehenden Angabe beziehe ich mich — auf $\frac{das}{mein}$ anliegende(s) ärztliche — amtsärztliche — Gutachten — auf das Zeugnis der nachbezeichneten Personen:

Ort: *Dachau* , den *15. XII* 193 *7*

Der Lagerkommandant K. L. D.

Des Antragstellers

SS - Oberführer

Der Standortarzt M. L. D.

Name und Vorname *Dr. Wid. . . .*

Stand ⚡⚡ - Hauptsturmführer

Wohnort *Dachau*

Straße *Lagerst. 29.*

An

die Geschäftsstelle des Erbgesundheitsgerichts

in *München*

[1]) Nichtzutreffendes ist jeweils zu durchstreichen.

Ge. Nr. 154
Verlag Carl Gerber, München.

What would the Nazi Party make of this?

Professor was behind gay vicar blackmail plot

Daily Mail
July 9
2000

By **Alison Gordon**
SOCIAL AFFAIRS EDITOR

THE gay vicar of one of the country's most exclusive parishes was being blackmailed by a professor based in Germany, it was revealed last night.

Father Neil Follett befriended the academic from Hamburg University over an Internet chatline. He visited the clergyman at his vicarage in Knightsbridge – just a stone's throw from Harrods in Central London.

But their friendship turned sour after a bill for several thousand pounds was allegedly run up on Father Follett's credit card.

It is understood the professor threatened to reveal details of the vicar's homosexuality to newspapers if the clergyman

'Some parishioners feel deceived'

pressed charges against him.

Father Follett apparently gave details of the gay blackmail plot to church elders when he also confessed to being homosexual. He fled the parish a few days later.

In a further twist to the scandal it emerged yesterday that churchwarden Captain Ian Powe has been arrested in connection with alleged anti-gay harassment against Father Follett.

The sorry saga of St Paul's has thrown parishioners into further shock over what is fast becoming a major embarrassment for the Church of England.

Capt Powe, a military hero who served in the Korean war, was described as 'a terribly nice chap, who is fair and without bias'.

Capt Powe, who founded the Gas Consumers' Council and

commanded HMS Yarmouth during the 'Cod War' has strongly denied 'any wrongdoing'.

Police sources revealed the investigation into blackmail threats was already under way and known to church elders before the alleged 'homophobic harassment'.

A Scotland Yard spokesman said: 'Officers from the Westminster community safety unit arrested a man in his 60s in connection with the homophobic harassment of a man in the Westminster area. He has been arrested on bail to return to Belgravia Police Station on August 8 pending further inquiries.'

Police were last night continuing an investigation into four allegations of blackmail and intimidation.

Father Follett, who is the father of three sons and is being divorced by his wife Pamela, is in hiding at a friend's house in the West Country. He was advised by police to leave his prosperous parish for 'his own welfare' about a fortnight ago and was given a month's leave by the Bishop of London, Richard Chartres. Detectives are guiding him on when it is 'safe' to return.

The vicar has let it be known he would like to stay at St Paul's if his congregation will accept him.

Rumours had been circulating in the parish about his sexual orientation before his confession. Until then, the well-heeled congregation only knew that he had separated from his wife.

One parishioner said: 'The congregation are divided. Some are willing to forgive but others are deeply hurt and feel they have been deceived and would like him to resign.'

Sir Kenneth James, a former ambassador to Poland, who is

IN HIDING: Father Neil Follett was a victim of anti-gay harassment

the senior church warden at St Paul's has told of the 'great feelings of sorrow and compassion for Father Neil and the parish at this difficult time'.

Father Follett, 50, was appointed in January after a job advert in the Church Times called for a family manof 'good social standing'.

His 'absolute charm' and Sandhurst officer training helped secure the coveted post, which comes with a large Victorian vicarage in the heart of Belgravia.

Before arriving at St Paul's in

April, Father Follett had been the vicar at Godmanchester in Cambridgeshire. He also served in the Army for seven years before a knee injury forced his retirement in 1978 when he was a captain in the Royal Artillery.

The Bishop of London is keeping in regular contact with Father Follett but no decision had been reached on the long-term future of St Paul's.

A spokesman said: 'No charges have been laid against anyone. We are waiting to see what develops from the police end. We are keeping an open mind.'

COP'S GAY THAI-MS

BY **JAMES MILLBANK**

TOP cop Brian Paddick, dubbed Commander Crackpot, has been relaxing in Thailand with his boyfriend as a storm raged over his weird views.

Paddick, 42, who told internet surfers he finds anarchy "appealing", spent a week in a £400-a-night hotel on the party island of Phuket.

He sunbathed with a tall pal in his 30s beside the Chedi hotel's pool. The couple have now left for a gay mardi gras in Australia.

Paddick, the £93,000 head of the Met in Lambeth, south London, pioneered the force's soft line on canna-

Soho, is a haven of cocaine use. Paddick pays £300 a year as a member of the club, also used by celebs including Sir Elton John and Michael Barrymore.

Our investigators took swabs from toilet lids there, because clubbers often snort drugs off them. On one night we found traces of cocaine on them ALL over three hours. Couples kissed and shared cubicles. Outside, VIPs hid in private rooms, some with mirror windows. Scotland Yard are already investigat...

HAUNT: the club

Those who wore the pink triangle patch (homosexuals) were brutally treated by camp guards. Death rates for homosexuals were much higher, perhaps three to four times higher, than for other non-Jewish categories of prisoners. While their overall numbers were small, their fate in the camps more nearly approximates that of Jews than any of the other categories, except, perhaps, Gypsies. And, homosexuals did not survive for very long, of those who were exterminated, most were exterminated within the first few months of the camp experience.

The contemporary Gay Rights Movement, both in the United States and in Europe, has led to a re-opening of the plight of homosexuals in Nazi Germany. The unparalleled treatment of homosexuals under the Nazi regime raises the same questions raised by the Holocaust itself: How could it happen? Can it happen again? And, how can its recurrence be prevented?

'WHAT ON EARTH HAS THE VATICAN AND THE CATHOLIC CHURCH GOT TO DO WITH THE NAZI HOLOCAUST??'

The Vatican and the pope remain defamed to this day over the controversy of the silence in the face of mass Nazi murder!

Astonishingly, the Vatican and Pope Pius XII felt that whilst being firmly aware of the Holocaust atrocities it was necessary they said, that the Vatican preserves its good name with the Germans!!

In the fall of 1943, the Nazis, without any intervention whatsoever from the Vatican or the Pope, began rounding up 8,000 Jews in Rome, 1,000 of whom, mostly women and children, were sent off to the extermination camp at Auschwitz death camp, in Poland.

Some 7,000 Jews in Rome went into hiding, 4,000 into monasteries. The Vatican again remained silent!! To add further insult to the misery and suffering, the silence continued when Italian law promulgated on 1st December 1943, provided for the internment of all Jews and the confiscation of their property!!

**Pope Pius XII
from 1939-58**

Undoubtedly, one of the most controversial moments in history!!

Whilst not condoning the silence from the Vatican, in all fairness, a lot of other countries and organisations also remained silent as well, for who knows what reason???

FILM "AMEN" REVEALS VATICAN SILENCE DURING NAZI HOLOCAUST

The film, "Amen", by director Constantin Costa-Gavras sheds light on the Vatican and Pope Pius XII's silence during World War II as millions of Jews were systematically being killed.

"This is an important film on one of the best kept secrets of the Vatican," said Rabbi Marvin Hier, dean and founder of the Simon Wiesenthal Centre. "The fact is that Pius XII knew as early as 1942 (from a letter he had received from Kurt Gerstein, an SS officer, who had provided Zyklon B to gas inmates at concentration and death camps), that Hitler had initiated a Final Solution but the Pius still continued his silence. Despite the overwhelming evidence, the film will obviously be attacked by Vatican officials but its veracity is unquestionable," continued Hier.

As a former Vatican official, Father Martin Malachi, wrote in one of his books that Pius XII had the Gerstein report, and as a result, he told the German Ambassador to the Vatican, Baron Von Weizsaecker that, "If such is true and if it continues, we will be forced to speak."

"But it continued," said Hier. "And even as late as 1945, Pius XII never issued a word of condemnation. Officially his name is Pius XII, but as far as the Jews are concerned, he will be known as Pius the Silent," concluded Hier.

In recent years, the media have accused the Catholic Church of either helping the Nazis or being silent during the Holocaust. As an example, the 26 January 1998 issue of Time magazine on page 20 claims that the Catholic Church apologised for *"collaborating with the Nazis during World War II."* Even the new Holocaust Museum in New York criticized Pope Pius XII for being silent during World War II. The Church has recently spoken on this topic.

The Israeli consul, Pinchas E Lapide, in his book, *Three Popes and the Jews* (New York: Hawthorn Books, Inc., 1967) critically examines Pope Pius XII. According to his research, the Catholic Church under Pius XII was instrumental in saving 860,000 Jews from Nazi death camps (p. 214). Could Pius have saved more lives by speaking out more forcefully? According to Lapide, the concentration camp prisoners did not want Pius to speak out openly (p. 247).

It should be noted that six million Jews and three million Catholics were killed in the Holocaust.

A Jewish woman is abused by the citizens of Lemberg, in the Ukraine, after the arrival of the Germans in the summer of 1941.

Adolf Hitler
(1889 - 1945)

Hitler was born in 1889 at Braunau-am-Inn on the Bavarian border. His father, Alois, was illegitimate, and carried his mother's name (Schicklgruber) until he established his claim to the surname Hitler in 1876. Adolf never used any other name. Mass agitation and propaganda, set against a government struggling with internal and external affairs, strengthened the Nazi party's influence. By the 1930 elections, the party received 6 million votes, making it the second largest party in the country. Hitler rose to power with the Nazi party, became dictator of Germany in 1933. By the end of 1942 the fortunes of the Reich had changed. Early on, the successes Hitler imagined had been pretty much realised. But now, to preserve his fantasies, he isolated himself from reality. Directing operations from his headquarters, he refused to visit bombed cities or read reports of setbacks.

When his planned offensive in the Ardennes failed, his hopes for victory began to revolve around the use of new weapons, the break up of the alliance, and the death of Roosevelt. Instead of trying to save what he could from defeat, he ordered mass destruction of materials and refused to allow surrender.

From January 1945 on, Hitler never left the chancellery. On 10 April 1945 he committed suicide by shooting himself. Eva Braun, his long time companion who he married just days before, took poison. In accordance with Hitler's instructions, their bodies were burned.

"The death of one man is a tragedy; the death of a million is a statistic." Joseph Stalin

Claims that Hitler left instructions that that his body should be burned is at odds with a photograph the Russian press released showing him to be dead...without scorch marks?

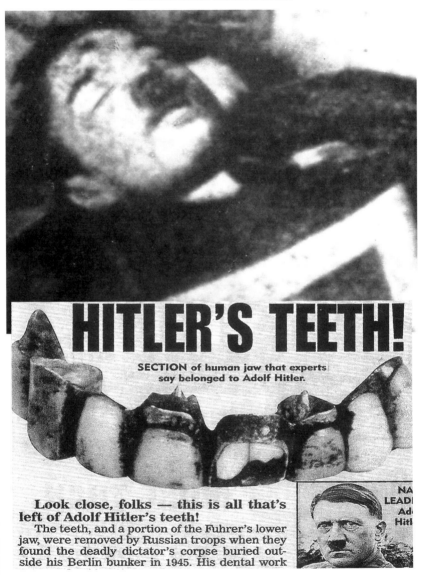

HITLER'S TEETH!

SECTION of human jaw that experts say belonged to Adolf Hitler.

Look close, folks — this is all that's left of Adolf Hitler's teeth!
The teeth, and a portion of the Fuhrer's lower jaw, were removed by Russian troops when they found the deadly dictator's corpse buried outside his Berlin bunker in 1945. His dental work

NA
LEAD
Ad
Hitl

Above, are these Hitler's teeth? A portion of the lower jaw of the alleged body of Hitler was removed by Russian troops when they supposedly found his body buried outside his Berlin bunker, his dental work, they say, was used to identify his body! Looking at the photograph above it seems at odds with that, why use dental work if the body was intact?

Hitler's signature, second from bottom, on an army awards document. The signature at the bottom is that of Rudolf Schmundt, Hitler's one time personal assistant who lost an eye and a leg, dying soon afterwards in an assassination attempt on Hitler's life on 20 July 1944. Museum displays original.

Jm Namen des Deutschen Volkes !

Mit Wirkung vom 1.Mai 1943 wird befördert:

N a m e	Friedens- truppenteil	Dienst- stellung	bisheriges Rangdienstalter	neues Rangdienst- alter

zum Generalleutnant
der Generalmajor

| Buschenhagen | Kdr.Pz.Gren.
Rgt. 5 | Kdr.e.
Jnf.Div. | 1.August 1941
(4) | 1.Mai 1943
(1 al); |

Mit Wirkung vom 1.Juli 1943 werden befördert:

zu Generalleutnanten:

die Generalmajore

| von
Oesterreich | Ausb.Leiter
Stargard(Pom)
2 | Führ.Res.
OKH W.Kdo.
XX | 1.April 1942
(22) | 1.Juli 1943
(2); |
| Kohlermann | Art.Schule | Kdr.e.
Jnf.Div. | 1.Juli 1942
(19b) | (3); |

zum Generalmajor
der Oberst

| Cuno | z.Vfg.Ob.d.H.
(Sonst.Offz.) | Kdr.d.Pz.
Tr.i.W.Kdo.
XIII | 1.April 1940
(9a) | 1.Juli 1943
(7); |

Führerhauptquartier,den *19.* Juni 1943

Der Führer

Oberkommando des Heeres
Jm Auftrage

Nr.4510/43 PA/Ag P 1/Ch/II/11

Generalleutnant und
Chef des Heeres-Personalamts

If Hitler faked his own death could Himmler have done the same?

The Modern day debate Goes on by historians as to whether or not the man in custody was really Heinrich Himmler, captured two weeks after the fall of Germany.

Himmler surrendered himself to the British on the evening of 23

The man they say was Himmler. Dead after committing suicide. Shown here propped up on a box.

May 1945, and was put into custody. The customary body search was carried out and when it came to Captain (Dr) C J Wells searching Himmler's mouth he gave Himmler's head a backward movement and saw, sticking to the inside of his left cheek, a capsule. The doctor slipped a finger into his mouth, but Himmler suddenly clamped his mouth around the doctor's finger!

After a short struggle Himmler wrenched the doctor's hand from his mouth and then quickly crushed the capsule between his teeth and took a deep inward gasp of air. He immediately became contorted with pain and his eyes glassed over.

The doctor shouted, "My God! It's in his mouth, he has done it on me." There was a smell of cyanide; Himmler was upended with his head in a bowl of water. They tried to seize his tongue, the doctor called for stimulants and got his tongue fixed, but after a few twitches, Himmler died at 11.14pm.

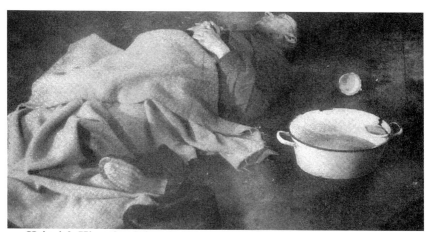

Heinrich Himmler, lying dead next to the bowl he was upended into.

The Gestapo

The Secret State Police (*Geheime Staatspolizei*) was universally known and feared by their more infamous name 'Gestapo'. The remit of the Gestapo was tracking down and eliminating political enemies and dissidents within Germany and applying the same remit to resistance organisations in occupied Europe.

The Gestapo owed its origins to Hermann Goering when he was the Minister-President of the Prussian State. The Prussian State Police Department (1A) (political activities) was converted by Goering into the secret police department. When Prussia was absorbed into the Reich, the Gestapo became a national organisation. Heinrich Muller replaced the former head of the department, Rudolf Diels, and the organisation came under the control of Heinrich Himmler and the SS.

The Gestapo had expanded rapidly and by October 1939 was incorporated into Reinhard Heydrich's integrated security apparatus, becoming Amt 1V of the RSHA. The Gestapo was indicted as a 'criminal organisation' at Nuremburg, but many members escaped prosecution, claiming they were simply policemen.

Hermann Goering commits suicide

During 1939, Goering was made Chairman of the Reich Council for National Defence and named as Hitler's successor. He planned the Luftwaffe's role in the invasions of Poland, Norway and France; in 1940, when Hitler made nine of his generals into field marshals, Goering was given the unprecedented rank of Reichsmarshall.

He had already reached the height of his career. The slide, when it began in 1940, was rapid, as his Luftwaffe failed to substantiate his boast to remove the British RAF from the skies. His tactical error had been to switch from attacks on RAF airfields and radar and to concentrate on the bombing of London.

In Russia the Luftwaffe was not to prove all-conquering, and Goering's inability to prevent the Allied bombing of German towns confirmed his decline. Self-indulgence softened him and more ambitious Nazis - Himmler, Bormann, Gobbels and Speer began to bypass him and reduce his importance.

The main rival to Goering (also the spelling of 'GÖring' is used with the 'O' having an amulet like so Ö) was Luftwaffe Field Marshall, Erhard Milch. Incidentally, Milch's father was Jewish, but he was 'Aryanised' by a statement from his mother that another man had fathered him!

Signed photo of Luftwaffe Field Marshall, Erhard Milch. Amazingly Milch's father was Jewish. He was sentenced at Nuremburg to life imprisonment, but was released in 1954. Genuine item on display in the museum.

On Hitler's birthday in April 1945, Goering left the Berlin Bunker, claiming urgent tasks in south Germany. When he telegraphed Hitler, offering to take command of the surviving German forces, Bormann interpreted this to Hitler as a treasonable act. Goering was ordered to be arrested and stripped of all offices and honours. Hitler's last will expelled him from the party.

In May 1945, from the SS house where he was detained, he despatched Field Marshal Brauchitsch to General Eisenhower to ask for protection from the SS. Then, dressed in a special uniform, he drove off to surrender, graciously acknowledging the salutes of the German soldiers walking to their imprisonment. At the 1946 Nuremberg trial, the effect of imprisonment and a normal improved diet showed, he was the star of the trial and clearly the leader of the accused.

He was found guilty on all counts and condemned to death. On the day before his execution was due in October 1946, the guards found him in his cell dead from poison.

Somehow (and still no one can explain how) he had managed to conceal about him a phial of cyanide on which he had bitten. There is an explanation as to how he came into the possession of poison and that was thought to have been from his second wife, Emmy, during the course of a visit. Incidentally, Goering was a big collector of pornography, boasting the largest collection of its kind in Germany and he had a great taste and understanding of art, which was unusual for a member of the Nazi party.

To be able to take your own life by taking poison must have either taken great courage or fear. Probably in the case of Himmler it was out of fear, but in direct contrast Goering was a war hero, he had won the Iron Cross after volunteering as a World War One fighter pilot, rising by the end of the war to command the elite Richthofen (Baron Von Richthofen) *Jagdgeschwader.*

After being awarded the Iron Cross (First Class) he also won Prussia's highest award for valour, *the Pour le Merite* or Blue Max. After Germany's defeat in the First World War, Goering went on to become a stunt pilot in Denmark and then went on to Sweden to fly for one of the first airlines.

Hermann Goering (Göring) took his own life on October 15th, 1946, two hours before he was to be hanged at Nuremburg. The order of the court was that his ashes were thrown into the last remaining incinerator at the Nazi Death Camp, Dachau.

Above, the signature of the Nazi Gestapo founder, Hermann Goering.

Goering in his cell at Nuremburg awaiting the veridct. He said, "If I am to die, I wish to face a firing squad in Berlin and die like a soldier."

Goering dead, like Himmler he had secreted a poison vial and robbed his prosecutors of a hanging.

"Peace in our time!" - Neville Chamberlain - 1938

Neville Chamberlain (1869 – 1940) was British Prime Minister from May 1937. His policy of 'appeasement' allowed Hitler's move into Austria and into the Sudetenland of Czechoslovakia.

Chamberlain believed that Germany had grievances from Versailles and that the concessions he made at Munich would satisfy Hitler's needs. He returned from Munich in September 1938 and at the airport, holding up the document he had signed with Hitler, declared, "Peace in our time!"

After Hitler occupied Czechoslovakia in 1939, Chamberlain abandoned appeasement and gave guarantees to Poland, which led to the declaration of war by Britain against Germany in September 1939. He resigned in May 1940, to be replaced by Churchill, and died shortly after.

Was Chamberlain sucking up to Hitler?

"Kill a man, and you are an assassin. Kill millions of men, and you are a conqueror. Kill everyone, and you are a god." Jean Rostand

The Munich Peace Conference October 1938, left, British Prime Minister Neville Chamberlain, second left, French Premier Edouard Daladier, Hitler and right, Italy's fascist dictator Benito Mussolini.

LORD HAW HAW – William Joyce
1906-1946

British Government hang USA citizen for High Treason!

And in modern day times, the USA can do what they want to British citizens if suspected of being involved in terrorism... Tit for Tat!!!

"Germany calling, Germany calling"
11th September 1939

**Joyce,
an Irish-
American
at a pre-war
fascist
meeting
in London
Lord Haw Haw**

The owner of the voice was William Joyce, an American, brought up in Galway, Eire who had taken up German citizenship during the Second World War before leaving England with a fraudulently obtained passport!

He was born of an Irish father and English mother in the United States in 1906. He went to Ireland with his parents in 1909, was educated at Catholic schools, and was brought up in a household that was fervently loyal to the British Crown.

For his pro-British stance his father suffered having much of his property burned in the Irish rebellion of 1916. Maybe this is what gave William the impetus to go against these ideologies?

As the situation in Ireland worsened, young William sought revenge by becoming a youthful informer for the para-military Auxiliaries, the hated "Black and Tans".

By 1921 Michael Joyce took his family to England. William, although not yet 16, joined the regular army; he gave his age as 18. Explaining that he had never been issued with a birth certificate. His Army career, however, was short-lived; his real age was discovered when he was admitted to hospital with rheumatic fever and he was discharged after serving only four months.

Joyce being a fighter, he was back and in 1923 Joyce entered London University, where he joined the Officer Training Corps.

A year later, he became involved in the embryonic British Fascist movement. In October 1924, during a scuffle with what he later called "Jewish Communists" at the Lambeth Baths Hall in southeast London, someone tried to cut his throat with a razor! The woolen scarf around Joyce's neck saved his life, but he was slashed across the right cheek from the corner of his mouth to behind his ear leaving a scar that marred his once handsome features and gave him a rather sinister appearance that enhanced his tough reputation on the political platform.

Double take – Sir Oswald Mosley, right, British Fascist leader imprisoned during the war for his beliefs seen at a Fascist conference in 1948. Hitler, left, in a similar stance to Mosley belts out his own sinister ideologies to the masses in Germany.

By the early 1930s, Joyce was heavily involved with the British Union of Fascists, led by Sir Oswald Mosley. But the Fascist cause made little headway in Great Britain and in 1939, as the clouds of war gathered, Joyce and his second wife, Margaret, emigrated to Germany.

Joyce founded the British National Socialist Party out of admiration of Hitler. He fled to Germany before the start of the war in August 1939 and was eventually employed by the Nazi regime in their propaganda war on Britain. The Joyces arrived in Berlin, with British passports, on 27 August 1939. Four days later, Germany invaded Poland! It was then that Joyce received a shock. A friend told him that if war broke out between Great Britain and Germany he and his wife would be separated and interned!

Joyce - The Road to Treason working at the German Radio Station

Joyce tried to leave Germany but a bizarre set of circumstances meant he couldn't use German currency to buy tickets for traveling outside of Germany – the Joyces stayed in Germany and eventually William and Margaret Joyce worked for the German Radio Corporation.

Lord Haw-Haw was the name given to Joyce by the Daily Express newspaper when referring to a journalist that had written of: '*A gent I'd like to meet is moaning periodically from Zeesen* (one of the main German transmitters). *He speaks English of the haw-haw, damit-get-out-of-my-way variety, and his strong suit is gentlemanly indignation.*'

And so, Lord Haw-Haw he became to the millions of Britons who, anxious for news of the war, tuned in to German radio broadcasts! The voice of Haw-Haw became the most hated voice to come out of Germany, but also was one of the most fascinating voices! The legacy of a broken nose, as the result of a childhood fight in Eire, gave him a unique twang. He would pronounce the word Germany with a peculiar intonation so that it sounded more like "Jairmany" - this became the identifying trademark of his upper-class drawl.

The British authorities became worried about Joyce's contribution to the German propaganda effort. He was clever; often enquiring about the welfare of British personalities he knew the names of.

Lord Haw-Haw made his last broadcast to Britain on 30 April 1945, the day Hitler is alleged to have committed suicide. *"Britain's victories are barren. They leave her poor and they leave her people hungry. They leave her bereft of the markets and the wealth that she possessed six years ago. But, above all, they leave her with an immensely greater problem than she had then. We are nearing the end of one phase in Europe's history, but the next will be no happier. It will be grimmer, harder and, perhaps, bloodier. And now I ask you earnestly, can Britain survive? I am profoundly convinced that without German help she cannot."*

Tentative plans had been laid to secrete the Joyces (William and his wife Margaret) out of Germany by Josef Goebbels, the German Propaganda Minister, but Goebbels died in Berlin and the plans came to nothing. They tried to escape to Sweden via Denmark, but Allied forces had landed ahead of them and they were forced to turn back. The end of the war found them in the village of Kupfermuhle, near the Danish border; their apartment was visited several times by British soldiers, who took them for an ordinary German couple and showed no interest in them.

Joyce was out walking one morning, soon after Germany's capitulation, in the woods. He stumbled upon two British officers who were gathering wood for a fire. He spoke to them in French and walked on. Their suspicions aroused, the officers followed him. One of them, Lieutenant Perry, an interpreter, called out: "You wouldn't happen to be William Joyce, would you?" Reaching into an inside pocket for his German passport Joyce looked to be reaching for a weapon. Perry fired his revolver. The bullet passed through both of Joyce's thighs and he fell to the ground.

He was taken to Luneburg, where he spent time in hospital recovering from his wounds, and then to Brussels, where he was detained while the British Parliament hurriedly passed the Treason

Act 1945, which made treachery a capital offence. This was obviously done in readiness for Joyce's trial. On 16th June he was flown to London and taken to Brixton Prison.

His trial began at the Old Bailey on 17 September1945. It was a complex business, much hinged on Joyce's possession of a British passport, which as you will recall was obtained by fraudulent means, and his allegiance to the Crown.

The outcome was never seriously in doubt, and no one showed much surprise when the jury, after only 23 minutes, found him guilty of High Treason.

Crowds gathered outside Wandsworth Prison to read the Notice of Joyces' execution

Joyce was executed on 3rd January 1946. To the end, he remained unrepentant. After the execution, Margaret Joyce was interned in Germany while her status was debated. She died in London in 1972, having regained her British nationality.

Even though there was solid evidence against Margaret (Lady Haw-Haw) to convict her of High Treason (treachery) by virtue of the fact that she had acted as assistant treasurer to her husband's National Socialist League. In reality she too was a German citizen although born in Manchester, England, she relinquished her British citizenship when moving to Germany.

Joyce's daughter, Mrs Heather Iandolo, a schoolteacher from Gillingham, England, fought successfully to have her father's body exhumed from the cemetery at Wandsworth prisons and buried in Eire.

The conclusion to this story could be that argued that because Joyce was not a legitimate British subject he could therefore not have been tried for treason. If the trial was to have taken place today maybe the outcome would have been 'not guilty'.

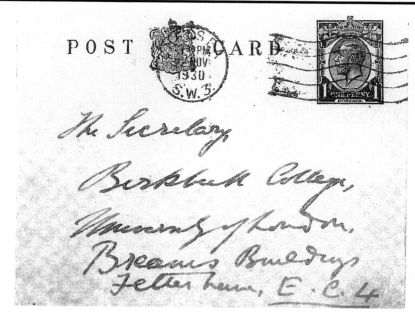

Above, an original item on display in the museum: A card sent to the
Secretary of Birbeck College, London by Joyce in 1930.

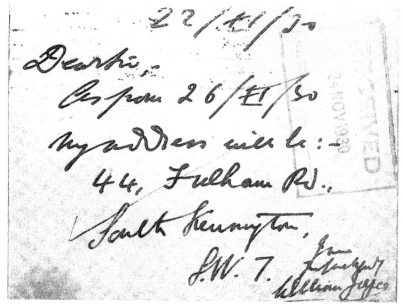

Above, the rear of the card, written in Joyce's own hand, indicates that
his new address will be 44 Fulham Road, South Kensington, SW7.
Signed by Joyce in the lower right corner.

NAZI HEADHUNTER

All original items are on display in the museum

Signature of
Nazi Headhunter
Simon Wiesenthal

Simon Wiesenthal – Head of the bureau in Vienna which tracks down and brings fugitive Nazi war criminals to justice. Many Nazis have escaped certain death by hiding out in 'friendly' countries around the world or changing their identities. It is the job of Simon Wiesenthal to track these butchers down. Who, though, is Wiesenthal working for? He certainly cannot be doing the job for nothing! Could he be accused of gaining financially from the Holocaust, has it become an industry in its own right?

FRIEDRICH MUSSGAY
SS-STURMBANNFÜHRER, HAUPTMANN D. LDW.
Kommandeur der Sicherheitspolizei und des
SD-Einsatzkommandos III/3

WAR CRIMINAL'S CALLING CARD

SS.STURMBANNFUHRER FRIEDRICH MUSSGAY, WAS COMMANDER OF SD-EINSATZKOMMANDO 3. AND SERVED IN RUSSIA IN EINSATZGRUPPE A, ARMY GROUP NORTH. HE DISAPPEARED AT THE END OF THE WAR AND WAS SENTENCED TO DEATH IN HIS ABSENCE.

What

If

The

Holocaust

Was

An

Invention

?

"The Holocaust Industry, is as I conceive in the book, is institutions, organisations and individuals who have put to use Jewish suffering for political and financial gain".

"These organisations frankly, bring to mind an insight of my late mother, that it is no accident that Jews invented the word "chutzpah". They steal, and I do use the word with intent, 95% of the monies earmarked for victims of Nazi persecution, and then throw you a few crumbs while telling you to be grateful".

"It is very hard to sink much lower than to turn the colossal suffering of the Jewish people during World War Two into an extortion racket ...but that's exactly what this gang of wretched crooks have done".

"...all the claims against the Swiss banks were a fantastic concoction of the Holocaust hustlers. But then after turning Jewish suffering into an extortion racket to then deny the actual victims these monies extorted it is very difficult to imagine sinking any lower on a moral level than that. If they were all put behind bars, it wouldn't be yet, in my opinion, a just punishment".

Professor Norman Finkelstein has been described as a dying breed of American maverick that relentlessly defies any attempt at easy categorisation. He is the son of Holocaust survivors but an unremitting critic of Holocaust reparation claims; a Jew but is a life-long anti Zionist; and though very much a Leftist, he is often praised by far Right revisionists of the Third Reich, such as Hitler-admiring historian David Irving.

Crime Through Time

http://www.normanfinkelstein.com/

Doctor Norman G Finkelstein is the author of four books: *Image and Reality of the Israel-Palestine Conflict* (Verso, 1995), *The Rise and Fall of Palestine* (University of Minnesota, 1996), with Ruth Bettina Birn, *A Nation on Trial: The Goldhagen Thesis and Historical Truth* (Henry Holt, 1998) and *The Holocaust Industry: Reflections on the Exploitation of Jewish Suffering* (Verso, 2000).

Finkelstein was born in Brooklyn, N.Y., USA in 1953. He is the son of Maryla Husyt Finkelstein, survivor of the Warsaw Ghetto, Maidanek concentration camp, and Zacharias Finkelstein, survivor of the Warsaw Ghetto, Auschwitz concentration camp.

Dr Finkelstein argues that most 'survivors' are bogus and that too much money is spent commemorating the Nazi genocide.

By using extracts from his book *The Holocaust Industry: Reflections on the Exploitation of Jewish Suffering* you can decide for yourself whether what is quoted has any weight to it. Obviously great weight is attached to the fact that Dr Finklestein is a Jew, and as some newspapers have noted, what if the book was written by, say, David Irving (see later in this chapter) or the leader of the US Muslims, Louis Farrakhan, probably war would have erupted in the courts or on the streets, so does Dr Finklestein have a licence to make such claims, see for yourself.

Genocide: Murder of a Nation

The Holocaust Industry: Reflections on the Exploitation of Jewish Suffering:

I sometimes think that American Jewry 'discovering' the Nazi Holocaust was worse than its having been forgotten. True, my parents brooded in private; the suffering they endured was not publicly validated. But wasn't that better than the current crass exploitation of Jewish martyrdom? Before the Nazi Holocaust became the Holocaust, only a few scholarly studies (by Raul Hilberg, Viktor Frankl and Ella Lingens-Reiner) were published on the subject. But this small collection of gems is better than the shelves upon shelves of shlock that now line libraries and bookstores. Both my parents, although daily reliving that past until the day each died, lost interest by the end of their lives in the Holocaust as a public spectacle. One of my father's lifelong friends was a former inmate with him in Auschwitz, a seemingly incorruptible leftwing idealist who on principle refused German compensation after the war. Eventually he became a director of the Israeli Holocaust museum Yad Vashem. Reluctantly and with genuine disappointment, my father finally admitted that even this man had been corrupted by the Holocaust industry, tailoring his beliefs for power and profit. As the rendering of the Holocaust assumed ever more absurd forms, my mother liked to quote (with intentional irony) Henry Ford: History is bunk'. The tales of 'Holocaust survivors' all concentration camp inmates, all heroes of the resistance were a special source of wry amusement in my home.

My parents often wondered why I would grow so indignant at the falsification and exploitation of the Nazi genocide. The most obvious answer is that it has been used to justify criminal policies of the Israeli state and US support for these policies. There is a personal motive as well. I do care about the memory of my family's persecution. The current campaign of the Holocaust industry to extort money from Europe in the name of 'needy Holocaust victims' has shrunk the moral stature of their martyrdom to that of a Monte Carlo casino.

The Holocaust only emerged in American life after Israel's victory in the 1967 Six Day war against its Arab neighbours. (Since then) too many public and private resources have been invested in memorialising the Nazi genocide. Most of the output is worthless, a tribute not to Jewish suffering but to Jewish aggrandisement. The Holocaust has proven to be an indispensable ideological weapon. Through its deployment, one of the world's most formidable military powers, with a horrendous human rights record, has cast itself as a 'victim' state, and the most successful ethnic group in the US has likewise acquired victim status.

The term 'Holocaust survivor' originally designated those who suffered the unique trauma of the Jewish ghettos, concentration camps and slave labour camps, often in sequence. The figure for these Holocaust survivors at war's end is generally put at some 100,000. The number of living survivors cannot be more than a quarter of this figure now. Because enduring the camps became a crown of martyrdom, many Jews who spent the war elsewhere represented themselves as camp survivors. Another strong motive behind this misrepresentation, however, was material. The post-war German government provided compensation to Jews who had been in ghettos or camps. Many Jews fabricated their pasts to meet this eligibility requirement. 'If everyone who claims to be a survivor actually is one,' my mother used to exclaim, 'who did Hitler kill?'

Even within the Holocaust industry, Deborah Lipstadt, for example, wryly observes that Holocaust survivors frequently maintain they were personally examined by Josef Mengele at Auschwitz. Because survivors are now revered as secular saints, one doesn't dare question them. Preposterous statements pass without comment.

In recent years, 'Holocaust survivor' has been redefined to designate not only those who endured but also those who managed to evade the Nazis. One contributor to a Holocaust website maintained that, although he spent the war in Tel Aviv, he was a Holocaust survivor because his grandmother died in Auschwitz. According to Israel Gutman, a former inmate of Auschwitz, director of Yad Vashem and a Holocaust lecturer at Hebrew University, '…it's not that important' whether Binjamin Wilkomirski's (now discredited) 'autobiographical' account of childhood in the camps, Fragments, is a fraud.

The Israeli prime minister's office recently put the number of 'living Holocaust survivors' at nearly a million. The main motive behind this inflationary revision is again not hard to find. It is difficult to press massive new claims for reparations if only a handful of Holocaust survivors are still alive.

Others involved in the preparations process have also done well. The reported annual salary of Saul Kagan, longtime executive secretary of the claims conference, is Dollars 105,000. Kagan rings up in 12 days what my mother received for suffering six years of Nazi persecution.

In recent years, the Holocaust industry has become an outright extortion racket. Purporting to represent all of world Jewry, living and dead, it is laying claim to Holocaust-era Jewish assets throughout Europe. Fittingly dubbed the 'last chapter of the Holocaust', this double shakedown of European countries as well as legitimate Jewish claimants first targeted Switzerland. (After a protracted campaign which enlisted the American political establishment) the Swiss finally caved in 1998 and agreed to pay $1.25bn.

Meanwhile, the Holocaust industry forced Switzerland into a settlement because time was allegedly of the essence: 'Needy Holocaust survivors are dying every day.' Once the

Swiss signed away the money, however, the urgency miraculously passed. More than a year after the settlement was reached there was still no distribution plan. By the time the money is finally divvied out, all the 'needy Holocaust survivors' will probably be dead.

The staggering dimensions of Hitler's 'Final Solution' are by now well known. And isn't the 'normal' history of humankind replete with horrifying chapters of inhumanity? A crime need not be aberrant to warrant atonement. The challenge today is to restore the Nazi Holocaust as a rational subject of inquiry. Only then can we really learn from it. The abnormality of the Nazi Holocaust springs not from the event itself but from the exploitative industry that has grown up around it.

The Holocaust industry has always been bankrupt. What remains is to openly declare it so. The time is long past to put it out of business. The noblest gesture for those who perished is to preserve their memory, learn from their suffering and let them, finally, rest in peace.

The Holocaust Industry by Norman G Finkelstein (Verso, £16 Sterling) is available from all good bookshops and

http://www.amazon.co.uk

"Both my father and mother were survivors of the Warsaw Ghetto and the Nazi concentration camps. Apart from my parents, every family member on both sides was exterminated by the Nazis."

Remember page 86, an extract

The Times newspaper reported that tourism officials are considering taking action against the Crime Through Time museum because exhibits on display relating to the Holocaust are of questionable taste and are considered "offensive" and "voyeuristic".

The article went on to say, 'Most have been upset about seeing Nazi memorabilia, which includes Nazi helmets, badges, SS rings, swastika flags and a bust of Hitler.'

Rabbi Julia Neuberger: "Programmes of Holocaust studies in universities, Holocaust museums, Holocaust days, are all relatively new. In London, we have the impressive Holocaust exhibit in the Imperial War Museum, put together, in my view, with great sensitivity and seen within the context of international and genocide as opposed to being free-standing."

Maverick attacks 'Holocaust industry'

Yesterday we published a summary of an explosive book that accuses the 'Jewish Establishment' of exploiting the Holocaust. Today the book's author, Norman Finkelstein, right, is himself taken to task by Rabbi **JULIA NEUBERGER**, left

Why he's wrong about the Holocaust

It would seem that so long as Jews appreciate such exhibits all is well, if that is the case then it can be said that many Jews have also appreciated the Holocaust exhibits on display at the Crime Through Time museum, even a Rabbi has visited the museum and has given positive comments as to the stylish layout and the sensitive way the displays have been designed. It would, though, seem that to gain national/international recognition you need the Queen to open such exhibitions. Strange, since the Royal family are descended from Germans!

The Downfall of a great historian

£1,000 if you can prove Hitler knew about the Holocaust!

David Irving - 1977

Making of a Monster

He taunts his lover with Hitler jibes and is 'improper' with his six-year-old child. Here David Irving, deserted by his first wife and

anti-Semite and a racist who twists history for his own ideological reason

by Mary Riddell

final reckoning

The family at war at a christening in 1965: Irving with, from left: Daughter Pilar (holding Josephine's baby Jules); his sister Carol; daughter Josephine, first wife Pilar; and daughter Beatrice

A broken marriage and three lost daughters, the awful price of obsession

David Irving: to shool

By Geoffrey Levy

FOR years David Irving has been telling a story about Hitler's right-hand man, Heinrich Himmler, watching a mass execution, and how a women held out her baby.

Obsession with discrediting Holocaust cost Irving £2m and bankruptcy

Defeated Irving may lose home

By **David Williams** Chief Reporter

HISTORIAN David Irving's libel defeat could cost him his Mayfair home as lawyers seek to recover £2.5million legal costs. Bailiffs are to be told to seize the £750,000 apartment where the 62-year-old author lives with his wife and two children within three months if the costs are not paid from a fighting fund. The fund was set up with anonymous donations to sue American academic Deborah Lipstadt, who said he had denied the Holocaust had ever happened, and her publishers Penguin books.
Irving has taken out five mortgages on his home in Duke Street. He also owns a property on Florida's Key West. Asked yesterday if he had sufficient funds to cover the costs, he answered: 'No.'

The pro-Nazi author David Irving declared bankrupt on 4th March 2002 after failing to pay £150,000 in costs after his monumentally disastrous libel action against Penguin Books that he was a Holocaust denier. Now facing the loss of his home, a flat in Mayfair, central London - estimated to be worth £900,000.

In 2000 the high court found he had falsified history to exonerate Adolf Hitler, driven by anti-semitism and his own pro-Nazi views.

Suing Penguin books and the author Deborah Lipstadt over her book that said he had persistently and deliberately misinterpreted and twisted historical evidence to minimise Hitler's culpability for the Holocaust Irving had hoped for a victory

Costs incurred by Penguin were £2m - for lawyers and experts they hired to defend the claim. In May 2000 Irving was ordered to pay an interim amount of £150,000.

After a 20-minute hearing the publishing firm was granted a bankruptcy petition against Irving who had failed to pay one penny of the outstanding costs. A trustee in bankruptcy will be appointed and a meeting of Irving's creditors will be held.

His prime assets is said to be his Mayfair flat, which has been his home for over 30 years. He, along with his partner Bente, shares it with their eight-year-old daughter Jessica.

Irving unsuccessfully appealed against the judgment by Mr Justice Charles Gray that stripped the author of his last shreds of credibility.

Signed photo of great historian, but great controversial figure, David Irving original. Don't fret – Andy Jones of Crime Through Time has no political involvement with David Irving. Incidentally, Irving exposed Hitler's diaries as fake. Original signed photo on display in the museum.

Penguin Books issued a statement via their lawyer: "Our client has been very patient but Irving was clearly not going to meet the interim payment which is a fraction of their total costs."

The costs, consequences of his failing with his libel action, have long been clear. It's another step from what happened in court in 2000. He was aware that we were incurring the costs at a high rate and he continued.

Penguin have been incredibly patient in waiting for the money to be paid, they're certainly not on a witch-hunt! One of Irving's financial backers is believed to be a former Nazi U-boat captain! Two offers were made by Irving to settle the interim costs order, both of which Penguin rejected, which surely shows it to be rigidity by Penguin in wanting their money!

Irving had offered to pay by instalments over six years, and also claimed that a supporter would pay the £150,000 on his behalf if Penguin accepted that as full and final settlement, but they turned this option down!

According to land registry records Irving had taken out five mortgages on his Mayfair flat, it is thought that there will be other claims on Irving's assets other than from Penguin.

Irving sued Deborah Lipstadt over passages in her book *Denying the Holocaust: The Growing Assault on Truth and Memory.* Lipstadt's description of Irving as a man prepared to bend historical evidence "until it conforms with his ideological leanings and political agenda," angered him enough to challenge her description of him.

Also challenged was the historical legitimacy of the Holocaust itself, Irving claimed there was sufficient reason to doubt large numbers of Jews were deliberately murdered by the Nazis at Auschwitz and other death camps. He also doubted the existence of gas chambers and at one stage addressed the libel case judge as "mein Fuhrer."

"Undoubtedly they will come for their pound of flesh, but will find I'm made of British beef."

David Irving, March 2002

Finklestein says is it right that Jewish leader Elie Wiesel, left, should charge $25,000 and demand a chauffeur driven limousine when he gives talks on the lecture circuit arguing that the Nazi extermination of the Jews was a unique event?

Is it right that Jews have sovereignty over suffering? What about the 10 million Africans slaughtered in the Congo as a direct result of the Belgian ivory and rubber trade – is the admittance of such a crime classed as Holocaust Denial?

Are Finklestein and Irving in Holocaust Denial?

Has the Holocaust become an industry?

Wartime British Traitor Unmasked
By Historian David Irving

Controversial right-wing historian David Irving has provoked fresh controversy with a claim that a former army officer may have passed British military secrets to the Russians during the Second World War!

Irving may have solved the puzzle of one of the few wartime conundrums left by identifying the spy previously known only by his Russian codename, Reservist.

At a conference at the Public records office in 2001 Irving stood up and said he believed the mole was probably Lieutenant-Colonel Kenneth Post, of the Royal Artillery, who died about 10 years ago.

It was during the Second World War that Post acted as a personal aid to Churchill's representative Duncan Sandys who also prepared Britain's military shield against Hitler's V-1 and V-2 rockets.

Post's widow, Diane from Tunbridge Wells, Kent, England, saying that her husband was "fiercely patriotic", angrily denied Irving's theory.

There is strong evidence to support Irving's claim, Post appears to fit the profile provided to us by intercepts from Russian intelligence.

Given that Irving also revealed the Hitler Diaries to be fake this sounds to be creditable stuff, although if you base this on his lost libel case it could be guesswork.

Has the Holocaust become a paradise for collectors?

Is it politically correct to collect SS ephemera from the Holocaust period? Collectors of memorabilia connected with the Second World War allegedly include Hollywood actor Clint Eastwood. Lemmy of heavy metal band Motorhead and singer David Bowie collect Nazi daggers. Bob Hope – collected Nazi daggers. Blondie's husband, Chris Stein – Nazi ephemera.

Signed poster of film High Plains Drifter - signed by Clint Eastwood

Czechoslovakia's Salute of tears

In 1938 on the morning of October 1st the German army marched across the Czech frontiers. A Czechoslovakian woman is in tears at having to give the Nazi salute. Many people still believe that the salute was freely given even by Germans to the SS, this was not so and in one incident a gun was pulled and put to the head of a German woman who refused to return the salute of SS officers entering a shop in Germany.

Germany's Salute of Evil

They are young, jobless, violent, they see no future.. and they're bringing Nazism back to Germany

THUGS' TIMETABLE OF TERROR

Germany's Salute of the new millennium

Museum lambasted over Hitler display

Newent Town Council condemned the display of swastikas outside the museum as "deplorable" and the items on display inside the museum relating to Hitler were lambasted at the Planning Committee meeting.

A bust of Hitler - "Deplorable"

Body cages - "Disapproval with disgust"

Ku Klux Klan display - condemned

Disapproval with disgust was also voiced over displays featuring Ku Klux Klan memorabilia and the body cages scattered around the grounds of the museum.

A new dawn, a new beginning?

NAZI COMPUTER GAME TO BE BANNED

BY KEITH GLADDIS
DEPUTY POLITICAL EDITOR

GOVERNMENT watchdogs are gunning for a World War II computer game that flaunts Nazi images and slogans.

Worried ministers want Day Of Defeat banned from Britain, fearing it will stir up racial hatred and provide a platform for fascists.

Players who choose to be Germans are "armed" with authentic-looking rifles, Luger pistols and Hitler Youth knives. They fight on battlefields draped with swastikas and Nazi posters.

At present Day Of Defeat is only available here on the internet. But a £20 disc version for PCs is already on sale in America.

Now the Department Of Culture, Media and Sports is investigating ways of barring it or ordering programmers to remove Nazi imagery.

An inside source

liced, especially as it's aimed at youngsters."

The business is worth more than £1.6 billion a year in Britain. Another World War II game, Return To Castle Wolfenstein, was given a '15' certificate because of its violent content but still topped the charts – selling more than a million

TORTURE: Castle Wolfenstein game scene — **CYBERHATE: Swastikas adorn war zone**

NAZI REF BANNED

By LUCY PANTON

RACIST thug Tony Stewart has been banned from refereeing children's soccer after the Sunday People revealed his former links with the Ku Klux Klan.

We told how Stewart, 34, burned fiery crosses, has a Nazi shrine at his home and spent nine months in jail for making death threats to an Asian family.

Now he has been shown the red card by embarrassed bosses of the junior football league in Batley, West Yorks, where he supervised weekend matches.

Stewart claims he regrets his racist past and is appealing against the ruling, which he branded a "knee-jerk reaction."

But parents of team members insist he must go and one said yesterday:

KU KLUX KLAN SHAME OF KIDS FOOTBALL REF

SHAME: Last week's story

"Now we know about his evil secret past there is no way we are letting him near our kids again. We want to thank the Sunday People for outing this monster."

League chairman Mike Wallace confirmed: "He has been removed from our current list of referees."

EXPOSED: RACE HATE NAZIS AT A TORY HQ

MESSAGE OF MENACE: Nick Cass, BNP organiser in Dewsbury, speaking at the meeting inside a Conserv

GENOCIDE JAIL

EXCLUSIVE

BNP thugs meet at party club

Daily Mail, Thursday, February 8, 2001

Page 39

From **Allan Hall**
in Berlin

A FRIGHTENING number of young Germans would welcome the Nazis back into power, a survey has found.

Half of 14 to 25-year-olds in the eastern part of the country believe the Nazis had 'good points' and, astonishingly, nearly one in six say the Nazi party itself was 'a good idea'.

The terrifying attitudes emerged as the German government revealed a 40 per cent rise in racist crime last year.

While much is made of the appeal of the Nazis to disillusioned youth in the former communist East Germany, the survey shows that youngsters from West Germany are just as attracted to the regime.

Some 35 per cent agree with their eastern neighbours that the Nazis had 'good points', while 40 per cent believe there are too many foreigners in Germany. Forty six per cent of easterners thought the same.

The survey of 1,106 youngsters conducted by a Berlin-based polling

Shock as half German youth back the Nazis

arson attacks on several refuges for asylum seekers.

The violence was concentrated in eastern Germany, Schilly told a newspaper. Roughly half of the crimes were committed there, even though only one-fifth of the population is resident in the area.

Experts often cite unemployment and a moral vacuum after the col-

in Germany but it is a fragile democracy, one that has been in existence for just 50 years. And the ghosts of the street battles between communists and Nazis are rattling their chains in the collective conscience all the time.

'That our youth still believe the perpetrators of the biggest mass slaughter in history had "good points" boggles the mind.'

Hitler in full rant: He and the Nazis still hold allure for many youngsters

Genocide: Murder of a Nation

British born comedian Ben Elton

Jewish employee ordered to dress as a Nazi by his bosses at Tulett, and Tokyo Liberty (stockbrokers). After refusing to wear the uniform as a punishment for being late for work Laurent Weinberger was demoted from his £125,000 year job. In an act of contrition the company offered a payment of £50,000 to a Jewish charity if Weinberger dropped the case!

But wasn't Weinberger's solicitor also being racist when he suggested that it was like forcing a black person to dress as a Klansman. Can you remember the British TV soap from the 70s, Love Thy Neighbour?

For all the obstacles in the way of progress the Jewish nation, it is not disputed, suffered more than any other race during the Second World War, in spite of this the Jewish race has produced some very clever individuals and some famous and infamous stars right from the days of Moses.

Albert Einstein – Probably the cleverest Jew in the world (Theory of relativity).

Robert Oppenheimer – Maybe the most infamous! In helping to develop the atom bomb he took part in the murder of 155,000 Japanese.

Jonas Silk – Without this man the vaccine against polio might not exist.

Steven Spielberg – Famous for his film about the Holocaust, Schindler's List.

Bob Dylan – The answer my friend is blowing in the wind.

Irving Berlin – Wrote White Christmas and many more hit songs.

Calvin Klein – Modern day designer.

Henry Heinz - 57 varieties of soup and more besides.

Estee Lauder – Cosmetics giant.

Barbara Streisand – Singing talents.

Harrison Ford – great actor, his mother was Jewish.

Henry Kissenger – American politician.

Michel de Nostradame (Nostradamus) – Jewish doctor, oh…and prophet.

Christopher Columbus (doubt exists that he was a Jew) – Famous discoverer.

David Beckham – Pro Soccer player (England). (Mother's father is Jewish.)

Harry Houdini – Escapologist.

Benjamin Disraeli - Former Prime Minister of Great Britain.

Goldie Hawn – American actress.

William Shatner (Captain Kirk) – Canadian actor.

Jerry Lewis – American comedian.

Leonard Nimoy (Star Trek) – American actor.

How many of the names did you recognise?

Museum curator, Andy Jones, questioned by anti-terrorism officers in connection with Nazi terror bomber!

Anti-terrorism squad officers questioned the owner, Andy Jones, of the controversial black crime museum, Crime Through Time, after his name was connected with Soho Nazi nail bomber David Copeland.

Police investigating the discovery of explosive devices in Gloucestershire questioned Andy twice.

His name, allegedly, appeared on a list of contacts found among David Copeland's possessions and police said Copeland had been trying to write to Mr Jones. This in itself is not unusual because in the course of collecting memorabilia certain sensitive communiqués are sent out to well known criminals in order to secure exhibits for the museum, it would seem that Copeland had wished to make some sort of statement to Mr Jones for display in the museum.

The museum does have some memorabilia linked to Copeland within the collection but after visiting the museum the police were satisfied that Mr Jones was a serious historian with no criminal intentions.

> **"I was a little bit put out because I am a serious collector."**
> **Andy Jones**

Andy said: "While I admit I felt a little bit offended I also respect the fact that it appeared to be of serious concern and the investigating officers had a job to do. Anyway, the investigations have been concluded, they were more than happy with their findings, and I wasn't arrested either."

Bearing in mind the size of the Nazi related collection at the museum it could certainly make the mind boggle if it wasn't a museum collection. Should Andy Jones have been named as a suspect and he had that little lot of memorabilia in his bedroom then it could certainly be taken as sinister! But rest assured, Andy is not a fascist, racist, terrorist, thug or part of any politically motivated movement.

Crime Through Time

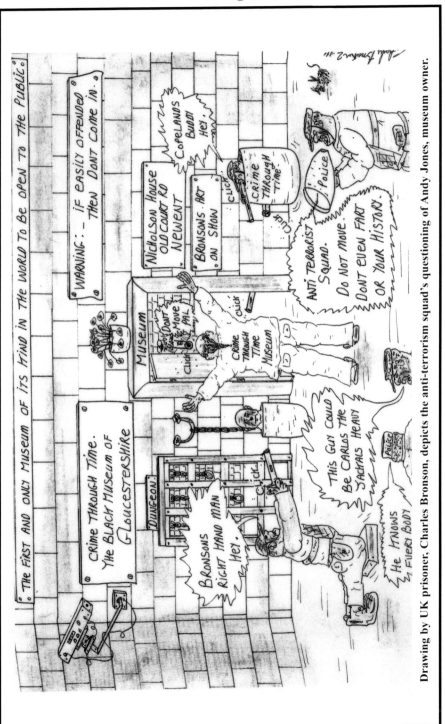

Drawing by UK prisoner, Charles Bronson, depicts the anti-terrorism squad's questioning of Andy Jones, museum owner.

Genocide: Murder of a Nation

David Copeland, 24, of Cove, in Hampshire, was sentenced to six life sentences in June 2000 after being convicted of planting nail bombs in Brixton, Brick Lane and Soho, in London. Three people were killed and 139 injured in the Soho bombing.

"… I believe it's my destiny…. political reasons … you know I am a Nazi I admit that." David Copeland

"A national socialist state… For this country, well for the entire world… it means the Aryan domination of the world."

David Copeland

"…I do predominantly say that the white race is the master race." David Copeland

"Adolf Hitler…And Sadam Hussein is one of my heroes….They're just real dictators. They're…strong people…" David Copeland

Genocide: Murder of a Nation

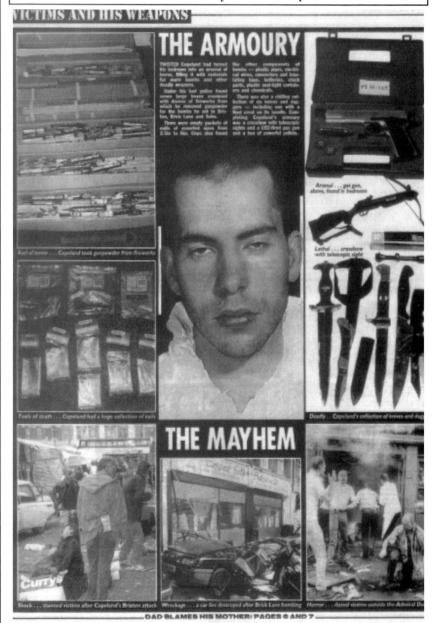

"That's right. My aim was political. It was to cause a racial war in this country." David Copeland

THE ARMOURY

THE MAYHEM

"I think perfectly British people have the right to ethnic cleanse." David Copeland

> "… I don't like them. I want them out of this country. I'm a national socialist. Nazi, whatever you want to call me. You know what I mean, I believe in a really master race…"
>
> David Copeland on asylum seekers

I AM AN SS COLONEL WHO RAPES AND KILLS WOMEN

By ADRIAN SHAW

BOMBER David Copeland had violent sex fantasies in which he drugged, raped and murdered women, a court heard yesterday.

He dreamed of being an SS colonel and playing God with the lives of women, said psychologist Jackie Craissati.

She said Copeland was a sexual inadequate who was terrified of

Fantasy of Soho bomber

having a normal heterosexual relationship in case he was "mocked and humiliated".

She told the Old Bailey: "He said he had violent fantasies, both physical and sexual, in which he would drug women so they were sexually compliant. In

the most common he would be God and he was able to choose the pretty women.

"In another he was in the SS and he[.....]'d pick a victim, rape he[.......] dead."

But [....] Craissa[.....]

obvious signs of mental illness". Defence psychiatrists claim he was insane when he planted three nailbombs at black, Asian and gay targets in London which killed three and injured 129.

Copeland, of Cove, Hants, denies murder but admits manslaughter on the grounds of diminished responsibility. The prosecution rejects the plea. The case continues.

[.....] shaw@mirror.co.uk

FEARS: Copeland

NAIL BOMBER

NOTHING EXCUSES THIS EVIL

Relatives' delight as judge cages [...]

'ethnic cleansing'

HELL

Horror movie drove Nazi bomber to kill

ng trail of carnag

> " I knew that Brixton was the focal point for the black community. I knew that Brick Lane was [the] focal point for the Aisan community. I knew that Soho was [the] focal point for the gay community…" David Copeland

"I'm just very homophobic … I just hate them."
David Copeland

" I, I chose the gays 'cos I hate them though. You know I mean that was personal, I'm sorry to say it was, but it was."
David Copeland

IRMA GRESE
1921-1945
Known as
Belle of Auschwitz, Angel of Death and Blonde Angel of Hell

The Sadistic Irma Greese

Irma Greese variously called the Belle of Auschwitz, Angel of Death, and Blonde Angel of Hell, became an SS *Hilferin* (Auxiliary) at the age of 18. The Angel of Death, at the age of 19, was appointed to look after the women's quarters of Ravensbruck concentration camp as an *aufseherin* (overseer), where she became case-hardened. After this, at the age of 22, she went on to Auschwitz, in charge of 18,000 female prisoners.

Greese had a reputation for sadistic beatings, using her riding whip (this is actually on display in the museum). She was the epitome of inhuman sadism and torture beyond belief!

Slipping on her heavy hobnailed boots, the big boned Irma Greese attacked the Nazi commitment to eradicate Jews with unswerving fanaticism. Strapping on her pistol and snatching up her whip she was ready for work at 7am every morning.

Applying psychological torture to her victims was inbuilt, she would pick up the lists of those due to be gassed, and toying with the inmates she would say to those awaiting their fate, "You're lucky – you have another two weeks." When the woman or child would appear relieved, Irma would smile and order the inmate killed at once! Doom was dangled like a worm before a trout, "Your turn comes on Friday, so think about it!"

The stories associated with Greese are beyond comprehension, reading about them detaches us from what it must have been really like to have someone like this evil Nazi at their side. Constant companions at the side of this nightmare figure were two savage Alsatian hounds. The dogs, kept half starved, would be ordered to attack and kill any prisoner that Greese felt displeased with. When the dogs pinned the inmate to the ground Greese would jump up and down on the inmate's stomach full force, then literally kick the woman or child to death. No one dared to intervene for fear of the same treatment being used against them!

Just like the perverse Buchenwald Bitch, Ilse Koch, she too would have the skin of dead prisoners made into lampshades! In the home of this hellish woman she had the skin of three victims made into lampshades because, "The skin let the light shine through in a pleasing way."

Just before the end of the war, in 1945, the heartless Greese moved on to Belsen. Described by some of her victims as of surpassing beauty and by others as a frowzy blonde, she acquired a reputation as a sadist who beat prisoners without mercy and who spent hours transfixed as she watched medical experiments, especially the removal of breasts.

Selecting women with large breasts she would cut their breasts open with her whip. She would then take them, bleeding, to a woman inmate who performed a painful operation on them while Irma Greese watched, cheeks flushed, swaying side to side and foaming at the mouth!

She was said to have had love affairs with Josef Kramer (the Beast of Belsen), the camp commandant, and Dr Josef Mengele, the head camp physician. After the war she was tried as a war criminal, condemned to death, and dragged screaming to the gallows on 13 December 1945, in Hamelin, Germany.

A child's potty found at Auschwitz death camp
On display in the museum

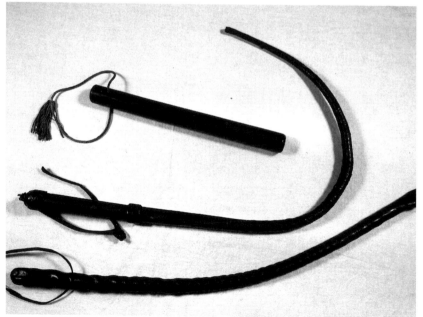

The horsewhips and cudgels used in Nazi death camps are on display in the museum

Genocide: Murder of a Nation

SS women camp guards, April 1945

Nazi horror camp at Belsen. When the 11th Armoured Division of the British Second Army reached the Belsen camp, in Hanover, Germany, in April 1945 about 60,000 helpless Jews and political prisoners were found. Two piles of bodies, dead inmates, lie exposed within the camp enclosure.

JOSEF KRAMER
1906-1945
Known as
The Beast of Belsen

Josef Kramer was the most notorious of the camp commandants, so-called 'Beast of Belsen' he received his training from Rudolf Hoess at Auschwitz and later had additional experience at Mauthausen, Dachau, and Birkenau.

In 1940 Kramer accompanied Hoess to inspect Auschwitz as a site for a new synthetic coal oil and rubber plant. He became notorious as a harsh taskmaster. Dr Franz Lucas, one of the defendants at the Frankfurt Trial (q.v.), testified that he tried to avoid assignments given him by Kramer by pleading stomach and intestinal disorders. When Dr Lucas saw that his name had been added to the list of selecting physicians for a large group of inmates transported from Hungary, he objected strenuously. Kramer reacted sharply: "I know you are being investigated for favouring prisoners. I am now ordering you to go to the ramp, and if you fail to obey the order, I shall have you arrested on the spot."

As an SS member, Kramer entered Eicke's fledgling concentration camp service as early as 1934. He served in Natzweiler camp and in the last months of Auschwitz commanded the extermination centre there.

Josef Kramer's driving licence - on display in the museum

Kramer after his capture in April 1941

In August 1943, Kramer received 80 inmates who were to be killed with gas. With the help of SS assistants, Kramer stripped the women and, when they were stark naked, shoved them in small groups into the gas chamber. "When the door closed they began to scream," he testified later. "I put in a small amount of salt through a tube and looked through a peephole to see what happened. The women breathed about a minute before they fell to the floor." Kramer repeated the performance until all were dead. When asked by his interrogator what his feelings were at the time, he replied; "I had no feelings in carrying out these things because I had received an order. That, incidentally, is the way I was trained."

In November 1944 he was transferred from Birkenau to Belsen, near the village of Bergen. The camp in northwest Germany had, up to this stage of the German collapse, been a detention camp holding Jews who (in theory at least) were to be exchanged for German nationals abroad. By a grisly irony it was also classified as a *Krankenlager,* a reception camp for sick prisoners - originally known as a small privileged camp Belsen was enlarged to serve as a convalescent depot for sick persons from concentration camps, factories, and farms and for displaced persons from the whole of northwest Europe.

There were no gas chambers in Belsen, but so hard was the rule inaugurated by Kramer that he became known as the 'Beast of Belsen'. Within a few months the camp administration began to break down, although Kramer ordinarily never took a step without filling out a form. On 1st March 1945, he wrote a report stating that he had 42,000 inmates in camp and that 250 to 300 had died from "typhus." On 19 March 1945, the number of inmates rose to 60,000; during the week of April 13th, some 28,000 prisoners were brought in. Roll calls were stopped, and the inmates were left to their own devices. Corpses rotted in the barracks, and rats attacked the living victims.

Irma Greese and Josef Kramer on trial for war crimes

From November 1944, conditions in the camp deteriorated rapidly. Evidence was offered at Kramer's later trial that he was responsible for selling off camp food supplies; more likely, the desperate food shortages in the last months of Belsen were the result of an increase in numbers from 15,000 to nearly 60,000. In the conditions of the time it is unlikely that any level of rations for the new arrivals would have reached the camp. The result was the complete breakdown of administration.

On an outbreak of spotted fever Kramer tried to close the camp but was refused permission. When British troops came into the camp 13,000 corpses were found, lying unburied in pits or in scattered heaps among the emaciated survivors.

Kramer, callous and indifferent, took them on a tour to inspect the scene. Piles of rotting bodies were lying all over the camp, mass graves were filled in, and the huts were crowded with prisoners in every stage of emaciation and disease.

A British military court tried him on 17 November 1945 and found guilty of war crimes, he was hanged on 13 December 1945.

"One has to see their emaciated faces, their slow staggering gait and feeble movements…they are dying and nothing can save them. Their end is inescapable. They are too far gone to live."

Peter Coombs – British Officer 1945

Dunkirk! 338,226 troops were evacuated from the beachhead at Dunkirk from 26th May to 4th June 1940 – the largest ever military evacuation!

"What luck for the rulers that men do not think."Adolf Hitler

The war ended with Germany's unconditional surrender on 7th May 1945. However, it was soon realised that this defeat was unlike any other in history. In addition to his war of military conquest, Hitler had also waged a war against defenceless civilians. The events of that war, revealed in the coming months during the Nuremberg trials, would stun the world, and even resulted in a new term to describe the systematic killing of an entire race of people - genocide.

"The Crime Through Time Museum hopes that the dying wishes of many of the murdered victims of the Holocaust has been met with this display." Andrew Jones – Curator and owner of Crime Through Time Museum

LEST WE FORGET!

"Everlasting peace will come to the world when the last man has slain the last but one."

Related web sites:

http://www.twafa.org.uk

http://www.crimethroughtime.com

http://www.anti-semite.com (Not anti Semitic)

Foreword to Doppelganger

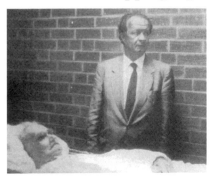

Hess is dead, Wolf looks on, 1987.

By Wolf Rudiger Hess

(Son of Rudolf Hess)

When my father flew to Scotland on 10th May 1941, I was three-and-a-half years old. As a result, I have only very few personal memories of him in freedom. One of them is a memory of him pulling me out of the garden pond. On another occasion, when I was screaming because a bat had somehow gotten into the house. I can still recall his comforting voice as he carried it to the window and released it into the night.

Rudolf Hess with his son, Wolf.

In the years that followed, I learned who my father was, and about his role in history, only bit by bit. Slowly, I came to understand the martyrdom he endured as a prisoner in the Allied Military Prison in Berlin-Spandau for 40 long years - half a lifetime.

What really happened between June 1940 and 10th May 1941, the day my father took off in a Messerschmitt 110 to Scotland, is known only in

220

outline because the relevant British documents still remain classified. The Hess papers that were released in Britain with great fanfare in June 1992 proved to be disappointing. Among these approximately two thousand pages was absolutely nothing of real substance about the secret contacts that existed between Britain and Germany, about the British peace group (which included members of the royal family) and its peace feelers to Germany, or about the role played by the British secret service prior to the flight. In short, these papers contained nothing that would show why my father seriously hoped that his mission might well turn out successfully.

In any case, it can be said with certainty that the still-classified British documents contain nothing that will reflect badly on Rudolf Hess or the policies of the German government of that time. Moreover, it can be stated with certainty that the documents that the British government continues to keep secret will reflect badly on the wartime British government of Winston Churchill. I will go further to say that these suppressed documents confirm that Churchill sought to prolong the war, with all the suffering, destruction and death that implies.

Some may dismiss this statement as unjustified and self-serving. In this regard, I would therefore like to cite the words of a British historian who has carried out extensive research on precisely this aspect of that dreadful conflict. In Ten Days To Destiny: The Secret Story of the Hess Peace Initiative and British Efforts to Strike a Deal with Hitler (New York: W Morrow, 1991), John Costello concludes that it would have been quite possible to bring the European war to an end before it turned into a world war, if only the British government had made even the slightest move to do so.

A general comment on the information available about my father's peace proposals is in order: during the entire forty-year period of his imprisonment in Spandau, he was prohibited from speaking openly about his mission. This "gag order" was obviously imposed because he knew things that, if publicly known, would be highly embarrassing to the British government, and possibly to the US and Soviet governments as well.

Doppelganger

(Revealed – the truth behind Hess' fatal attempt at peace.)

These were my father's proposals submitted to Churchill:

One: Germany and Britain would reach a compromise on world-wide policy based on the status quo. That is, Germany would not attack Russia to secure German *Lebensraum* ("living space").

Two: Germany would drop its claims to its former colonies, and would acknowledge British hegemony at sea. In return, Britain would acknowledge continental Europe as a German sphere of interest.

Three: The then-current relationship of military strength between Germany and Britain in the air and on the sea would be maintained. That is, Britain would not receive any reinforcements from the United States. Although there was no mention of land forces, it can be assumed that this balance of forces would be maintained in this regard as well.

Four: Germany would withdraw from "Metropolitan France" (European France) after the total disarmament of the French army and navy. German commissioners would remain in French North Africa, and German troops would remain in Libya for five years after the conclusion of peace.

Five: Within two years after the conclusion of peace, Germany would establish satellite states in Poland, Denmark, the Netherlands, Belgium and Serbia. However, Germany would withdraw from Norway, Romania, Bulgaria and Greece (except for Crete, which German parachutists had taken in May 1941). After some rounding-off in the East, North, West and South (Austria and Bohemia-Moravia were apparently to remain within the Reich), Germany would thus concede Britain's position in the Eastern Mediterranean and the Middle East.

Six: Germany would recognise Ethiopia and the Red Sea as a British sphere of influence.

Seven: The person to whom the Deputy Führer was speaking was somewhat confused about whether Italy had approved Hess' peace proposals. Hess himself said nothing about this, although points four and six would have considerably affected Italian interests.

Eight: Rudolf Hess admitted that Hitler had agreed in advance to the official "cover story" put out in Germany that he was of "unsound mind."

This peace proposal would indeed have brought peace to the world in 1941. If Britain had negotiated with Germany on this basis, the German attack against Russia - which began less than three weeks later, on 22nd June 1941 - would not have taken place, because Hitler would have obtained what he needed for survival: control of the continent. The war would have withered away on all fronts.

Instead, as we know, the war continued - bringing destruction, suffering and death on an almost unimaginable scale - because Churchill and Roosevelt rejected the outstretched hand of peace. The peace they sought was a Carthaginian one. Their sole war aim was the destruction of Germany.

After initial interviews with Rudolf Hess conducted by the Duke of Hamilton and Sir Ivone Kirkpatrick in Glasgow, my father was interviewed on 9th June 1941 by Lord Simon, the Lord Chancellor, and on 9th September 1941 by Lord Beaverbrook, Minister for Aircraft Production. A few days later, Beaverbrook flew to Moscow to arrange for military aid to the Soviet Union. These two interviews were motivated not by any desire for peace, but were instead merely to pry out any possible military secrets from my father.

Wolf Rudiger Hess

b.Nov. 18, 1937, d.Oct. 24, 2001

5

Doppleganger

Amazing revelation! Father of Rudolf Hess, courts his first wife in Gloucester, England!!!!

1894-1987

Did Britain do this man an injustice when he fled Germany and landed in Britain to try to broker a peace deal, what really went on? Signed photo of Hess, as on display in the museum along with related items.

Crime Through Time

An article in the WESTERN MAIL & SOUTH WALES NEWS - dated Thursday 26th June 1941.

'NEW WELSH LINK WITH RUDOLF HESS'

(The article is reproduced with incorrect spellings of names)

Facts given me on Wednesday give further colour to the suggestion that Carl Hess, father of Rudolf Hess, Hitler's deputy, formerly lived in the vicinity of Cardiff and has a brother-in-law now living in retirement in a Cottage in Michaelstone-y-Fedw, Cardiff.

Carl Hess was highly educated, and a fluent master of several languages, and a man who spent much time travelling. In 1890 he met at **Gloucester** a Miss Elizabeth Mackie, born and bred in Michaelstone-y-Fedw, but of Scottish descent, and the couple were married at Bystock, Exmouth, Devon. Their happiness was short-lived, for in 12 months Mrs Hess died, and Carl Hess, foregoing any share in the few hundred pounds left by his wife, resigned his position and left for Germany.

The body of his wife was taken back to Michaelstone-y-Fedw and buried in the parish churchyard by the then Rector (the Rev W Jenkins)

officiating. A tombstone *(Note: photo was included in this feature, but too far gone to reproduce here.)* was put up by Carl Hess, and reads 'Erected by Carl Hess, of Schleswig, Germany, in memory of his wife, Elizabeth Mackie, who died at Exmouth, Devon, June 13th: 1891, aged 35. In life beloved, in death never forgotten.'

BROTHER-IN-LAW'S STORY

The present Rector of the Parish, the Rev D Hopkin Evans, showed me the register of deaths, recording the burial of Mrs Hess, and then introduced me to Mr Edward Mackie, brother of Elizabeth. Mr Mackie is 77 and has a sister living with him, Miss Jane Mackie, who is aged 88. "If Elizabeth had lived she would have been 85," said Mr Mackie, "When she met Carl Hess she was in service in the household of the **Bishop of Gloucester**, and he was steward in the Bishop's palace, Hess could speak several

225

languages and in summer did a lot of travelling abroad. He made no secret of the fact that he was German, and shortly after he met my sister, he took a position with a Mr Bryce, a rich American, and went with him to Exmouth. My sister followed later and they were married there. Twelve months later I had a letter from Hess saying that my sister had gone out boating, had caught a chill, and had since died of pneumonia."

Mr Mackie said Hess had always been determined to go into business on his own, and when his wife died he bought the Hotel Cecil in Hamburg, Germany, sometime later Hess wrote him saying he was to marry again and that he and his new wife intended to travel a lot.

GOING TO EGYPT

"I believe he mentioned something about going to Egypt in his letter," said Mr Mackie, who added that if Carl Hess were still alive he would be 90 years old. He never heard whether Hess had been a schoolteacher in Cardiff or anywhere else. A brother of his, Mr Wilhelm Hess, a photographer, had been present at the funeral of Mrs Elizabeth Hess in Michaelstone-y-Fedw.

"Rudolph Hess who landed by parachute in Scotland is the son of Carl Hess by his second marriage," said Mr Mackie. "He is certainly a different sort of man from his father, Carl Hess and his brother Wilhelm, they were two of nature's gentlemen, refined, and well educated, and with gentle loving nature's."

END OF ARTICLE

****

In 1945 some 2 million civilian Germans were evacuated from East Prussia. This was the biggest civilian evacuation ever!

Crime Through Time

As a German soldier, Rudolf Hess was shot twice in the chest. Soon he joined other disgruntled war veterans who found a spokesman in Adolf Hitler. Hess became Hitler's loyal second-in-command throughout the early years, even spending time with Hitler in Landsberg prison when Hitler was serving five years for a failed coup, taking down the Fuhrer's dictation of his autobiography, *Mein Kampf.* During the first years of World War II Hess' influence waned and his deputy, Martin Bormann, and other Nazi leaders were outshining him. In an act that allegedly astounded both sides in the war, Hess took off from Augsburg on 10th May 1941 and flew non-stop to Scotland, where he parachuted, carrying peace proposals. Hitler quickly disowned his mission as that of a man with "pacifist delusions," and the British treated him as a prisoner of war.

Shortly after 11pm on 10th May 1941, 45-year-old ploughman David McLean heard an explosion, looked out of his window, and saw a parachutist float into a meadow of Floors Farm near Eaglesham, Scotland. He ran out to find a crashed and burning Messerschmitt and a slightly injured German officer – "Hauptmann" (Captain) Albert Horn. Horn turned out to be Rudolf Hess, Adolf Hitler's deputy!

There is a suggestion that British military intelligence unit S - 01 lured Hitler's deputy with the false notion he'd be greeted by a peace faction – a stalling move to delay a feared invasion by Germany. Hitler, who wanted peace with Britain so he could devote his energy to invading the Soviet Union, had supposedly blessed the trip. Although once Hess bailed out of his plane, neither Churchill nor Hitler would own up to their plans.

Hess is one of the great World War II mysteries, evidence shows that Hess was shot through the lung in the Great War and scarred for life on his chest, front and back. Yet at Buchanan Castle Military Hospital on 13th May 1942, the man from Eaglesham showed no scars whatsoever! Hess had a large gap between his front teeth whereas the published 1941 dental plan of the man shows no sign of that gap?

A map, printed on silk, carried by Hess on the flight came into the possession of the Home Guard. It was a standard issue for SAS agents, not German issue! There are startling claims that the real Hess was captured by Special Operations Executive in Scandinavia and interrogated in a house near Fort William.

Claims are that the real Hess was kidnapped by SAS in Sweden and smuggled back into Scotland. This, say researchers, was to prevent a German massacre of hostages, it was crucial to have the Germans believe Hess had gone mad, flown to Scotland, instead of a peace mission to Sweden with Samuel Hoare, Britain's ambassador in Spain. This, if true, would have made the *doppelganger* (double) trapped.

A letter from Ambassador Archibald Clerk-Kerr to Stalin supports the liquidation of Hess in November 1942 who told him, *Any enemy leaders caught before the end of the World War Two will be liquidated.*

Proof - British Intelligence knew of Hess' mission.

A claim that two Aldergrove (Ulster) pilots were ordered to break off their attack on Hess' plane, adds fuel to allegations of collusion between England and its German enemies. Hess - Hitler's faithful servant - flew over 800 miles to Scotland on an apparent lone peace mission, without being intercepted by the RAF?

How Hess' Messerschmitt fighter plane managed to crash land near Glasgow, without being attacked by British air defences has never been established! Ulster-based pilots' logbooks recorded their flight from Aldergrove, to intercept Hess' twin-engined plane. No official record of the pilots' search and destroy mission exists?

A piece of evidence that verifies Sgt Vaclav 'Felix' Bauman's story is in the form of his logbook that was signed by his squadron leader - apparently verifying the Czech pilot's version of the bizarre incident.

An interview from a man who served with the 245 Squadron for a year at Aldergrove, said he later realised "...some more shady work had been going on." He added, "My own personal opinion now is that our people knew that Hess was coming. When you reflect on it, how on earth was a person like Hess allowed to come over the country, over northern England and over the borders without being intercepted?"

Was Hess searching for fools gold?

Was Hess on a Mission to Find the Holy Grail?

Nazis thought religious icons were hidden in Scotland.

Witchcraft, black magic and worshipping strange gods might seem far-flung from the Hess story, but when you refer back to the chapter containing details of the Knights Templars (forerunners of the Freemasons) who were welcomed to Scotland when the rest of Europe outlawed them it might not sound so strange. What is the Link between events in the Holy Land, 700 years ago, and Rudolf Hess' puzzling flight to Scotland in May 1941?

The items the Knights Templars brought with them to Scotland may solve one of the Second World War's most bizarre incidents. It's well known that leading Nazis had a fascination for the occult. Hitler consulted astrologers and would only invade on a day when the omens were good. Top Nazis also believed that certain objects possessed mystic power. The spear, which pierced Christ's side as he hung on the cross, had supposedly passed into the hands of the rulers of Austria, Hitler's birthplace, and was seen as a prized possession able to create powerful magic.

What would the Nazis have given to get hold of the Holy Grail, the cup (or plate) passed around by Christ at the Last Supper? Its paranormal powers are legendary, as are the tales of its whereabouts. According to one story, a friend of Jesus took it to Glastonbury. But stronger evidence suggests that it came into the possession of the Knights Templars during their stay in the Holy Land. Whilst looking for buried treasure, they supposedly dug it up below the ruins of the temple at Jerusalem. An event of some 700 years ago seems far-fetched but might help explain the puzzling and unsolved mystery of Rudolf Hess' flight to Scotland?

One of the most bizarre explanations for Hess' flight was that he was out to get hold of the Holy Grail - he was told it had been hidden at Rosslyn Chapel in the Lothians. Strange, though, why no one has secured the Holy Grail since then, assuming this information might have some strength to it?

Doppelganger

Hess might have been aware of the tales that a treasure trove of mystical objects had been taken by the Knights Templars to Scotland in 1307. So it's not altogether impossible that Hess hatched a scheme, as some think, to get hold of such a supernatural prize, but it still remains a bizarre idea at that!

MI6 helped orchestrate the arrival of Hess?

Suggestions have been made that MI6 were expecting Hess on the night he parachuted near East Kilbride, Scotland. This argument is at odds with other research, but it has been said that M16 actually lured Hess to Scotland.

A new twist in the puzzle comes in the shape of a suggestion that Hess was on a mission to form an alliance between Britain and Germany in order to form a new 'golden age'. Another romantic notion - this might have been Hitler's plan but certainly if that was the case then MI6 were only playing for time in order to capture Hitler's deputy!

MI6 allegedly got experts to forge statements in an ancient book and then made sure it got into the hands of Hitler. Subsequently as a consequence of the statements in this fake ancient book Hess was lured to Scotland, which sounds closer to the truth!

Although plausible, the alleged scheme by MI6 or wartime agencies was rejected by the very modern day historians who took it upon themselves to say the Hess in Spandau prison was a fake Hess planted by MI5! Historians still stand by the story that Hess took it upon himself to fly to Scotland after his own position was becoming less important in Germany and in a last gasp bid to restore his position within the Nazi party he had hoped to broker a peace deal.

The Duke of Hamilton, was he a pawn used by Churchill to flush out the 'peace mongers'?

Hess missed his target, Dungavel House, outside Glasgow, the country home of the Duke of Hamilton, whom he believed would organise an audience with the king and help plan peace terms. Instead, Hess bailed out over Eaglesham Moor, only to land in a field near Floors farm, not far from Dungavel. A ploughman, David McLean, helped the injured man to his farmhouse, where he was offered tea.

Going back to the two Polish pilots, Sergeant Vaclav Bauman and Sergeant Leopold Srom, the discovery in the Czech republic of their personal logbooks shows that they were ordered not to fire on Hess' Messerschmitt.

The claim that the British government was aware of Hess' plan was given added support by allegations that Churchill's own secret services colluded in Hess' arrival in Britain.

When James Douglas-Hamilton, now Lord Selkirk, the son of the Duke of Hamilton, published his book 'Motive for a Mission' in 1971 he explained that the connection between his father and Hess lay with mutual friends, the Haushofers. Professor Karl Haushofer, the father of geopolitics, was Hess' teacher and mentor, and his son Albrecht was Hess' friend. They all shared a view that peace with Britain was desirable, if only so that the German army could focus on defeating Russia.

Around midnight, the Duke of Hamilton arrived with Yvonne Kirkpatrick; head of BBC European section, who had been a first secretary at the British Embassy in Berlin, to identify Hess and question him in German. Hess was taken to Buchanan Castle Military Hospital and during the course of his stay he met the Duke of Hamilton for one hour. The Duke and Hess had previously met only once at the Munich Olympics in 1936.

It has to be remembered that at this point in the war Germany had domination in Europe. With the fall of Crete in that spring, was one of the lowest ebbs of British morale. Britain was close to breaking at this period, which doesn't fit the heroic myth!

The military adviser Basil Liddell-Hart believed that Britain would lose the war and should sue for peace at once, getting the best terms they could. Those who disliked Churchill - Beaverbrook and Halifax in the Cabinet, Lords Bedford, Brocket and Buccleugh, even the Australian Prime Minister, Stewart Menzies, might have been persuaded that despite the holding exercise of the Battle of Britain - some kind of deal must be made with Hitler!

Doppelganger

Amazing letter that shows Duke of Hamilton was on the 'suspect list'.

COPY.

Box 5,
EDINBURGH.

Gen.6/95/B.R.11.   12th May, 1941.
BR to A.S. MacIver, Esq.

Dear MacIver,

This is to confirm our telephone conversation this
morning, when I informed you that on Saturday-Sunday,
May 10th-11th, about midnight, a Messerschmidt 110 came
down in Renfrewshire. It appeared to be a new machine
and the guns had not been used. It was piloted by one
man, who stated that he had a message for the Duke of
Hamilton. He was taken in charge by the R.A.F. Intelligence and is now in Maryhill Barracks, Glasgow.

This information was passed to me by the Scottish
Home Department who received it from the Renfrewshire
Police. I contacted the Supervising D.A.P.M. for Scotland, F/Lt. Sime, D.A.P.M. No. 18 Group, and the R.A.F.
Omte;;ogence Scottish Command, in an endeavour to obtain
further information. I was able to confirm that the
facts as stated above were substantially correct and I was
informed by the R.A.F. Intelligence, Scottish Command, that
the matter had been passed to a higher authority.

I pass this information to you as the Duke of Hamilton
is on the Suspect List.

Yours sincerely,

R. Watt (?)

for Major P.C. Perfect.
Scottish Regional Security Officer.

AS MacIver, Esq.,
Box No.500,
Oxford.

Original in PF 54592 HAUSHOFER 68x Y Box 487 Held R.3.6.

Crime Through Time

Hess – Peace emissary, or was he shit on by the British?

The Nazi-Soviet Pact, which Hitler had signed secretly with Stalin, was merely a lull, masking Hitler's ambition to achieve his *lebensraum* (living space) in the East. Having delayed at least twice, the Fuhrer launched Operation *Barbarossa* a month after Hess' flight and exposed Germany to the worst of nightmares - the war on two fronts. Hess' flight was designed to prevent this by dealing with a peace party he imagined to exist in Britain who would oust the warmongering Churchill and do a deal with Germany. A conspiracy was hatched by the most secret of Secret Service institutions, Special Operations One, based in 1941 at Woburn Abbey. Files released by the Foreign Office in the summer of 1998 tell of extraordinary schemes of black propaganda, to "set Europe alight" with words, in Churchill's famous phrase. One of the files not released though is that relating to Rudolf Hess!

Under the aegis of Hugh Dalton - was a Walter Roberts. Roberts' aunt, Mary Violet, was an old friend of the Haushofer family. And the Haushofers were friends of Rudolf Hess! Is it becoming clearer?

Certain papers also show that Albrecht Haushofer was a friend of the Duke of Hamilton, a Scottish peer serving in 1941 with the RAF in the Lowlands! There were a number of potentially influential people, many of them Peers of the Realm, who were pacifists and possibly pro-German in outlook.

(Haushofer wished to make contact with King George VI through the Duke. But when Haushofer was unable to contact the duke, Hess desperate to regain Hitler's favour, flew off to secure the peace alone.)

It is known that Haushofer attempted to contact the Duke through a post box number in Lisbon used by Roberts, but it is now believed her nephew, a member of the Political Warfare Executive, composed a series of letters to attract Hess!

The Duke of Bedford had preached peace repeatedly in the late 30s, following up peace initiatives as late as 1940. Many of these pacifists owned property within a 50-mile radius of the spot where Hess crashed his Messerschmitt.

Doppelganger

Papers released recently by British Intelligence are boring!

A i 7F54591 Haushofer 68a Y Box 487

COPY.

/X

I went over to the Air Ministry yesterday afternoon and saw Air Vice Marshall Medhurst A.C.A.S.I. He asked me whether I knew anything about the case of HAUSHOFER. I told him that I did and gave him a brief outline of the story as I knew it and the connection between HAUSHOFER and the Duke of Hamilton. Medhurst then asked me if I had heard of the recent developments, to which I replied that I had not and he told me the following story:-

On Saturday night an M.E. 110 had landed in Scotland and the airman who had been injured was taken to hospital. When he got there he asked if he could see the Duke of Hamilton as he had a message for him from HAUSHOFER. Unfortunately Medhurst did not know the name of the airman.

Owing to bad communications Medhurst was unable to get through to Wing Commander Felkin through whom he hoped to learn further details. In addition to all this Air Vice Marshall Medhurst told me that Sir Archibald Sinclair had been spending the week-end with the Prime Minister and that they had sent for the Duke of Hamilton on Sunday.

It was as a result of Sir Archibald Sinclair's enquiries that Medhurst wished to know more about HAUSHOFER. I said that I would try and make enquiries through our Regional Officer in Edinburgh in order to find out more details about the case and in particular the name of the pilot. I also told Medhurst that we had received no information about this man. Medhurst said that the Foreign Secretary, Mr. Eden was also interested in the case.

I returned to the Office and reported this to Mr. White and subsequently rang up Mr. Watson, Assistant Regional Officer, Edinburgh, who said he would make enquiries about the case and let me know.

On the 9 o'clock news last night the German Communique reported that Rudolf HESS had mysteriously disappeared in an aeroplane, and in today's papers it appears that the pilot of the aeroplane was none other than Rudolf HESS. I spoke to Mair of Edinburgh who rang me up this morning and told me that HESS was in the custody of the Military at Maryhill Barracks, Glasgow and that the Duke of Hamilton had seen him for one hour on Sunday morning, after which he left to see the Prime Minister.

B.2.a./13.5.41.

Sd. T.A. Robertson.

Crime Through Time

Woburn Propaganda unit set trap for Hess.

Mary Roberts was used as a pawn, apparently writing to the Haushofers in the middle of a war, sending her greetings. But was this correspondence really the work of the black propagandists at Woburn, feeding Hess the false information that an active peace party was at work, spearheaded by Beaverbrook or Lloyd George.

Should this have been so then all Hess had to do was to get to Britain and offer Hitler's terms. Then, perhaps, a march on London to overthrow Churchill and the West would be secure for Germany before the Americans could be brought in. So what British Intelligence did was to play for time and this was by luring Hess to Britain. They gave the illusion of wanting peace. The British held out an olive branch, but behind that was a sub-machinegun.

Because of the Foreign Office's refusal to release files, because of the non-appearance of Jack Straw's (former Home Secretary of England) promised *Freedom of Information Act*, we do not have the conclusive proof of the British Intelligence lure, neither do we have the nitty-gritty details of how it was all to happen. What has been established, though, is Mrs Roberts' link with Special Operations and new evidence has been uncovered about mysterious aircraft over Scotland on the night that Hess arrived - incidentally, a night that saw the heaviest blitz on London of the entire war!

The American President, Roosevelt, was itching to know the truth behind the Hess story, as was Stalin, the Russian dictator. When one of those directly involved, the Duke of Hamilton, was due to visit the States soon after the war, Churchill forbade him, in case matters relating to the Hess case should come out. What did Churchill have to hide?

The Duke of Hamilton was tarred with the brush of distrust, but many believe the Duke to have been an honourable man. Suggestions as to why the Duke was singled out by Hess are that a nephew of Violet Roberts, the widow of a Cambridge professor and a friend of the Haushofers set the bait.

Hess explained to an orderly in the military hospital in Scotland that the war had started because the Poles had refused the Germans use of their deep-water port, and said that the atrocities people were beginning to hear about were not typical of the German people. Hess went on to say that Germany and Britain should join forces to defeat Russia.

The Doppelganger Theory

Hess always maintained that what he did was done without Hitler's knowledge. Hitler, in person privately and via Goebbels' propaganda machine, publicly disowned his deputy, claiming he was suffering mental degeneracy. Hess himself gave the opt-out. In his last letter to Hitler, delivered on the morning after the flight, he wrote '...*simply say I was mad.*'

MI5 Blast Dads Army Interrogation of Hess.

A Boy Scout hall in Giffnock was the location of a Dads Army style interrogation of Hess within hours of him sensationally parachuting into Scotland.

Secret papers (again they revealed very little and were boring, the main ones are being kept back until 2017) that were published in 1999 reveal MI5 chiefs were furious when they learned that all initiative had been lost through the Home Guards "amateurish" quizzing of Hess, who had demanded to be taken to the Duke of Hamilton, and that the MacMainwairings of the day had employed the services of a Polish consul official based in Glasgow to act as interpreter.

Wartime papers from MI5, now made public, show how intelligence chiefs became even more concerned when they received a report from Montevideo citing Argentinean fascists and declaring that Hess could have been sent to Scotland in connection with a projected German invasion planned for the following month which the Nazis hoped would coincide with a coup in Scotland.

Even so, this seeming fanciful, the report was passed to Prime Minister Winston Churchill's intelligence adviser and the secretary of the War Cabinet and other top officials. At the time, the whole world - not least British intelligence - was attempting to work out why Hess had embarked on his extraordinary solo flight in a

Messerschmitt 110 from Ausberg. This really wasn't too difficult to work out since they already knew it was a peace mission, but plenty of shovelling smoke made it look good!

> Hess, they say, hoped for backing from British Fascists to help oust Churchill – if what we know is true then it would have saved millions of lives if Churchill was kicked out of office.

A most secret intercept decrypted report from the Japanese ambassador in Rome to Tokyo described a meeting between himself and Germany's foreign affairs minister Joachim von Ribbentrop which took place seven days after Hess had flown to Scotland! The ambassador was assured by Ribbentrop that Hess had no treasonable intention whatsoever when embarking on his flight. "Although his action has been eccentric, it is clear that his intentions were excellent." He explained to the ambassador that Hess had got it into his head he could minimise the number of victims in the attack on "England" and bring an end to the war with the aid of British fascists who would help bring about the downfall of Churchill. Hess had the idea that if he could win over Hamilton, the British fascists would be all out for Rudolf Hess and would at once flood to him.

As intelligence continued to arrive from various parts of the globe, MI5 chiefs began a limitation exercise over Hess' initial interrogation by interviewing those involved - in particular the Polish consular official, whom they reckoned should never have been allowed anywhere near Hess. Obviously frightened that people would find out the truth about it all! At the time of the interrogation, nobody allegedly knew who the mysterious pilot was, although it was clear he was not your normal run-of-the-mill airman and there were those who reckoned he bore a resemblance to Hess.

Roman Battaglia, a Polish assistant consul from Glasgow who was called by the Home Guard, had some experience of interviewing suspects and fully realised the importance of the first interrogation, had himself gained a poor impression of the techniques adopted by the Home Guard in the scout hut. About 20 people were in the room at the time and questions were fired from all corners.

Some he considered offensive and refused to put to Hess. People wandered around the room inspecting the prisoner and his belongings. No accurate note was taken during the two-hour interview.

Throughout the interview Hess remained calm and controlled. The only sign of distress was when he leaned forward at intervals and sunk his head in his hands. He realised the people present were only Home Guard and therefore Battaglia was hardly surprised that the answers he gave were evasive. Hess had come to meet the people who would have known about the peace mission, yet here he was sitting in a hut full of lowly servants! He insisted the flight had been at his own volition, volunteering that he had been forbidden to fly because of his age and his health, but nevertheless had gone ahead. If only Hess had of known what lay ahead!

Hess, remarking on his feat, he jokingly asked the interpreter: "Don't you think it was a fine performance?" He emphatically denied he was a deserter. He had come with a message for the Duke of Hamilton, which was in the highest interest of the Royal Air Force. All hell broke loose when it was realised later who the prisoner really was. After the fiasco of the first interrogation in the scout hall, intelligence officers never did learn anything of importance from Hess throughout his incarceration, although it was not for want of trying.

Battaglia was described by MI5 as "extremely shrewd." Hess was asked if he knew the Duke, he replied: "I saw him at the Olympic Games in Berlin and we have a friend in common." The consul gave a personal opinion that the friend - now known to have been Albrecht Haushofer, a young Munich intellectual - might have been acting as an intermediary. He had invited the Duke in 1941 to meet Hess in Lisbon. The telegram was intercepted, embarrassing the Duke, who had been air controller of the sector into which Hess parachuted. Churchill's suspicions were aroused, but Hamilton later defended his honour successfully in a libel action. The Haushofer "plot" is believed to have been the German response to a double-cross plot to lure a leading German to Britain. When the security men met Hess, the mask of insanity, feigned or not, survived until the Nuremberg Trials were in place.

Until the trials Hess was swiftly interned in 'Camp Z' (See later pages referring to Maindiff Court Hospital, near Abergavenny), a secret location near Aldershot, Hampshire, according to personal papers and Second World War files released by MI5.

The Death of Hess

There are those who romantically believe the 'Hess' incarcerated in Spandau for 40 years was an impostor planted by British Intelligence, which is total twaddle – who would have pretended to be Hess for 46 years? Some historian researchers believe that Hess may have been kidnapped by the Special Operations Executive, interrogated in a secret location in the north of Scotland and then executed. Again this is utter nonsense since it would have meant a fake Hess playing the part for 46 years – who in their right mind would be willing to do this? Photographs of Hess prior and during to his incarceration in Spandau prison support the fact that it is the same man throughout!

The miracle of the missing scars.

A consultant surgeon, Dr Hugh Thomas, in the Royal Army Medical Corps lends weight to the doppelganger theory. Dr Thomas was responsible for looking after Hess, or prisoner 'No 7'; as he was known in Spandau prison. Hess had been shot through the left lung in the First World War, but Thomas found no scar tissue during examinations! When Hess was told that his scarring had disappeared he scurried off into his cell and refused any further examinations!

Hess in Spandau Prison.

Doppelganger

Hess would have borne the distinctive scar tissue in his lungs from the wounding, and they could not have been eradicated, say historians. Governments involved in the Hess case stoutly denied any foul play while Hess was imprisoned in the Tower of London throughout World War II. Were there were two different men involved? Very unlikely!

Hess, aged 91, in Spandau.

When Hess died in 1987, aged 93, at first, the jailers said it was from natural causes. After a few days an official story emerged that Hess had strangled himself with some electric wire. Although it has been suggested by romantics that shortly thereafter, Hess was buried furtively at night without an autopsy having been performed, there were actually two autopsies performed, one by a British doctor and a further autopsy two days after this by a German doctor.

Some other arguments for the romantic notion that it was not Hess who died in Spandau say that on his death he showed no body scars or internal scar tissue on X-ray and therefore he could not possibly be Rudolf Hess!

Hess - Original X-Ray request.

Using a length of electrical extension cord, Rudolf Hess, a frail 93-year-old, allegedly hanged himself in the garden of Spandau prison, Berlin, on 17 August 1987; or did he? Like so much of his life, Hess' death remains a puzzle. Why should a man who had survived 40 years in an Allied-controlled prison commit suicide when an international campaign for his release looked like succeeding?

A senior Scotland Yard detective, Howard Jones, thought there was sufficient evidence to suggest Hess had been murdered, and submitted a report to the Director of Public Prosecutions saying so. But, not surprisingly, the DPP did not agree and nothing happened.

Did British Government have motive for murder?

There was certainly a motive for Hess' murder. Once free he might have spoken out and told the real story of why he crash-landed his Messerschmitt in a field near Glasgow. And what a story it would have been!

Hess planned to meet with British leaders, persuade them that it was madness for Britain and Germany to continue to fight each other and convince them that they should unite against the Soviet Union. How different history would have been if Hess had succeeded.

Should the SIS (Intelligence Service) not have *lured* Hess to Britain, it had certainly *invited* him! Why had Hess reason to believe that he would be welcome in Britain, we have to go back to the last months of 1939.

The war at that time was considered a tragedy by a substantial minority of Britain's leaders and some still admired Hitler. Others believed that there were powerful opposition groups in Germany anxious to overthrow Hitler and sue for peace and that these should be encouraged. The desire for peace, with or without the overthrow of Hitler; grew rapidly.

Reports of dissension in Germany were put to Foreign Secretary, Lord Halifax by the SIS. Leaving it to see what happened was a disaster. The SIS believed it had made contact, through two of its officers in Holland, with a German group that wanted Britain on its side for an invasion of the Soviet Union. (Substantiating what Hess had said.) For a while the contact progressed, and there was even some agreement on peace terms - Hitler would remain in power for the time being. Austria, Czechoslovakia and Poland would be restored and there would be a united anti-Soviet front. Halifax approved all this and there was talk of a meeting in London to finalise matters.

Could Churchill have averted war in 1940?

On 1st November 1939, with the war two months old, the War Cabinet was told about these secret SIS negotiations for the first time - with some deliberate fudging by SIS on whether Hitler would be removed. The War Cabinet was far from happy, Churchill for one demanding that all contact with the Germans be broken off immediately.

In the end it was the Germans who terminated the operation. Himmler, the head of the Gestapo, who had, with Hitler's approval, authorised the contacts with the SIS, sensed his leader's second thoughts. German plans for an offensive against France and Britain were well advanced, Britain had spurned Hitler's offer of a compromise peace on October 6th; now further talk of peace smacked of defeatism. Himmler arranged a meeting with the two British SIS officers at the Dutch town of Venlo on the German border and there the Germans kidnapped them at gunpoint!

This was too much for Churchill and the moment he became Prime Minister in May 1940 he clamped down on all further peace feelers.

But there were Germans who still thought there was sufficient support in Britain for a compromise peace. Hess was one of them and when he arrived in Scotland he had with him a list of prominent British leaders who he believed would be sympathetic to his mission.

The Germans had had a series of successes in North Africa and Greece. The U-boats appeared to be winning the Battle of the Atlantic. The Blitz was at its peak. Britain was running out of money to pay for arms from the United States, which was showing no signs of joining the war. According to the former American ambassador in London, Joseph Kennedy, Britain was finished. President Roosevelt badly needed to know how strong Britain's stomach was for the fight. How would he have reacted if he had learnt that the Germans believed - rightly or wrongly - that some of Britain's leaders were ready for peace? What would such a revelation have done to his chances of persuading congress to enter the war on Britain's side?

If the British public were to learn the reason for Hess' mission then it would be a blow to Britain's morale, especially since so many prominent people were involved. No wonder the story was hushed up, no wonder Churchill decided to play down what could have been the propaganda coup of the war, no wonder successive governments have kept the lid on the affair.

Doppelganger - Boring theory goes on

Another story goes that it was not Hess but a double who landed in Scotland, that the SS intelligence chief, Reinhard Heydrich, had intercepted the real Hess at Alborg, in northern Denmark where Hess was either changing planes or refuelling, executed him on the spot for treason and then sent a trustworthy look-alike to test the extent of the plot.

There must certainly be something murky in the British archives to embargo them for so long. This is why some Germans think Hess deserves credit for a peace plan that, if it had come off, would have changed the course of the war and saved millions of lives.

Whilst the riddle of the doppelganger theory goes on, the claims made that the Hess who was locked up in Spandau was a double put up by British intelligence after the real Hess had died continue to keep the fairytale alive.

Did Churchill sabotage peace deal?

There is a suggestion that Churchill was aware of and effectively sabotaged a peace deal with Germany. A wide range of characters had roles to play in the affair, including the Dukes of Kent and Hamilton and the former Glasgow Lord Provost, Sir Patrick Dollan.

Doppelganger

It was essential to maintain the pretence that Hess was still alive, assuming you believe the story that he has been killed in Scotland, because of fears that should the Nazis suspect he had been ill-treated or even murdered this would have an adverse effect on the treatment meted out to captured British officers. But, when you consider that the Holocaust began in earnest after Hess was kidnapped by the British then maybe this was a reprisal by Hitler for the way Hess was locked up? Could the Holocaust have been averted?

A key that opened the door to further previously undisclosed documents lay in a box of documents bought at auction in Bonhams in London. The box had been the property of the late Daniel McBride, a regular soldier who had been at Floors Farm, near Eaglesham, when Hess was first taken into custody. McBride, it appears, had taken a keen interest in the Hess affair and had carried out his own, lone, research.

The documents have led to evidence that not only was Churchill aware of the Hess flight 24 hours before he took off - through spies working at the Messerschmitt plant at Augsburg - but that the Duke of Kent and the Duke of Buchanan were among a party waiting at the Duke of Hamilton's Dungavel estate to receive Hess, having spent the previous evening at Balmoral.

A woman who served with the ATS and was at Dungavel on the night of 10 May 1941 claims the landing lights at the Dungavel airstrip were switched on, ready to receive an incoming aircraft, but later switched off!

Hess having begun his descent, 'lining up' the distant brightly lit strip. The lights suddenly went off! Hess, low on fuel, rapidly began to climb until he achieved height enough to allow him to bale out of his aircraft. He "stood" it on its tail, and dropped from the cockpit. Churchill would not entertain proposals for peace, so it must be assumed that the Hess mission managed to smoke out the peace conspirators!

The Duke of Buccleuch was later put under virtual house arrest for the remainder of the war, while the Duke of Kent was killed in a mysterious air crash in Caithness in August 1942. Hess may also have been on this flight. Theories have abounded over the years as to the cause the crash of the Sunderland aircraft, with some claims that the flight may have been deliberately sabotaged!

The official records hold that the Duke, who was serving in the RAF as a group captain in the welfare branch, was en route to Iceland. However, the destination was actually Sweden, where, through the offices of a Swedish diplomat, a plot had been hatched for the Germans to return Poland - apart from Silesia - to the Poles and place the anti-Bolshevik Duke of Kent on the Polish throne!

Book held the key.

The Polish General Sikorsky, who was also killed in a mysterious air crash - off Gibraltar - in 1943, was allegedly a party to this plot. Evidence allegedly also claims Glasgow Lord Provost, Sir Patrick Dollan - a friend of Sikorsky - had commissioned a re-write of a book he had written in 1941 on 501 Squadron. The new book was to incorporate details of the Hess and Kent affiliation.

However, before the book could be published the author died in yet another mysterious air accident, in September 1942, when the Sunderland aircraft he was in crashed after apparently running out of fuel off Tiree.

The Duke of Buccleuch's chauffeur and a handyman, meanwhile, were both later killed in a road accident.

Hess peace proposals blanked!

The Hess peace proposals were never taken seriously and after periods of incarceration and interrogation at the former Maryhill Barracks, in Glasgow, Buchanan Castle, near Drymen; the Tower of London and Mytchett Place, near Aldershot; he was confined for the rest of the war at Maindiff Court Hospital, near Abergavenny, Wales.

It has never been satisfactorily explained, however, who this mysterious 'double was. Who would be prepared to spend 40 years in Spandau prison just for the sake of keeping a stiff upper lip? Nor has it been satisfactorily explained why the fiction had to be maintained right up until the death of Prisoner No 7 in Spandau on 17 August 1987.

****

Doppelganger

Epilogue
By
Wolf Rudiger Hess

On Monday, 17th August 1987, a journalist informed me in my office that my father was dying. Later, at home, I received a

Rudolph Hess with his son, Wolf.

telephone call at 6:35 pm from Mr Darold W Keane, the American director of the Spandau Prison, who informed me officially that my father had died. The official notification, which was in English, read as follows: "I am authorised to inform you that your father expired today at 4:10 pm I am not authorised to give you any further details."

The next morning I was on a plane to Berlin, accompanied by Dr Seidl. When I arrived at the prison, a fairly large crowd had gathered in front. Berlin police were blocking the entrance, and we were obliged to show identification papers before we were allowed to approach the green-painted iron gate. After ringing the bell, I asked to speak with the American prison director, Mr Keane. After quite a while, Mr Keane finally appeared, looking extraordinarily nervous and unsure of himself. He told us that we would not be allowed inside the prison complex, and that I would not be permitted to see my dead father. He also told us that he was not able to provide any further information about details of the death. A new report with details of my father's death was allegedly being prepared, and would be made available at about 4pm. Then, after we gave him the address and telephone number of a Berlin hotel where we would be waiting for further news, he left us standing in front of the gate.

Crime Through Time

The long-expected telephone call to the hotel finally came at about 5:30 pm Keane said:

"I will now read to you the report that we will release immediately afterwards to the press. It reads":-

'Initial examination indicated that Rudolf Hess attempted to take his own life. In the afternoon of August 17, 1987, under the customary supervision of a prison guard, Hess went to a summerhouse in the prison garden, where he always used to sit. When the guard looked into the summerhouse a few minutes later, he discovered Hess with an electric cord around his neck. Attempts were made at resuscitation and Hess was taken to the British Military Hospital. After further attempts to revive Hess, he was declared dead at 4:10 pm The question of whether this suicide attempt was the cause of his death is the object of an investigation, including a thorough autopsy, which is still in progress.'

My father was a frail 93-year-old man with no strength left in his hands, who could just barely drag himself from his cell into the garden. How was he supposed to have killed himself in this way? Did he hang himself with the cord from a hook or a window latch? Or did he throttle himself? Those responsible would not immediately provide a detailed explanation about this point. We had to wait a full month for the final official statement about the circumstances of the death. It was published by the Allies on 17th September 1987 and reads as follows:

1. The Four Powers are now in a position to make the final statement on the death of Rudolf Hess.

2. Investigations have confirmed that on August 17 Rudolf Hess hanged himself from a window latch in a small summerhouse in the prison garden, using an electric extension cord which had for some time been kept in the summerhouse for use in connection with a reading lamp. Attempts were made to revive him and he was then rushed to the British Military Hospital where, after further unsuccessful attempts to revive him, he was pronounced dead at 4:10 pm.

Compare the handwriting above to the thank you note, below, written by Hess to Sergeant Frank Jenkins RMC in 1970.

Doppelganger

The Suicide note.

Please would the Governors send this home. Written a few minutes before my death. I thank you all my beloved, for all the dear things you have done for me. Tell Freiburg, I am extremely sorry, that since the Neuremberg trial I had to act as though I did not know her. I had no choice, because otherwise, all attempts to gain freedom would have been in vain. I had so looked forward to seeing her again - I did get pictures of her, as of you all

Your Eldest.

3. A note addressed to Hess' family was found in his pocket. This note was written on the reverse side of a letter from his daughter-

It reads:-

Sergeant Frank Jenkins RMC, with thanks for untiring, ceaseless, careful looking after me and many other kindnesses.

Rudolf Hess

8.11.70

in-law dated July 20, 1987. It began with the words 'Please would the governors send this home. Written a few minutes before my death.' The senior document examiner from the laboratory of the British government chemist, Mr Beard, has examined this note, and concluded that he can see no reason to doubt that it was written by Rudolf Hess.

4. A full autopsy was performed on Hess' body on August 19 in the British Military Hospital by Dr Malcolm Cameron. The autopsy was conducted in the presence of medical representatives of the four powers. The report noted a linear mark on the left side of the neck consistent with a ligature. Dr Cameron stated that in his opinion death resulted from asphyxia, caused by compression of the neck due to suspension.

5. The investigations confirmed that the routine followed by staff on the day of Hess' suicide was consistent with normal practice. Hess had tried to cut his wrists with a table knife in 1977. Immediately after this incident, warders were placed in his room and he was watched 24 hours a day. This was discontinued after several months as impracticable, unnecessary and an inappropriate invasion of Hess' privacy.

The report of the autopsy carried out by the British pathologist Dr Cameron on August 19th was later made available to the family. Concluding that my father's death was not due to natural causes, it was consistent with point five of the Allied final official statement.

Autopsy and Burial

On the basis of a 1982 agreement between the family and the Allies, the body of Rudolf Hess would not be burned, but instead would be turned over to the family for burial "in Bavaria quietly in the presence of his immediate family."

The Allies kept this agreement - something they have most probably since regretted emphatically. Accordingly, my father's body was turned over to the family on the morning of 20th August 1987.

The coffin was accompanied by the three Western governors and two Russians, whom I didn't know, as well as a certain Major Gallagher, chief of the so-called "Special Investigation Branch,

Doppelganger

Royal Military Police." The turnover was brief and to the point. We then immediately brought the body to the Institute for Forensic Medicine in Munich, where Prof Dr Wolfgang Spann was waiting at our family's request to conduct a second autopsy. Throughout the entire journey from the military training grounds to the Institute for Forensic Medicine in Munich, the transport was guarded by a contingent of Bavarian police.

In the conclusion of his report of 21st December 1988, on the second autopsy, the renowned Munich pathologist Professor Spann

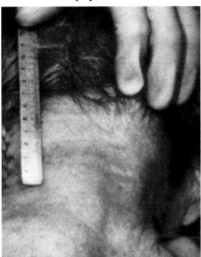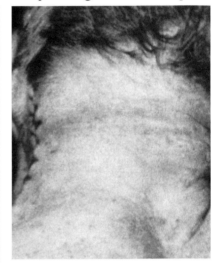

Hopefully, the mono stills showing the 'cord' marks on the neck of the dead Hess are clear?

pointed out the difficulties he encountered because he did not have any information about details of the alleged hanging. In particular, he had no information about details of the condition of my father after the supposed discovery of his body. In spite of these limitations, Dr Spann, nevertheless, was able to arrive at the following remarkable conclusions:-

Dr Cameron's further conclusion that this compression was caused by suspension is not necessarily compatible with our findings ...

In forensic medicine, the course which the ligature mark takes on the neck is considered a classic indicator for differentiating between forms of hanging and throttling ... If Prof Cameron, in his assessment of the cause of death, comes to the conclusion that the cause of death was asphyxiation caused by compression of the neck due to hanging, he neglects to consider the other method of strangulation, that is, throttling... Making this distinction would have required an examination of the course of the ligature mark. The precise course of the mark is not given in Prof Cameron's autopsy report ...

Here, neither the course of the strangulation mark on the neck, as we have described it, nor its course on the throat, nor its position relative to the prominence of the larynx has been described and assessed ... Since on the uninjured skin of the neck, where the possibility of distortion through the suture of the dissection incision is ruled out, an almost horizontal course of the strangulation mark could be identified, this finding, as well as the fact that the mark on the throat obviously was not located above the larynx, is more indicative of a case of throttling than of hanging. Under no circumstances can the findings be readily explained by a so-called typical hanging. The burst blood vessels which were observed in the face, caused by blood congestion, are also not compatible with typical hanging.

A Tunisian medical orderly, Abdallah Melaouhi, was a civilian employee of the Spandau prison administration at the time of my father's death. He is not a citizen of one of the four Allied occupation powers, nor; even more to the point, a member of their armed forces. As a result, he could not be silenced or transferred to some remote corner of the world like the others who were present at the scene of the crime. After the death of my father, Melaouhi got in touch with our family. From a note that my father wrote to him, it is clear that there was a relationship of personal trust between the two men. The core of Melaouhi's account, which he set down in an affidavit, is as follows:

'When I arrived at the garden summerhouse, I found the scene looking as though a wrestling match had taken place. The ground was churned up and the chair on which Hess had usually sat lay on the ground a considerable distance from its usual location. Hess himself lay lifeless on the ground: He reacted to nothing, his respiration, pulse and heartbeat were no longer measurable. Jordan (an American guard) stood near Hess' feet and was obviously quite beside himself.'

Melaouhi noticed to his surprise that besides Anthony Jordan, the black American guard, two strangers in US military uniform were present. This was unusual, since no soldier was normally permitted access to this part of the prison, and above all, because any contact with Rudolf Hess was most strictly forbidden. In Melaouhi's opinion, the two strangers seemed reserved and calm, in sharp contrast to Jordan.

Murder, Not Suicide.

On the basis of Prof Spann's autopsy report, the affidavits of the Tunisian medical orderly and the South African attorney, as well as the supposed "suicide letter," I can only conclude that the death of Rudolf Hess on the afternoon of 17th August, 1987, was not suicide. It was murder.

Although US authorities were officially in charge of the Allied Military prison in Berlin-Spandau in August 1987, it is noteworthy that British citizens played such a major role in the final act of the Hess drama. The American director, Mr Keane, was permitted by the British merely to call me and inform me of my father's death. After that his only duty was to keep his mouth shut.

To sum up here:-
* The two men the Tunisian orderly Melaouhi saw in American uniform, who were most probably Rudolf Hess' murderers, were from a British SAS regiment.
* The death was established in the British Military Hospital, to where my father was brought in a British ambulance.
* The death certificate is signed only by British military personnel
* The autopsy was carried out by a British pathologist.
* The British prison director, Mr Antony Le Tissier, supervised the prompt destruction of all tell-tale evidence, such as the electric cable, the garden house, and so forth.

Crime Through Time

* The officials of the Special Investigation Branch (SIB) that investigated the death were all British citizens, and were headed by a British Major.
* The alleged "suicide note" was supposedly found two days later in the pocket of Hess' jacket by a British officer, and was examined by a British laboratory.
* Mr Allan Green, the British Director of Public Prosecution, halted an investigation into my father's death begun by Scotland Yard, which had recommended a "full scale murder investigation" after officials there had found many inconsistencies.

The same government, which tried to make him a scapegoat for its crimes, and which for almost half a century resolutely sought to suppress the truth of the Hess affair, finally did not shrink from murder to silence him. My father's murder was not only a crime against a frail and elderly man, but a crime against historical truth. It was a logical final act of an official British conspiracy that began in 1941, at the outset of the Hess affair.

But I can assure them, and you, that this conspiracy will not succeed. The murder of my father will not, as they hope, forever close the book on the Hess file.

I am convinced that history and justice will absolve my father. His courage in risking his life for peace, the long injustice he endured, and his martyrdom, will not be forgotten. He will be vindicated, and his final words at the Nuremberg trial, "I regret nothing!," will stand forever.

Rudolf Hess, my father, did not commit suicide on 17th August 1987, as the British government claims. The weight of evidence shows instead that British officials, acting on high-level orders, murdered my father.

Wolf Rudiger Hess

b. Nov 18, 1937, d. Oct 24, 2001

Doppelganger

A previously undiscovered and unpublished letter from the British Broadcasting Corporation sheds further light on the capture of Rudolf Hess on 10th May 1941. This letter provides hard evidence that the official account of Hess' capture remains, for whatever reason, far from the truth.

It seems remarkable that an innocuous letter detailing a £2 fee destined for a member of the Royal Corps of Signals could be of importance, but even more remarkable is the fact that the British government has found it necessary to conceal the truth surrounding the capture of the Deputy Fuhrer for this length of time.

Whilst the identity of the soldier remains undisclosed the content of this letter is clear, it says:

The British Broadcasting Corporation

20th May 1941

Dear Sir,

I have much pleasure in enclosing herewith £2 0s 0d in payment of expenses incurred by you on your visit to Broadcasting House, Glasgow, on Tuesday, May 13th, [1941], when you gave an interview to us on the capture of Rudolf Hess.

I shall be grateful if you will sign and return at your convenience the enclosed receipt.

Yours sincerely,

(Ena Quade)

Programme Executive

(Note the validity of the government's account is seriously questioned. This document provides proof that the arrival and capture of Rudolf Hess was *not* a complete surprise, nor was it due to the combined actions of David McLean, a local farmer, and the Home Guard, as official records have led us to believe. The deception became all the more apparent when, as the soldier explained in his interview, the reason he was in the vicinity of the landing was to capture Hess. The soldier goes on to explain that all leave had been cancelled and a state of alert declared. Someone was clearly expecting the Duke of Hamilton to receive a visitor even if, as the Duke himself claimed, he was expecting no one.)

Rudolf Hess faced these Indictments

Count One: Conspiracy to Wage Aggressive War

This count helped address the crimes committed before the war began, showing a plan to commit crimes during the war.

Count Two: Waging Aggressive War, or "Crimes Against Peace"

Including "the planning, preparation, initiation, and waging of wars of aggression, which were also wars in violation of international treaties, agreements, and assurances."

Count Three: War Crimes

These were the more "traditional" violations of the law of war including treatment of prisoners of war, slave labour, and use of outlawed weapons.

Count Four: Crimes Against Humanity

This count involved the actions in concentration camps and other death rampages.

THE VERDICTS		
Count I:	Indicted	Guilty
Count II:	Indicted	Guilty
Count III:	Indicted	Not Guilty
Count IV:	Indicted	Not Guilty

Sentenced to: Imprisonment for life.

"This is another example of German justice gone berserk. What will have happened (from my own experience) is this: the Munich judge put in the usual phone call to the Minister of Justice in a lunch adjournment to warn that the country's most prestigious institute of history, the IfZ, had confirmed long ago there were never any homicidal gas chambers at Dachau; and the Minister will have told him to find Hess guilty nonetheless. Eventually Real History will prevail, but no thanks to the German government of today."

David Irving – War Historian   http://www.fpp.co.uk

Doppelganger

Mr Melaouhi describes, what he saw, when he entered the summerhouse: "When I entered the summerhouse, the scene was like a wrestling match had taken place; the entire place was in confusion. The straw tiled mat which covered the floor was in disarray, although only the day before I had cleaned the floor and had left the straw tiled mat carefully arranged in its usual place. A tall lamp had fallen over, but I clearly remember that the cable attached to the lamp was still connected to the main socket. It was this lamp cable, which the authorities later said that Mr Hess had used to hang himself. ..."

Mr Melaouhi continues, "The body of Mr Hess was lying on the floor of the summerhouse, apparently lifeless. Near to his body stood two soldiers dressed in US Army uniforms. I had never seen either soldier before. I also saw an American guard, whom I knew as a Mr Tony Jordan. There was no cable anywhere near the body of Mr Hess; as I have said, the only cable was attached to the fallen lamp which was still plugged into the wall."

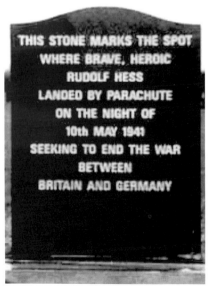

This memorial stone was erected in 1992 at Floors Farm, Scotland, at the ground where Rudolf Hess first touched Scottish soil on the night of 10th May 1941.

During the war, Hess was held for two years at Mytchett Place, Surrey, in Britain. This property was reportedly up for sale for 650,000 British pounds. According to an article in Psychic News, London, there are 'numerous reports of figures moving up and down the staircase, lights going on in locked rooms and photographs moving inexplicably.'

During his imprisonment at Mytchett Place, Hess attempted to commit suicide by hurling himself over the balcony into the hall below.

Crime Through Time

Hess' grandson denies existence of gas chambers.

A grandson of Adolf Hitler's deputy Rudolf Hess, Wolf Andreas Hess, a 23-year-old student, was fined for public incitement after putting remarks by Hess on the internet. Hess was quoted as saying there were no gas chambers in Dachau concentration camp near Munich during the Second World War and that the Americans installed them afterwards to scare tourists.

Counsel for the defence said Hess was not trying to incite anyone, adding that he had paid attention in his history lessons and knew there was a Holocaust. Hess was fined $1,184.

Anniversary of Hess' death marred by Nazi extremists.

A group of German right-wing extremists stabbed two foreigners in a Bavarian village. The attack came a day after a neo-Nazi rally in another Bavarian village to mark the anniversary of the death of Adolf Hitler's deputy, Rudolf Hess. Police in the southeastern town of Cham, near the Czech border, said four Germans attacked two refugees from Iraq and Jordan in the early hours of the morning.

The German youths jumped out of a car, shouted insults and then slashed the victims across their arms and hands, authorities said. The assault came without any warning or provocation. The two men were treated in a nearby hospital. The assailants escaped. Germany said there had been an increase in far-right crimes.

A report showed there had been 7,729 incidents in the first six months of 2001, including 430 acts of violence. The figure also included 5,200 criminal acts involving far-right propaganda such as displaying the outlawed swastika or using the "Heil Hitler" salute.

Interior Minister Otto Schily vowed the government would redouble its efforts against extremists. The leader of Germany's Jewish community, Paul Spiegel, said he was appalled by the rise in far-right crime. "It's deeply disturbing. The report shows there is no reason to sit back and relax. We cannot simply turn our backs to the gradual rise in racist crimes." Spiegel said, aside from the violence it was a "disgrace for Germany and a slap in the face to the victims of the Nazis" that criminals could paint swastikas on German buildings.

Germany, haunted by the shadow of its Nazi past, has been plagued by an eruption of far-right crime since unification in 1990. About 100 people have been killed in violence directed at foreigners in the last decade. The attacks have been especially virulent in the formerly communist East, where extremists have even set up "nationally liberated zones" where they have banned foreigners.

Police said about 800 right-wing extremists marched in Wunsiedel to mark the 14th anniversary of the death of Hess who is buried there. Authorities said the demonstration, about 200km west of Cham, was peaceful but 11 demonstrators were detained for carrying outlawed weapons such as clubs. Hess continues to hold a fascination for German neo-Nazis, who treat him as a martyr

The Nuremburg war crimes trial, Hess is front row left – described by Wolf Hess as a "kangaroo court."

http://www.rudolf-hess.de/

6

Celebrity Scandals

" INSANITY. "

FROM
" BEAUTY TO BEAST".

" SHE PAID THOUSANDS OF POUNDS.
TO LOOK LIKE THIS..
THATS WHAT DRUGS DONE TO HER.
WHAT A BLOODY WASTE...

Charles Bronson 2,000

A drawing by UK prisoner Charles Bronson.

Introduction to
Celebrity Scandals
By
Sid Vicious

Nancy Spungeon breast feeds Sid Vicious!!

Crime Through Time

Lyrics from Sid Vicious song... "My Way"
A rebel till the end!!

And now, the end is near

And so I face the final curtain
You cunt, I'm not a queer
I'll state my case, of which I'm certain
I've lived a life that's full
And each and every highway
And yet, much more than this
I did it my way

And yes, I've had a few
But then again, too few to mention
But dig, what I have to do
I'll see it through with no devotion
Of that, take care and just
Be careful along the highway
And more, much more than this
I did it my way

There were times, I'm sure you knew
When there was nothing fucking else to do
But through it all, when there was doubt
I shot it up or kicked it out
I fought the just as before
And did it my way

Knocked out in bed last night
I've had my fill, my share of looting
And now, the tears subside
I find it all so amusing
To think, I killed a cat
And may I say, oh no, not their way
But no, no, not me
I did it my way

For what is a brat, what has he got
When he finds out that he cannot
Say the things he truly thinks
But only the words, not what he feels
The record shows, I've got no clothes
And did it my way

SEX PISTOLS

27th May, 1977, 'God Save The Queen' is released by punk band The Sex Pistols. Athough banned from daytime play by the BBC and leading chain stores.

The record sells some 150,000 in a matter of days and by 11th June it reaches the No 2 spot, although there are claims that it is out-selling the No 1 spot held by Rod Stewart's 'I Don't Want To Talk About It'!

It was in the early morning hours of 12 October 1978, in room 100, of New York City's fabled Chelsea Hotel that Sid Vicious ended his tempestuous 21-month relationship with Nancy Spungen by allegedly stabbing her to death with a hunting knife. Four months later, in agony without her, he ended his own tortured life as well.

Sid, real name John Simon Ritchie, was 21 years old and was the bass player for the punk band the Sex Pistols, which had broken up a year earlier; he was a member of one of Britain's most influential and explosive punk-rock bands.

Nancy, 20, had been his most ardent fan. Together, the couple were in the forefront of rock's avant-garde, two dog-collared nihilists who brought their twisted, gothic romance to its ill-fated end.

Sid Vicious
10th May 1957 – 2nd February 1978

Crime Through Time

Doesn't look like Nancy is enjoying this very much??

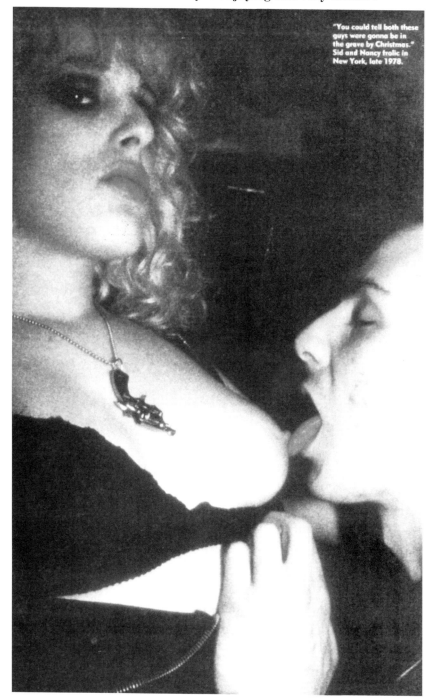

"You could tell both these guys were gonna be in the grave by Christmas." Sid and Nancy frolic in New York, late 1978.

SEX PISTOLS

Very very scarce... unaware of another signed photograph by both of them. Signed under the influence of drugs. On display at Crime Through Time

Vivienne Westwood admits perverting the course of justice!: "It was a terrible, awful thing that happened. Sid threw that bottle, but we pretended to the police it was someone else. He was arrested, and put into some kind of young person's remand home. We felt bad but Sid didn't feel guilty about it. I think he'd managed to convince himself of his own innocence."

Crime Through Time

Main photo is signed rear sleeve of 'Holidays in the Sun' record. Signed by all members of the Sex Pistols including alleged murderer Sid Vicious, signed 'Sid V' in bottom left corner.

Celebrity Scandals

Ronnie Biggs (who was a fugitive then) performed with the Sex Pistols.

The last signed photograph of Ronnie Biggs in Rio before he returned to his fateful reunion with Her Majesty's prison.
www.ronniebiggs.com

Crime Through Time

Is Eminem the modern day Sid Vicious?

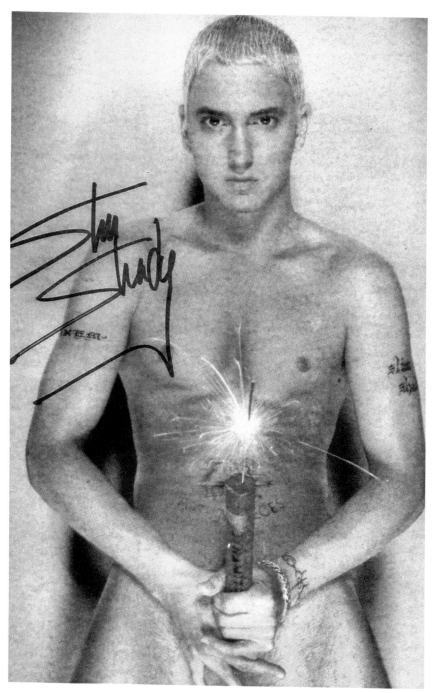

Celebrity Scandals

These boots are on display in the museum

29 Finch Lodge
Carlton Gate
Admiral Walk
Harrow Road
Maida Vale
London
W9 3TB   (U.K.)

August 5th 2000.

☠ SID VICIOUS MOTORBIKE BOOTS ☠

Dear Sir or Madam,

In 1989 I was commissioned by Omnibus Press Publishers to write the official biography of Sid Vicious (aka Simon John Beverley), I wrote this book with Keith Bateson and Vicious' now deceased mother Anne Beverley.

During the research period I spent quite a lot of time at Mrs Beverley's home in Swadlincote (Burton) often staying for weeks at a time. My time with Mrs Beverley is covered in full in the book 'Satellite' (Abstract Publishing) and it goes on to tell of all things she showed me in her home which belonged to her late son.

These motorbike boots where among three pairs owned by Vicious which I often saw at Mrs Beverley's home, one pair had been worn by himself and Nancy Spungen at various times, but all three pairs were worn under foot. Following Mrs Beverley's death by Vodka and sleeping pills overdose in September 1996
I hadn't seen anything much which belonged to her late son.

These boots were presented to me on Sunday July 30th at my home by George X Slattery (King of the punks) who himself is mentioned in Vivienne Westwoods Biography as a punk expert, I recognised them immediately as the boots owned by Sid Vicious which I hadn't personally seen in four years.

Yours faithfully

(Alan Parker)

268

Crime Through Time

Song written by Ronnie Biggs and performed with the Sex Pistols.

NO ONE IS INNOCENT

God save the sex pistols they're a bunch of wholesome blokes
They just like wearing filthy clothes and swapping filthy jokes
God save television keep the programmes pure
God save William Grundy from falling in manure

Ronnie Biggs was doing time until he done a bunk
Now he says he's seen the light and he sold his soul to punk

God save Martin Borman and Nazis on the run
They wasn't being wicked God that was their idea of fun
God save Myra Hindley God save Ian Brady
Even though he's horrible and she ain't what you call a lady

Ronnie Biggs was doing time until he done a bunk
Now he says he's seen the light and he sold his soul to punk
Ronnie Biggs was doing time until he done a bunk
Now he says he's seen the light and he sold his soul to punk

God save politicians God save our friends the pigs
God save Idi Amin and God save Ronald Biggs
God save all us sinners God save your blackest sheep
God save the good Samaritan and God save the worthless creep

Ronnie Biggs was doing time until he done a bunk
Now he says he's seen the light and he sold his soul to punk
Ronnie Biggs was doing time until he done a bunk
Now he says he's seen the light and he sold his soul to punk
Sold his soul Sold his soul Sold his soul to punk

Celebrity Scandals

Marilyn Monroe, errrrr…not quite? But certainly Marilyn.
Signed photograph of alleged anti-Christ Marilyn Manson.

Did he do a Sid Vicious and top himself?

(So say perverted??) Michael Hutchence, signed photo
on display in museum,
see related piece.

Celebrity Scandals

Below, the nightstand next to Monroe's bed reveals the star's drug dependency.

Above, Monroe in her heyday ...hopelessly insecure and dependant on drugs.

Ganja King - The Legendary Bob Marley died so young. What an assassination attempt failed to do cancer did.

Drugs junkie - The Legendary Jimi Hendrix choked on his vomit when in a barbiturate induced state.

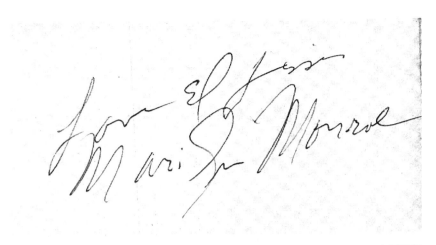

TRULY ONE OF THE MOST SCARCE AND HIGHLY SOUGHT AFTER SIGNATURES IN THE WORLD - A LEGENDARY FIGURE WHO WAS NOT SCARED TO ADMIT THAT SHE HAD SLEPT HER WAY TO THE TOP.

GENUINE SIGNATURE OF SCANDAL RIDDEN FILM SCREEN LEGEND - MARILYN MONROE, WHO INCIDENTALLY CONVERTED FROM HER ONCE PROTESTANTISM RELIGION TO JUDAISM AS A CONSEQUENCE OF HAVING MARRIED HER JEWISH HUSBAND, ARTHUR MILLER IN A HIGHLY ACCLAIMED JEWISH CEREMONY ON THE 1ST OF JULY 1956.

THIS SIGNATURE ALONG WITH ALL OTHERS CONTAINED WITHIN THIS AUTOGRAPH BOOK WAS PERSONALLY ACQUIRED DURING THE TIME OF HER ONLY UK VISIT IN THE YEAR 1956, BY HER THEN BRITISH CHAUFFEUR FOR THE WORLD FAMOUS PINE WOOD FILM STUDIOS - LONDON.

MARILYN MONROE ARRIVED IN THE UK ON THE 14TH OF JULY 1956, SHE MET HM THE QUEEN ELIZABETH AT THE ROYAL COMMAND PERFORMANCE IN LONDON'S LEICESTER SQUARE TO PROMOTE HER PERFORMANCE ALONGSIDE LAWRENCE OLIVIER, IN THE FILM 'THE PRINCE AND THE SHOWGIRL.'

SHE LEFT THE UK TO RETURN TO AMERICA ON THE 20TH OF NOVEMBER 1956 AFTER A 4-MONTH STAY. MARILYN MONROE ALLEGEDLY COMMITTED SUICIDE ON THE 4th OF AUGUST 1962???

CONSISTING OF SOME 60 GENUINE AND PERSONALLY ACQUIRED SIGNATURES WHICH INCLUDE THE LIKES OF OTHER LEGENDARY FILM SCREEN SEX SYMBOLS WHO MANY CLAIM HAVE SLEPT THEIR WAY TO THE TOP, BETTE DAVIES, THE BUSTY JANE MANSFIELD, CLAUDETTE COLBERT, JEAN KENT, KATHERINE HEPBURN, ALONG WITH MANY OTHER BEAUTIFUL WOMEN WHO HAD VISITED THE UK DURING THIS PERIOD.

THE BOOK ALSO CONSISTS OF MANY LEGENDARY ACTORS SUCH AS BOB HOPE, DAVID KOSSOFF, RICHARD TODD, DAVID NIVEN, ALEC GUINNESS, JACK WARNER, MICHAEL REDGRAVE, BILL OWEN, TERRY THOMAS, AND MANY, MANY MORE, WHICH CAN BE SEEN IN THE MUSEUM.

TURN THE PAGE TO SEE MARILYN AS VERY RARELY SEEN BEFORE!!!!

Celebrity Scandals

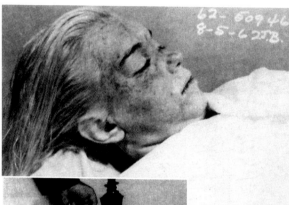

Marilyn in death, this photo was taken after the autopsy was carried out on her, which caused her face to sag. Previous to the pathologists work Marilyn remained beautiful.

The table, as it was left beside Marilyn's bed - in an incomplete investigation!

Frank Sinatra was accused of acting as a pimp when he fixed up President John F Kennedy and his brother Bobby with the ill fated Marilyn Monroe.

Is this what it was all about? Did she bonk her way to the top?

Crime Through Time

Body Beautiful...Marilyn Monroe nude shots!!

A signed photo of Monroe, on display in the museum.

Crime Through Time

**Marilyn Monroe...
with falsies!**

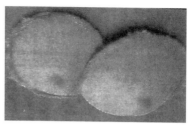

The Falsies
Marilyn's Breasts were falsies...never! The screen legend boosted her classic pose with a pair of falsies.

Specially made for her were these flesh coloured chest pads... including being complete with nipples! Her already ample figure of 36C was boosted in order to give her the "provocative look". The man who stole them later sold the falsies at auction for £3,450! Alan Abbot was given the job of making sure the body of Monroe had them fitted, even in death, but he nicked them...naughty boy!!!

On display in the museum is a stunning black basque that was once worn and belonged to Miss Monroe.

A very stunning and priceless piece. The item was purchased privately from a genuine show business friend (The Barrymore family - USA) of the sexy star. The chequered past of Miss Monroe has been claimed to involve taking part in blue movies, being a hooker and of course her affair with John F Kennedy, the President of the USA and family man!

MARILYN MONROE - USED MEN TO GET TO THE TOP

Remember what it was that got this man in big trouble...his dick

As with JFK and Archer...most men's dicks rule their brain.

SEX, SEX, SEX, SEX, SEX, SEX, SEX, SEX, and more SEX

Jeffrey Archer

House of Lords

Men who abuse their positions of power, Archer and JFK, always seem to get their comeuppance...go to jail and work in a theatre...or be shot.

Lady Nicholson told the BBC: "Clearly, both the Red Cross and Jeffrey Archer, deliberately or not, misled the Iraqi Kurds at their time of greatest need." Lady Nicholson's comments triggered a fraud squad investigation into the campaign.

Scotland Yard said detectives were still carrying out a "preliminary assessment" of Lady Nicholson's complaint before deciding whether to carry out a full investigation.

A spokeswoman for the charity commission said: "We are aware that allegations have been made to the police and we are monitoring the situation."

NORMA JEAN

BORN

TO BE

WILD

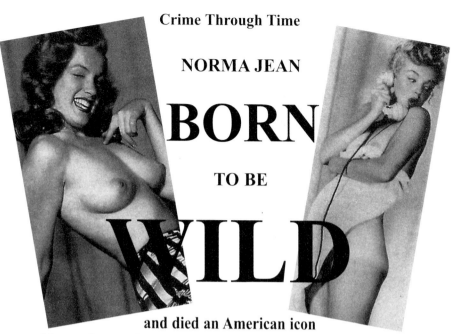

and died an American icon

Norma Jean Baker grew up in orphanages and foster homes, her resume included stints as a nude model and a prostitute before she morphed into Marilyn Monroe.

As an up and cuming (coming) starlet Marilyn never let the casting couch stand in her way. She shagged her way to the top, up and down! "It wasn't any big dramatic tragedy," she shrugged. By the end of the 1950s, she'd soared to stardom in such films as 'Gentlemen Prefer Blondes' and reigned as Hollywood's hottest sex bomb.

A censor was determined to snip a scene in 1960's "Let's Make Love" because Norma Jean's "horizontal position implied sex." "So what?" Marilyn cooed. "You can do that standing up." The suggestive scene stayed in. Marilyn's darker side ultimately destroyed her. Her chronic lateness on movie sets became legendary. Her marriage to second husband Joe Di Maggio lasted just nine months. She gulped pills to sleep and pills to wake up, washing them down with booze.

There were affairs with two married Kennedy brothers, John and Robert. Many onlookers thought she was high on more than life when — wrapped in a skintight, almost transparent gown — Marilyn sang "Happy Birthday" to President Kennedy at his 19 May 1962 birthday bash. None of the 22,000 people on hand at the

New York, Madison Square Garden bash suspected they'd been having an affair since 1955! It has been suggested that it was screen idol Frank Sinatra who was the pimp and got the two together.

The affair was called off by JFK when he learned Teamster boss Jimmy Hoffa had sent a wiretapper to bug Marilyn's phone, seeking ammunition in his feud with the Kennedy's. Maybe he had something to do with Kennedy's death assassination?

Marilyn became frantic when the affair looked to be ending, what could JFK do, he sent his brother Bobby to break the news gently to her and Bobby ended up in bed with her, although there are suggestions that he had been dallying with the blonde bombshell even before his brother JFK had 'sexual relations with her.' Would semen stains have been found on Marilyn's dress, obviously Marilyn wasn't as prepared as Monica Lewinsky (sexual liaison with President Bill Clinton – she'd been Clintoned!).

Less than three months later — after being fired from her last movie - the 36-year-old sex goddess was found dead, nude, facedown on her own bed. The death was ruled a suicide by barbiturate overdose. But rumours of foul play persist to this day. The romantic notion that JFK and Bobby had her murdered seems to carry much weight with romantics, but in reality her life was a mess.

Goodbye,
Norma Jean

Monroe and others find a home in Gloucestershire

Stars' scribbles
sold for £3,300

Marilyn Monroe's signature bought for £3,300 by crime museum!

Robertson-Justice. The autographs were collected by a former chauffeur to the stars during the 1960s.

Taxi driver Robert Bird was originally asked to drive several of the stars from Bath to the nearby picture postcard village of Castle Combe where the classic film Dr Dolittle was being shot.

He did as well that Pinewood Studios asked him to be their chauffeur between Bath and the studios in Buckinghamshire.

He got to know many of the celebrities and started collecting their signatures.

The result was the palm-sized autograph album which went under the hammer following instructions from Mr Bird's son.

■ Above ...
Dominic Winter, left, auctioning the Marilyn Monroe signature which is being held up by porter Roger Frost.

■ Left ... Andy Jones is delighted with his purchase

Pictures: SAM FROST
Ref: 5194

PAULA YATES - AS TRAGIC AS MONROE

**FROM THE
CRADLE TO
THE GRAVE
TRAGEDY
CHASED
THIS
WOMAN**

**DRUGS
+SEX
+ROCK
+ROLL**

Authentic signature of tragic Paula Yates.

Celebrity Scandals

ALWAYS A POPULAR CHARACTER FOR THE TABLOIDS

SHE COURTED DISASTER WITH BLIND IGNORANCE

PAULA'S TERROR AS HER CRAZED STALKER ESCAPES

Police fear mania is out to get star

BY LEE BROWN

'Paula Yates threatened to murder Tiger Lily'

She was destined to be with her Hutch

Signed photo of Bob Geldof

DUMPED GELDOF IN SUICIDE AGONY

BY MYDRIM JONES

ROCK hero Bob Geldof has confessed that he considered killing himself after his late wife Paula Yates dumped him.

Celebrity Scandals

Paul Yates + Michael Hutchence =
An accident waiting to happen??

PAULA: BURY ME WITH HUTCH ASHES

EXCLUSIVE

TRAGIC Paula Yates was laid to rest yesterday with her dying wish unfulfilled.

The tormented TV star wanted to be cremated with her head resting on the pillow stuffed with lover Michael Hutchence's ashes.

But undertakers said it would have breached strict funeral laws about what can be placed in a coffin.

● Continued on Page 4

PAULA OWED £2,000 FOR DRUG DEALS

EXCLUSIVE by ALUN PALMER

DESPERATE Paula owed more than £2,000 to drug dealers for heroin, cocaine and cannabis the day she died, the Sunday People can reveal.

She ran up the debts with neighbourhood pushers who thought the tragic mother's celebrity status meant her credit was good.

Paula had even given two dealers their own keys to her mews home in London's Notting Hill.

Friends changed the locks the day after her death, fearing the pushers would get in to grab goods for the cash they were owed.

Residents said Paula would never have had a problem getting hold of narcotics as her home is a stone's throw from All Saints Road, an area notorious for drugs. It is dubbed "The front line" by locals.

One source said: "Paula knew quite a few faces who dealt in drugs. There are hard or soft drugs – you can get whatever you want if you have the cash."

A CELEBRITY DRUG MUG CONFESSES

Ex-Soap star Danniella Westbrook, once the star of Eastenders (UK soap) has had plenty of time to consider the consequences of her actions during the course of being addicted to cocaine for many years. The price she's paid for this addiction is the loss of her septum - the gristly membrane which separates the nostrils - has apparently disappeared, leaving Danniella's pretty face impaired and her once-pert nose in need of serious surgery.

"I'm an addict. I can't help it."

The cost of Danniella Westbrook's addiction has also had an affect on other people, like when she sold her mother-in-law's vacuum cleaner for drugs money and had dealers turning up at the set of the soap demanding she settle her bills.

Cocaine users' hearts age twice as quickly as non-users. Cocaine use has been linked to many types of heart disease and has been found to: trigger chaotic heart rhythms called ventricular fibrillation; accelerate heartbeat and breathing; increase blood pressure and body temperature. Physical symptoms may include chest pain, nausea, blurred vision, and fever. Regularly snorting can lead to loss of sense of smell, and nosebleeds. Heavy use can also lead to a 'Danniella Westbrook' type hole between the two nasal passages!

Celebrity Scandals

THERE'S NOTHING CLEVER ABOUT USING DRUGS!

Cocaine can also cause problems with swallowing, hoarseness, and an overall irritation of the nasal septum, which can lead to a chronically inflamed, runny nose.

Ingested cocaine can cause severe bowel gangrene, due to reduced blood flow. And, persons who inject cocaine have puncture marks and 'tracks,' most commonly in their forearms.

It can also lead to a bulging weakness in the wall of the branch point of the arteries in the brain, often called a 'berry aneurysm'. Eventually this aneurysm bursts, and blood pouring out of the leak is known as a subarachnoid haemorrhage. It can cause major damage to the brain which can be permanent leading to difficulty with sight, thought, speech or movement. Some may recover, some people die.

Liver damage is more common and the risk of sudden death is 18 times greater when alcohol and cocaine are used together than when cocaine is used on its own.

Legendary George Best - Self confessed alcoholic
A NEW LIVER AND HE CAN DRINK FOR IRELAND

**Isn't it odd how even the greatest legends turn to alcohol, etc!
Hey...but on the other hand don't most of us love a drink too!**

Crime Through Time

CELEBRITY DRUG SCANDALS!!

Carrie Fisher, who is, perhaps, best known for her role as Princess Leia in the Star Wars trilogy, became addicted to prescription drugs.

Frank Zappa: "A drug is neither moral nor immoral - it's a chemical compound. The compound itself is not a menace to society until a human being treats it as if consumption bestowed a temporary license to act like an asshole."

Celebrity Scandals

George Michael...Homo Scandals

He had little trouble keeping his name in the papers.

Born Georgious Kyriacos Panayiotou, Finchley, in London, 20 June 1963 – Better known as George Michael. And he enjoys a wank in public toilets too!

> "Do they really think they have a chance of shagging me?" George Michael on the public's never ending fascination with his sexuality.

Pop's randy George Michael's father was a Greek restaurateur and his mother is English. George, or Yog as his family call him, grew up listening to Motown, Queen, and Elton John. Maybe these were the influences that decided his sexuality? His original childhood aspiration was to be a pilot, but near-sightedness and colour blindness ended that dream turning his hopes to a musical career.

His contribution to the Beverly Hill's Cop 2 movie soundtrack, 'I Want Your Sex', caused uproar on both sides of the pond. The BBC banned the track, which, rather perversely, gave the track an extra boost chartwise, reaching No 3. Many radio stations refused to play the song or would only play it late at night, so while the song reached No 2 in overall record sales, it was kept from the No 1 spot by lack of airplay.

George had a run in with his record company Sony and it wind-ed up in court, with Sony emerging victorious. Pundits say that George never had a chance of winning in the first place, because a ruling in his favour would have turned the music industry upside down, with every artist suing to get out of their contract.

As a part of the generous settlement, George was released from his contract with Sony and allowed to sign with Dreamworks, owned by record mogul David Geffen, director Steven Spielberg, and Hollywood player, Jeffery Katzenburg. Sony paid George $40m for his song catalogue!

On Tuesday 7 April 1998 Los Angeles detective, Marcelo Rodriguez, arrested George Michael for lewd behaviour in a public lavatory, in Will Rogers Memorial Park, in Beverly Hills, USA. The event became a big story, particularly in the tabloid newspapers. On 9 April 1998 the front page of The Sun was taken up entirely by the story with the banner headline almost filling the page 'ZIP ME UP BEFORE YOU GO GO'. (A reference to the Wham! hit single Wake me up before you go go, 1984.)

After the arrest, George Michael was quoted as saying: "I feel stupid, reckless and weak for having allowed my sexuality to be exposed in this way, but I don't feel any shame whatsoever, and neither do I think I should."

The incident might have been expected to be George Michael's fall from grace, but he turned the outing into something more to his own advantage. His cottaging (public toilet cruising – gay slang) seemed to work miracles for his flagging career and he underwent a metamorphosis from a scared closet queen to an open, relaxed and happy homo.

In subsequent interviews he became very ready to talk about his arrest and his sexuality. The video for the single Outside featured an irreverent reconstruction of events leading up to the arrest. A television interview by Michael Parkinson received some acclaim for its frankness...well, Michael is always accommodating and prepared to be frank for people like George.

There are rumours that every actor with a flagging career is doing some cruising around the cottages in the hope that the press might do a story on them too!

"No, Gary that doesn't mean you have a chance of making a cumback, puffs are acceptable but not paedophiles…sorry."

> **Wherever you go, mate, the press will follow!!!**
> **Below, signed photo of Glittering paedophile.**

Gary Glitter, last seen cruising around a school yard in Cambridgeshire, but someone had got there before him. Monsters, should they hang? Go to www.myrahindley.com

In September 1999, Marcelo Rodriguez sued George Michael for 'the humiliation and shock to the system' that he had suffered after the arrest when George Michael mocked him in interviews and in his video. And he seemed like such a nice boy too!

> **"I want people to know I haven't been exposed as a gay man, I don't feel any shame."** George Michael

Michael didn't have a relationship with a man until age 27; wrote love songs for women for the first half of his career; then wrote love songs for men. This isn't the first time Michael has dropped his trousers in a public toilet, it would seem he likes to wank himself whilst being watched by a man while he bashes his bishop.

292

Crime Through Time

George Michael finishes off

(Do you want some tissue?)

"This is as good as time as any, I want to say that I have no problem with people knowing that I'm in a relationship with a man right now. I have not been in a relationship with a woman for almost 10 years.

It has been humiliating, embarrassing...funny to some degree, but I can't be angry with anyone but myself. I mean, the only people I've really hurt are myself, the people who love me and my partner who has been absolutely amazing and understands me, thank God. I'm Okay and I want my fans to know that this is not going to finish me off." (Good on you, Michael, there's plenty more toilets left around the world to conquer yet.)

Right, what follows on the next eight pages is going to break a lot of peoples' hearts, so please skip the next eight pages if you don't want to feel disillusioned. There are those of you who have known of this man for some time, his real name is Cyril Louis Goldbert, he's starred in films from as early as the 1950s and was once, and probably still is until you turn the page, a heart throb of great magnitude. Men would copy his hairstyle and his sense in fashion prompted boutiques to copy his clothes, whilst women swooned over him, often fantasising about him to the point of orgasm.

Do you want a few more clues as to who it is, okay then...he was born in France, Marseille, in southern France to be exact, but he hasn't a trace of a French accent so that rules out Sacha Distelle. Any closer to helping you? His father worked in the British Diplomatic Service and his mother was French. Have you guessed, okay then here's another clue he donned plenty of velvet shirts and was the flashiest and most flamboyant screen detective ever since Sherlock Holmes stopped wearing long johns. He had a Zapata style moustache...closer now aren't we? Turn over.

http://www.georgemichael.com

Celebrity Scandals

Peter Wyngarde

Signed photo of Peter Wyngarde, on the left.

The most famous of roles played by actor Peter Wyngarde (Cyril Louis Goldbert) is that of Jason King, the author-cum-investigator) out of televisions Department S.

The macho woman chasing Jason King came across as the typical woman hungry predator.

Wyngarde's career, as an actor, goes back to 1946! Starring in many of the now classic cult series of the 60s and 70s: 'Department S', 'The Avengers' and 'The Prisoner', even starring in four episodes of 'Dr Who'.

Actor Peter Wyndgarde, 47 years old at that time, was caught in the public toilets of Gloucester bus station on the evening of 8 September 1975 committing an act of gross indecency with another man, Richard Jack Whalley, 24.

Caught red handed in the act by police, the pair were arrested, most embarrassing for Mr Wyngarde! Appearing at Gloucester magistrates' court on Friday 17 October 1975 under his real name of Cyril Louis Goldbert he was fined £75 for the gross indecency.

When Wyngarde was arrested he told the police that he was a native of Singapore and a writer by profession! Obviously he had hoped that none of this would come out, although it did appear in a tiny Gloucestershire newspaper it seems to have been missed by the national press and never made big time news. At that time if it had of been discovered by the national press then maybe the headlines would have looked something like this:

Jason King caught in
Department 'S'ex drama
As he has toilet sex with man half his age!

Photographs of the toilets were shown to the bench presiding at the court by Lawrence Keen, defending Peter Wyngarde, who said, "We are concerned at the state of these lavatories and very much hope they will be repaired as quickly as possible." Mr Keen referred to the state of disrepair the cubicles were in, they had faulty partitions.

Lawrence Keen defending
"The toilets are notorious for homosexuals."
"It's like a trap to catch a poacher."

Submitting the photos of the faulty toilet cubicles Mr Keen said the police had made between 15 and 20 arrests that year at the toilets. Going on to describe the toilets as "bait" said there were no locks on the cubicle doors enabling the police to burst in.

In a further bizarre plea to the bench Mr Keen went on to say: "This may produce an impressive crime detection record in Gloucester, but it would be better for the bus company to take protective steps by erecting a substantial partition and thereby relieve the police from an obviously distasteful task." This seems to be advocating 'safe sex' areas for homosexuals and obviously Mr Keen saw no real danger of making this known to the court bench!

Mr Cecil Bruton, the presiding magistrate seemed to be taking up what Mr Keen had said when he advised: "We are concerned at the state of these lavatories and we very much hope that they will be repaired as quickly as possible." It would seem that Mr Bruton was sympathetic to the cry for larger partitions; maybe they could get more in to the cubicle that way?

"Heterosexuality isn't normal, it's just common"
Oscar Wilde

Piss off babe!
I've got other things
on my mind just
now!!

Apparently, on the afternoon of the indecency offence Mr Wyngarde was shopping in Gloucester for curtain fittings, although it was said he was not familiar with Gloucester, Mr Wyngarde seemed to make a beeline straight to the gay haunt of Gloucester's bus station toilets! However, at one time it is thought that Mr Wyngarde lived in the Gloucestershire/Stroud district, named 'Camp'.

The defence said, "…but the defendant is not a homosexual. The offence was committed in a moment of mental aberration." Well this mental lapse certainly came back to haunt Mr Wyngarde, did it destroy his successful TV career in the UK, well it would seem that in 1976 he went to Austria, working in the English theatre in Vienna, starred in an obscure Austrian film and briefly returned to the UK to star in further stage plays.

Crime Through Time

It wasn't until 1984 that Mr Wyngarde returned to the TV screen in four episodes of 'Dr Who' – Planet of Fire, a four part series.

In one of pop's more bizarre offerings - Peter Wyngarde's one and only recording venture - an album steeped in myth and controversy, was withdrawn within weeks after it first appeared back in 1970, and mired in contractual complications until RPM were able to offer it a more than suitable home.

The record, in its day, was outrageous and would certainly be in the top ten of the most bizarre moments in pop history.

The song (no singing in this one) 'Hippie And The Skinhead' has Wyngarde reading out a letter written to The Times newspaper by two Home Counties skinhead girls.

Rape can happen to homosexuals too!

Also on the record you can hear Billy the Queer, Pilly Sexy Hippie, sung over a Nashville backing. And there's even something for discerning lovers of late Sixties English rock as he takes on the Attack's 'Neville Thumbcatch', written by Vic Smith.

The Bizarre song titles of Wyngarde's vinyl love letter

1 Come In, 2 You Wonder How These Things Began, 3 Rape, 4 La Ronde De L'Amour, 5 Jenny Kissed Me, 6 The Way I Cry Over You, 7 Unknown Citizen, 8 It's When I Touch You, 9 Hippie and The Skinhead, 10 Try To Remember To Forget (Riviera Cowboy), 11 Jenny Kissed Me And It Was…, 12 Widdecombe Fair, 13 Neville Thumbcatch, 14 Once Again (Flight Number 10), 15 Pay No Attention, 16 April

---

Released in 1970 when the actor was at the peak of his prowess. The album included songs, which exploded into rampant rages of male sexuality, in gay abandonment that was permissive for those times. Record producers had long been sniffing around, hoping to get Wyngarde into a studio; getting a top TV personality to cut an album was a sure-fire way to make a quick buck, regardless of their musical abilities. They told Wyngarde that he could do what he liked. The central idea was to string the songs together into one long suite and none were more interesting than the opening quartet of 'Come In' (cum).

The songs, 'You Wonder How These Things Begin' and 'Rape' are the album's centrepiece, this has given the record such cult notoriety that collectors happily shell out up to £400 for a copy. Wyngarde defends this piece of musical infamy. (Is it politically incorrect?) He says, "I've really no idea. It's about all kinds of rape. There is so much rape going on, rape within bureaucracy, rape at so many government levels, rape of countries. You know, even attempting to explain it totally defeats its purpose."

True crime books are of interest to Mr Wyngarde, maybe this one will be of even greater interest. If George Michael came out then what is wrong with Peter Wyngarde coming out, both were flushed out by incidents that took place in public toilets - George Michael used it to his advantage! The most terrifying moment in Mr Wyngarde's life came when, he says, 30,000 women at Sidney Airport, Australia, mobbed him in 1971. Obviously being arrested for gross indecency wasn't the most terrifying moment! When asked if there were any experiences in life he'd have rather missed, he says "None at all. Every experience, even a bad one, has its advantages."

"I don't feel as if I belong to any strata of society. I never did. I can be at home with anyone, whether it's at an ambassadorial dinner party, or with a gang of building labourers. Mind you, people say I try too hard to be one of the boys." Peter Wyngarde

---

With his Zapata moustache and bushy sideburns, Wyngarde was the culmination of all that was "fab" about British television in that all-too-brief period during the late Sixties and early Seventies, when gentlemen's wardrobes the world over went into overdrive in continual salute to the one true guru of style.

Crime Through Time

Wyngarde on Wyngarde

"I loved every minute of being in The Avengers. It was obviously very kinky and it was meant to be. Since the Cathy Gale days, there was this always slightly camp and kinky side to The Avengers. Before ('A Touch Of Brimstone') I had this reputation of being a bit of a sadist, quite unfounded of course. After that episode I was in great demand. Off screen too!

I have a loner instinct; maybe my childhood has something to do with it. (He had spent the war years in an internment camp - without his parents, and stranded from all other relatives, in Shanghai.) It taught me to be self reliant from a very early age.

I'm a very solitary person. Although I'm not self-sufficient. I like to be on my own. I ruminate a lot. Maybe I'm frightened of getting too close to people. I don't want to get hurt and I don't want to hurt other people. But I do think I need a permanent relationship. The trouble is that the sorts of people who are attracted to me don't seem to be all that intelligent. They start being petty and squabbling, and jealous. What I need is someone who can be entirely independent - and there aren't that many around.

If I ever got married again, I'd want to live in a separate house to my wife. Then we could just see each other when we wanted to, instead of all the time.

I've always had people staring at me in restaurants because of my appearance. I always wore slim trousers, and I always wore boots. A while ago, someone in Hollywood recognised me walking past a shop - he just remembered me from the clothes I wore when he knew me in London 10 years before.

I had no thought of becoming an actor until I tried law, which was a disaster. But I suppose that was theatrical in a way. Then I went into advertising, and if I'd stayed in that I probably would have done pretty well. The partner I used to work with is a millionaire in America now.

The real acting began when I met a chap I knew outside a theatre in London. He was the only actor I'd ever met and I asked him what he was doing, he said he'd just been to an audition, and I wished him good luck with it, and then walked in myself! I had no idea what an audition was like, and just announced myself as Wyngarde and said I'd come about the part.

They asked me which part and I just said, well, THE part. Then they gave me this script to read, and I read all the parts. I thought that's what you had to do at an audition! Then they asked me what experience I'd had, so I said Old Vic and Birmingham Repertory, because they were the only companies I'd ever heard of! Oh, I told a lot of lies!"

1957 ITV broadcast a play that was from the London stage.

Julian Green's 'South' - a controversial play about homosexuality was screened by ITV on 24 November 1957. This was a brave step and shows how ITV were a little bit adventurous way back then. When you consider how raunchy C4 and C5 in the UK has been classified as it might be worth looking back on such events as being part of our social history.

This small screen version, set in America's deep south just prior to the start of the Civil War, starred Peter Wyngarde in the lead role of Jan - a man who falls hopelessly in love with Eric MacClure. This is uncanny, was Wyngarde made for this part?

Jan breaks down in front of Broderick, the man that introduced them, and confesses his feelings for Eric, saying *"I'm not ashamed, but alone. Hopelessly alone."* This may well have been quite poignant and reflected on Wyngarde's own life!

Jan then forces a duel on MacClure, being killed was better than facing life without him.

This was a play straight down the line about homosexuality presented to a mass of viewers maybe not quite ready to grasp the nettle. This thinly veiled sexual drama was ahead of its time.

ITV (Independent Television) should have been congratulated for screening 'South', if Peter was brave enough to tackle this part back then it should have resulted in him being used as an icon by the gay activists of the time. Wyngarde, a gay icon?

Peter Wyngarde was, by far and away and without a shadow of a doubt, the grooviest, flashiest bastard and most flamboyant icon ever to don a frilly shirt, apart from Liberace!

Crime Through Time

Was Wyngarde the tough puff?

He was no more than a baby when he was captured by the Japanese in Shanghai, surviving four years in a concentration camp. Convincing enough!

Shanghai was a city that left lasting impression on him. He had been temporarily left in the care of a Swiss family, whilst his father was away in India on business. The Japanese had captured the city in 1941 and before long Peter and his surrogate family were locked up in Lung-hai concentration camp!

Confined in barbaric and brutal conditions for four years, Peter somehow managed to prevent his family and friends from dying at the hands of the cruel and evil soldiers in the camp.

Peter would often run errands between the camp huts, but he was discovered and punished by the soldiers – they broke both of his feet with a rifle butt! As if this wasn't enough he was also put into solitary confinement for two weeks!!!

In order to occupy himself he worked in the camp laundry and gardens, and began to write and appear in plays he organised to keep the morale of the prisoners up.

His acting career effectively began when he was a little boy in the camp, he would play with homemade puppets - Dr Jekyll and Mr Hyde.

Eventually, in 1945, when the camp was finally liberated Peter was found to be suffering from malnutrition, berry berry and malaria, he was taken to a sanatorium in the Swiss mountains where he spent the next two years.

Peter's nickname at school was 'Juicy' and he used to be the mascot at Stamford Bridge football ground, obviously he supports Chelsea football club.

What a shame he's been out of favour with the TV world for so long, maybe they'll make a film about his life...warts and all!

Peter Wyngarde appreciation Society site:

http://www.hermes58.freeserve.co.uk/

Celebrity Scandals

TV's favourite rag and bone man takes in more than bed knobs. You dirty old man...how could you!

BBC's 70's television series *Steptoe and Son* made an unlikely soap star out of Wilfred Brambell, who in real-life was a perv...a "Dirty Old Man." Teenage boys gave the actor - who played rag-and-bone man Albert Steptoe - the hots.

Corbett and Brambell - 70s icons.

Lusting for teen sex, his urges took him to Hong Kong, a regular haunt for gay perverts. Brambell used to cruise the gay bars looking for teenage rent-boys.

Once caught by the police "cottaging" in public toilets (ironically near to the BBC studios, in Shepherds Bush, London) his craving for young men was to know no bounds. Harry H Corbett, 57, who played the forever henpecked son in the series died from a massive heart attack in 1982, three years later Brambell, 75, died of cancer.

The Beatles were said to be great fans of the show, and it was their choice that Wilfred Brambell would play Paul McCartney's grandfather in the film *A Hard Day's Night.*

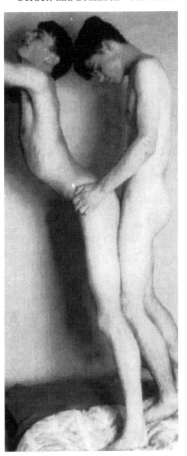

Brambell lusted for gay teen sex.

In real life - both loathed each other.

Crime Through Time

The next subject

Bullied at School
As a child he was shy
Grew up with no friends
Loved playing with dolls
Real name Marshall Mathers III
Sued by his mother for ridiculing her
Accused his mother of drug addiction
Some critics call him the devil incarnate

His wife tried to commit suicide by slitting her wrists
Has tattoos on his wrist that read 'slit me', on his stomach
is his wife's name, Kim, alongside a tombstone and the
inscription 'Rot in Flames'
Publicly supports two youths who shot dead 12 classmates
and their teacher at Columbine high school, in USA
Was threatened to be sued by Christina Aguilera after he
suggested, in explicit terms, that she slept her way to the top

> **"In twelve years he has gone from 'Grandma I love you,' to 'Go to hell'. It breaks my heart."**
> The subject's grandmother

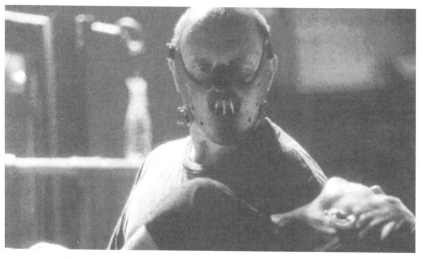

Could this be the man, turn the page to find out?

Eminem
Probably the best role model any child could have?!!?

EMINEM NO.1

The Mail's Parliamentary sketch writer – a man used to unedifying public performances – saw Eminem live. So what did he make of it all?

REVIEW
from Quentin Letts

Hardcore rapper or just a big girl's blouse?

Born Marshall Bruce Mathers III on 17 October 1972, in Kansas City, USA. His childhood was spent moving back and forth between Kansas City and Metro Detroit.

In spite of court cases and divorce that have plagued his private life he has still managed to carry on with his solo career, tour and manage to produce another rapping band.

The mother of rapper Eminem (aka Slim Shady) sued her son for defamation, claiming he portrayed her as stoned white trash in media interviews. Debbie Mathers-Briggs recently filed a lawsuit in Michigan's Macomb County courthouse.

The rapper has also come under fire for his sexist, anti-gay lyrics and violent lyrics that include raping a 15-year-old girl.

Grammy-winning rapper Eminem was one of four people arrested outside a suburban Detroit nightclub in June 2000 after a disturbance that began when a crowd in the parking lot recognised the rapper. They wanted to get an autograph or just talk with him. A fight broke out and three bar security guards rushed in and detained someone with a gun!

His lyrics are said to be depraved! He urges fans to take drugs! He has been compared to polio, as the biggest threat to the young! Sings of killing his father! He preaches hatred and glorifies violence!

Yet the public can't get enough of him!

Celebrity Scandals

Eminem was arraigned on 7 June 2000 on two felony weapons charges stemming from the disturbance outside a Detroit night-club. The Grammy winning Eminem is accused of pulling a gun and fighting with a man after he spotted him kissing his then-wife, Kimberly Mathers.

Witnesses told prosecutors that Eminem, then 27, pointed the gun at the other man and shouted, "I'm going to kill you." The gun was unloaded. Eminem applied for a gun-carrying permit but failed to attend a required safety course.

In April 2001, the Grammy-winning rapper was given two years' probation in a plea bargain for carrying a concealed weapon. The great white rapper faced further weapons charges in court in June 2001 when the rapper was sentenced to a further year of probation (to run concurrently with the first probation order imposed) on weapons charges stemming from an argument in June 2000 with an associate of rivals Insane Clown Posse.

In April 2002, the controversial rapper agreed to pay John Guerra $100,000 (£69,574), less legal costs, according to the Macomb Daily newspaper. This was in connection to one of the gun charges. (His mother unsuccessfully tried to sue for $10m (£6.9m) for lyrics in the song *My Name Is*, which she said were defamatory.)

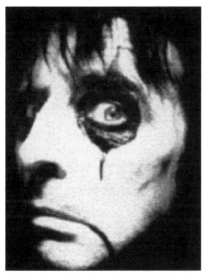

If Eminem shocked then, certainly, he was only following others.

On a good day, Alice Cooper would have eaten Eminem for breakfast and on a bad day he might have just bitten his head off! Downing two pints of whisky a day and drinking with the legendary Keith Moon and Doors singer Jim Morrison meant he didn't have to worry about splashes of blood because he was often up to his neck in gallons of the stuff. Long before rapper Eminem used a stage prop electric chair Alice Cooper was leading the way.

Black Sabbath front man Ozzy Osbourne would bite the head off a bat at press conferences and from then on his fans would throw dead animals on stage. One night Ozzy bit into something that was thrown at him, it was a live bat and he ended up having to have a series of painful anti-rabies injections! The beard of drummer, Bill Ward, was often set alight on stage by Ozzy and one night when on tour he was arrested in San Antonio, Texas for pissing on the Alamo Fort – a symbol of American freedom.

Dubbed the most shocking band in history, the Sex Pistols. Bass guitarist Sid Vicious would often attack himself on stage …slashing himself with a knife or broken bottle!

Which takes us nicely on to…

Celebrity Scandals

Hugh Grant...suck on this, Divine!
("Expensive blow job mate.")

What a naughty, naughty boy, Hugh!

Tuesday, 27 June 1995 1:45 am Hugh Grant, 34, arrested in Hollywood and booked 'on suspicion of lewd conduct in a public place' after being caught having his knob end polished by a prostitute, Stella Marie Thompson, aka Divine Brown, 25, in a rented white BMW convertible! Fancy that, was the roof down? The act took place off Sunset Boulevard. A tearful Grant called his girlfriend of eight years, Estee Lauder model and actress, Elizabeth Hurley, 29, from jail, crying that the arrest was "all a mistake." (Is this what Hugh Grant might have said to Liz: "I was only having some polishing done, honest, Liz.") Grant released a statement apologising to his loved ones, calling his actions "completely insane." The big rumour that sweeps Hollywood is that the prostitute is a man in drag - which later turns out to be false, but imagine if it wasn't!

Grant flies home to Britain to face his partner, Elizabeth Hurley, Estee Lauder says Hurley will continue as their "face" in a multi-million dollar cosmetics campaign. British tabloids banner the story with headlines such as 'Hugh Blows It With Hooker,' 'You've Blown It, Hugh,' and 'Hugh Naughty Boy, Hugh!' The New York Post, in classic style, blares: 'Hugh Dirty Dog!' All feature the Grant mug shot, some in full colour.

Thursday, June 29th Grant and Divine Brown charged with lewd conduct in Los Angeles City Court. Grant could have faced up to a year in jail, while Brown, who is on probation, could have faced a stronger sentence.

Crime Through Time

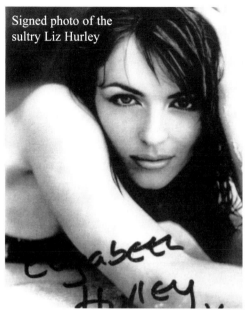

Signed photo of the sultry Liz Hurley

Elizabeth Hurley released a statement from Sudeley Castle, where she had been staying with a close friend, Lord Brocklehurst, saying, "I am very much alone." Grant, who boarded a British-bound airplane in LA went to ground.

Friday, June 30th
Grant returned to England and met with Hurley in their rented mansion near Bath. Dozens of reporters and photographers descend on the tiny village of West Littleton, and spot the couple having lunch in their back garden. Earlier, reporters noted that flowers had been delivered, as well as a double bed!!! Was reconciliation in the making!

British tabloids print photos of the glamorous Hurley next to photographs of Divine Brown in various stages of undress. Grant hired ex-OJ Simpson and Michael Jackson attorney Howard Weitzman to defend him. Friends blamed Grant's lapse on the exhaustion of promoting Nine Months, and especially dozens of interviews done on the day of the incident. Grant is quoted from an interview with US Magazine conducted before the arrest as saying that, even with fame, his life is empty. It is also revealed that he paid Brown $50 for the polishing job!

Divine Brown's exclusive story was bought by the News of the World newspaper in the UK for a reported $158,000 (£100,000). Elizabeth Hurley, heavily disguised with a blonde wig, was seen speeding away from their mansion in a Mercedes, followed by a car packed with luggage. Maybe she had found the double bed too hard! Speculation about the double bed was quelled when a store manager was quoted as saying that Hurley had ordered the bed hours after news of Grant's arrest, saying that she wanted it for the spare room.

Celebrity Scandals

Sunday, July 2nd The News of the World publishes its interview with Divine Brown, giving details of the encounter. Brown relates that Grant picked her up on Sunset Boulevard and handed her three crumpled $20 bills, saying, "I've always wanted to sleep with a black woman. That's my fantasy." (What a wonderful big pair of lips you have, Divine.)

Grant was in too much of a hurry, she said, to pay the extra $40 for a hotel room. Maybe he was a bit premature! After her arrest, Brown wanted to know "Who the hell is Hugh Grant?" Well now the whole world knows, great publicity and the rest they say is history. It seems such conduct can be used to help your career along…if done in the right way!

Nice lips, Divine!

Brown poses in a revealing Versace dress identical to one worn by Hurley, as well as like Julia Roberts in Pretty Woman. Coverage of the arrest knocks Prime Minister John Major's battle to retain leadership of the Conservative party off the front pages. Leonard Lauder releases a statement that the company's relationship with model Hurley remained unchanged.

A poll by on-line site 'Mr Showbiz' indicates that two out of five people are more likely to see the movie, Nine Months, that starred

Hugh Grant than they were before Grant's arrest…brilliant stuff. Has this man an agent working for him?

July 8th Video orders for Grant's films are up 30%, but sadly on the following day, Sunday, July 9th, the Sunday Mirror of London reports that Grant and Hurley are to split after eight years together. Industry experts doubted that the arrest would hurt his career.

Anything Divine can do I can do better!

Grant stutters and twitches when asked on a USA TV show what he was thinking of, but answers wittily, announcing, "I'm not one to go around blowing my own horn," as the crowd goes wild. One Hollywood insider speculates that Grant's most elusive audience, young adult males, are now more likely to want to see his film than before.

Hugh, how could you do this to such a gorgeous woman, you must be bonkers letting your dick rule your brain!

Tuesday, July 11th Grant pleads "no contest" to a charge of having sex with a Hollywood prostitute and is fined $1180 (£800), given two years probation, and ordered to submit to an AIDS test. Later, Grant appears at the Nine Months premiere in Los Angeles, with Elizabeth Hurley on his arm. Nine Months writer/director Chris Columbus, is quoted as saying, "I think America re-fell in love with Hugh Grant last night." He also adds that Grant's arrest and honesty about the incident would probably boost the film's fortunes at the box-office.

After Liz dumped Hugh Grant she seemed to be getting her own back on him when she's spotted by the News of the World in what looks to be a compromising position with her then-new boyfriend, Steve Bing, who is the father of their love child.

Friday, July 14th On NBC's Today Show, Grant denies that he frequents topless bars and appeals to the press to quit "hounding me." Grant takes another swipe at the British press later on Live with Regis and Kathy Lee, saying that they "are not the kindest in the world." About Hurley, he adds, "I don't particularly think I deserve to be forgiven, but she's really working at it."

July 20th In a taped deposition, actor Charlie Sheen, (star of Platoon and Wall Street), jumps in on the act saying that he hired prostitutes employed by Heidi Fleiss, the alleged Hollywood Madam, approximately 20 times between 1991 and 1993 and paid them at least $20,000 per encounter, (was he being mugged off, because Hugh Grant paid nowhere near that for his evening of relaxation) in cash and cheques. His spokesman reads a statement apologising to his family, friends, and his future wife for "any embarrassment these incidents may have caused." This looks like a play for publicity but the press weren't having any of it, if he wanted publicity then he was sure as hell gonna have to pay for it.

There's no such thing as bad publicity

Divine Brown – Crime pays!
And the hours are good!

July 31st A Brazilian lingerie company announces that it has signed Divine Brown to do an advertisement. Brown will warn women of the risks ignoring their husbands' sexual fantasies and be paid $30,000.

August 7th Divine Brown films a commercial for soft-rock radio station KXEZ-FM, Easy 100.3. The commercial features a montage of the Grant headlines, then cuts to Brown, who says, "I began to realise that he had the radio tuned to easy 100.3."

Here's Gerrrrrrrrrrrrri...the shoplifter

The gorgeous Geri Halliwell, ex-Spice Girl (signed photo).

Fact File

In Spain, during a news conference she called one of the journalists a queer, because he booed her. She left the group the Spice Girls when she was allegedly challenged by Melanie Brown (Scary Spice) to be front woman.

She smokes, has a pierced belly button and has a black panther tattooed on her lower back. At 17 she was convicted of theft, shoplifting and handling stolen goods. She was ranked in People Magazine's 25 Most Intriguing People (1998). She ranked #8 in 1997, #58 in 1998, #43 in 2000 and #28 in 2001 in FHM's 100 Sexiest Women. She was a topless model. She was the first Spice Girl to hit #1 with a solo song (Lift Me Up) in Britain.

Party political pop star Geri Halliwell was not eligible to vote at the general election. The former Spice Girl had urged everyone to "use their vote" on 7th June 2001, was not actually able to use her own, as her name did not appear on the electoral register, which is against the law with a fine of £1,000!! Geri appeared on a party political broadcast for the Labour party. A spokesman for the singer said that she was not on the Electoral Register for "security reasons", as it could make it easier for stalkers to find her home address...yes. But will she receive her £1,000 fine?

Crime Through Time

Geri makes a clean breast of things

Related website: www.dailysport.net

Confession Time

Geri's confession that she has a criminal record may end her American dream! Geri Halliwell has revealed her secret criminal record, as a warning to the deprived children she is helping through Comic Relief. The blonde diva and UN goodwill ambassador was convicted for shoplifting and handling stolen goods when she was just 17.

Geri confessed: "It's not something to be proud of, but if talking about it prevents one kid from making the same mistakes then it's got to be worth it." Geri may not have realised what she has got herself in to, as she now may be facing a lifetime ban from entering America, because of their strict rules on entering the country.

Officials at the American Embassy in London indicated yesterday that they want to interview Geri to decide whether her convictions for shoplifting, theft and handling stolen goods mean she should be banned. A ban would come as a tremendous blow to Geri, who loves the States and spends much of her time there. Geri's American dream has also encompassed trips to New York as a British "ambassador" for the United Nations' Population Fund.

"Let he who is without sin, cast the first stone."
Jesus of Nazareth

"Rob from the rich to give to the poor."
Robin of Sherwood

316

Crime Through Time

They'll do anything for publicity

The pain of fame!!

Celebrity Scandals

Bruno...went the distance

Bruno...Divorce is price of unreasonable behaviour.

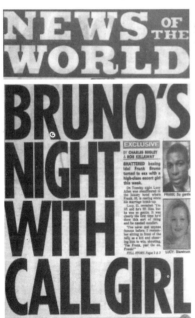

One of Britain's greatest boxing heroes Frank Bruno found comfort in the arms of a common prostitute after facing the cold stark reality of life without his wife, Laura. Frank, licking his wounds from the final round after the bust up with his wife picked from three prostitutes who were lined up as contenders for some all night ring work.

Bruno chose Lucy Allen, a busty 21-year-old blonde who looked likely to go the distance.It was a close call and went to a judges' decision, but first cumer Bruno was satisfied with the outcome. For £150 Bruno got to make whoopi with Lucy to the background sounds of Gabrielle playing on a CD player.

Gillian Taylforth - You naughty, naughty woman
Surely what she was doing was only normal!!

GILLIAN TAYLFORTH
as Kathy Mitchell

> There is the chance of great riches if a **High Court**
> jury finds in favour of a libelled party.

The Sun newspaper ran a story that was to eventually ruin the reputation of Miss Taylforth, as well as costing her in excess of £500,000. The implication of the story was that Miss Taylforth was performing oral sex on her lover, Geoff Knights, when a police officer, per chance, came upon the vehicle parked in a slip-road off of the A1, at Borehamwood, Herts. The Sun quoted police as saying Knights had been cautioned for an indecent act. The story from Miss Taylforth was simply that she had been leaning over to rub Mr Knights' stomach because he had drunk too much champagne at Royal Ascot and was feeling rather queasy.

Should Miss Taylforth prove to the jury beyond reasonable doubt that she was telling the truth then she stood to gain a big payout and all legal tabs would have to be picked up by The Sun. But a loss could prove catastrophic - yet it was a risk she was willing to take in order to clear her "good name." The trial went on for 11 days and provided further tabloid drama for Britain.

Witnesses, explanations and a final, dramatic 11th hour video produced on behalf of The Sun providing evidence that Miss Taylforth had used a wine bottle to imitate oral sex would finally clinch the case against her. The case was the talking point of

Celebrity Scandals

Britain. The cost to Miss Taylforth was not only financial — it also raked over a story that most people in the country, save those who read The Sun, had never heard of and gave it to an audience of tens of millions.

January 1994 - Representing The Sun was the late George Carman. QC - a man with a rapier sharp mind and an even sharper turn of phrase and he hardly ever lost a libel case.

Miss Taylforth was to find out for herself just how brutal George Carman could be as he chipped away for the truth.

Her evidence was that Knights had suffered a "pancreatic attack" after drinking the champagne and that she was relieving the pain by rubbing his stomach. "How could anyone think I would stop on the A1 to have oral sex?" She asked the court quizzically. "It was cheap and really made me feel sick to my stomach." Her QC, Michael Beloff, tried to suggest that the policeman, whose unhappy lot it was to tumble across the couple, was doing it for some kind of glory, of making the story up "and reveling in the limelight."

Police Constable Terry Talbot was a man whose evidence was firm, he told the court that he had approached the parked car and saw Taylforth's head "moving slowly up and down" over her lover's lap. He also said he saw Mr Knight's exposed manhood!

After being cross-examined time and time again he said, "If I stood here until Christmas I would not change anything I said or saw." PC Talbot said he should have arrested her and Knights instead of merely cautioning them.

Left, Miss Taylforth was seen to suck on a big German sausage. Seen here with Geoff Knights.

320

Crime Through Time

"I give very good head." The damning video evidence.

The trial suddenly changed in the favour of The Sun newspaper, dramatically, when a video was produced. Without the video it might have been that the newspaper had to make a massive payout for damages, as it is you could have heard a pin drop in the court as the tape was played. It destroyed Taylforth's carefully cultivated image of a woman wronged by both the police and a press report. Miss Taylforth could be seen simulating oral sex on a wine bottle! And also performing what is commonly known as 'sucking off' on a large German sausage and the words "I'd like to state, I give good head. I give very good head," could be heard above the party noise!

The video was made during a lunchtime party with some showbiz friends at a small theatre in north London. It would have remained a private video forever had Gillian Taylforth not chosen to take the newspaper to court. The jury found in favour of The Sun and Miss Taylforth had to be taken to hospital in shock at the prospect of having to pay a legal bill of £1/2m.

Celebrity Scandals

The Bobbitt Case

Every man's nightmare…!

The tatty sausage was a human penis, lying in a puddle of water, its last resting place after being chopped off!

Lorena Bobbitt decided to cut off her husband's penis in a mad rage. Policemen found John Wayne Bobbitt's penis in a puddle where Lorena had thrown it. It was packed in ice and reattached after a marathon nine-hour operation.

It was only during her trial in February 1994 — three months after a jury had cleared him of rape that the facts emerged about what had happened that night. Lorena remembered going to the kitchen to get a glass of water, looking at the knife, grabbing it in her hand and marching back to (the sleeping figure of her husband). She lifted the sheets and with one stroke, his manhood was severed…. ouch!

Bobbitt, 26, was the first witness on the stand at the trial of his wife. The prosecutor was told that he had downed five beers and two cocktails in a pub-crawl on the night of the attack. He had had the night off work as a bouncer and had decided to hit the bars of his hometown in Manassas. Bobbitt claimed that he went to bed naked and then fell asleep immediately, only to be woken up by his wife wearing sexy Victoria's Secret silk lingerie.

"I remember responding, caressing her," he said. "But part of me was still asleep, part was not. I don't think I got an erection.

Crime Through Time

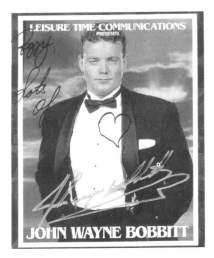

JOHN WAYNE BOBBITT

" I was too exhausted. Then I remember rolling on top of her. But I was really too exhausted to perform. I don't really remember anything else happening. At that point I opened my eyes. She was checking to see if I was able to perform for her. I must have fallen asleep again. Then I felt a couple of jerks on my penis. I felt a lot of pain and thought she had pulled it off. I shot up, real quick, I was bloody."

Surgeons said, "He should regain use of it for his sex life, although it was quite badly damaged."

Lorena's testimony at her trial certainly had a profound effect outside the courtroom on those jurors who had acquitted her husband of rape in November, four of them said they would convict him in a shot if they were trying him now.

Testimony from Lorena and his friends about his brutal behaviour convinced them, as it did much of America that Bobbitt got his just desserts.

As rough as her justice was on him, the jury was finally with her at the end of her two-week trial with a verdict that essentially judged her "mad not bad." They found that Lorena acted on an "irresistible impulse" in a moment of temporary insanity and that, therefore, she was not guilty of maliciously wounding her husband. But she was led away to a mental hospital for a 45-day stay where she underwent tests to gauge when she should be returned to society. In the end she stayed less than 45 days and is now free, pursuing the American dream.

Lorena Bobbitt

Celebrity Scandals

Michael Jackson

THE PRESS DUBBED HIM A HOMOSEXUAL CHILD MOLESTER. JACKSON RETALIATED BY SAYING PEOPLE WERE JEALOUS OF HIS RECORD SALES BEATING ELVIS'.

Signed photo of Michael Jackson - hundreds of original signed photos like these can be seen in the museum.

"I made a terrible mistake ..." Jackson on holding his child dangerously over a balcony in Berlin. Not an act for caring parents to imitate.

Until 1992, his refusal to undergo probing interviews had allowed the media to portray him as a fantasy figure, a hypochondriac who lived a twilight existence cut off from the rest of humanity. He attempted to dispel this image, and succeeded to a degree, with a carefully rehearsed interview with US chat show host Oprah Winfrey in 1992. The televised programme was shown all over the world, during which viewers saw his personal funfair in the back garden, and watched as Jackson spoke of his domineering father.

However, the unthinkable happened in 1993, just as Jackson's clean-cut image was at its peak. Allegations of sexual abuse were made by one of Jackson's young friends and the media had a riotous time!

Police raided Jackson's home while he was on tour in the Far East and the artist, clearly disturbed, cancelled a number of performances due to dehydration. No charges were made, and things began to quieten down until November 1993, when Jackson left the USA and went into hiding. Additionally, he confessed to being addicted to painkillers and was seeking treatment. After this admission, Jackson's long-time sponsors Pepsi-Cola decided to pull out of their contract with the now damaged career of the once world's most popular superstar.

Controversial Rabbi Shmuley Botech – the best selling author of the Jewish handbook on sex – Kosher Sex, accompanied Michael Jackson to the Oxford Union debate for a talk he was giving on childcare.

Abused children, Wacko Jacko, the Kosher Sex rabbi and how the Oxford Union was taken for a ride.

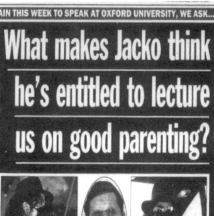

IN THIS WEEK TO SPEAK AT OXFORD UNIVERSITY, WE ASK...

What makes Jacko think he's entitled to lecture us on good parenting?

MY PALS ... Jacko, with son Prince, left, and a young friend, right. Above, Rabbi Boteach

WACKO

THE THREE AMIGOS: Below, Jacko and rabbi Boteach

JACKO, THE RABBI, BLOW JOBS AND DILDOS

SHOWBIZ EXCLUSIVE

325

Celebrity Scandals

The, so say, King of Pop is reigning supreme in yet another legal tangle. Michael Jackson's victory tour came in a California court in July 1999. He won a lawsuit filed by the father of the teen boy the singer allegedly molested years ago!

Jacko was officially deemed the winner, July 26th, when an arbitrator ruled in the pop star's favour. The lawsuit had its roots in the early 90s investigation by authorities in Santa Barbara and Los Angeles after Jackson was alleged to have molested a 13-year-old boy at the Neverland Ranch. Criminal charges were never filed, but the boy's father filed a civil suit against the 'Gloved One'.

In 1994, Jackson settled that suit - while the terms were confidential, the amount was estimated between $15 and $50 million!

But! Two years later the father (his name has not been released to protect the identity of his son) filed another lawsuit, after Jackson went on ABC's Prime Time Live and told Diane Sawyer the molestation charges were "lies, lies, lies, lies." The comment, the father said, violated the terms of the original lawsuit and damaged his family's reputation. The arbitrator disagreed and found for the entertainer.

Jacko is, of course, no stranger to courtrooms – in April 1998, he won a $2.7 million judgment against a freelance writer, Victor Gutierrez, who claimed he had seen footage of Jackson having sex with a boy. In March 1997, Jackson beat several ex-employees who claimed they were wrongfully fired from Neverland after cooperating with authorities in the child-molestation probe. (Two of the former workers were actually ordered to pay Jackson $60,000.)

The singer filed the lawsuit in 1995, seeking $100 million in damages. Jackson's complaint alleged that Gutierrez told Hard Copy reporter Diane Dimond that he'd seen a 27-minute video of the King of Pop in a compromising position with a boy. Dimond later repeated those comments on a Los Angeles TV station, the suit said. During the trial, Gutierrez said another boy's mother had shown him the tape. But he refused to produce any evidence of the X-rated footage. He invoked a California law that allows reporters to protect sources. In the end, even Gutierrez's attorney said, "Some of the jurors wanted to send a message to tabloids."

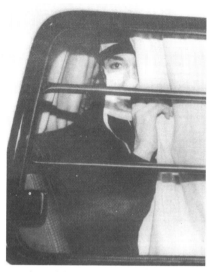

Gutierrez is the author of Michael Jackson Was My Lover, a book that claims to be the "secret diary" of the 13-year-old boy whose family once sued the singer for sexual molestation. Jackson denied any wrongdoing. He settled the suit out of court in the 1994 Jody Chandler case. A criminal investigation into the case ended without any charges being filed. Back to the lawsuit in which Jackson's former employees brought an action against him. According to their lawsuit, an administrative assistant, a maid and three bodyguards who formerly worked for the pop star claimed Jackson and six other employees harassed, threatened and fired them.

The plaintiffs say they were forced out of Neverland because they testified against Jackson before a grand jury investigating whether the singer molested a 13-year-old boy. The lawsuit

Lawyer Johnny Cochran announces settlement of the sex abuse claim.

alleged Jackson was so paranoid that he bugged his home to find out what employees were saying about the charges.

The singer's attorneys filed a countersuit, saying the five quit voluntarily and were not harassed. It also claimed two of the former workers - the maid and a bodyguard - stole sketches, personal notes, hats, toys and candy from the ranch, selling some items to tabloid newspapers.

The jury of 10 women and two men agreed with Jackson. They ruled that there was no evidence to support the allegations brought against Jackson or the six aides mentioned in the lawsuit by his former employees. Jurors also decided that items were stolen and awarded Jackson the 60 grand. "We're happy to be finally and fully vindicated," said Jackson's attorney, Johnny Cochran.

False Allegations of Child Sexual Abuse web site
http://www.falseabuse.com

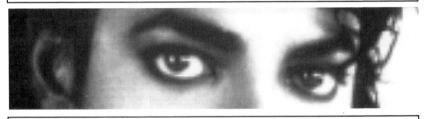

False Memory Syndrome Foundation (FMSF) web site
http://www.fmsfonline.org

The reclusive Jackson bought an enormous California ranch, which he dubbed Neverland, and filled the grounds with amusement park rides, inviting children to visit and even stay with him. His penchant for plastic surgery, mysteriously lightening skin tone, and often bizarre behaviour (such as wearing a surgical mask in public Howard Hughes-style) made him a frequent target for tabloids. Furthermore, Jackson's reluctance to grant interviews encouraged groundless gossip, such as stories that he slept in an oxygen chamber and tried to purchase the Elephant Man's skeleton. In 1985 he bought ATV Publishing, which owned the rights to many Beatles songs (as well as material from Elvis, Little Richard, and others), a profitable business decision but a move that ruined his friendship with ex-Beatle member, Paul McCartney.

The media were handed more bait when he married Lisa Marie Presley in May 1994, perhaps in an attempt to rebuild his image. The marriage collapsed nineteen months later, giving further rise to allegations that it was merely a set-up to improve his soiled image.

He did, however, enhance his reputation with History: Past, Present And Future - Book 1. One half of the double set chronicled his past hits, but there was the equivalent of a new album forming the second half. Lyrically, the new material was strong, and Jackson very cleverly gave himself a forum to respond to his critics. The downside of this return was a sickening display of self-aggrandizement at the UK's 1996 BRIT Awards. Controversy surrounded Jarvis Cocker (of Pulp), who invaded the stage in protest while Jackson, dressed in Messiah-white, was surrounded by, among others, worshipping children and a rabbi. Blood On The Dancefloor - History In The Mix was a collection of remixes and new material that spawned further hit singles. It appears that, despite the allegations of child abuse and the constant media attacks, particularly surrounding his unexpected second marriage to Debbie Rowe (which ended in October 1999) and the birth of two children, Jackson's fans are destined to remain loyal to the "King of Pop."

On visiting his controversial friend, Mr Al Fayed, of some 20 years standing, Jackson gave an impromptu interview to London radio station Liberty, a huge publicity coup for the station. (Owned by Mr Al-Fayed.) It has had a troubled history, and despite the tycoon's backing, it has only 156,000 listeners for its diet of 70s music and gossip.

Jacko then went on to visit Fulham; the west London football club owned by Mr Al-Fayed. He stayed to watch the Division Two side beat Wigan 2-0.

Michael Jackson faced worldwide humiliation in 1993, it would seem that certain acts of kindness were taken to mean something else and led to numerous court cases that did Jacko no favours, even though he won them all. They say mud sticks, but maybe Jacko can bounce back from it all and remain a pop icon.

Celebrity Scandals

Signed painted portrait of Al Fayed, the Egyptian born, and controversial business tycoon. A great man who is prepared to take on the establishment, signed original can be seen in the museum. The British government refused to give Al Fayed a British passport, but the establishment was willing to take his cash for questions!

Barrymore...what a gay day!

Signed photo of TV star, Michael Barrymore.

Is being gay a crime, is it deemed to be politically incorrect or correct in the society we live in today? Is the act of a man pushing his penis up another man's backside against what nature intended? Christianity looks upon homosexuals with distaste, Hitler outlawed them – would he be turning in his grave now, they say they call him 'Revolving Hitler' down in hell!

What about the gay couple (males) who adopted a baby and are bringing it up right now this minute as you read this? Is it in the public interest that gay men should be given political positions of power – gay power? Are we in danger of becoming a gay nation, where the straights are the minority? It would seem that just about every closet has a gay ready to pop out and reveal him or herself, look at the winner of Britain's TV 'Pop Idol' show, 'Will', the winner of Pop Idol, came straight out with it and admitted he was gay...but only after winning! Would it have made a difference to the voting if he advised the population of this, say, a few weeks before the final show to decide on a winner? Would all the women desiring his body have made such efforts to lift the telephone and vote for him so many times, maybe not?

Celebrity Scandals

"I WILL"   ## "I WILL NOT"

"If only I was a royal butler, all this could be taken care of."

"When torn between two evils I take the one I haven't tried before."
Mae West

Crime Through Time

The swimming pool where Stuart Lubbock drowned, after having sex with a number of men.

The victim, Stuart Lubbock

Mad or sad, is that Michael Barrymore? In March 2001, the part naked body of Stuart Lubbock, 31, was found floating face down in the swimming pool of Barrymore's luxury home. Before Lubbock drowned he was party to some rough gay sex, which had caused some internal damage to his anus. There was reference to the date rape drug Rohypnol, which is commonly used among gay men. Police suspect Mr Lubbock of having purchased some.

A late night party developed after Barrymore and his gay lover, John Kenney, claimed that after Mr Lubbock was discovered in the pool he ran off with two other men into the nearby village. Kenney called his lover, Barrymore, a coward for running off.

> ## "I freaked. I'm sorry. I ran."
> **Michael Barrymore**

Barrymore faced the next few weeks wondering what charges, if any, would be served to him, as it turns out the death was put down to nothing more than a mad night of sex and drugs. Barrymore now tries to rebuild his career as a TV host, but he will have to live with this moment of madness for the rest of his life.

Behind every clown's smile there is sadness and in this case it is true. What sort of self-destruct mechanism is brought to life when TV stars are unleashed form their daily grind at the studio, only Barrymore can answer that one!

Puff Daddy

G
U
N

R
A
P

Rapper Puff Daddy, the millionaire performer, pulled a gun out and opened fire in a crowded nightclub after a rival 'dissed' him by throwing money in his face, a court heard. Puff, who was with his girlfriend, Jennifer Lopez, was said to have fired a single shot into the ceiling of a New York rap venue!

Puff, real name Sean Combs, was then said to have offered his driver £30,000 to say he owned a handgun found by police in their car!

After a lengthy trial Sean "Puffy" Combs was found not guilty on all five charges of gun possession and bribery. The singer and music producer had been charged with possession of a weapon in connection with a 1999 shooting at a New York club, in which three people were injured. He had also been charged with trying to bribe his driver to take the blame.

When the verdict came in there was brief applause and cheers in the packed Manhattan courtroom, before the judge silenced the public.

However, Mr Combs' co-defendant and associate Jamal Barrow, 21, was found guilty of first-degree assault and reckless endangerment, charges that carry a maximum sentence of 25 years in prison. He was found not guilty on charges of attempted murder for the injuries suffered by the three club patrons, one of whom was severely wounded in the face.

A third defendant, Mr Combs' bodyguard Anthony Jones, 34, was cleared on all the charges he faced. Mr Combs' then girlfriend, Jennifer Lopez, was initially arrested, but never charged.

The jury had spent three days deliberating, following a six-week trial. The court heard evidence from nearly 60 witnesses, including Mr Combs himself, who spent a day giving testimony. In court, Mr Combs said that he never carried a weapon on the night of the shooting - instead, he believed he was the target.

Although he has been cleared in this case, he may now face other lawsuits from parties seeking more than $1bn in damages over the incident.

Gun Rapping Mad

And one month after Puff Daddy was acquitted, American rapper Jay-Z has also been arrested for illegal gun possession in Manhattan, New York. The Grammy-award winning singer - real name Shaun Carter - was arrested with three other men when a loaded handgun was allegedly found in their car. Sounds like a re-run of the Puff Daddy scenario!

Undercover police officers saw an armed man climbing into a car outside the club Exit in New York in the early hours of the morning. Police then stopped the car close to the club and found a gun.

Four men were charged with third-degree criminal possession of a weapon - Hamzah Hewitt, Romero Chambers, and Tyran Smith were arrested along with the singer.

Celebrity Scandals

"My daughter was dating Frankenstein!"

Nancy Spungeon with Sid Vicious

Nancy Spungeon, the murdered girlfriend of the notorious punk rocker Sid Vicious, was as addicted to him as he was to drugs.

Nancy was the wild child of a well respected and wealthy Jewish family – her father was a solicitor and her mother very committed to the Jewish faith and church – in Philadelphia, America.

Responding to a report of a domestic dispute, police entered the hotel room where Nancy and Sid were staying and found Spungen, clad in blood-soaked bra and panties, crumpled under the bathroom sink, dead of a single, deep stab wound to her abdomen. Sid, in a drugged haze, as we know he was charged with her murder and released on $50,000 bail. In several telephone calls to Deborah Spungeon, Nancy's mother, after his arrest, Sid "never said he was sorry," she recalls, "He never said anything about it happening at all." Ten days later, Sid attempted suicide, slashing the full length of his forearm with a knife and reportedly screaming, "I want to be with my Nancy! I want to be left alone!"

After Nancy's death, Sid's mother, Beverley, flew to Manhattan to be with her son who, despite a stint in rehab, was still nursing his drug habit. On 1st February 1979, fearful that he would be arrested in a drug buy on the street, she bought a supply of heroin for him, and was with him in the Greenwich Village apartment of a friend that night while he injected it. Afterwards, "I swear to God he appeared to have a pink aura around his whole body," she remembers. The next morning, when she brought him a cup of tea, "he was lying there quite peacefully. I shook him until I realised he was very cold and very dead." Sid had got his wish!

Some say that Sid had taken his life after being gang raped whilst held on remand in prison before being granted bail, this whole experience had taken its toll on him and the only solace he could get was to be with his beloved Nancy!

There are claims that the ashes of Sid Vicious were dropped accidentally on the runway at Heathrow Airport, but in an equally bizarre, but true story, late one night, a few days after Sid's death, Beverley climbed the wall to a Jewish graveyard outside Philadelphia – this being done in a commando style raid – as this type of desecration would not have been allowed or accepted by the Jewish community. And, against the wishes of the Spungeon family, scattered her son's ashes in the snow over Nancy's grave.

Although authorities never officially determined whether Sid's death was by accident or design, Anne Beverley has little doubt. As evidence, she offers the worn piece of paper on which Sid scrawled a poem, simply titled 'Nancy', to his departed love: 'You were my little baby girl/And I knew all your fears/Such joy to hold you in my arms/And kiss away your tears/But now you're gone/There's only pain/And nothing I can do/And I don't want to live this life/If I can't live for you.' Part of the poem was used as the title for a book written by Nancy's mother, Deborah Spungeon, titled 'And I don't want to live this life'. That the book's title is taken from a poem Sid wrote for Nancy suggests Deborah's uneasy truce.

Deborah, "My daughter was dating Frankenstein." Deborah's treatment of Nancy's death is particularly troubling as she describes the insensitivity of public officials, the press and the public. There is also Sid's communications with Deborah following Nancy's death - not the Sid seen in the media. Sid called Deborah once and sent her two notes, always expressing his devastation at Nancy's death as well as his need for Deborah's understanding and support.

Inxs

Autoeroticfantasy death theory.

"You keep me hanging on."

The entertainment world was in mourning over the tragic death of rock superstar Michael Hutchence who at the height of his powers had inflamed a generation with the passion of his music.

But the flamboyant front man for the Australian rock band INXS thought his magic was fading and friends believed he had become fearful of the future as he tried unsuccessfully to revive it. He hated the paparazzi that constantly hounded him, thought London had become a difficult place to live in and, as he told his last interviewer, believed that "people were putting the boot in left, right and centre." He even felt let down that his home country had failed to give his band the recognition he thought it deserved, although Prime Minister John Howard described him as one of Australia's most gifted and talented performers. Hutchence revealed some of his anxieties to his parents as he dined with them and at one stage his father, Kell Hutchence, was worried enough to ask if he was all right and he replied: "Dad, I'm fine." But a few hours later the 37-year-old wild man of rock had followed a well-trodden path to self-destruction behind a line-up of rock legends that included Kurt Cobain, Jimi Hendrix, Jim Morrison, Janis Joplin and Brian Jones.

He was found, hanged from a leather belt attached to a door of a suite, in an exclusive harbour side hotel.

Hutchence had only just returned to Australia for a 20th-anniversary tour and his devastated band members broke down when they learnt he had hanged himself. Empty alcohol bottles were found in the suite and prescription pills on the floor, but no note or illegal drugs were discovered.

At the peak of its success the album 'Kick' sold more than five million copies, staying in the British charts for more than 107 weeks, and INXS was able to fill London's 80,000-seat Wembley stadium for a single concert.

'Kick' proved the musical peak and would not be repeated, the focus of media attention turned to his private life, his romances with glamorous women such as 'Neighbours' star Kylie Minogue, model Helena Christensen and, finally, Bob Geldof's ex-wife Paula Yates.

Ms Yates and the girls loved Sydney and toyed with the idea of returning to live in the place he described as "the greatest city in the world for the 21st century."

Ms Yates' lawyer denied press allegations in the media that the singer died while engaging in sado-masochistic sex. "I condemn the scurrilous and grossly irresponsible speculation and fiction trailed as fact in some tabloids that 'kinky sex' led to Michael's tragic death," Mr Anthony Burton said. Police also dismissed London tabloid press speculation that he died while engaging in a sex bondage game.

All those close to the singer report that he had been in high spirits in the days prior to his suicide, although he had been linked with a notorious reputation of cocaine and opium use. He was also planning to marry his girlfriend, Paula Yates, the mother of his 18-month-old daughter, Tiger Lily.

The great problem with people of a normal sexual persuasion is that they cannot empathise with those that need to experience another type of high other than ordinary sex. For instance, we might need our regular fix of coffee for our mid-morning refresher, but would never think of taking amphetamine sulphate (speed) to perk us up! So it is with the libido (sexual appetite), we all have a different need and in the case of Michael Hutchence only he would know what would fix his sexual appetite.

The Full Report Of The Coroner – Michael Hutchence

Full transcript

The following is a complete transcript of the Coroners Report handed down into the death of Michael Hutchence by NSW Coroner, Derek Hand.

INQUEST INTO THE DEATH OF MICHAEL KELLAND HUTCHENCE

I have received a completed police brief into the death of Michael Kelland Hutchence on 22nd November 1997, at Ritz Carlton Hotel, Double Bay. I am satisfied that the cause of death was "hanging." I am also satisfied that there was no other person involved in causing the death.

The question of whether the death was a suicide or not has to be considered. The deceased was found at 11:50am naked, behind the door to his room. He had, apparently, hanged himself with his own belt and the buckle broke away and his body was found kneeling on the floor and facing the door. It has been suggested that the death resulted from an act of autoeroticism. However, there is no forensic or other evidence to substantiate this suggestion. I therefore, discount that manner of death.

With regard to the question of suicide I have to be satisfied on a strong balance of probabilities before I am able to come to such a conclusion. There is a presumption against suicide. Having considered the extensive brief I am satisfied that the standard required to conclude that this death was a suicide has been reached for the following reasons:

(1) Michelle Bennett, a former de-facto of the deceased, received two telephone calls from him on the morning of the 22nd November. The first

was on an answering machine and Mr Hutchence sounded "drunk". During the second call at 9:54am the deceased commenced to cry and according to Ms Bennett sounded "very upset". She was concerned about his demeanour and for his welfare and told him she would come immediately. However, when she arrived at the hotel she was not able to rouse him neither by knocking loudly on his door nor by ringing him. She wrote a note and left it at reception. Ms Bennett stated that Mr Hutchence never expressed previous inclinations regarding suicide.

(2) The deceased's father, Kelland Hutchence, dined with him the previous night. The deceased was in good spirits, however appeared very worried in regard to the outcome of a custody suit in London. Mr Hutchence could offer no explanation as to why his son would take his own life.

(3) Ms Kym Wilson and Mr Andrew Rayment were with the deceased in his hotel room from sometime after 11pm and left about 5am. According

to Ms Wilson the deceased appeared to want both of them to remain with him to offer support if the result of his custody hearing was unfavourable. His mood was described as "elevated, however pensive when discussing court proceedings." All three persons consumed alcohol, including vodka, beer and champagne together with cocktails during this time.

(4) Whilst Ms Wilson and Mr Rayment were in the room (when) Ms Martha Troup, the deceased's personal manager, rang from New York. Then later at 9:38am she received, via voice-mail, a call from Michael Hutchence in which he said: "Marth, Michael here. I fucking had enough." She rang the hotel immediately and the telephone rang out. A further call was received at 9:50am on Ms Troup's telephone answering machine. The deceased sounded as if he was affected by something and was slow and deep. This call worried Ms Troup and (she) spoke to John Martin the tour manager for INXS about her concerns. Mr Martin refers to a note received from

the deceased stating that he was "not going to rehearsals today." The rehearsal was to be the last one prior to the start of the tour and was quite important.

(5) Ms Paula Yates provided a statement. She provided background to the custody dispute between her and Sir Robert Geldof. She stated that she rang the deceased at some time prior to 5:38am on the 22nd November and he told her he was going to beg Geldof to let the children come out to Australia. She had told the deceased that the custody matter had not been finalised and was adjourned until the 17th December and she would not be bringing the children out. Ms Yates stated that the deceased sounded "desperate" during the conversation.

(6) Sir Robert Geldof received two telephone calls from the deceased, the first at about 6:30pm London time on (the) evening of 21st November. It was of a short duration and Geldof asked the deceased to call back. Geldof received the second call about 5:30am on 22nd November,

Sydney time. This call was of some length. Geldof refers to the deceased's demeanour as being "hectoring and abusive and threatening" in nature. He refers to the deceased as "begging" to allow him to let the children come to Australia. He did not sound depressed during the conversation. A friend of both Geldof and Paula Yates, Ms Belinda Brewin, confirms the substance of the conversation between the two. A statement obtained from a Gail Coward, the occupant of the room directly next to the deceased's room, alludes to her hearing a loud male voice and expletives emitting from the deceased's room about 5am that morning. I am satisfied that she was hearing the telephone conversation between the deceased and Geldof.

(7) A statement obtained from the mother of the deceased, Mrs Patricia Glassop, confirms her opinion that the deceased was in a depressed state.

(8) In December 1995, Michael Hutchence was first prescribed Prozac by Dr J Borham, a London medical

practitioner, to treat a pre-existing depressive problem. He was last so prescribed on 1st November, 1997. A London psychiatrist, Mr Mark Collins, was consulted by the deceased on 17th October, 1997 in regard to a minor depression being experienced by him. According to the doctor there was no hint of suicidal thinking by the deceased.

(9) An analysis report of the deceased's blood indicates the presence of alcohol, cocaine, Prozac and other prescription drugs. On consideration of the entirety of the evidence gathered I am satisfied that the deceased was in a severe depressed state on the morning of the 22nd November, 1997, due to a number of factors, including the relationship with Paula Yates and the pressure of the on-going dispute with Sir Robert Geldof,

combined with the effects of the substances that he had ingested at that time. As indicated I am satisfied that the deceased intended and did take his own life. I am also satisfied that this death is one in which nothing will be gained by holding a formal Inquest. The identity of the deceased, the date and place of death and the manner and cause of death are clearly set out and the time and expense of holding an Inquest is not warranted and therefore such will be dispensed with. May I offer to the family of Michael Hutchence my sincere condolences on their sad loss.

INQUEST DISPENSED WITH.

(D.W. HAND) NSW STATE CORONER Glebe.

6th February 1998

The report could be taken to mean that this was a straightforward case of suicide, but given the high mood Hutchence was in and the way the answer phone messages are interpreted then it does, on the surface, seem like a straightforward suicide. Was Hutchence referring to the battle for the children when he left these messages, maybe so? His conversation with Mr Geldof was of such a magnitude to show he had fight left in him, let's look at an alternative to suicide.

Celebrity Scandals

Autoerotic Asphyxiation Syndrome

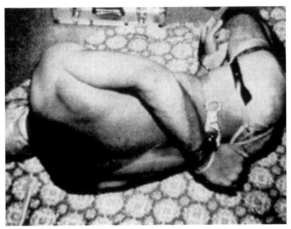

Fatal asphyxiation during an autoerotic event.

Survivors of those who die by auto-erotic asphyxiation are puzzled and troubled by what must seem to them bizarre behavior on the part of individuals whom they believed to be free of abnormal sexual behaviour. The surviving family members and friends are left struggling with the sudden tragedy of death, along with having to cope with the bizarre, embarrassing practice of autoerotic asphyxiation. Families are left with lingering questions of; why did he do this? Who taught him this? Why didn't he get help? The grim task of answering these enigmatic questions is usually left to law enforcement investigators or medical professionals who, most likely, have only limited explanation for the autoerotic practice. There are psychoanalytic and physiological theories that can explain some of the reasons for the practice; however, families are still left with unanswered questions, along with feelings of guilt and embarrassment. Of the various types of abnormal sexual behaviour, or "paraphilias" as defined by medicine, probably the most bizarre and dangerous is autoerotic asphyxiation, also known as sexual hanging. Autoerotic asphyxia is the practice of inducing cerebral anoxia, usually by means of self-applied ligatures or suffocating devices, while the individual masturbates to orgasm. The most common practitioners of this paraphilia are adolescent and young adult males. Despite its long documented history, this bizarre practice is still an enigma for most in society, including medical and law enforcement personnel. Tragically, the asphyxiator's sexual practice is usually first discovered when he dies from accidental hanging!

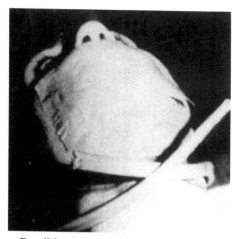

Possible sexual/masochistic hanging.

Examples of Autoerotic Fatalities

Autoerotic Fatalities (AEFs) are unintentional deaths caused by solo sexual gratification activities. AEFs focuses on noose-based autoerotic asphyxiation. However, many deaths are actually due to complications arising from physical restraint (self-bondage). Any person who engages in solo physical restraint should be fully aware of the risks involved. If a person decides to engage in self-bondage in spite of the risks, they should prepare a current legal will, in case of accidental death!

In 1931 a 37-year-old male shop assistant was found dead in his bed. Lying under the covers, gagged with handkerchiefs, head tightly wrapped in a towel. Legs tied with towels, hands tied up behind his back. He was clutching a nail scissor in his left hand to free himself, but the tight laces around the wrists cut up the arteries, and he bled to death. Source: Schackwitz

This time a 'Compression Victim' – a male winched himself up off the ground by a rope wrapped around his abdomen. High blood alcohol content probably contributed to his inability to release the winch. Pressure continued unabated on his abdomen until breathing became impossible. Sources: R.R. Hazelwood, et al., Autoerotic Fatalities, Lexington Books, 1983, Lexington, MA. / J Forensic Sci 1984 Apr; 29 (2) 679-84. "An unusual autoerotic death asphyxia with an abdominal ligature." Thibault R, Spencer JD, Bishop JW, Hibler NS.

Compression/asphyxiation – a Yale graduate constructed an airtight vinyl bag that he zipped himself into. He bound his hands behind his back with a short length of chain. Penis was wrapped with a saran-wrap/ rubber-band condom, found dead of asphyxiation.

Asphyxiation Victim - enclosed his body into plastic with an airway out of his 'cocoon' in the form of a snorkel tube. He was engaged in masturbation when he apparently lost his mouthpiece or airway. He attempted to use a knife to cut himself out, but did not succeed in time. Source: Am J Forensic Med Pathol 1985 Jun;6(2)151-2. "Wrapped to death. Unusual autoerotic death." Minyard F.

Choked on gag – a 30-year-old female found dead in her locked apartment. Nude and lying supine on a blanket on the bedroom floor. A pillow beneath her buttocks elevated them. (Many women use pillows as masturbation tools.) Legs were slightly spread, arms by her sides. Blouse lodged in her mouth and covered her face. Next to body was a dental plate belonging to the victim. Near left foot: empty beer can, an ashtray, and a drinking glass. Neither the body nor the scene exhibited signs of a struggle. Victim's clothes and purse containing her keys were on bed. Vibrator and leather bondage materials were found in her closet. Door was locked with a spring bolt. The autopsy report indicated that she had choked to death. Source: Hazelwood, Burgess, and Dietz

Compression/asphyxiation – a 40-year-old male, 1973, airplane pilot drove his Volkswagen to a secluded, roughly circular, flat clearing, he removed his clothes and put on a self-manufactured harness, which connected him via a ten-foot length of chain to the car's rear bumper. He tied a belt to the steering wheel and strapped it down so that the wheel was completely counter-clockwise. He started the engine and placed it in first gear, so that the car circled the clearing slowly with him being led walking behind. He had performed this ritual previously. On this final occasion, however, when he approached the car to end the scene, the chain began winding around the left rear axle; he was pulled in toward the left wheel area, and died of compression against the car. Source: J.C. Rupp, "The Love Bug," Journal of Forensic Sciences, vol. 18, 1973. pp. 259-262.

DON'T TRY THIS AT HOME!!

Compression/asphyxiation – the victim was in a dustbin (garbage can). He'd intended to use a roll of chicken wire as an escape mechanism. The mechanism failed and the man died of compression. (In chest compression, the movement of the ribcage is restricted or the diaphragm movement is cut off.) Source: R.R. Hazelwood, et al., Autoerotic Fatalities, Lexington Books, 1983, Lexington, MA.

Compression/asphyxiation – a 62-year-old male was found dead in his barn, pinned under the hydraulic front scoop of a John Deere tractor. A neighbour found him lying prone on the ground with the scoop of the tractor on his back. The tractor engine was no longer running, but the ignition was still in the 'on' position. Victim nude except for a pair of red women's shoes with eight-inch heels and knee-high nylons. Duct tape was wrapped around ankles. Ankles were bound to a four-foot-long segment of pipe such that legs were spread. A yoke was attached to the centre of the pipe, which was attached to the front loader bucket by a chain. Two ropes led from the victim to the tractor's control lever for raising and tilting the bucket. Fully raising the hydraulic bucket would have caused complete suspension of his inverted body by the ankles. He died when accidentally pinned to the ground under the shovel after intentionally suspending himself. Source: J Forensic Sci 1993 Mar; 38 (2) 359-64. "Autoerotic fatalities with power hydraulics." O'Halloran RL, Dietz PE. Ventura County Medical Examiner Office, CA, USA.

One Canadian researcher studied 117 males aged 10-56 who had died accidentally during autoerotic asphyxial activities.

Asphyxiation – male victim found in 1988 lying on side in semi-foetal position. Right wrist bound behind, in small of back. Left wrist handcuffed in front at crotch level. Legs bent up at knees. Ropes, straps, belts, rings combined for restraints. Undressed but wearing women's shoes. Source:Wetli Mittleman, Rau. Practical Forensic Pathology.

Scenarios and activities become more elaborate over time - more experience leads to greater danger of death, not less danger!

Victim, male, 23, died while suspended by leather wrist restraints from a hook in the ceiling. Was wearing a commercially produced 'discipline mask' and had a bit in his mouth. A length of rope was attached to each end of the bit and ran over his shoulders, going through an eyelet at the back of a specially designed belt he was wearing.

The pieces of rope ran to eyelets on both sides of his body and were connected to wooden dowels that extended the length of his legs. The ropes were attached to two plastic water bottles, one on each ankle. The bottles were filled with water and each weighed 7 pounds.

The victim's ankles had leather restraints about them. A clothes-pin was affixed to each of the victim's nipples. The victim's belt had a leather device that ran between his buttocks and was attached to the rear in front of his belt. This belt device included a dildo that was inserted in his anus and an aperture through which his penis protruded. His penis was encased in a piece of pantyhose and a toilet-paper cylinder. A small red ribbon was tied in a bow at the base

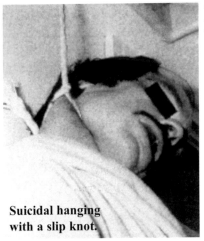

Suicidal hanging with a slip knot.

of his penis. Source: Hazelwood, Burgess, & Dietz.

Given the way Michael Hutchence died compared to the common consensus of opinion, autoeroticism, and given the examples used it is possible that Mr Hutchence was carrying out a means of private self-gratification to comfort himself over the battle for custody of Ms Yates' children.

---

500 to 1,000 autoerotic deaths occur annually in the United States.

Related web site

http://www.openmindmedia.com/self-bondage/

Crime Through Time

"We all have skeletons in the cupboard don't we??? Celebrities are no different!!!"
On a lighter note...do you recognise any of them, which ones are dead and which
are gay and who is straight? All original signed photos on display in the museum.
What have they been up to...visit the museum and see!!!

Which one is the Crime Through Time Security Guard?

Celebrity Scandals

Autographed Celebrity Nudes

Why are so many women prepared to strip off for the camera??? Not complaining...but let's face it...it does help in earning them a few bob or two??

Colour originals on display in the museum - bring your white stick. Here's just a brief insight on the great many on display!

Crime Through Time

Autographs

**The museum has a vast selection of celebrity related autographs on display
What's this lot been up to??? Visit the museum and find out!!**

Celebrity Scandals

Autographs

Real or fantasy crime is always a good earner, without crime would we be stuck in a dull world?

Thousands of genuine Autographs on display in the Museum.

Foreword to
Sporting Scandals
By
Jesse Owens

"Hitler's worst nightmare?? Do you remember this geezer??"

Jesse Owens
1913-1980

On the first day of school, my first-grade teacher asked me my name and I said, 'JC Owens'. And she said, 'Oh, Jesse,' and I've never considered changing it since.

People always ask me about the 1936 Olympics (when he won four gold medals and established three world records). But don't get me wrong - I'm glad they do it. If people forget the Olympics, they forget what Hitler did there and they forget me. When I came back to my native country, after all the stories about Hitler, I couldn't ride in the front of the bus. I had to go to the back door. I couldn't live where I wanted. I wasn't invited to shake hands with Hitler, but I wasn't invited to the White House to shake hands with the President, either!

Sporting Scandals

Hitler presents an award, 1936 Olympics.

The Olympics is the major league of amateur sports. It's the greatest success one can claim in the field and I consider myself very lucky to have achieved what I did.

My greatest accomplishment? That would have to be marrying my wife, Ruth. We met in junior high school and were married senior high. Since then, she's been more than just a wife - she's been a confidant and inspiration.

We have three daughters. One's a teacher, one's a social worker and one's a bank executive. The youngest was the Homecoming Queen at Ohio State in 1961. I'm very proud of that, she's the only black girl to be the queen. I wouldn't want to change anything in my life and there's nothing else I'd rather be doing now. Sure, I've had ups and downs, but God has been very good to me. If I had a pencil and eraser and could start over again, I couldn't improve anything. I feel I'm a lot richer than most people - not in money, but in many aspects of life. The people I work with and meet in my job and travels (over 150,000 miles a year) are great. They made my work enjoyable.

My junior-high track coach, Charles Riley, had the most influence on my life - everyone loved him and he loved everyone. He made a lot of things possible for a lot of kids.

Bart Starr, Gale Sayers, Mike Garrett and Bob Gibson - they all are symbols with which kids can identify. Even Cassius Clay is a symbol. I know Cassius, but I only know him by his devotion to his life style. I never argue about religion or politics. After all, Jesus Christ was the most perfect man who ever lived and they nailed him to a cross.

Jesse Owens

Crime Through Time

Many people believe that all Germans were as equally as bombastic as Hitler was, but a story here shows that not to be the case. In the 1936 Olympics in the long jump competition, with one jump remaining, Luz Long, a tall, blue-eyed, blond German long jumper who was Owens' stiffest competition, introduced himself. He suggested that Owens make a mark several inches before the takeoff board and jump from there to play it safe. Owens took the advice, and qualified.

In the finals that afternoon, Long's fifth jump matched Owens' 25ft 10in. But Owens leaped 26ft $3^{3}/_{4}$in on his next attempt and won the gold medal with a final jump of 26ft. $5^{1}/_{2}$in. The first to congratulate the Olympic record holder was Long, who looked like the model Nazi but wasn't.

Jesse Owens said, "It took a lot of courage for him to befriend me in front of Hitler. You can melt down all the medals and cups I have and they wouldn't be the plating on the 24-carat friendship I felt for Luz Long at that moment. Hitler must have gone crazy watching us embrace. The sad part of the story is I never saw Long again. He was killed in World War II." Owens, though, would continue to correspond with Long's family.

Owens did not speak of Hitler's alleged rebuff without probing. And when he does, he dismissed it as a minor incident. To him, Hitler's reference to "America's black cargo" meant little. Jesse Owens allowed his performance to speak for itself. Jesse Owen faced racism in his own country, the country he won at the Olympics for, the country he so loved! He wasn't given any preferential treatment by the white Americans, not until in 1976, President Ford presented Owens with the Medal of Freedom, the highest honour the USA can bestow upon a civilian. Owens was a pack-a-day smoker for 35 years; he died of lung cancer at age 66 on 31st March 1980 in Phoenix, Arizona, USA. Four years later, a street in Berlin, Germany was renamed in his honour!

A decade after his death, President Bush posthumously awarded Owens the Congressional Medal of Honour. Bush called his victories in Berlin "an unrivalled athletic triumph, but more than that, a triumph for all humanity."

Sporting Scandals

Born James Cleveland Owens in Decatur (although some claim 'Oakville'), Alabama, USA, on 12th September 1913 to Henry and Emma Owens he moved with his family to Cleveland, Ohio, as a young boy. When he enrolled in grade school, he acquired the name Jesse.

He was one of the first men to change the way people viewed black athletes and more importantly black people. The youngest of ten children, "Jesse" defied the beliefs of racism in the USA and around the world.

In 1922, he moved to Cleveland and attended Fairmont Junior High School where he started his track career. He grew up much like the other black kids of his time. His parents were sharecroppers and whites mistreated him. When he was seventeen, he attended East Technical School. After breaking records in the 100-yard dash and 200-yard dash, he was accepted to Ohio State University. While travelling with the track team, Jesse and his black teammates experienced the cruelty of prejudice. When they stopped to eat at a diner they were denied service because they were black.

In 1936, Owens qualified for the Olympics by setting a record in the 100-yard dash. He won four gold medals in the 100-metre, 200-metre, long jump, and 400-metre relay. The gold medals that he won at the Olympic games in Berlin were achieved with Adolf Hitler in attendance. Owens success disproved Hitler's theory that there is a supreme Aryan race and that blacks were not on the same level and therefore inferior to this master race.

Jesse Owens is an example to all races in the world that you can overcome adversity by using the gifts of nature. We're all unique in that we're all different to each other, therefore we all possess special qualities that are unique, Jesse Owens' qualities were, though, just that little bit more special than most.

Related web site

http://www.jesseowensmuseum.com/

7

Sporting Scandals
When off the field antics go wrong.

Greatness doesn't mean forever!!!

LEEDS STARS ARRIVE ON TEAM BUS FOR GBH CASE

WOODGATE
England man denies GBH and affray

BOWYER
Midfielder allegedly attacked student

DUBERRY
Injured ace denies conspiracy charge

Jonathan Woodgate's promising career is unclear after he was found guilty of affray in connection with the attack on an Asian student, Sarfraz Najeib, in Leeds. During the trial fellow team mate, Michael Duberry, dramatically turned the tables when he changed his story from a previous version given.

Sarfraz Najeib's father, Mohammed, spoke about a civil action the family propose, which is to be headed by Mike Mansfield, QC. The action is thought to include a private prosecution claiming damages for assault against two Leeds players, Lee Bowyer and Jonathan Woodgate.

The action is also planned against Paul Clifford, 22, who was given a six-year jail sentence for the attack, and Neale Caveney, 22, who was convicted of affray but cleared of assault.

In December 2001, Bowyer, 24, and Woodgate, 21, were both cleared of causing Sarfraz grievous bodily harm. Bowyer was also cleared of affray but Woodgate was found guilty and ordered to do 100 hours community service.

Lee Bowyer had been accused of punching and kicking a fellow holidaymaker in Cyprus in 1999. Although found not guilty of the serious assault of Asian student Sarfraz Najeib in January 2000, Bowyer has been severely reprimanded by the club for being drunk on the night of the attack.

359

Sporting Scandals

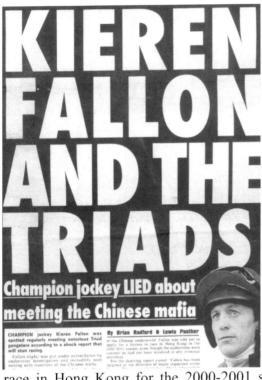

KIEREN FALLON AND THE TRIADS

Champion jockey LIED about meeting the Chinese mafia

CHAMPION jockey Kieren Fallon was spotted regularly meeting notorious Triad gangsters according to a shock report that will stun racing.

Fallon (right) was put under surveillance by undercover investigators and incredibly seen mixing with members of the Chinese mafia

By Brian Radford & Lewis Panther

of the Chinese underworld Fallon was told not to apply for a licence to race in Hong Kong in the 2000-2001 season, even though the authorities were content he had not been involved in any criminal activities.

But the damning report stated: 'Fallon has been targeted at the direction of major organized crime

Triad gangsters were seen meeting regularly with champion jockey Kieren Fallon according to a shock Hong Kong Jockey Club report that will stun racing!

Surveillance by undercover investigators was put on Fallon and he was seen to mix with Triads. When Fallon was asked about these meetings he denied they took place, but later changed his story! Fallon was told not to apply for a licence to race in Hong Kong for the 2000-2001 season, even though the governing body were satisfied he had not done any dodgy deals.

Legendary football manager George Graham had to pay back the bung he received whilst manager at Arsenal. Although such practice is frowned upon what's wrong with earning a bit of cash on the side as a backhander, especially if you're a great manager and your team are performing?

Crime Through Time

Glen Hoddle...when the shit hits the fan!!!

At odds with identifying himself as a Christian, Glen Hoddle the ex-England football team manager claimed to have a firm belief in former lives. Being committed to the idea that we have lived many times on this earth, he ventured the view which millions of reincarnationists hold, that our experience of this life is a consequence of our behaviour in earlier incarnations. He then suggested that people with disabilities should accept that their afflictions in this life were related to the character of their lives in the past. For a reincarnationist this is by no means a controversial remark, but it brought down a storm around Hoddle's head that led to him losing his post.

Glen Hoddle was fired as manager of the English soccer team four days after it was reported in the *Times of London* that he had said disability was caused by deeds in former lives. Hoddle, who believes in reincarnation, was attacked for insulting disabled people and most of the mass media, politicians and representatives of disability organisations mounted a massive and successful attack.

Hoddle had been given to this sort of voodoo thing over the last couple of years. During the campaign for the World Cup, he set tongues wagging when he called on a spiritual healer, Eileen Drewery, to inspire some positive thinking in his charges.

That supreme spoon-bender, Uri Geller, was also asked to give some 'unofficial' help to the England squad. Mr Geller claimed that the World Cup trophy was taken to his home to be "energised positively for England." Geller also said that he visited the Marseilles stadium in France, where England played their first game, so that he could leave "positive energy crystals." For reasons that were not made clear, this was meant to imbue the lads with mystical energies!

The cheerful message devotees of reincarnation bring to disabled persons is that in a previous existence they might have been an Adolf Hitler, and they are being punished for it in this life by physical and mental handicaps which work out their karma. Hoddle is not alone in believing these ideas. Alternative therapists in their hundreds practise "past-lives therapies" to help people get rid of the stress of their present existence. It is much easier to blame everything on a former existence than take responsibility for one's own behaviour today. The Hindu religion has believed in reincarnation for centuries. The classic question, "Who am I?" has been replaced by the question "Who was I?" And there is no one in the world that can tell him or her the answer to that.

Who were these disabled people who wanted Glen Hoddle sacked for expressing a religious belief that might be thought outlandish here (though John Lennon was never ridiculed for adhering to it) but which commands great respect and a strong and widespread adherence in Asia?

If you ask enough people a question you will get the answer you want from one of them and it wasn't difficult to find somebody with half a brain saying that Hoddle had to go, and that just happened to be a wheelchair user. There was also a scattering of protest from spokespersons from various organisations representing disabled people who said that Hoddle should be sacked.

The British Minister for Sport called for Hoddle's resignation, representatives of disabled persons groups were deeply aggrieved and insulted, the ravenous British press bayed for his blood and Tony Blair put the boots in. There were a couple of voices off to the side saying that Hoddle was a kind and gentle man, highly respected within the world of soccer. But it was to no avail. He was forced to resign.

Crime Through Time

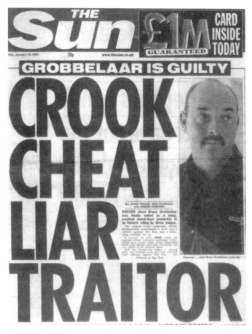

Former Liverpool goalkeeper Bruce Grobbelaar won £85,000 in libel damages from The Sun newspaper over match-fixing allegations in the High Court in 1999.

Grobbelaar, 41, had asked for substantial damages over a series of articles published by The Sun in November 1994. It was alleged he took £40,000 to make sure Liverpool lost 3-0 away to Newcastle in 1993. It also said he had blown his chance of £125,000 more in a 1994 game against Manchester United, which ended in a 3-3 draw, by accidentally making a sensational save in a match he was trying to lose.

In an amazing turnaround, the Court of Appeal, in January 2001, reversed the decision made against The Sun and also ordered that £85,000 damages paid, to the former Liverpool keeper Bruce Grobbelaar over match-fixing allegations, was to be paid back.

Grobbelaar said he is "devastated" by the judgement, in which his 1999 victory was described as "a miscarriage of justice."

> **"I am absolutely astounded and absolutely devastated at what's happened, and I feel very sorry for my family who have stuck by me through thick and thin."** Bruce Grobbelaar

Grobbelaar maintained he had never helped fix a match and said his solicitor would be making a petition for leave to appeal to the House of Lords.

Sporting Scandals

David Jones – Innocent until proven guilty!!!

'Jones' dark secret'

Former soccer boss preyed on vulnerable boys in his care, says QC

My sex with soccer boss, by boy who is now a girl

The former manager of Southampton football club, David Jones, was cleared of care home child abuse when his trial collapsed because an alleged victim refused to give evidence, campaigners for falsely accused carers said the "dip sampling" method used to collect evidence could lead to people fabricating stories of abuse to get compensation.

Police defended the trawling methods used in investigating past abuse in children's homes and said they would continue to use them despite criticism that they were touting for victims.

The assistant chief constable, Mike Tonge, of Merseyside police, said: "There is no other method of doing it."

Harry Fearns, whose brother-in-law was convicted after an Operation Care investigation, is chairman of the Campaign for Falsely Accused Carers and Teachers. "We feel that trawling methods are equal to touting for allegations. By the nature of police methodology they will collect false accusations as well as true," he said. David Jones' solicitor, Stephen Pollard, said, "Child abuse allegations must be more rigorously investigated to ensure innocent people did not suffer."

Ian Botham…it's just not cricket

Right, signed photo of Botham

Why do women stay with two timing rats?
Because they presumably love them of course???

The mighty Beefy sword awaits…

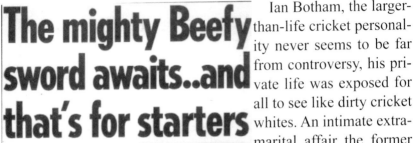

The mighty Beefy sword awaits..and that's for starters

EXCLUSIVE

BY LOUISE OSWALD & FRANK THORNE

What Ian said in e-mail to secret Bondage

Ian Botham, the larger-than-life cricket personality never seems to be far from controversy, his private life was exposed for all to see like dirty cricket whites. An intimate extramarital affair the former England all rounder reportedly had with an Australian waitress was emblazoned on newspapers around the world

Botham made a public apology to his wife and family after the News of the World went public with revelations of his romance with single mother Kylie Verrells, 31.

Two years of sex and bondage and all he can say is:

I'M SORRY KATH

"This is obviously a very difficult time for my family and friends. I am extremely sorry for the distress and embarrassment I have caused to them and in particular to my wife. I would like to take this opportunity to apologise to them all."

Ian Botham

Crime Through Time

It was reported that Botham, who has three children, met Ms Verrells when she served him lunch at a restaurant in Sydney on New Year's Eve 1998. Botham, was commentating on the Ashes tour, began an affair with her and then asked her to go with him when the tour moved to Adelaide and Melbourne. Six weeks after they met, Botham returned home to his loyal wife Kathy, 42, in Yorkshire. But a few months later he met Ms Verrells again when filming a television programme in New Zealand.

Horny e-mails – Do they arouse passion?

Beefy Botham sent Ms Verrells "saucy" e-mails:

'Babe, you ain't seen nothing yet!!! The mighty Beefy sword awaits...and that's just for starters. XXXXX'

Another kinky e-mail from Botham:

'As we both agree, I'm in charge of discipline...all spankings and other forms of punishment selected exclusively by me and administered by me to be conformed with in total at my discretion. We are an item bigger than Ben Hur. Love you for EVER XXXXXX'

"I bought black Velcro wrist and ankle ties, a leather whip and a tube of willy gel. I also got some quick-release handcuffs. Ian likes to be tied to the bed and teased but I'm not that keen myself. I wanted to make sure I could get out of it if I had to." Kylie Verrells

Sporting Scandals

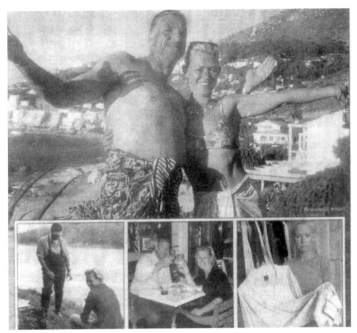

News of the World feature Beefy and Kylie.

In the late 80s the British Press went to town with another England captain's peccadilloes with a barmaid, Mike Gatting.

Indian cricketer Azharuddin also strayed, the Indian media did not blow it out of proportion. Before the former Indian cricket captain divorced his first wife, by and large the press, looked the other way even though he was often seen in the company of Ms Sangeeta Bijlani, his current wife.

Men seem to be so promiscuous, yet if a man's wife commits the foul deed she becomes an outcast. What gives? Why should a man want to go off with a mistress forsaking his lovely wife? How is it that women are too quick to forgive such men, taking them back at the drop of a hat? What was once scandalous has become the norm, the more in depth stories we hear the less they seem to mean.

If a vicar was to run off with his cleaner it wouldn't make big news, not unless he was a bondage merchant and all the succulent details were in print would it be worth reading about. The more salacious, randy and pervy the better we seem to like the story – does that reflect on what society has become today?

When a hero falls...ouch!

B U N C H

O F

F I V E S

H O W S

T H A T

TCCB · 40 GEOFF BOYCOTT · Yorkshire N Transvaal England

Dishonoured

Boycott fails to clear his name over assault of former lover

The 58-year-old former Yorkshire and England opening batsman, Geoff Boycott, was dropped as a commentator by newspapers and broadcasters following the outcome of a court case in France. He was found guilty of punching Margaret Moore 20 times after an argument in a hotel, in Antibes, in the south of France in October 1996.

Sporting Scandals

Alas, poor Yorath, for I knew him well!

> ### "Mine honour is mine life, take away mine honour and my life is gone."
>
> **Mr Boycott, who was allowed to speak in court, he quoted Shakespeare.**

Both the BBC and BSkyB dropped the former England cricketer as a commentator pending the outcome of the appeal heard in France.

During a 10-hour retrial he said Mrs Moore had slipped after flying into a rage when he refused to marry her. Mr Boycott faced a three-week wait before judge Dominique Haumont-Daumas at the Palais de Justice, in Grasse, southern France, gave her guilty verdict in May 2000.

The court saw the former opening batsman present former girl-friends as witnesses to his character and medical experts discounting the evidence of Mrs Moore.

During the retrial Mr Boycott continually battled against language barriers as the marathon court session went on, occasionally losing his temper. At one point he caused his former lover to flee in tears when he told her solicitor to "shut up." He told the judge: "I will answer if he will shut up and let me speak."

Crime Through Time

When the judge asked Mr Boycott about the method of payment of the hotel bill, he shouted: "Everybody's talking French - I don't understand!" His barrister had to shake Mr Boycott's shoulder and remind him that he was in France!

BASHER BOYCOTT DOWN AND OUT

Margaret Moore, was she lying?

Earlier in the trial a number of medical experts spoke for the defence, they said photographs of Mrs Moore's injury did not support her version of events. And there was an allegation that the pictures used to help convict Mr Boycott had been digitally enhanced to make the bruising look worse! After he lost the retrial, the Sun newspaper immediately sacked him as a columnist and both the BBC and Trans World International, for whom he has commentated in the past, said they had no intention of using him again. The defence, to demonstrate the injuries that could be sustained in an accident, also called two women who had sustained bruising in falls rather than assaults. Talk Radio were not put off by the appeal verdict and immediately signed up Geoff Boycott as chief cricket correspondent. The proceedings are thought to have cost Mr Boycott up to £500,000 in costs. Geoff Boycott, a man for all seasons, but for beating up a woman...what do you think?

Sporting Scandals

Vroom, Vroom! - Cor blimey they're all at it???

Formula one racing driver, David Coulthard seduced Ruth Taylor, 20, in a hotel hot tub, telling her he didn't have a girl-friend! When Coutlthard's fiancée Heidi Wichlinski found out about the night of carnal exploration Coulthard had performed with Ruth, a model, she gave him the elbow and immediately phoned her father in the USA.

HOW COULD YOU DO THIS TO ME, DAVID?

Cheated Heidi blasts love-rat Coulthard

EXCLUSIVE
BY STUART WHITE & CHARLES BEGLEY

THE devastated fian-cée of Formula One race ace David Coulthard rang him in anguish after he sneaked a voluptuous model into his hot tub for a night of sex.

"I've only got one question for you," Heidi Wichlinski seethed into the mouth-piece. "Why? Why, and how could you do this to me?"

The News of the World re-vealed last Sunday that McLaren-Mercedes driver Coulthard told 20-year-old Ruth Taylor he was spar-ticked then kissed her "from head to toe" as gallons of bubble-bath frothed around them.

Then he took her to bed. "He kept asking if I enjoyed certain positions," said Ruth. "He gave me an experience I'll never forget."

Not will Heidi. After she re-alised the depth of his be-trayal the 20-year-old called off their marriage plans and dumped him. Then, from her Chelsea flat, she called her parents in America.

Foreword to
Sexual Scandals
By
Benny Hill

Benny Hill - British Comedian/Actor
1924-1992

I want the show to be a joyous thing. I want everyone to have a giggle. Just as the fat man comes on to the stage and makes people giggle I want to be the man who makes people laugh and is loved by everyone.

To tease and titillate my audience pleases me. I know I play the part of men wearing Macs and chasing women and I know what people think, but I am not gay! I know that one day I'll be famous - maybe in a 100-years from now. What does it matter!

Playing the part of the lecher or the shortsighted oaf is serious business. With Hill's Angels the chasing scenes would always be funny, and a lot of the stuff was ad-libbed. Most of my work has been of my own invention, it was based on titillation, each sketch lasted a few minutes and often it would involve a lady with a low cut dress or wearing a bikini.

I won awards for what was fun, getting awards for something you enjoy doing is fun. Inventing ever more daring routines was challenging. We didn't use full nudity, but we got close one or two times and based on the daring of the girls the show would be classed as smutty or sexy, it was a fine line!
"Don't do anything I wouldn't do!"

Benny Hill

> **"Just because nobody complains doesn't mean all parachutes are perfect."** Benny Hill

Benny Hill was born on 21st January 1924 in Southampton, England. His real name was Alfred Hawthorne Hill. The chubby, youthful-looking, brown-haired British comedian of leering innocence was once known as 'Britain's brightest boy.'

An enthusiastic performer in school shows, he was a milkman, drummer and driver before finding employment as an assistant stage manager. Despite the promising star debut in his first movie, no big career in the cinema followed.

During World War II he appeared in 'Stars in Battledress', and later followed the traditional comic's route of workingmen's clubs, revues and end-of-the-pier shows.

An early convert to the potential of television, he appeared in 'Hi There' (1949), and was named TV personality of the year in 1954. He gained national popularity with the saucy *The Benny Hill Show* (1957- 1966), and spent over two decades writing and performing in top-rated television specials that were seen around the world.

His periodic TV-shows are rough-edged celebrations of picture-postcard vulgarity, with Hill himself doing broad impressions and singing. Hill's television career was launched in 1955 and his show ran, off and on, on the BBC until 1968 with a brief season with ATV in 1967. In 1969 he moved to Thames Television and it was there that he was to make the programs on which most of his fame rests.

This series picked up a cult following, making Hill the most popular British comedian to appear on U.S. television. The compilation series was sold in over 90 other foreign language markets, including Russia and China that normally did not buy British comedy. However so much of Hill's series was based on sight gags and humour that audiences in many parts of the world came to appreciate the comedy. In point of fact, the early series of *The Benny Hill Show* appeared on the BBC. His early work was inventive, local in its references. Some of the BBC shows are fondly remembered for his many inspired and usually hilarious impersonations of such icons of British television such as Hughie Green (of the talent series *Opportunity Knocks*) and Alan Wicker of the travel/foreign correspondent series *Wicker's World.*

The Fred Scuttle Character

Hill himself often played a series of stock figures such as the shortsighted Professor Marvel, a cowboy, Captain Fred Scuttle and a member of the fireman's choir. His characteristic trademarks included a broad accent, whether Southern American, Devon or other British versions, an oafish salute and often a jacket buttoned too tightly across the chest. His songs and rhymes were rendered with the look of a happy idiot that constantly broke into a leer.

Benny Hill had also some accomplishments on the radio. His greatest hit 'Ernie' (*The Fastest Milkman In The West*), released in winter 1972, topped many British music charts. This album alone sold 700, 000 copies during Christmas sales.

Hill was adept at playing buffoons who, on a slightly closer inspection, turned out to be both sly and lecherous. Indeed lechery and smuttiness were a hallmark of many of the shows, in which tall, beautiful girls were constantly being chased or ogled by Hill and a group of stereotypical males such as Henry McGee, Bob Todd, Jackie Wright and Nicholas Parsons. Wright in particular, as the small, bald man, invariably cropped up in a comic fire brigade sketch or as a cowboy in several of the slapstick sketches.

Benny Hill never married, although he says he was proposed to twice, never owned a car and left no will when he died on 20th April 1992 from a heart attack, leaving some £10m, which was shared between distant relatives. His body is buried at Hollybrook Cemetery, Southampton, England.

Benny Hill – Titillation!

8

Sexual Scandals

Genuine signed photo of Anna Nicole Smith – Former nude Playboy girl and movie star. The busty blonde married an ageing billionaire who oddly enough then went on to pop his clogs and die soon after.

Sexual Scandals

And the rest they say is history!

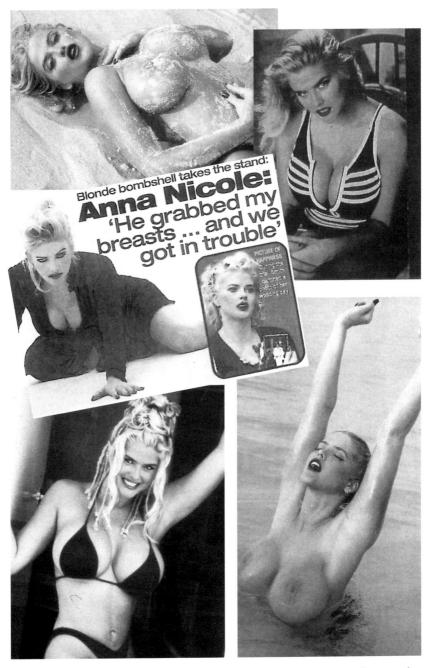

Anna Nicole Smith – A very rich lady, with plenty of assets!

Crime Through Time

Madonna

Pop star Madonna has taken on many incarnations. Through sexual scandal, re-invention and redemption, she has kept fans and critics alike intrigued for nearly 20 years. Many have criticised Madonna as being more flash than substance. But her defenders point to her long-running popularity and her seemingly endless ability to stay one step ahead of the game.

Her mother died of cancer in 1963, a defining moment in Madonna's childhood. In 1992, Madonna released her most controversial work of art - a book. The book was called 'Sex' and was devoted to photographs of Madonna in different sexual poses and situations. Although the book caused uproar, *Sex* sold out worldwide within a few days. "This book is about sex. Sex is not love. Love is not sex. But the best of both worlds is created when they come together," said Madonna.

Although thousands of complaints were lodged about the book it was deemed a work of art.

Sexual Scandals

Deep Throat

Linda Lovelace claimed that she was coerced into performing in 'Deep Throat,' claiming that her husband Chuck Traynor beat her repeatedly on and off the set.

There was no corroborating evidence that she was beaten on the set. Much of her body was not shown during the movie because she had scars from going through a car window during a car accident.

A question remains, was she beaten or were the scars caused by her 1970 car accident. She became a feminist and testified that pornography was dangerous. Despite her anti-pornography stand, she posed for 'Leg Show (2001).'

She attended Catholic school as a kid and actually wanted to be a nun. She had silicon injections in her breasts.

Died 22nd April 2002, as a result of a car crash at the age of 53.

Crime Through Time

Demi Moore, signed photo

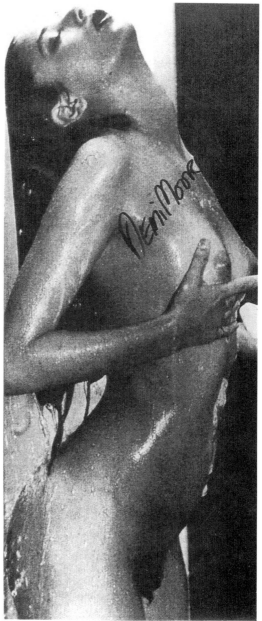

Emmanuel Star, Slyvia Kristal

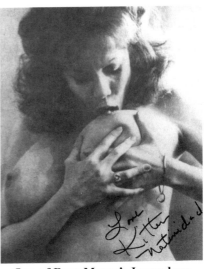

One of Russ Meyer's Legendary girls - Kitten Natividad

Crime Through Time Cleaning lady! Really though, Pandora Peaks is her name www.pandorapeaks.com

Ex Charlie's Angel Farrah Fawcett

Bobbitt

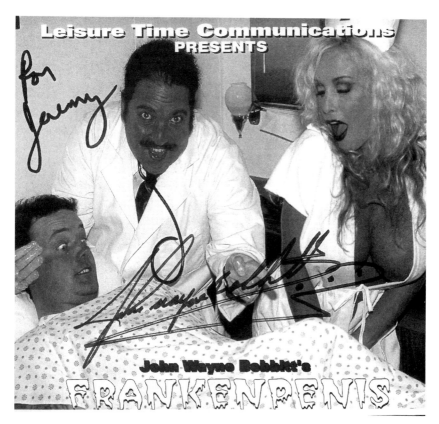

The moonlight glints off the razor sharp knife Lorena holds in her hand. She steps closer to the bed, where her husband sleeps unsuspectingly. Slowly and deliberately she pulls the covers away from his naked, unprotected body...exposing his penis! He lies still, not knowing the damage about to be inflicted upon his body. She raises the knife and brings it down upon his...

It was the story that shocked the world. Overnight John Wayne Bobbitt was the man everyone was talking about, but who no one wanted to be. It was a story that sent fear into the hearts and groins of men everywhere!

And it was probably the best thing to happen to Mr Bobbitt, it put him on the road to fame and riches, and on the tongue of every female is... "What does it look like?" Well...you'll have to buy the video to find out girls!

Sexual Scandals

Randy Footballers

IT DOESN'T STAND UP

...and that's not just your lies about the Thai massage, Joe

Ashton ... rubdowns

GREEN MILE STAR VOWS TO WIN REAL-LIFE AIDS BATTLE

★GLOBE
THE AMERICAN
HOLLYWOOD'S HOTTEST SECRETS

DI'S DEATH: IT'S ALL CAMILLA'S FAULT -SAYS QUEEN

EXCLUSIVE

'MARTIN LUTHER KING PAID FOR MY BIRTH'

JULIA ROBERTS SHOCK

X ON SCREEN

REVEALED — Runaway **Bride's** baby secret...

MARTIN LUTHER KING PAID FOR JULIA ROBERTS' BIRTH

'I will always be grateful to the Kings. Whenever I hear'

THE Sun **WORLD PICTURE EXCLUSIVE**

SOPHIE TOPLESS

Star Tarrant's sexy fun with Edward's bride

Sexual Scandals

Here's Jerrrrrrrrrrrrrrrrrrry

Controversial Jewish chat show host. The rampant Jerry Springer

The beautiful people always seem to die so young!!

THE BIGGEST TITS IN THE WORLD???

She died so young!! Here on display, is an authentic signed photo of the legendary Lolo Ferrari (real name Eve Valois). Lolo, incidentally, is French slang for tits!! **(Signature is difficult to see due to it being signed on a black background, original can be seen in the museum... in full colour of course!!!)**

Be warned!!!! Unprotected sex and AIDS can kill!!!!

He died so young... legendary gay rock singer Freddie Mercury died of AIDS on 24th September 1991. Here is a scarce and, certainly, highly sought after signed photograph of, undoubtedly, one of the world's finest and best known live performers... front man of Britsh rock band...Queen. A man with his immense talent and wealth could have potentially had almost any woman that he so desired... yet he preferred the company and sinister, sadistic sexual relationships with many men instead!!

Courtesy News of the World

If the body sells more records... flaunt it!!

REVEALED: The convent girl who gave her name to Britain's first ever sex shops: Ann Summers

by Richard Pendlebury

Courtesy Daily Mail

SECRET SEX CLUB

Vault located at 565 W. 23 st. in New York City, USA

From the outside it's an unassuming building, 5 floors of ancient pink brick, but once inside it doesn't take long to get interesting - namely, the stairs leading down to the entrance. You descend into the unearthly blue glow of backlights, the darkened walls on either side painted in big orange and yellow flames six feet high, all the way down to the bottom. Once through the main door, it ceases to be just impressive and becomes positively erotic. Unmistakable odours of burning flesh drift around.

A woman in an evil black leather harness dangles a blood-soaked tampon above a guy on his knees in front of her. "Bark for your dinner!" she commands, and when he does she feeds him the thing, the string hanging out of his mouth like spaghetti as he commences happily to chew the juices out.

Another man in leather chaps and long hair is busy working a toilet plunger in and out of the pussy of a pretty brunette spread-eagled on the floor; it's hard to tell whether she's howling in agony or orgasm, or maybe a little bit of both.

Set deep into the rear wall is a series of shower stalls, and in one of them a naked woman is getting sick... all over another naked woman who sprawls there masturbating with a dildo. Two women in short skirts take turns at a waist-high metal railing, the one leaning forward on it while the other, who is facing her, reaches over her and lifts her skirt from behind for any man who would like to stop and partake - while she watches.

Crime Through Time

Heather Locklear

Harrison Ford

Naomi Campbell

There's a prim-looking sorority type on her knees in front of a line of six men, sucking one of them off and then moving to the next without bothering to wipe the cum off her face. People lie in restraints with their faces, the soles of their feet next to the flames. The stink of singed hair fills the air, and something not unlike the smell of bacon. One poor wretch is even bound to a spit and being rotisseried over a 6-foot bed of coals, one person at his head, another at his feet, turning the spit, while another bastes him with some kind of gooey syrup and a paintbrush. Tied face-down on some kind of trestle is a naked man with a gag in his mouth, while behind him stands a tall, beautiful blonde in fishnet stockings and leather bustier and heels. And she's holding what looks like a branding iron of all things, the business end of it glowing an ominous red in the dim light. Then, she takes it and, standing between his spread legs, proceeds to press it into the sensitive flesh of his bare butt. She really leans into it, until he's bellowing like a bull through his gag, his body a quivering knot, the sweat collecting in little puddles on the floor. And still she holds it there, hissing, for what seems like forever: the angry hissing of an overheated radiator, smoke climbing in thick ropes to the ceiling. When finally she does stop, the skin is an awful, blistered white, the wound an unrecognisable mass, though on the other cheek is another burn, not quite so fresh, this one already congealing into what appears to be…a perfect 3-inch 'V'.

391

Sexual Scandals

http://www.clubvault.com/   http://www.clubhellfire.com/

Crime Through Time

Mick Hucknall…Simply Framed

Why is it that when a man is charged with rape or even just inter-viewed or accused he gets his name plastered all over the newspa-pers whilst the alleged victim is sure of securing anonymity by the protection of the law.

People are always arguing that the case of the victim is under-stated, but what about the Hamilton's (British case) who were plas-tered all over the press and eventually vindicated of claims that they carried out sexual crimes against a female.

Shouldn't there be laws to protect alleged perpetrators of sexu-al offences from such exposure until it has been fully proven in court that they are, indeed, guilty.

The case of Mick Hucknall highlights the flaw in the law. Although! It can also be argued that the prospect of a woman fac-ing a barrage of questions and the glare of courtroom officials can also put women off from coming forward and reporting sexual crimes carried out against them.

The prospect of facing a team of barristers employed by an afflu-ent person can be daunting!

Crime Through Time

Ursula Undress, err…Andress

0
0
7

O
O
SO
NICE!

In her heyday Ursula Andress has appeared nude in Playboy, starred in love scenes for the 1962 James Bond Film, 'Dr No'. The Swiss born sex bomb played the part with enthusiasm on and off screen. She was linked with the big name stars such as Sean Connery, Marlon Brando, James Dean, Peter O'Toole and a string of other well-known celebrities.

Ms Andress was asked again by Playboy to reveal her assets for a $250,000 payday but she said, "To pose in the nude at my age is a scandal."

Sexual Scandals

Tyson…mean sex machine!

The Tyson everyone loved – World Champ 1987

Michael Gerard Tyson was born on 30th June 1966 in Brooklyn, New York. After run-ins with the law and expulsion from high school, Tyson was taken out of reform school by boxing trainer Cus D'Amato. Cus saw the potential in this troubled kid and knew what he could become if given the right influence and training. With Cus' guidance, Mike Tyson became the hottest young heavyweight in professional boxing and was soon on the road to the heavyweight crown. Cus D'Amato's tragic death from pneumonia in 1985 was a blow to Mike Tyson, but he continued the journey to the heavyweight title with trainer Kevin Rooney at his side along with promoters Jim Jacobs and Bill Cayton. The death of Mike Tyson's mentor, Cus D'Amato, may have been the beginning of Tyson's moral downfall.

Mike Tyson became the youngest heavyweight champion in heavyweight history (20 years, 144 days) when he knocked out the then WBC Champion Trevor Berbick in the second round of their match up on November 22, 1986, breaking Floyd Patterson's claim to the record.

396

> "They said I was emotionally disturbed. I don't know what emotionally disturbed is. Charles Manson – I guess he's emotionally disturbed." Mike Tyson

The bathing-suit belles giggled nervous lying their in skimpy suits, wobbling on their high heels as their hero hove into view. Mike Tyson, ex-heavyweight boxing champion of the world, was even more awesome close-up than he was on the screen punching his opponents to kingdom come. Tyson, a born-again bachelor since his highly publicised divorce from Actress Robin Givens. But today these girls were all his own — black girls competing in an all black beauty pageant at an exposition in the Midwestern city of Indianapolis in 1991.

Tyson's comments to the girls were crude and lewd, but some of these girls were from the ghetto like Tyson, some of them under-stood the language of the streets. Few were offended by the boxer's purple language and off-hand sexist remarks.

One particular 18-year-old among the contestants that day was overawed at being in the presence of boxing's maestro. Desiree Washington, a vivacious beauty, a girl from a nice middle-class home, didn't hear the risqué banter; she just hoped with baited breath that the Tyson would stop to speak with her – he did.

Tyson exchanged telephone numbers with Desiree, the girl from Rhode Island, and they met later that night for what she thought was going to be a nice sightseeing tour of the bright lights of Indianapolis – with no makeup on and wearing lose clothes? Her tour, however, ended in room 606 of the plush Canterbury Hotel where she claims Tyson raped her. Throughout the ensuing trial Tyson proclaimed his innocence, but it became clear to a watching world that he was a brutish man who took what he wanted, when he wanted it.

The hushed court on the first day of proceedings heard that hours before the attack he had knelt in prayer with the Rev Jesse Jackson. But after midnight, the lust for the young beauty he had met earlier in the day welled up inside him. The attraction between the former champ and the beauty queen changed from innocence to a nightmare rape ordeal in a split second on 19th July 1991.

"She was asleep when Tyson phoned to invite her for a ride around town in his limousine," said the prosecutor. "He told her he was leaving town the next day. So she gets up and decides to go and see the town with one of her heroes. She was excited. She thought: 'I am out on the town with Mike Tyson!' But then he said something about going back to his hotel.

The morning after, Desiree's roommate asked: "What was he like?" Desiree replied: "He raped me." A day later Miss Washington complained to police and when doctors examined her, they found two wounds "clearly visible 25 hours after the attack. It is beyond reasonable doubt that he callously and viciously raped her."

Tyson's lawyer, Vincent Fuller, to try and defend his client from such shattering testimony, portrayed Tyson as a brute. Yes, he was tough, he was crude, he was brutal – his argument was that any girl who went into a hotel room after midnight with a hulk like Tyson should have known they weren't going there to play scrabble. "There is no denial on Mr Tyson's part that sex took place," he said. "But we will prove that sex was consensual." He argued that the fact that Tyson didn't call a cab after the brief encounter with Miss Washington led her to concoct the rape story: "Miss Washington left his room in anger — not because of rape, but because of disillusionment."

"I asked her if she wanted to fuck me the first time I met her."
Tyson on the witness stand

Desiree Washington

"I was kissing her neck, her cheeks, kissing her chest, kissing her shoulders and her nipples. She had taken off her shorts and I had taken my shirt off. She had taken off her underwear, and the underwear had dropped to her knees and then I took it all off. I started having oral sex with her. We had oral sex for a little while. She told me to stop, saying 'come up, come up.' That indicated she wanted sex. We had sex. It lasted for 15 or 20 minutes. She was not on the pill so I didn't climax inside her. I offered her to stay the night because her and a girlfriend had a 5am wake-up call. I said my limo would take her home and that I was not going to walk back down the stairs. She was irritated because I would not walk her down the stairs."

TYSON OUT OF HIS MIND
Did this cost him dearly when he lost to Lewis?

Sexual Scandals

I say, I say, I say

Man charged with stabbing Fred Elliott was former rent boy

By Andrew Chapman

MANIAC ATTACKS CORRIE'S FRED

I've been stabbed!

I say, I've been stabbed!

WHY BUTCHER FRED?

Street stars in shock at knife attack on their pal

By PHILIP CARDY, KIRSTY STORRAR and JULIE MOULT

MADONNA BURGLED

By EMMA JONES

STAR FLED THE NAZIS WHEN HE WAS JUST 3

Crime Through Time

A man he invited back to his flat after they met at a notorious guy haunt stabbed Coronation Street soap star John Savident, 62, twice in the neck. The incident happened in December 2000 in the luxury apartment of Mr Savident.

The married father of two invited former rent boy, Michael James Smith, 28, after they met in Napoleons Bar in the heart of Manchester's gay scene. A conversation was struck relating to acting and it was with this in mind that the former rent boy was invited back to the flat, where they talked of the theatre.

This is when the alleged unprovoked attack took place! Smith forced Mr Savident to hand over the keys to his luxury sports car along with various credit cards. After the attack Smith was unable to open the garage door and made his escape on foot. Soon after this Mr Savident managed to close the flat door and contact the police. In the early hours of the morning the police apprehended Smith who was still lurking by the flat.

Mr Savident's wife lives in high society Muswell Hill, London, in a £900,000 luxury home.

Sexual Scandals

We're very happy

We're leaving to live in America say gay fathers

By **Gordon Rayner**

A HOMOSEXUAL couple who fathered twins by a surrogate mother are emigrating to escape what they see as hostility from the public.

Millionaires Tony Barlow and Barrie Drewitt have sold their home and will move to a 15-bedroom mansion in Miami next month while they await the birth of triplets by a second surrogate.

Mr Drewitt, 31, said: 'We have been deeply upset by the amount of criticism levelled at us here. It is very disturbing when little old ladies attack us verbally in supermarkets.

'But in America we will not be the only gay dads with surrogate babies. People there have had time to get used to the idea and gay dads are treated more as celebrities than freaks.'

Mr Drewitt admitted that, despite having battled with the authorities for the right to British citizenship for

Left: Barrie Drewitt (on the right) and Tony Barlow with their daughters. Above: Egg donor Tracie McCune

'We're very happy'

A millionaire homosexual couple that fathered twins by a surrogate mother decided to emigrate to America to escape what they see as hostility from the public. Tony Barlow and Barrie Drewitt, 31, sold their home and proposed to move to a 15-bedroom mansion in Miami while they awaited the birth of triplets by a second surrogate. Mr Drewitt said: "We have been deeply upset by the amount of criticism levelled at us here. In America we will not be the only gay dads with surrogate babies."

Despite having battled with the British authorities for the right to British citizenship for their daughters, they had changed their mind and wanted them to be American.

Babies Aspen and Saffron were born after the two men spent £200,000 on surrogacy fees and medical expenses to buy their daughters. They made legal history after winning a court battle to allow them both to be named as fathers on the birth certificate. A fertilisation technique that is banned in Britain was used to ensure that each of them was the biological father of one of the babies.

Is it right that gay a gay couple should be allowed to do this, maybe money talks? But it is their life after all and maybe they can give their children a better upbringing on their £millions!

Crime Through Time

Sex Madames

€7M SEX MADAME'S VICE LITTLE EARNER

■ by PETER DYKE

AN AGEING vice-queen raked in an estimated £7.5 million in two years after advertising sex parlours in police magazines.

Wheelchair-bound Josie Daly, 64, was arrested after undercover cops visited one of her saunas and found they were a front for brothels.

Bespectacled Daly was brought before court yesterday and could now lose her fortune.

Contrite

Her bank accounts have been frozen and a judge has warned her she faces a hefty fine.

Harrow Crown Court was told the grey-haired madame cheekily flaunted the sleazy services in 999 Magazine and The British Transport Police Diary.

Prosecutor Brendan Kelly said officers had posed as punters and gone to one of her saunas paying a flat fee for a massage.

He said they were then approached by one of the girls and offered sexual services from £15 up to £50.

Up to 500 customers a week visited her three premises in London – The Aqua Sauna, Ishka Bath and The Lanacombe

SEX FOR SALE: Daly made millions

STEAMY: Her Lanacombe sauna

Sauna. Daly's girls, aged between 18 and 30, came from all over the world to work at her brothels and included immigrants from Eastern Europe and Thailand.

Mr Kelly said 85 per cent of customers went there for sex and each sauna earned around £750,000 to £1 million a year.

The court was told how clients would wander in looking for more than a relaxing rub-down.

They were asked to pay a £10 to £15 "entrance fee" and then taken to another

room where they would fork out a further £15 to £50 for "sexual services".

The menu on offer consisted of £80 for "French", £40 for "sex" and £15 for "hand relief". The brothel receptionist was paid £20 for a 12-hour shift and also got additional tips from the prostitutes.

Officers estimated Daly would have made £7.5 million from the business over two years.

And they claimed she had about £3 million worth of "realisable assets" including property.

Daly, who has a daughter from a brief marriage to a Ghanaian, pleaded guilty to three charges of controlling prostitution for gain.

Suffering

The madame, who lives in a £700,000 Victorian villa in north London, also admitted to advertising her sex parlours in the police magazines.

Gilbert Gray, counsel for Daly, said she had not been able to visit the saunas personally to see what was going on because she had been suffering heart problems.

He said: "She sits before your honour in that wheel-chair... utterly contrite and profoundly bewildered."

She was freed on unconditional bail until a confiscation hearing in September.

Josie Daly raked in £7.5m from her prostitution racket.

The Luncheon Voucher Madame - Cynthia Payne.

London : Monday
April 21, 1980
Price : Ten pence

STANDARD CLOSING PRICES

THE PEER, THE VICARS AND SEX

Amazing story of police raid on the 'luncheon voucher' brothel

THE HOUSE Streatham raided police — amon "guests," a peer an

A MEMBER of the House of Lords, several vicars and an M from Ireland were among 53 m

403

Sexual Scandals

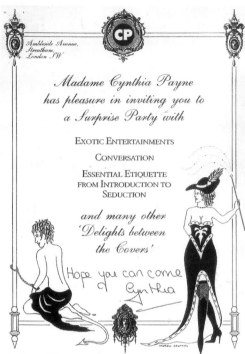

A signed invitation to a surprise party from Madam Cynthia Payne

The luncheon voucher took on a new meaning when used as currency at wicked sex Madame Ms Cynthia Payne's establishment. Vicars, members of Parliament, judges and big businessmen gathered together in Streatham for a Christmas party when to their surprise and dismay the police burst in and arrested Ms Payne.

The phrase, he jumped out of the room faster than a priest jumping out of a brothel window during a police raid, equally applied during this police raid. Films, devices and hastily dressing people were taken to the station.

At her trial Ms Payne was given sympathy from the public and was sentenced to 18-months imprisonment, in Holloway. The charge of 'keeping a disorderly house' found distinguished supporters falling over themselves leaping to her defence. *Cynthia Payne's story can be read in 'An English Madam' by Paul Bailey.*

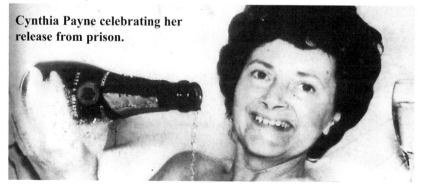

Cynthia Payne celebrating her release from prison.

Foreword to
Paedophile Scandals
By
Fred West
1941 – 1995

And what I'm saying is, for God's sake put it together... My life means nothing to you, but it means a lot to me... and if the police sorts it out then I haven't said anything. I thought, shit, I can't get her down through there. I thought, I'm going to have to cut her up again, and by this time I'm realising that's three, no two, not three, where is this going to stop? I've got to give myself up, I've got to tell Rose so I don't do this again. When the police searched Cromwell Street the spirits come up to me, when they come up into you it's wonderful, it's when they go you are trying to hold them, you feel them flying away from you and you try and stop them.

Anne-Marie said about Rose tying them up, I said to Rose about it, she said she was only playing with them.

I remember we had to clean the garage out; she (Rose) was shitting herself. She said "Rena's in bags in that skip." I lifted some asbestos sheets off the skip, and the smell... We took the bags and buried her.

It's been going on for 30-years! I still believe that these girls ended up at parts right in Bristol. They were drugged, sexually abused and then taken back to where Rose was and they were taken away and someone else killed them!

I can remember taking a breath and swallowing, I said, 'What do you mean there's others (bodies) out there?'

I should go to hell for what I've done.

Fred West

Above item, not in museum exhibits

9

Paedophile Scandals

Fred West came from a long line of Herefordshire farm labourers. He was born in 1941, in the village of Much Marcle, approximately 120 miles west of London, to Walter and Daisy West. Fred began life as a beautiful baby, with huge piercing blue eyes and blond hair.

War brought poverty, but in spite of this the Wests had six more children. Fred and his mother enjoyed a particularly close relationship. He was her pet and did everything she asked. Fred admired his father as a role model.

Fred West the beautiful swan grew up into a scruffy-looking duckling. His blond hair turned to a dark brown and became curly and unkempt. He had inherited some of his mother's less attractive facial features: an overly large mouth and a gap between his large teeth. He had a simian look about him.

Fred was not a promising student and was constantly in trouble for which he was regularly caned, as if hitting him would make his brains work! Daisy, seriously overweight and dressed unattractively, would go to the school to yell at the teacher for disciplining her favourite son - an action that made Fred the butt of many jokes. He was a "mammy's boy." He left school at age fifteen - almost illiterate - and went to work as a farm hand. By the time he was sixteen, he cleaned himself up enough to be attractive to girls. He was extremely aggressive with the opposite sex and soon went after any girl that caught his fancy.

Fred claimed that his father had sex with his daughters, using the logic, "I made you so I'm entitled to have you." But then, Fred was a habitual liar. It's hard to say if his father ever was ever guilty of incest or that Fred made his sister pregnant, as he later claimed.

At the age of seventeen, he was seriously injured in a motorcycle accident, which left him in a coma for a week and resulted in a metal plate being put into his fractured head. His leg was also broken and was permanently shorter than the other leg.

His head injury, some thought, had made him prone to sudden fits of rage and that he seemed to have lost control over his emotions.

After his recovery from the accident, Fred met the pretty 16-year-old Catherine Bernadette Costello, nicknamed Rena, an accomplished and experienced thief who had been in trouble with the police since early childhood. Almost immediately they became lovers.

The affair ended a few months later when she went back to Scotland. Fred's attentions quickly turned elsewhere and in an act of sexual assault he stuck his hand up the skirt of a young woman standing with him on a fire escape at a local youth club. She knocked Fred off the fire escape, banging his already damaged head even further. The lasting impact on Fred's behaviour suggested that he might have suffered some brain damage.

In 1961, Fred and his friend stole a watchstrap and cigarette cases from a jewellery store, both were caught with the merchandise on them. Fred and his accomplice were both fined. A few months later, he was accused of impregnating a 13-year-old girl who was a friend of the West family. Fred was surprisingly uncooperative and didn't see that there was anything wrong with molesting little girls.

His attitude of "Well, doesn't everyone do it" and the ensuing scandal caused a serious break with his family. Fred was ordered to find somewhere else to live. Distanced now from his family, he went to work on construction projects. It wasn't long before he was caught stealing from the construction sites and having sex with young girls.

At the trial for having sex with the 13-year-old girl, his doctor claimed that West was suffering from epileptic fits. Consequently, he escaped a jail sentence, but the die was cast. At age 20, Fred West was a convicted child molester and petty thief - and a total disgrace to his family.

In 1962, Fred's parents relented and let him come back to live with them at Much Marcle. That summer, his girlfriend Rena Costello came back from Scotland and took up with Fred immediately. They seemed well matched. Rena was the average run of the mill girl, but rather an experienced delinquent that as a teenager had a record for prostitution and burglary. That Rena was pregnant by an Asian bus driver introduced a complication into their relationship and to the acceptance of her by his parents.

In November 1962, Fred secretly married his girlfriend and moved immediately to Scotland. His parents believed that the baby she was carrying was Fred's.

In March of 1963, when Charmaine was born, Fred had Rena write to his mother saying that their baby had died in childbirth and that she had adopted a mixed-race child. Already West was devious in his ways.

Rena had been a prostitute at various times and she was not happy to be a prisoner to the voracious sexual appetite of Fred West - oral sex, bondage and…sodomy…at all hours of the day and night.

Fred's politeness, apparent trustworthiness and sincerity, and his ability to spin interesting tales made him attractive to the teenagers who flocked around his ice cream truck.

By 1964, Rena bore Fred's child, a daughter they named Anna Marie. They had a roller coaster marriage for several years. During that time, Rena and Fred met Anna McFall, whose boyfriend had been killed in an accident. At that time, Fred was involved in an accident with the ice cream truck that killed a young boy, so he and Rena and their two children, plus Anna McFall moved back to Gloucester. Fred had a job in a slaughterhouse.

Rena wanted to take the two children back with her to Glasgow, but Fred refused, so she went back to Scotland alone. But she was miserable without her daughters and, in July of 1966, returned to Gloucester to find Fred and Anna McFall to be an item –living in a caravan.

Rena told Detective Constable Hazel Savage (mentioned later on in this section) that her husband was a sex pervert and unfit to raise their children. Coincidentally, at that time there were eight sexual assaults committed in the Gloucester area committed by a man of Fred's description!

In early 1967, Anna McFall became pregnant to Fred. She was trying unsuccessfully to get Fred to divorce Rena and marry her. Fred responded to the stress of her demands by killing her and burying her near the trailer park sometime in July. Not only did he kill his mistress and their unborn child, he slowly and methodically dismembered her corpse and buried her along with the foetus. Oddly enough, he cut off her fingers and toes, which were missing from the gravesite. It would be his modus operandi (calling card) in future crimes.

After McFall's disappearance Fred acted very nervously. Rena moved back into the trailer and Fred became his old self again. Fred happily sent Rena out to earn some pocket money as a prostitute and began to openly fondle the young Charmaine!

In January of 1968, pretty 15-year-old Mary Bastholm was abducted from a bus stop in Gloucester. There were a number of links between Fred and Mary Bastholm: he was a customer at the Pop-in (where Mary worked) and Mary often served him tea; Fred had been employed to do some building work behind the café; Mary had been seen with a girl fitting the description of Fred's former lover, Anna McFall; and one witness claims to have seen Mary in Fred's car. In February, the death of Fred's mother launched him into a series of petty thefts, which caused him to change jobs frequently.

On 29th November 1968, while he was working as a bakery delivery driver, he was to meet the girl who would become his next wife and accomplice in at least 12 murders - Rose Letts.

25 Cromwell Street is a name etched on the memories of the survivors of those that escaped the evil hands of Fred and Rose West. As the layers of the three-storey house were peeled away the grisly goings on that had taken place over the years gone by were revealed. 24th February 1994 was the beginning of the end of the macabre things that had been going on.

That afternoon, the police came to find the owner of the house, Frederick West. Instead, they found his heavy set, sullen wife

Crime Through Time

Rosemary, who called her husband on his mobile phone the minute they handed her the warrant. "You'd better get back home," she barked at Fred when he answered from his van. "They're going to dig up the garden, looking for Heather." West, a dark haired swarthy looking character was described by the legendary UK prisoner, Charles Bronson, as "Looking like one of the Wurzels." (British pop group from the 70s.)

West showed no outward signs of worry except that the police wouldn't clean up the mess they were sure to make lifting up the patio stones in his garden, looking for the body of their daughter. He stopped by the police station on his way home from work. He told them he and Rose had no idea where Heather was, but he was not worried. "Lots of girls disappear," he explained, "take a different name and go into prostitution." He said she was a "lesbian" and had problems with drugs. Rose West told a similar story. (Heather disappeared at the age of sixteen, back in 1987.) She repeated the story about Heather being a disagreeable and lazy person and a lesbian.

Fred and Rose stayed up all night and talked. The next morning, he stepped into a police car and confessed to the murder of Heather, "I killed her," he told DC Hazel Savage. When he got to the station, he told the police in minute detail how he had cut Heather's body into three pieces and buried them. Rose, he said, had known nothing about the murder at all.

Fred West had retracted his confession, but on hearing that "bones" had been found he changed his mind and once again confessed to Heather's murder.

Fred told how it happened - the argument, slapping her for her insolence and grabbing her throat to stop her from laughing at him. He must have grabbed too hard because she turned blue and stopped breathing. He tried to revive her, but he didn't have the training, so he dragged her over to the bathtub and ran cold water over her. He took off her clothes, lifted her out of the tub and dried her off. Then he tried to put her in the large garbage bin, but she didn't fit.

So it was back in the bathtub where he knew he would have to make her smaller. But first, he strangled her with some tights just to make sure that she was dead. "I didn't want to touch her while she was alive. I mean…if I'd have started cutting her leg or her throat and she'd have suddenly come alive…"

He closed Heather's eyes before he dismembered her. "If somebody's sat there looking at you, you're not going to use a knife on that person are you?"

When he cut off her head, he found the sound - a "horrible noise…like scrunching" - very unpleasant. But, once her head was off, he started on her legs, twisting her foot until he heard "one almighty crack and the leg come loose, like." Cut into pieces, she fitted nicely into the garbage bin.

West said that he buried Heather's body in the garden that night after the remainder of his family was asleep.

Fred was covering for his wife, Rose, formerly Rosemary Letts prior to marrying. Rose West was born in November 1953 in Devon, England with a less than auspicious heritage.

"Fred West said, 'There are 20 other bodies out there, not in one place.' They were spread around and he'd give them (the police) one every year." Janet Leach

---

Rose's father, Bill Letts was a schizophrenic and her mother, Daisy Letts, suffered from severe depression. Bill Letts was a violent domestic tyrant who demanded unconditional obedience from his wife and children. He enjoyed disciplining them and seemed to look for reasons to beat them. Given Bill's psychotic trysts and rigid Victorian behaviour he was not an ideal employee - drifting through a series of low-paying, unskilled jobs.

The family was always short of money. His son Andrew recalled, "If he felt we were in bed too late, he would throw a bucket of cold water over us. He would order us to dig the garden, and that meant the whole garden. Then he would inspect it like an army officer, and if he was not satisfied, we would have to do it all over again…We were not allowed to speak and play like normal children. If we were noisy, he would go for us with a belt or chunk of wood. He would beat you black and blue until mum got in between us. Then she would get a good hiding."

Crime Through Time

So it would seem that the seeds had been sown in terms of Rose West probably having some sort of mental deficiency. After giving birth to three daughters and a son and trying to cope with her violent husband, Daisy's deepening depression resulted in hospitalisation in 1953. She was treated with the controversial electroshock therapy (ECT). Shortly, after a number of these treatments, which delivered electric currents into the brain, Daisy gave birth to Rosemary! Maybe there lies the answer to some of the later problems that came out!

As a baby, Rose developed a habit of rocking herself in her cot; if she was put in a pram without the brake on, she rocked so violently that the pram crept across the room. As she became a little older, Rose only rocked her head, but she did this for hours on end. It was one of the first indications that, in the family's words, she was "a bit slow." As Rose grew from a baby to a toddler to a little girl, she would swing her head for hours until she seemed to have hypnotised herself into semi consciousness.

By now Rose had become known as Dozy Rosie, due to her lack of intelligence, although she was a pretty girl.

Rose was smart enough, however, to make herself her father's pet, always doing whatever he wished immediately. Thereby, she alone received paternal affection and escaped the beatings. She was overweight, which made her the butt of cruel jokes at school. She lashed out at them and attacked anyone who teased her. Consequently, she became known as an ill tempered aggressive loner.

As a teenager, Rose showed signs of being sexually precocious, walking around naked after her baths and climbing into bed with her younger brother and fondling him sexually. Her father's rules forbade her to date boys her own age so she focused her interest in sex on the older men of the village.

In January of 1968, a fifteen-year-old girl named Mary Bastholm disappeared from a bus stop in Gloucester. Mary had been on the way to visit her boyfriend, carrying a Monopoly set. All that the police found at the bus stop were a few pieces of the Monopoly set. The disappearance was thought to be linked to several other rapes in the area.

413

Paedophile Scandals

Rose was cautious of falling foul to the same end but she soon went in search of the older man and paid for it by being raped by an older man.

Early in 1969, Daisy Letts became tired of being her husband's punching bag, took fifteen-year-old Rose and moved in temporarily with her daughter Glenys and her husband. Without her father watching her, Rose spent a lot of time out at night.

In mid-1969, Rose moved back with her father, an action that surprised everyone. Some said that Rose and her father had an incestuous relationship and that Bill Letts had a reputation for molesting young girls, but all of this was unsubstantiated rumour.

Then she met Fred West. However limited Bill Letts was as an ideal parent, he saw Fred West as a completely undesirable boyfriend for Rose. When Bill found that Rose was sleeping with Fred, he raised a fuss with the Social Services. When that was ineffective, he showed up at Fred's trailer park and threatened him.

Meanwhile, Fred West was sent to prison for various thefts and failure to pay fines for previous offences. Rose went back to stay with her father until he found that she was pregnant with Fred's child. At age sixteen, Rose left her father's house to take care of Charmaine and Anna Marie, as well as deal with Fred, who seemed to always be in trouble with the law.

In 1970, Rose gave birth to Heather. One day in the summer of 1971, Charmaine was suddenly missing and Rose told her sister Anna Marie that Rena had come to get her!

Since Fred was in jail when Charmaine was murdered, his involvement probably only extended to burying her body under the kitchen floor of their home on 25 Midland Road where it lay undiscovered for over 20 years. Before he buried Charmaine, he took off her fingers, toes and kneecaps. Fred would hold this criminal secret over Rose for the rest of her life.

Fred would always remind her: "Come on, Rosie, you know what we've got between us," when her father Bill Letts tried to take Rose away from Fred. Rose told her parents, "You don't know him! There's nothing he wouldn't do - even murder!"

Gloucester had a large population of West Indians that created entertainment and income for both Rose and Fred. Rose invited

House of HORRORS

In 1994, the arrest of a seemingly ordinary Gloucester couple living in a seemingly ordinary Gloucester terraced house sparked off a series of extraordinary – and horrifying – revelations.

Cromwell Street is a narrow road of Victorian houses, within a few hundred yards of the main railway station in central Gloucester. It is not a 'good' area – police are often called there to intervene in domestic disputes and brawls. However, to their neighbours, the Wests who lived in number 25 seemed a perfectly normal couple living in a three-storey, semi-detached house, situated at the end of a terrace, that was usually crammed with children and teenage lodgers.

Fred West was a swarthy, slightly simian-looking man with long sideburns, piercing blue eyes and a gap between his front teeth. He seemed to spend most of his spare time dressed in overalls, adding various extensions to his house. His wife Rosemary, 12 years her husband's junior, was plump, bespectacled and plain. To her friends she was known as Rose.

A few neighbours may have remarked upon the unusual number of male callers, many of them black, and the fact that three of Rose's younger daughters were of mixed

South West News Service

The Citizen newspaper, Gloucester

DATE file 24–25 Feb 1994

24.2.94
1.25pm Police arrive at 25 Cromwell Street to dig up the rear garden

7.40pm Fred West goes to Gloucester police station to make a statement

7.55pm Rose West interviewed

25.2.94
11.15am Fred admits his daughter Heather is buried in the garden

11.20am Fred arrested for the murder of Heather

12.25pm Rose arrested on suspicion of the murder of Heather

6.34pm Police officers accompany Fred to the back garden of 25 Cromwell Street, where he indicates the place his daughter is buried

▲ 25 Cromwell Street was the perfect house for Fred and Rosemary West – it was a broken-down place that Fred could do up, located in a once-desirable neighbourhood.

1

many West Indian men to their house on 25 Midland Road to have sex with her - either for cash or fun. Fred encouraged this behaviour and would voyeuristically watch through a peephole. Sex with Fred involved bondage, vibrators, acts of sadism or 987 lesbianism to get him involved, Fred took erotic photos of Rose and ran them as ads in magazines for 'swingers'.

By murdering Charmaine, Rose had created both a monster in that it was both a problem and an opportunity for Fred regarding his first wife Rena. Rena came around looking for Charmaine and sought out Walter, Fred's father, in the hope that he could tell her what had happened to Charmaine.

Fred had no choice but to kill Rena. After killing her he then followed his usual format of dismembering her body and mutilated it in the same odd way that he had Anna McFall's body: he cut off Rena's fingers and toes! Then he put her remains into bags and buried her in the same general area as he buried Anna McFall.

Later that year, Fred and Rose became friendly with Elizabeth Agius, who babysat for them several times. When Fred and Rose returned home, Elizabeth asked them where they had been? The surprisingly candid answer was that they were cruising around looking for young girls, hopefully young virgins. Fred thought that with Rose in the car that a young woman would not fear taking a ride with them. Elizabeth assumed at the time that they were joking. Another time, Fred openly propositioned Agius.

In June of 1972, Rose had another daughter by Fred. They named her Mae West. This time, the child was legitimate, Fred and Rose having married in January of that year at the Gloucester Registry Office.

Fred and Rose decided they needed a house to raise their growing family and also to accommodate Rose's prostitution business. 25 Cromwell Street was just the place. Fred had plans for the cellar and told Elizabeth Agius that he was either going to make it into a place for Rose to entertain her clients or he would soundproof it and use it as his "torture chamber."

Fred's eight-year-old daughter, Anna Marie, was the first victim at Cromwell Street. He and Rose undressed her and told her that she was lucky that she had such caring parents who were making sure that when she got married she would be able to satisfy her husband. Anna Marie's hands were tied behind her and a gag put in her mouth.

In a sickening paedophilic attack, Rose held the girl down while Fred raped her! The pain was so severe that the girl could not go to school for several days. She was warned that she would be beaten if she ever told anyone about the rape. Another time, Anna Marie was strapped down while her father raped her quickly in his brief lunch hour!

In late 1972, Fred and Rose picked up a 17-year-old girl named Caroline Owens, who went on to become a beauty queen, and hired her as a nanny. They promised Caroline's family that they would watch out for her while she lived with them.

Caroline was very attractive, so much so that Rose and Fred competed with each other to seduce her. In short, Caroline found the Wests to be repugnant and told them she was leaving. The couple abducted, stripped and raped her. Fred told her that if she didn't do what he wanted, "I'll keep you in the cellar and let my black friends have you, and when we're finished we'll kill you and bury you under the paving stones of Gloucester." Terrified, she believed him.

When Caroline's mother saw her bruises, she got the truth from her and called the police. Rose West had assaulted her. She had her legs prised open and Rose was beating her between the legs.

In January 1973, there was a hearing - Fred was 31-years-old and Rose a mere nineteen, and pregnant once again. Fred was able to dupe the magistrate into believing that Caroline was a willing partner. Despite Fred's criminal record, the magistrate did not believe the Wests were capable of violence and fined them each £20.

The Wests had been carrying on a friendship with seamstress, Lynda Gough, she eventually moved into 25 Cromwell Street to take care of the children. Lynda became a victim and was murdered. Fred carried out the task of dismembering her and buried her in a pit in the garage. True to his ritual, he removed her fingers, toes and kneecaps.

Paedophile Scandals

When Lynda's family came looking for her, they were told that she had stayed there but had left. By now a hideous pattern was emerging. Young women would come to stay at 25 Cromwell either as lodgers or friends or nannies, but so few ever made it out of the front door alive. The house was slowly becoming a monument to the depravity of the Wests.

A year to celebrate for the Wests was 1973, they walked away from the Caroline Owens rape and abduction charge with only a fine and they had murdered Lynda Gough with no police repercussions at all.

In August that same year, Rose gave birth to their first son, Stephen. Empowered by their success, they went on to abduct 15-year-old Carol Ann Cooper in November and amused themselves with her sexually - until she outlived her entertainment value and was snuffed out by strangulation or suffocation, dismembered and buried. 25 Cromwell Street was starting to become a graveyard to the Wests' victims.

Fred, persistent in his DIY, had enlarged the cellar and was demolishing the garage to build an extension to the main house.

A little over a month later, university student Lucy Partington had gone home to her mother's house to spend the Christmas holiday. On December 27th, she went to visit her disabled friend and left to catch a bus shortly after 10pm. She had the misfortune to meet up with Fred and Rose, who probably knocked her out and abducted her. Like Carol Ann Cooper, she was tortured for approximately a week and then murdered, dismembered and buried in Fred's concreting projects. While dismembering Lucy he accidentally cut his hand and had to go to the hospital for stitches on 3rd January 1974.

Between April of 1974 and April of 1975, three young women - Therese Siegenthaler; 21, Shirley Hubbard; 15, and Juanita Mott; 18, met the same sad ending as Carol Ann Cooper and Lucy Partington. Their tortured and dismembered bodies were buried under the cellar floor of the West's house.

Bondage was becoming a major thrill for Fred and Rose. Shirley's head had been wrapped entirely with tape and a plastic tube was inserted in her nose so that she could breathe.

Crime Through Time

Juanita was subjected to even more extreme bondage: Juanita was gagged with a ligature made from two long, white nylon socks, a brassiere and two pairs of tights, one within the other. She was then trussed up with lengths of plastic-covered rope, of the type used for washing line. It seems that some sort of autoeroticism was sought to be induced? The rope was used in a complicated way, with loops tied around her arms and thighs, both wrists, both ankles and her skull, horizontally and vertically, backwards and forwards across her body until she could only wriggle like a trapped animal – suspended bondage. Then the Wests produced a seven-foot length of rope with a slipknot end forming a noose. This was probably used to suspend Juanita's body from the beams in the cellar.

Fred felt at ease with what he had done and continued to attract the police with continuous thefts and fencing stolen goods. Obviously it was necessary for Fred to keep stealing to pay for his home improvement projects.

In 1976, the Wests enticed a young woman, designated as 'Miss A' by the courts, from a home for wayward girls. At Cromwell Street, Miss A was led into a room with two naked girls who were prisoners there. She witnessed the torture of the two girls and was raped by Fred and sexually assaulted by Rose.

One of the girls that Miss A saw was probably Anna Marie, Fred's daughter, who was a constant tool for the release of the couple's sexual sadism. As if Fred's rape and torture of his daughter was not enough, he brought home his friends to have sex with her. Who were these so-called friends? A paedophile ring is thought to have existed in Gloucester, of which both Fred and Rose were members.

In July 1977, the Wests owned a café at 214 Southgate Street, Gloucester, which they rented out to others at £80 per month. The premises, The Green Lantern, have since been demolished and it is speculated on that more bodies may have been buried there! The actual rent book for this property is on display in the museum, signed by both Fred and Rose – a very rare item.

Mary Bastholm, 15, went missing in 1968 and a TV company procured the services of a reclamation company - Ronsons

Paedophile Scandals

Reclamation - to dig up the basement floor of another café a few hundred metres up the road from The Green Lantern (Tavern) Café. Fred West was a regular client and visitor of Ronsons Reclamation for many years as a local DIY builder. Although Andy Jones of the museum knows certain members of the West family and a living victim, he has remained silent, wishing to respect family wishes.

In 1977, the upstairs of the house at Cromwell Street had been

Above, the front and inside of the rent book for The Green Lantern Cafe, signed by both Fred and Rose West. A very rare item, can be seen on display in the museum.

SAL

REGISTRATION OF BUSINESS NAMES ACT, 1916

as amended by the Companies Acts 1947 and 1976

CERTIFICATE OF REGISTRATION

I hereby certify that pursuant to section 3 of the above-mentioned Act a statement of particulars in respect of

THE GREEN LANTERN

was this day registered.

Dated the **21st July 1977**

(F. WHIPP)

Registrar of Business Names

Regn. No. **2146782**

Above, the Certificate of Registration for a sole Proprietor registering the business name of The Green Lantern.

420

remodelled to allow for a number of lodgers. One of them was Shirley Robinson, 18, a former prostitute with bisexual inclinations. Shirley developed relationships with both Fred and Rose. Shirley became pregnant with Fred's child after Rose was pregnant with the child of one of her black clients.

While Fred was pleased that Rose was carrying a mixed child, Rose was not comfortable with Shirley carrying Fred's child. Shirley foolishly thought that she could displace or even replace Rose in Fred's life and, in the process, jeopardised her own existence. Rose was jealous and made it clear that Shirley had to go – one way or the other!

And go she did, seven months after Rose gave birth to Tara in December of 1977, Shirley joined the rest of the girls buried in Cromwell Street. The cellar being full, Shirley was put in the rear garden along with her unborn child. This time, Fred dismembered Shirley and their unborn baby!

In November of 1978, Rose and Fred had yet another daughter who they named Louise, making a total of six children in the bizarre and evil household. Fred also impregnated his daughter Anna Marie, but the pregnancy, which occurred in her fallopian tube and became an ectopic pregnancy, which had to be terminated.

In May of 1979, Rose's father died of a lung ailment. Several months later, the Wests were up to their old tricks and murdered a troubled teenager named Alison Chambers after they raped and tortured her. Like Shirley, Alison was buried in the alternative cemetery in the rear garden.

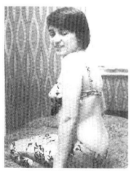

Above, Rose West's Swingers Advert

The children were now becoming aware of some of the ghastly gruesome goings on in the home. They now knew that Rose was a prostitute and that Anna Marie was being serial raped by her father. When Anna Marie moved out to live with her boyfriend, Fred focused his sexual advances on Heather and Mae. Heather resisted her father and was beaten for it.

Paedophile Scandals

In June of 1980, Rose gave birth to Barry, Fred's second son. Then again, in April of 1982, Rose gave birth to Rosemary Junior, who was not Fred's child.

In July of 1983, Rose gave birth to another daughter who they named Lucyanna. She was a half-caste, like Tara and Rosemary Junior. Rose became increasingly irritable and systematically beat the children without provocation. The stress was starting to take its toll on Rose.

In 1986, the wall of family silence that had protected the Wests was broken. Heather told her girlfriend about her father's advances, her mother's prostitution and affairs and the beatings she received. The girlfriend in turn told her parents, who were friends of the Wests! Heather's life was now in jeopardy.

Heather West - Murdered

After her parents murdered her, they told the children that she left home. Fred asked his son Stephen to help him dig a hole in the rear garden, where Fred later buried Heather's dismembered body.

Rose built up her prostitution business by advertising in special magazines. She and Fred were on the lookout for women who they could get to participate in their various perversions as well as prostitute herself under Rose's direction as a whorehouse Madame. One such woman, Katherine Halliday, fitted the bill and became a fixture in the West household and saw first hand the kinky black bondage suits and masks that they had collected, plus the various whips and chains. With good reason, Katherine became alarmed and quickly broke off her relationship with them.

The Wests carnival of killing was coming to an end. One of the very young girls that Fred had raped, with Rose's assistance, told her girlfriend what happened. The girlfriend didn't tell her parents, she went to the police! The case was assigned to a very talented and persistent D C named Hazel Savage. Hazel knew Fred from his days with Rena and remembered the stories that Rena had told her about Fred's sexual perversions.

Crime Through Time

On August 6th 1992, police arrived at 25 Cromwell Street with a search warrant to look for pornography and evidence of child abuse. They found mountains of pornography and arrested Rose for assisting in the rape of a minor. Fred was arrested for rape and sodomy of a minor.

Hazel Savage went to work interviewing family members and friends of the Wests. When she talked to Anna Marie, she heard for the first time the shocking story about how she had been so severely abused. She also expressed her concerns about Charmaine, who Hazel had known from her experiences with Rena.

Hazel had all she needed to bring child abuse charges, but she needed to further investigate the disappearance of Charmaine, Rena and Heather. Hazel was not satisfied that Heather had disappeared without a trace. Insurance and tax records showed that Heather had not been employed nor had she visited a doctor in four years. Either she had left the country or was dead.

The younger children had a care order placed on them and were taken from Rose and put into government care. With Fred in jail and the police closing in on her, Rose couldn't face the pressure and took an overdose of pills and attempted suicide, her son, Stephen, saved her. Later, she escaped from her loneliness and found sanctuary by stuffing herself with candy and watching Disney videos.

The case against the Wests collapsed when two key witnesses decided not to testify against them. But the seeds of their discovery had been sown. The strange, inexplicable disappearance of Heather was firmly implanted in Hazel Savage's mind.

An inquiry into Heather's whereabouts was actioned. When no sign of the girl was found, Hazel feared that that the rumour was true that Heather was buried under the patio. The West children were questioned repeatedly. Fred had threatened them that if they didn't keep their silence that they would end up the same way as Heather - under the patio!

Detective Superintendent John Bennett was in charge of the by now media-sensitive case. Finally, the warrant to search the Cromwell Street house and garden was signed, but the logistics of digging up a six hundred square foot garden were nontrivial. Fred's extension to the house was built over a portion of the garden. The search would be very expensive and be certain to attract attention of the media.

Things improved for the investigation after Fred confessed to killing his daughter and after human bones other than Heather's were found in the garden. When Rose was informed of Fred's confession, she claimed that Fred had sent her out of the house the day Heather disappeared and had no knowledge of Heather's death.

Recieved from Mrs Wagner the sum of £2 for Water Heating date: 1/8/77

signed Mrs R.P. West.

Recieved from Mrs Wagner the sum of £4 for Water Heating date: 5/9/77

signed Mrs R.P. West.

Above, two authentic receipts signed by Rose West in respect of payment received for water heating in 1977, original items on display in the museum.

The living room after it was stripped. Note the scenic mural on the wall.

The cellar of 25 Cromwell Street.

Fred was temporarily released on bail, but with the police digging up the garden he knew it was only a matter of time before the final piece of the jig-saw was in place, which would be the discovery of Heather's body!

Fred confessed to his son that he had done something really bad and would be going away for a while. Stephen remembered, "He looked at me so evil and so cold. That look went right through me."

> **"They'd be drugged out of their brains, if they were girls or boys it didn't matter what."** Fred West

The police found the remains of a young woman in the garden, and then they found another body – the scope of the investigation now widened.

To protect Rose, Fred claimed responsibility for the murders himself. He was charged with the murders of Heather, Shirley Robinson and the as yet an unidentified third woman.

An investigation was opened into the disappearance of Rena and Charmaine. For some reason, Fred decided to tell the police about the girls buried in his cellar? Fred admitted to murdering the girls, but not rape. These girls, he maintained, wanted to have sex with him.

Nine sets of bones were discovered in the cellar and the police did not know whose they were. Fred was not much help since he could not remember the names and details of some of the women (probably because he'd killed so many over the years) he had picked up. Considering the many women who go missing every year, extensive work had to be done to match up missing person's reports with the remains.

Rose abandoned Fred in order to save herself, but this may have been helpful in her downfall. She tried to position herself as the victim of a murderous man, but she was not particularly convincing or clever enough to carry this out.

The bodies of Rena, Anna McFall and Charmaine were found as Fred continued to cooperate with the police. On the Mary Bastholm case, Fred decided to quit cooperating and her body was not found. (See earlier reference to The Green Lantern Café.) It has, however, been suggested to Fred's solicitor by Fred that Mary got into a car and is buried at Bishops Cleve.

At their joint hearing, Fred attempted to console Rose, but she avoided his touch. She told the police he made her sick. The great killing partnership was over.

Fred was devastated by Rose's rejection and at such a time when he needed a shoulder to cry on it made him bitter. On 13th December 1994, he was charged with twelve murders. Again, Rose brushed him off. He had written to her, 'We will always be in love...You will always be Mrs West, all over the world. That is important to me and to you.'

> ## "I should go to hell for what I've done."
> **Fred West**

LIVING VICTIMS

Fred West: Still loved by his children

Rose West: Only Mae visits her in jail

Above: The Wests with six of their children

...adow of their parents: Stephen and Mae West and (right) their half-sister Anne Marie Davies

Fred's brother, Doug West, "I think he (Fred) was prepared to take the wrap, but when she (Rose) ignored him..." (Talking about when Rose stood next to Fred in the magistrates' court dock and ignored him when he touched her shoulder to speak to her.)

Just before noon on New Year's Day, 1995, at Winson Green Prison, in Birmingham, when the guards were having lunch, Fred hanged himself with strips of bed sheet. He had clearly planned his suicide well in advance so that he would not be discovered.

Despite the shortage of direct evidence linking Rose to the murders, Rose went to trial on 3rd October 1995. A number of witnesses - including Caroline Owens, Miss A, and Anna Marie - testified to Rose's sick sadistic sexual assaults on young women.

The goal of the prosecution, led by Brian Leveson QC, was to construct a tight web of circumstantial evidence of Rose's guilt. The defence, led by Richard Ferguson QC, tried to show that evidence of sexual assault was not the same as evidence of murder. That Rose did not know what Fred was doing when he murdered the girls and buried them in various places.

Ferguson made the big mistake of putting Rose on the stand, which at the end of the day was a decision she would have had to agree to. Her defiance came through very clearly to the jury. Furthermore, the prosecution learned to extract damaging testimony from her by making her angry, which wasn't difficult. The jury were left with beliefs that Rose had treated the children badly and that she was completely dishonest.

Rose in king size bed with lace canopy.

When the recordings of some of the 124 police interviews Fred had given the police were played in court describing how he had murdered the victims when Rose was out of the house, unfortunately for Rose, Fred was shown to be lying on key issues, which threw his entire statement into doubt.

Paedophile Scandals

The most damning evidence was given by Janet Leach, who was called as the "appropriate adult" (witness) to Fred West's police interviews.

Privately, Fred had told her that Rose was involved in the murders - and that Rose had murdered Charmaine and Shirley Robinson without him - but that he made a deal with his wife to take all the blame on himself.

Janet was so stressed by this confidential confession that she suffered a stroke. It was only after Fred's death that she felt that she could tell the police what he had said to her. After her testimony, she collapsed and had to be taken to the hospital.

Rose was called the strategist and the dominant partner in Leveson's prosecution summary, "The evidence that Rosemary West knew nothing is not worthy of belief." Ferguson, in his defence summary, stressed that the evidence only pointed to Fred.

Finding Rose West guilty didn't take the jury too long. The judge sentenced her to life imprisonment on each of ten counts of murder.

Serial killer Fred West's police interviews, which suggested he killed more women than previously thought, were to be broadcast for the first time. A TV company had allegedly paid £100,000 (Sterling) for audiotapes, videotapes, photographs and other related material.

But the ruling by the Attorney General to allow Channel 5 to broadcast the taped interviews as part of a documentary has angered Gloucestershire Police, considering such a large sum was handed over in an indirect way it seems a surprising move by Gloucestershire Police when they must have known the items were not going to be sitting gathering dust in some television company's archives!

The interviews were to form part of a programme that would criticise the police for failing to investigate fully the claims that West committed more murders than the 12 for which he was charged. The force has repeatedly dismissed similar allegations in the past.

Gloucestershire's Chief Constable, Tim Brain, wrote to the Attorney General expressing concern about the material being used

End of a NIGHTMARE

The plot took on a new twist when Fred West committed suicide. This turned the spotlight on Rose. Was she a partner in their murderous career

As it slowly dawned on Fred West that he had no hope of ever being freed from jail, he became increasingly depressed. Rose had also been in prison since 21 April 1994, but when they had been brought together in the dock on 30 June to be charged jointly with nine murders, Rose had refused to look at him and shrank away when he tried to touch her. Leaked press

Winson Green Prison, Birmingham, to eat his lunch. Using the needle and thread he had been given for his job of sewing buttons on prison shirts, he stitched into a rope strips of the green blanket from his bed, and hanged himself from a bar on the ventilation shaft above the door. When found, less than an hour later, he failed to respond to any attempts at resuscitation.

in a programme or series of programmes. (Have since been broadcast.)

Mr Brain appealed to programme makers to adopt a "sensitive" approach, following the decision of Lord Goldsmith not to intervene. Mr Brain told BBC Radio 4's *Today* programme: "Emotions are still very raw in the county of Gloucestershire and beyond. For victims' families these are still very, very current memories for them and consequently we feel that somebody ought to speak up for them."

Mediawatch-UK, formerly known as the National Viewers and Listeners Association, wants Independent Television Commission (ITC) chairman Sir Robin Biggam to investigate how Channel 5 gained possession of the tapes.

This is a reasonable request, considering that Crown Copyright would be applied to the actual interview tapes and other evidence the police developed for the prosecution case. Only the Crown could assign such copyright, the Crown in this case being the police authority concerned! The other items such as video recordings, made by Fred, of course could not have Crown Copyright applied to them nor the family photoset, etc.

Mediawatch-UK director John Beyer said the ITC should nvestigate whether the programme was in the public interest. In a letter to Sir Robin, he said: 'Given that these police interviews were never intended for transmitting on free to air television, I believe that it is appropriate for the ITC to fully investigate how they were acquired by Channel 5 TV.' But on the other hand it is in the public interest that the full story be told and if there are failings in the investigation then these should be fully investigated. Since it is now in the public domain the audiotapes may well find their way around the globe.

West was charged with 12 murders, including those of his first wife and eldest daughter.

Objectors to the plans by Channel 5 to broadcast the controversial programme handed in a 5,000-signature petition to TV producers. Fred West's daughter, Anne-Marie Davis, was among the families of victims and MPs who handed in the protest to bosses at Channel 5. She said at the time: "I am absolutely out-raged. I find it most distressing when these television companies try to boost their ratings on the back of so many families' grief." In direct contrast to this, her brother, Stephen, appeared in the Channel 5 broadcast of the finished TV documentary. Stephen West indicated in the documentary that another farm was used to carry out torture on kidnapped victims.

> ## "It was a house of abuse, constant abuse!"
> **Stephen West**

It has been further claimed that another farm, in Gloucester, separate to the one Stephen West mentions, was frequently a busy place with plenty of parked cars there. Supposedly used by a cult that held girls there for days on end, torturing them and burning their fingernails, as well as the use of a biff stone slab being involved in some sort of torture routine.

Given that one of Fred's brothers also hung himself it would indicate that some sort of paedophile ring did exist and that the brother, not Doug, took part in the activities of the ring. Fred mentions Bristol, saying girls were drugged and taken there?

Some of the videos seized by police actually show Rose West being involved in bestiality. (Sex with animals.) Given then the serious nature of the claims made by those seeking further arrests it does seem logical that someone knows more than they're telling. There is evidence out there, people have talked but given the complexity of the paedophile ring it is not in the interests of public funds to investigate the matter. The police seemingly being happy at the suicide of Fred and the conviction of Dozy Rosie.

One of the deaths most frequently attributed and admitted to by Fred West to his solicitor was that of 15-year-old Mary Bastholm, who disappeared in 1968 as she waited for a bus in Gloucester. Her body has never been found. Her brother, Peter Bastholm, said: "I have no objections whatsoever providing they do get the facts correct."

Gloucester Social Services admitted to losing track of some 400 files relating to children and that out of them 100 of the children could be missing! Sharon Compton, who claims she took part in sex and bondage games and was also assaulted by Fred and Rose claimed that police officers were having sex with Rose at a time when girls were being tortured and killed. She further claimed that the police had paid Fred for their sexual activities with Rose.

After an official inquiry the police were cleared and the report said that Sharon wasn't ever at the home of Fred and Rose West and that her claims that she'd been assaulted by the pair was also unfounded? Strange though, because again this claim was again aired in the Channel 5 documentary in which Ms Compton also appeared!

> ### In 1996, 25 Cromwell Street was demolished.

> ### There are a hundred young women unaccounted for in the Gloucester area between 1970 and 1995.

Paedophile Scandals

Rose West, last heard, was in HMP Durham on the notorious 'She' wing. Perhaps what fascinates many people about the Cromwell Street murders is that it exposes the dark side to us all, maybe we are intrigued by the darker side?

The Crime Through Time museum has many genuine articles on display relating to the murders of Fred and Rose West, all sympathetically displayed. Crime Through Time museum is based in Gloucestershire, amidst the area frequented by Fred West, in fact the actual prison cell that once had Fred West locked up in is the one at the museum - the museum formerly being the police station and courthouse.

ROSE'S EVIL ART

Jail pictures expose the sick mind of serial killer

EXCLUSIVE

By CHRIS TATE

HOUSE of Horrors killer Rose West has started drawing pretty pictures in her prison cell – and even THEY reek of evil, the Sunday People can reveal today.

Rose, 46, serving life for murdering 10 girls, has turned to art in a desperate attempt to occupy her lonely days.

She spends most of the time in her cell doing coloured chalk drawings because she is too scared to mix with other female inmates.

Rose fears they will attack her for the hideous crimes at 25 Cromwell Street, Gloucester, committed by her and now-dead husband Fred. Her pictures are signed "Lots of love, Rose" with two kisses.

But when the Sunday People showed the one above supposedly of flowers to top psychologist Martin Lloyd-Elliott, without revealing who had drawn it, his verdict was damning. He said:

6 I've seen some horrific images over the years but this really did give me the shivers.

And when I showed it to three colleagues without telling them who had done it they all agreed with me – it gave us the shivers.

The drawing is a grotesque

TWISTED: Rose's drawing made a psychologist shiver

GROTESQUE: Rose's sign-off

charade. It tries to be bright and friendly but it is done by someone who has no normal emotions. Look at the strangeness of the plant, like some kind of Venus fly-trap.

Her dark murderous nature has hijacked her attempt to paint something loving and has per-

verted it into a distorted view of life. Something meant to be loving is revolting, distorted and perverted.

Rose, who has launched a legal battle against her convictions, started drawing after she complained she was suffering from stress and a psychiatrist at Durham jail advised her to take up art.

A source at the jail said: "She thinks her pictures are wonderful but they are not fit to wrap fish and chips in."

● PeopleHotlinks
e-lab@people.co.uk
For more on the Wests:
www.crimelibrary.com

MONSTER: Evil Rose West

"By using these tapes, they brought him back to life."
Caroline (Owens) Roberts - Living Victim

Crime Through Time

All that glitters is not gold

F A L L E N

I D O L

RETURN OF THE SEX MONSTER

Evil Glitter breaks ban to sneak into Cuba

BLOATED FACE OF A FALLEN IDOL

EXCLUSIVE: PAEDOPHILE

SICKENING, REPULSIVE

LIFE IN JET-SET Sex beast Glitter walks past a flashy motor parked close to where his boat is moored in Spanish port

DISGRACE Singer after being freed from prison

TWISTED glam rocker Gary Glitter is

THE Sun

THE PEOPLE'S PAPER

GLITTER A fat, bald, evil pervert in paradise

433

Paedophile Scandals

Bloated and bald, the paedophile of pop now that the glitter has gone

By Nick Craven

Glitter's new face

Changing face of the star who went from Leader to loser

Left: Gary Glitter performing on stage in his heyday as the king of glam-rock

Above: Leaving his yacht Voyager in a dinghy

Right: The £45,000 yacht at its moorings in the resort of Sotogrande, where the shamed star has been for seven weeks

Cuba doesn't want him, and in 2003 Cambodia kicked his ass out of their paedophile welcoming country.

Warped world of Wonderland

Victims tortured and tormented to satisfy the sickest of desires

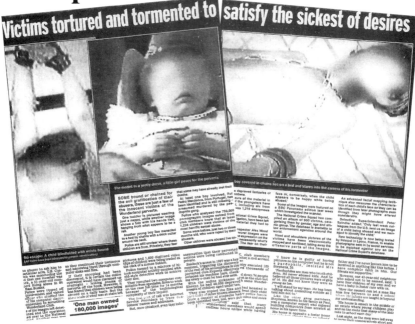

434

Has King gone to the moon...or is it prison?

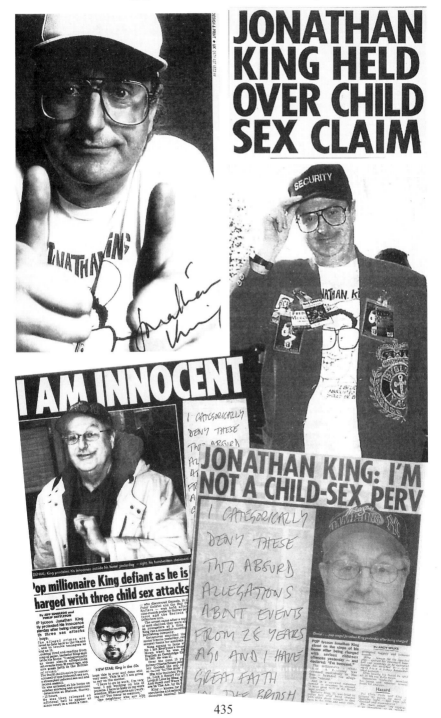

435

King faces court on sex charges

By CHARLIE BAIN

POP tycoon Jonathan King appeared in court yesterday accused of a string of sex offences against young men nearly 30 years ago.

The 55-year-old record producer faced three sexual assault charges, including one on a boy under 16. They are alleged to have happened between 1970 and '71.

Bachelor King was charged under his real name of Kenneth George King.

Wearing a black suit and trainers, he spoke only to appear again at Staines Magistrates Court in Surrey on January 2.

King won fame in 1965 with the chart hit Everyone's Gone To The Moon and later became a successful TV presenter and columnist.

He was arrested last week when police swooped on his luxury home in Bayswater, west London.

SEX FIEND KING TO NAME HIS PERVERT PALS

JAILED sex fiend Jonathan King is threatening to expose other high-profile paedophiles.

King has told inmates at Maidstone prison in Kent that he wants to name and shame a top sports personality and a showbiz star.

A prison insider said: "Both men have whiter than white reputations and the public would be shocked if they knew who they were."

King, jailed in December for seven years for offences against boys, says he won't apply for parole if his appeal fails because he refuses to admit his crimes.

A prison insider said:

BY **MATTHEW ACTON**

"He contradicts himself. First he's protesting his innocence, but then he's threatening to expose paedophiles who are in the public eye and still free."

John Lennon abused me, rants King

JAILED pervert Jonathan King is boasting he had under-age sex with ex-Beatle John Lennon in the 1960s.

The pop paedophile, who is serving seven years for

THE WEB OF PURE EVIL

 Andrew Sadler was a popular prep school teacher. But as this chilling investigation reveals, he was at the centre of a vast and sophisticated network of paedophiles, many of them occupying top jobs, who with sickening cunning have infiltrated our public schools ...

by **Jo-Ann Goodwin**

Caption: Andrew Sadler (top right), who has been jailed in Romania for child sex offences, and, left to right, schoolmaster Adrian Stark, convicted paedophile Morris Vasar, child sex apologist Tom O'Carroll and Ric Gabriel, Sadler's Romanian 'fixer'

Crime Through Time

The most evil paedophile duo ever!

Brady and Hindley dancing on the moors not far from where at least four bodies were buried.

Photo courtesy of James Nicholson

She has her own 'suite', TV and laptop – and secret letters from Brady

ALL MOD CONS: Highpoint Prison where Hindley, right, is the only inmate to be served her meals in a specially decorated cell

Revealed: Luxury lifestyle of child murderer Hindley

By **Thomas Penny**

EXTRAORDINARY details of the privacy and unparalleled luxury enjoyed by Moors murderess Myra Hindley emerged last night.

After years in prison, Hindley lives in conditions which make other inmates jealous and have angered some prison officers guarding her.

Hindley, whose affair with Ian Brady turned into a sadistic child-killing spree in the Sixties, has two cells to herself and round-the-clock access to a television and a laptop computer. She sleeps on an orthopaedic bed bought for her by well-wishers and enjoys regular visits in her cell from a hairdresser. Her suite is even carpeted and fitted with curtains to match her blue and white duvet covers.

She has private access to showers, a phone and an exercise yard, and is served meals in her cell.

And, in an astonishing new twist, The Mail on Sunday can reveal Hindley has also been carrying on a secret correspondence with Brady.

Last night, the news was met with fury from the families of her victims. A spokesman for the family of ten-year-old victim Lesley Ann Downey, whose mother, Ann, died from cancer last year, said they were sickened by Hindley's treatment.

'When she was ill, Ann had to be washed downstairs at a sink because she didn't have the strength to walk upstairs,' he said. 'Alan [Ann's husband] is absolutely livid that his poor wife was not even provided with the basic facilities of a bed and a bath while she was suffering with cancer – and then there's no expense spared when it comes to Hindley.'

Prison sources say Hindley, jailed for life in 1966 and currently held at Highpoint Prison, Suffolk, wrote to and received letters from Brady, who is in Merseyside's Ashworth High Security Hospital,

HATE MAIL: Brady started writing to Hindley again

up until three years ago. Until now, they were known only to have written to each other in the Sixties and Eighties.

It is believed the latest exchange of letters ended in 1998 when Brady threatened to publish letters showing that Hindley's claims he had led her into the killings were untrue and to demonstrate that she

The hairdresser visits regularly

was capable of cold-blooded murder without his influence.

A prison source said: 'The contents of the letters could be explosive. It's not known who started the correspondence, but she has a lot of letters from him.'

Hindley has managed to keep the letters away from the light fingers of fellow inmates because of the extraordinary conditions in which she lives.

Secluded from her fellow prisoners, she lives in splendid isolation in a suite of two cells joined by a corridor sealed off from the rest of the prison.

Shuffling between the cells she looks more like a 75-year-old than the 58-year-old she is. Crippled by osteoporosis, back pain and angina, she is also in constant pain as a result of a pin in her leg which has slipped and trapped a nerve.

A source close to Hindley said: 'In the mornings she is brought breakfast and newspapers in the cell which acts as her bedroom and living room. She reads and writes letters, some by hand and others using the laptop computer which she has in her cell and has access to around the clock.' Her morning routine also includes Buddhist chanting under a poster of the Dalai Lama.

The cell has a toilet and a sink piled high with face creams and moisturisers. Her hair is also cared for during regular visits from a hairdresser. If she wants a shower, other inmates are locked away while she uses the communal showers.

Unlike the cells in the rest of the prison, Hindley's 'living room' is decorated to her own tastes. It is painted pale pink and has a fitted carpet. Her bed has a £750 orthopaedic mattress

and pillow, and was un... recently receiving treatme from a visiting osteopath.

Two weeks ago, as she c... elerated her 58th birthday, h cell was filled with fresh flo ers and cards from well-wis ers, believed to include Lo Longford and David Astor, t former editor of the Observ who is said to provide her wi £250 a month pocket money.

'Her cell is like Steptoe's ya in the TV series Steptoe A Son – she's a "collectomania and never throws anythi... away,' a jail insider said.

'She has kept all the ne... paper cuttings and books abc her case and hundreds of l ters from well-wishers a from Brady.'

In her two wardrobes are t brightly coloured caftans s likes to wear. She rolls her o cigarettes, keeping her tobac in an engraved silver box.

The second cell acts as t work room, where she repa library books for £7 a week.

Unlike other inmates, Hi... ley receives visitors in private room. If she wants use the telephone, other pr oners are locked in their ce as she chats to friends and t lesbian girlfriend, Nina Wil

In the evenings, she watcl her own 14in colour televisi she has her own collection videos – or listens to her sou system or Walkman. T power is left on in her c... throughout the night. She is t only prisoner who is free decide what time she turns t lights off and goes to sleep.

Norman Brennan, of the V tims of Crime Trust, sa 'Charities like ours find it ha enough to find £50 to pay for hour's counselling for famil bereaved by murder, and to see no expense spared the comfort of someone w killed.'

The test case that could free Hindley

By **Michael Clarke**
Home Affairs Correspondent

BRITAIN'S most notorious killers, including Myra Hindley and Rose West, could walk free from jail if a landmark court case launched yesterday succeeds.

The move, which could trigger a huge rebellion by MPs, is being brought under the terms of the Human Rights Act.

Two killers have claimed that the decision on how long they stay behind bars should be made by a judge and not the Home Secretary, Jack Straw.

Double murderers Anthony Anderson and John Taylor say allowing the Home Secretary to decide their tariff, or minimum jail term, is a breach of their human rights.

They claim they should be treated in the same way as the killers of James Bulger, who could be released this summer. Mr Straw has already conceded the principle in the cases of juvenile murderers, after Robert Thompson and Jon Venables took him to the European Court in Strasbourg.

Hindley: Told 'life must mean life'

Court: 'These are sentencing functions which should not be performed by a politician, but by the judiciary.'

He said judges have to explain their reasons in open court and their decisions can be challenged, while the Home Secretary makes his rulings in secret.

David Pannick QC, for Mr Straw,

437

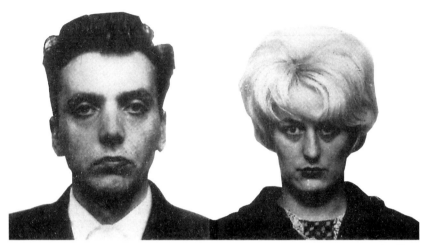

MOORS MURDERS - Ian Brady, aged 28, and Myra Hindley met in 1961, she was a 19-year-old typist, he was a 23-year-old stock clerk.

By 1966, both were tried at Chester Assizes for multiple murder. The trial lasted 15 days; Brady and Hindley were convicted on 6th May 1966, sentenced to life imprisonment. To date, in the new millennium, there has not been a Home Secretary brave enough to even talk about their release.

Brady and Hindley worked in the same office. After hours, they developed a violent appetite for sadism, Nazism and pornography. In September 1964 the couple went to live with Hindley's grandmother in Hattersley. They were friendly with Hindley's sister Maureen and her husband 17-year-old David Smith. With his books on sadism and handguns Brady sought to impress Smith. Between them they talked of robbing banks and even worse, murder!

Not wishing to look like an idle boaster, Brady picked up 17-year-old Edward Evans, a homosexual, in Manchester on the evening of 6th October 1965 and took him home. Later that night, 11.30, Hindley went to Smith's house and asked him home. Smith was shown a murder! On the sofa in the living room was a young man. He was still alive, but Brady, wielding an axe, proceeded to smash his head in. He said, 'It's done. It's the messiest yet. It normally only takes one blow.'

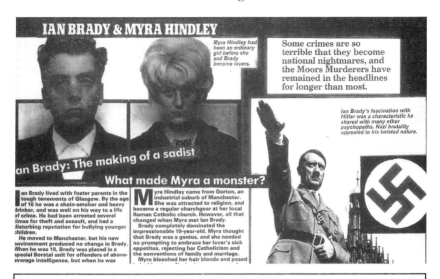

IAN BRADY & MYRA HINDLEY

Myra Hindley had been an ordinary girl before she and Brady became lovers.

Some crimes are so terrible that they become national nightmares, and the Moors Murderers have remained in the headlines for longer than most.

Ian Brady's fascination with Hitler was a characteristic he shared with many other psychopaths. Nazi brutality appealed to his twisted nature.

Ian Brady: The making of a sadist

What made Myra a monster?

Ian Brady lived with foster parents in the tough tenements of Glasgow. By the age of 16 he was a chain-smoker and heavy drinker, and was well on his way to a life of crime. He had been arrested several times for theft and assault, and had a disturbing reputation for bullying younger children.

He moved to Manchester, but his new environment produced no change in Brady. When he was 18, Brady was placed in a special Borstal unit for offenders of above-average intelligence, but when he was

Myra Hindley came from Gorton, an industrial suburb of Manchester. She was attracted to religion, and became a regular churchgoer at her local Roman Catholic church. However, all that changed when Myra met Ian Brady. Brady completely dominated the impressionable 19-year-old. Myra thought that Brady was a genius, and she needed no prompting to embrace her lover's sick appetites, rejecting her Catholicism and the conventions of family and marriage.

Myra bleached her hair blonde and posed

Cigarette loving Hindley smoked her way to a chest infection/heart attack and died 15th November 2002.

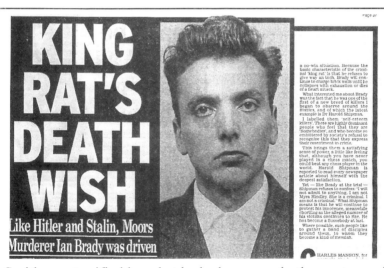

Page 47

KING RAT'S DEATH WISH

Like Hitler and Stalin, Moors Murderer Ian Brady was driven

a no-win situation. Because the basic characteristic of the criminal 'king rat' is that he refuses to give way an inch, Brady will continue to charge brick walls until he collapses with exhaustion or dies of a heart attack.

What interested me about Brady was the fact that he was one of the first of a new breed of killers I began to observe around the Sixties, and of which the latest example is Dr Harold Shipman.

I labelled them 'self-esteem killers'. These are highly dominant people who feel that they are 'Somebodies', and who become so embittered by society's refusal to recognise this that they express their resentment in crime.

This brings them a satisfying sense of power, a little like feeling that, although you have never played in a chess match, you could beat any chess player in the world. Harold Shipman is reported to read every newspaper article about himself with the deepest satisfaction.

Yet — like Brady at the trial — Shipman refuses to confess: 'I will not admit to anything. I am not Myra Hindley. She is a criminal. I am not a criminal.' What Shipman means is that he will continue to protest his innocence, meanwhile chortling as the alleged number of his victims continues to rise. He has become a Somebody at last.

Where possible, such people like to gather a band of disciples around them, to whom they become a kind of messiah.

CHARLES MANSON, for

Smith was terrified by what he had seen; early the next morning he telephoned the police. At the house police found the body of the dead youth in a bedroom. A search produced two 'left luggage' tickets that corresponded with two suitcases at Manchester Central Station. The police found the cases and within them was one of the most revealing discoveries that would haunt them for the rest of their lives. Amongst the coshes, wigs, papers and photographs were two tape recordings.

Paedophile Scandals

Some of the photographs were of a little girl - 10-year-old Lesley Ann Downey, who had been missing from her home since December 1964. The child's screaming voice was identified on a tape recording pleading to be allowed to go home. The tape went on to a reveal the heart rending cries of pain coming from the little girl, as she was brutality tortured with pliers. Commands were heard been given from Brady telling her what to do, this took place in a bedroom. When they had finished with her she was killed. Her body was found disposed of on Oldham moors, north of Manchester.

Another child, 12-year-old John Kilbride, missing from home since November 1963, featured in some of Brady's notes - notes which were a plan of murder. From photographs showing Brady and Hindley on the moors, police were able to identify search areas. John Kilbride's moorland grave was found a few hundred yards from that of Lesley Ann Downey.

The Moors Murderers continued to excite interest, first with suggestions that Hindley had become a socially reformed character fit to be paroled and, secondly, by persistent rumours that there were more bodies to be found on the moors. Despite a strong campaign on her behalf by the late Lord Longford, Hindley remained in prison; Brady, who is detained in Park Lane High Security Hospital, Liverpool, has said that he never wants to be released. Having gone on various hunger strikes, wanting to die he seems to have survived for quite some time.

A private confession in 1986 by Hindley to two more killings led to searches on Saddlewoth Moor for further graves. Her confession was made public in April 1987 and it became known that she and Brady admitted killing Keith Bennett, 12, and Pauline Reade, aged 16. Some 24 years after the girl was murdered her body was found in August 1987, 24 years after she had disappeared. At different times both Hindley and Brady assisted the police in their searches by being taken to the moors in a helicopter.

The Director of Public Prosecutions announced in January 1988 that no further charges would be brought against the Moors Murderers. Since then Brady has written a manuscript, relating to the murders, that he has given to his solicitor, in the event of

Brady's death he has asked for the manuscript to be sold to a publisher and made into a book. Brady courted more controversy when he wrote a book on serial killers, although he didn't mention his own crimes it caused an outcry, but still sold well. His royalty cheques went to his aging mother. Hindley hopes she might be freed. Her body ravaged by the effects of chain smoking will be her only way out of prison. In a bizarre move, UK prisoner Charles Bronson sent her a pack of cigarettes... to speed up her death!! Ian Brady and Myra Hindley killed for kicks. They developed a sick, mutual thrill from killing innocent children.

Brady was well on the way to being a full-blown psychopath. He had a private library of books about torture and ritual killing, his favourite being the works of the Marquis de Sade. (Sadism) Hindlsy was quickly influenced and dominated by her older boyfriend, whom she regarded as an intellectual genius, as did he too. She soon took an avid interest inhis books on leather fetishism, sexual sadism and bondage, at a time when pornography was outlawed more strictly than it is now.

Brady had a fascination with Hitler, a thing he shared with many other famous psychopaths. Nazi brutality seems to appeal to people that have a sense of wanting to grasp power by any method they can. Apart from idolizing Hitler, Brady had a favourite movie that he and Hindley would watch time and time again... the 'Nuremburg War Trials'.

Brady was obsessed with Hitler
The museum has a vast display of items relating to
serial killers and paedophiles.

Paedophile Scandals

Dirty Rotten Perverts

442

Dirty Rotten Perverts

THE FILTHY FRIAR

Monk groped mum in secret sessions, court told

By ROB CHAPTOR

A MARRIED woman was seduced into a six-year affair by a Catholic monk, a court heard yesterday.

PERVERT MAGICIAN PREYS ON GIRLS AGE 4

TAGGED FROM SPACE

Perverts to be tracked by satellite

PREDATOR: Green was tagged

PREDATOR: Dangerous Oliver

Catholics turned a blind eye to perverted priest

By Michael Seamark and Neil Sears

BRITAIN'S most senior Roman Catholic, the Archbishop of Westminster, was under attack yesterday for allowing a known paedophile to continue working as a priest.

MY PERVERT DAD IS FREE TO WORK WITH CHILDREN

ALERT: Dentist Bromley still practices

DIRTY DENTIST TREATS KIDS

DISGUSTED: 'Men like my dad don't get better,' warns Sarah

EXCLUSIVE

By NADIA COHEN

Paedophile Scandals

No Cure

Is it right that the wife of a political leader should defend a paedophile on the grounds that the law infringes his human rights? Ask any parent whose child has been sexually assaulted or even murdered by a paedophile if a soft option should be considered, they'll tell you bloody different Cherie!

Soham, in Cambridgeshire, England, was the scene of a double child abduction when Holly Wells and Jessica Chapman went missing in August 2002. The partially skelitised bodies of the two missing girls were found within weeks. A man, Ian Huntley, was arrested and charged with the double murder, but was sectioned off under the mental health act, his girlfriend, Maxine Carr, faces charges of attempting to pervert the course of justice. Coverage of the case continues in the national press.

Foreword to
Suffer Little Children
By
Caroline Roberts

A surviving victim of the

Fred and Rose West scandal

1977 – Caroline the Beauty Queen.

It was horrifying and shocking. I've always thought it will happen to me, I'm stronger now. In my dreams, for years, I would see my face on the front of newspapers, but when these bodies started coming out I thought it should have been me, how come they died instead of me, I felt so guilty.

By using these tapes they brought him back to life.* The victims were overlooked; they were never portrayed as having personalities behind their faces. Instead of using just the photos they should have given an insight into the victims' lives. (*Audio and videotapes secured from the prosecution and made into a documentary shown on Britain's Channel 5 TV.)

If a film was made about Fred West then I would like to see it focus on each girl instead of just showing the victim being dragged off and killed and featuring the activities of the other things that went on.

I'm a perpetual victim, it took me years before I could even go on a plane, you see, I thought because I was going to go on it that I would make it crash, simply because I was going to bring bad luck to everyone in it! I always thought I was going to be killed or something, I had relationship problems as a direct result of the crimes carried out against me, but I'm over that now.

I remember when everyone wanted stories about the Wests, they were chasing me, and then afterwards, once they got what they wanted, I was discarded, I felt used. They could forget about it but it would bring it all back for me and when I was left alone it came back to haunt me.

I'm stronger now and can even fly on a plane, things are getting better, but you never forget, it's always with you!

Caroline Roberts

Perpetual Survivor

Caroline Roberts (formerly Caroline Owens) is a sexual abuse survivor, having suffered at the hands of Fred and Rose West in the 70s. Caroline has written a book, yet to be published, called '*Life's a Bitch, and then you Survive.*' When asked about what she thought about a film being made on the Wests, Caroline suggested it would be better to make a film about the victims, giving each one a personality, which has yet to happen. The media portray the victims as strange faces peering at us, named but empty characters.

Caroline, present day

Indeed, the thought of making a film that animates the victim's personalities sounds an interesting one, maybe, instead of the focus being on Fred and Rose West a film should focus full on in to the victim's life. (Author's note: I am trying to secure the backing to make such a film that relates to the lives of the victims (living and dead), Andy Jones of the Crime Through Time museum has agreed to act as executive producer.)

10

Suffer Little Children

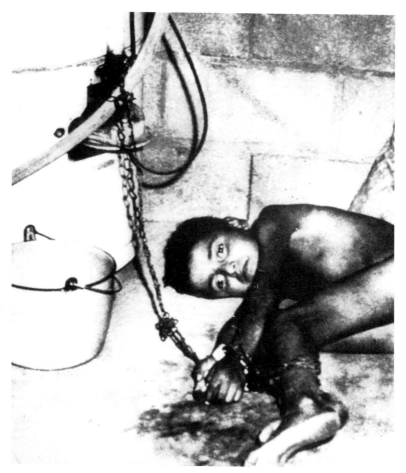

Texas, USA, 9-year-old Antonio Valenzuela told police who found him naked and chained to a washing machine, "Whenever mother leaves the house she ties me up."

Miami, Florida, USA – 4-year-old Kelly Puente weighed only 15 pounds and needed the aid of a nurse to stand. His parents kept him locked in a cage.

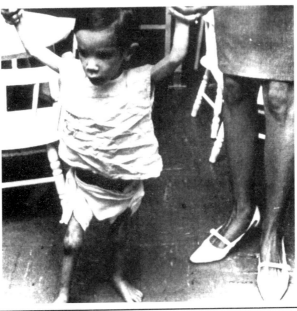

It is estimated that before they reach the age of 18 at least 1 in 6 males and 1 in 4 females will have suffered from some form of sexual abuse or serious sexual assaults.

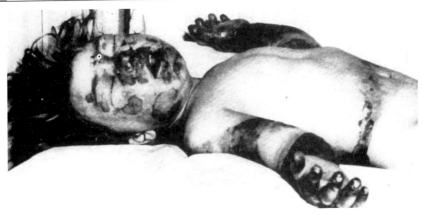

Lakeland, Florida, USA – 4-year-old Sharon Kay Hamil has 25 percent burns over her body. Their mother set her and her brother alight. Gasoline was poured over them, locked in the bathroom while the mother waited for the flames to end their lives because they were getting on her nerves.

Suffer Little Children

Denver, Colorado, USA – 15-year-old Karen Knight lies on her bed…dead. During a robbery Karen was bound hand and foot, placed on the bed and shot twice by David Early.

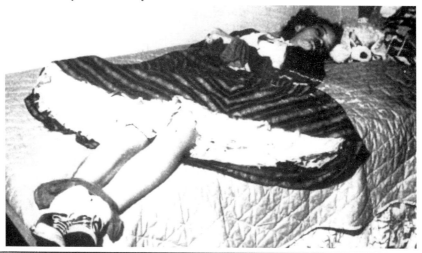

"Child abuse is a great evil and we believe that the church should be an example of excellence in rooting it out." Lord Nolan

St Paul, Minnesota, USA – 4-year-old Sonja Peterson had her right hand amputated by her father, who at first said it was an accident. He was arrested on charges of maiming.

Between 1974 and 1984, Bryn Estyn (Wales), became "the worst centre of child abuse" in north Wales over a period of 10 years, undetected by outsiders.

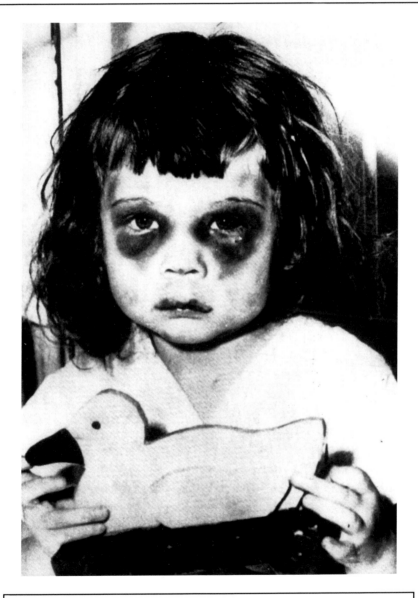

Approximately one in three girls are sexually abused before the age of 18.

Suffer Little Children

Neighbours took this photograph of Michael Aexias, 6, and his brother Casmer, 7, as they found them...gagged and lashed to a bunk. Their parents had gone out for the evening and tied them up so that they wouldn't get into the peanut butter.

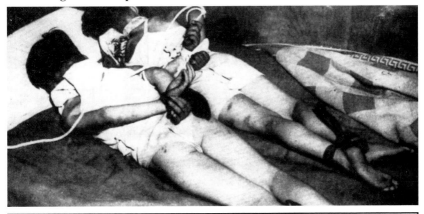

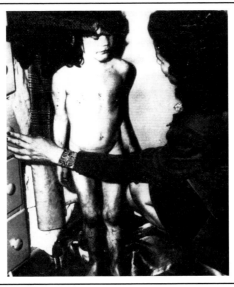

5-year-old Sharon Steward was found naked in a filthy closet, suffering from malnutrition. The father was on a fishing trip, the mother was at the beach with her two other children.

> **"I was at Bryn Estyn for two-and-a-half years and the name it got was the Colditz of care. It was abusive and threatening."**

By MARY MARSH
Director and Chief Executive of the NSPCC

THE whole country has been deeply shocked by the death of little Anna Climbie.

Burned with cigarettes, beaten with bicycle chains, starved of food, tortured. Horrific.

A government inquiry is set to look into the role of all the agencies involved in Anna's case.

The NSPCC welcomes this. Everyone needs to learn the lessons.

The government must insist that the inquiry's remit ensures this and that the lessons are applied effectively across the country.

There have been failings, no doubt. But the nation needs to wake up to the fact that at least one child a week dies from abuse or neglect.

Anna's death was extreme. These cases, thankfully, are the rare ones. They hit the headlines.

But, keep remembering: ONE CHILD A WEEK, EVERY WEEK.

Preventing children dying from abuse and neglect is a core element of the NSPCC's FULL STOP campaign to bring about an end to cruelty to children.

FULL STOP is a long-term ambition. The objectives will take many years.

But we need to develop a national strategy now to reduce the level of fatal child abuse.

Our call in the wake of Anna's death is for the government to take the lead and develop this strategy, including targets to reduce child killings.

This country is making real progress in reducing the numbers of children dying from accidents or illness.

Preventing deaths from drink-driving is now engraved on the public's consciousness. But nationally we are failing to cut the overall number of children

'Real toll of killings may be double'

who die from abuse or neglect. Why? Home Office figures show that the rate of child homicide in England and Wales has not dropped for 25 years.

In each generation more than a thousand will be killed before reaching adulthood. Most will die at the hands of violent or neglectful parents and carers.

But these figures underestimate actual fatal child abuse, as many such deaths are put down to other causes.

It's been estimated that the real incidence of child killings in England and Wales may be DOUBLE the official rate.

But lack of information on the causes and circumstances of many unexpected or suspicious child deaths means the full extent of problems remains hidden.

A national strategy–involving everyone, government, profession-

One child dies of abuse or neglect a week. EVERY week

to help monitor outcomes for all maltreated children, ensure improvements and set future policy goals.

These should include national targets to reduce deaths from abuse and neglect.

■ CHILD DEATH REVIEW TEAMS to look at all cases where children die and review the causes and circumstances of all unexpected or suspicious deaths.

The teams should provide full reports on reviewed deaths to local and central government, outlining the changes in policy and practice required to prevent future deaths.

Made up of professionals from different disciplines, the teams should have statutory powers.

■ INDEPENDENT CHILDREN'S COMMISSIONS in each of the UK countries which would act as champion and watchdog for children.

One of the duties would be to oversee all inquiries and reviews into child deaths.

The government needs to consult widely on the legislative and policy changes needed to implement such a strategy.

The NSPCC is about to publish an important report on these vital issues as we continue to campaign to keep cruelty to children at the top of everyone's agenda.

There is a need to look again at how all the agencies can work together to protect children from fatal abuse.

Child protection services cannot be expected to bring down the level of child abuse deaths working alone.

What terrible tragedies we have seen over the last few months.

Sarah Payne, Damilola Taylor and now poor Anna Climbie.

All these young children died needlessly–in different ways and from different types of violence.

Yet they have not been the only ones to die.

In the same week little Sarah was found dead a number of other children also died violently. The numbing figure grinds on.

AT LEAST ONE A WEEK, ONE A WEEK.

Ours is a modern country, filled with caring and loving people. Filled, too, with dedicated

'Public mood is right to end child cruelty'

social workers who work marvels to protect children and save lives every day.

Let's never forget that it was Anna Climbie's so-called carers, her great-aunt and her partner, who killed her.

Yet all of us, whatever our job, whatever our position in life–politician, parent, businessman or young person–must reassess our fundamental attitudes to children.

We must all work towards a time when all forms of cruelty to children, and, emphatically, all cases of child deaths from abuse or neglect are consigned to history.

The public mood is ripe to work towards this change of culture. The response so far to the Full Stop campaign has been huge. People all over the country want to see cruelty end.

More than 650,000 people have

Pin Down Inquiry in Staffordshire, Frank Beck case in Leicestershire, Waterhouse inquiry in North Wales.

http://www.nspcc.org.uk   http://www.preventchildabuse.org

Foreword to
Gangland
By
Al Capone
1899 – 1947

This American system of ours ... call it Americanism, call it capitalism, call it what you like, gives to each and every one of us a great opportunity if we only seize it with both hands and make the most of it. Don't get the idea that I'm knocking the American system. Don't you get the idea I'm one of those goddam radicals.

When I sell liquor, it's called bootlegging; when my patrons serve it on silver trays on Lake Shore Drive, it's called hospitality. I am going to St Petersburg, Florida, tomorrow. Let the worthy citizens of Chicago get their liquor the best they can. I'm sick of the job – it's a thankless one and full of grief. I've been spending the best years of my life as a public benefactor. There's a lot of grief attached to the limelight.

You can get more with a kind word and a gun than you can with a kind word alone. I have always been opposed to violence – shootings. I have fought, yes, but fought for peace. I don't pose as a plaster saint, but I never killed anyone.

The income tax law is a lot of bunk. The government can't collect legal taxes from illegal money.

Al Capone

Alphonso Capone, nickname-Scarface, was born on 17th January 1899, in Brooklyn, New York, USA. Equally, as everyone knows of Mohamed Ali or Jesus this was the same of Al Capone in the days of prohibition, when America tried to become alcohol free, which was a gift to such men as Mr Capone. The prohibition era in the 1920s was rich pickings for those involved in bootlegging or speakeasies.

Along with the territory though came gang fights between the mobs and such names as the *Saint Valentine's Day Massacre* spring to mind when writing of such men.

Eventually, the only way Al Capone could be convicted was for tax evasion. An eleven-year prison sentence was imposed on Al and it was in 1939 that he was released from prison suffering from syphilis, which he'd contracted as far back as the 1920s from a waitress.

Being a shadow of his former self, he was left to live his life "nutty as a fruit cake" until he died of a stroke on 25th January 1947 at Palm Island, Fla., USA. The once 'Public Enemy Number One' has become a legendary figure. Having served some of his time in the equally legendary Alcatraz prison it would seem that the biggest icon from the crime world was destined to be held in the biggest icon in the American penal system, an apt scenario for the authorities.

Al Capone's life was equated with that of Adolf Hitler in Berthold Brecht's satirical play *The Resistible Rise of Arturo Ui.* Would Mr Capone have turned in his grave at that comparison?

Crime Through Time

IN THE DISTRICT COURT OF THE UNITED STATES
FOR THE NORTHERN DISTRICT OF ILLINOIS
EASTERN DIVISION.

UNITED STATES)
        VS) NOS. 22852)
                     23232) Consolidated.
ALPHONSE CAPONE)

We, the Jury find the Defendant NOT
GUILTY as charged in Indictment No. 22852 and we find the
Defendant GUILTY on Counts _one - five - nine - thirteen - eighteen_
and NOT GUILTY on Counts _2 - 3 - 4 - 6 - 7 - 8 - 10 - 11 - 13 - 14 - 15 - 16 - 17 - 19 - 20 - 21 - 22_
Indictment No. 23232.

[jurors' signatures]

Above, the actual jury verdict handed to the judge in the Al Capone tax-
evasion case, with the signatures of all the jurors, given at 11pm on 17th
October 1931.

11

Gangland

Anyone look familiar, a coloured drawing by Paul Bridgeman original painting on display in museum.

NEWS WORLD PICTURE EXCLUSIVE

Biggs finally serves a life sentence

AND HE DID

↓

STROKE RAVAGES ROBBER'S BODY

BIGGS' DYING WISH IS TO MARRY HIS EX

BY AMANDA STOCKS

GREAT train robber Ronnie Biggs' dying wish is to marry former lover Raimunva de Castro— the mother of his son Michael – in jail.

He has written to the prison authorities asking for permission and hopes to be able to go ahead as soon as possible. A prison source said: "Ronnie feels it's something he should do. We are delighted for them."

Raimunva, 52, who lives in Switzerland, will fly into Britain for the ceremony once a date is set.

A simple service will take place in top security Belmarsh Prison in south-east London, where Biggs is being held.

Biggs, 72, and Raimunva were together for four years. They met when Biggs

THE GREAT TRAIN ROBBERY On 8th August 1963, the Glasgow to London night mail was stopped by a faked signal in Buckinghamshire, and men in balaclava helmets uncoupled the engine and high-value packages coach from the rest of the train, clambered aboard the engine, and beat down the driver who resisted them, causing him concussion and trauma. They forced him to take them forward another 1.6km (1 mile) to Bridego Bridge. There the robbers broke into the hvp van, intimidated the Post Office workers with axe handles and, forming a human chain, unloaded £2¹/₂m in old used notes being taken for destruction at the Mint. After working for half an hour, the gang made off in a convoy of vehicles, leaving mailbags containing further huge sums, but escaping into the dawn before they could be detected. The audacity and skilled planning of the crime impressed the public as much as the huge booty (still the largest amount ever seized in used notes).

Above items all signed or in Ronnie Biggs' handwriting are on display in the museum along with much memorabilia relating to the robbery.

Is it true????? (once behind bars your defence is ignored!!!)

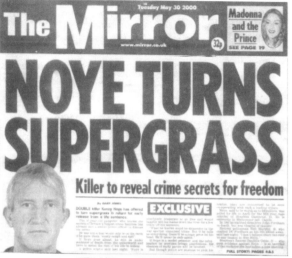

459

TAXMAN'S REVENGE

USIVE by GARY JONES

axman is targeting
ne bosses who have
worth £220million.

me sleuths will hand over
nfidential tax returns so
oceeds of crime can be

keaman for the National
al Intelligence Service
This will send a shiver
i crime bosses with big
yachts and flash cars.
x return was considered
not, but now the Inland
e will be sharing their
dge. It will enable us to
iminals more effectively."

Inland Revenue targets luxury lifestyle of 39 major criminals

Prime Minister Tony Blair has ordered that a National Confis-cation Agency be set up to seize crime bosses' assets.

The agency, will also have powers to tax "front" businesses used for money laundering.

An Inland Revenue spokes-woman said: "Criminals should

not escape justice because the right hand of government does not know what is in the left hand.

"We will negotiate sensible arrangements to ensure disclo-sures take place in accordance with the law."

Customs, police and Inland Revenue investigators will work

together under one roof to target high-living criminals.

They will ask a judge to decide "on the balance of probability" whether an individual's wealth was legally obtained.

If he finds against the suspect, the trappings of their life of crime will be taken away and sold, with profits ploughed back into crime fighting.

One target will be Kenneth Noye, jailed in April for the road-rage killing of Stephen Cameron.

Noye still rules a £10 million crime empire from jail.

g.jones@mirror.co.uk

JAILED: Noye

NOYE'S LITTLE EARNER

We reveal killer's secret millions

ROAD-rage killer Kenneth Noye has stashed away a massive se-cret fortune—hidden in bricks and mortar.

We can reveal that the jailed gang-land boss who pleaded poverty and claimed £298,650 legal aid at his trial—owns at least SIX properties worldwide worth nearly £3 million.

But after Noye has made sure his name can never be linked to them.

For the underworld mastermind has covered his tracks by using false names, bogus companies, members of his fam-ily and criminal associates to hide his ownership of the properties.

He's laughing really," a gangland source told us. "You could call it Ken-ny's pension policy. He's made sure every-thing he's financed in Britain is now in other people's names.

"He reckons he'll be out of prison inside 15 years and he wants to make sure he doesn't have to struggle."

Both Scotland Yard and the government are desperate to get their hands on missing Noye's ill-gotten millions gleaned from massive drugs deals and his part in the aftermath of the £26 million Brink's-Mat bullion robbery in 1983.

CUNNING: Road-rage killer Noye

NEWS OF THE WORLD INVESTIGATES

BY JULIA TIMMS

Trail

They are pinning their hopes on a new National Confiscation Agency which will have powers to go after criminals' assets—even abroad.

death by the M25 in 1996. It is registered to a firm called Trumong Ra-coded Limited—a Noye front. He sunk business assets on the register of Spanish companies.

HOTEL, Atlantera, Spain, £200,000 invested: Noye bought into it for £100,000 then pumped an-other £100,000 into the venture before his arrest. Its owner is listed as a Spanish businessman.

TWO penthouse flats,

really sold off more than £1 MILLION in UK assets including...

The Racquets Sport And Leisure Ifitness club in Dartford, Kent, which he bought for Brenda in 1993. It fetched £150,000.

The Noye family home, Hollywood Cottage, near Sevenoaks. It was sold for £490,000.

An interest in a contro-versial London wine bar which sold for £200,000 earlier this year.

Noye is foiled over plot to flee jail with 'heart attack'

by Chester Stern
CRIME CORRESPONDENT

SECURITY around Kenneth Noye has been stepped up after a prison doctor thwarted a plot by the road-rage killer to escape by faking a heart attack.

The 52-year-old gangster, jailed for life at the Old Bailey in April for the £25 stabbing of Stephen Cameron, was set week told he will have to serve a minimum of 15 years before being considered for parole.

The police killer has reportedly offered £million to underworld contacts to free an and prison authorities intend to move in regularly between six top-security attractions to reduce the risk of escape.

Last week a faction at Whitemoor igh-security prison in Cambridgeshire, where Noye is being held in the special secure unit—a prison within a prison—overheard the gangland millionaire plotting a prison escape.

Noye wanted to know details of the routine adopted when an inmate has a heart attack, in particular he wanted to know to what extent...

FORTRESS: Top-security Whitemoor jail

HIGH RISK: Kenneth Noye asked about 'pr

escaped conviction after stabbing undercover police-man John Fordham to death in the grounds of his Kent home. A key member of the gang behind Britain's biggest armed robbery in 1983, Noye served time for handling the £26 million stolen Brink's Mat gold bullion.

After he murdered 21-year-old Stephen Cam-eron in front of his fiancee during a road-rage clash on the M25 in 1996, Noye fled

Superintendent 'po McGluckky said evil man. He ha for life and tha should remain.

Detectives w view him to gra evidence which linked to the dru

The body of dealer John M had been shot and chest, was I under tables of back of his Rang days after Noye

£1,300,000

FLAT RATE: Penthouses in Cyprus

£1 million

POOL RESOURCES: Timeshare flats

Treasure hunt

Officers search for Brink's-Mat gold (in a village named Ore)

GIVEN its name, Ore is per-haps the perfect place to hunt for hidden gold.

Yesterday 33 Scotland Yard Fly-ing Squad officers descended on the tiny Sussex village searching for loot from Britain's biggest rob-bery—the £26million Brink's-Mat bullion raid carried out more than 13 years ago.

Astonished villagers suddenly found themselves the centre of

By Stephen Wright
and Duncan Gardham

revenue today in the village on the outskirts of Hastings.

"We have executed a search warrant on the premises,' he said. 'We have looked through a couple of ware-houses there with builders' materials and started to dig.

'Mr Winchester has been helping with our enquiries. He has not been

and threatened them with a bit match for the combination of the vault. More than £1.5million realised from the gold have been syphoned off to police, with the rest allegedly invested in property in Britain and Spain or in drugs.

Lloyd's of London, which paid out for the stolen millions, is believed to have forced 20 people linked to the robbery to secretly pay back every penny stolen.

M25 road rage killer Kenneth Noye served 13 years for his role. Police found gold bars at his mansion in Kent.

s.wright@dailytelegraph.co.uk

Centre of attention: Police at the yard in Ore

Crime Through Time

When all about you are running around like lunatics and throwing themselves off bridges, this man is so cool he sweats ice cubes!

Hire Dave Courtney for afternoon dinner luncheons and barmitzvahs.

www.crimebiz.co.uk

Gangland

How many famous faces from the underworld do you recognize?

Dave Courtney is suing the Metropolitan police, claiming the force has tried to get him shot. The claim emanates from a trial at the Old Bailey in which the prosecution alleged Dave to be an informer. Dave says this misinformation amounts to an intent to endanger his life.

See more of Dave and the chaps at
www.crimebiz.co.uk

Crime Through Time

Reg Kray's own handwriting, a short note to his prison lover, Bradley.

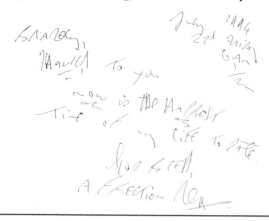

Bradley, Thanks to you now is the happiest time of my life to date. God bless, affection, Reg. Dated Friday 22nd July 1994.

REGGIE KRAY CONFESSES FROM GRAVE: I AM GAY

Letter to PEOPLE man reveals gangster's darkest secret

Will the real daughter of Reg Kray stand up... Sandra Ireson misses her dad.

I'M REGGIE KRAY'S SECRET DAUGHTER

Sandra tells of her mum's fling with gangster and a moving prison reunion

Gangland

Born 'Monek Prager' (Alias Mickey Duff, boxing promoter) on June 7th 1929, with a strict Jewish upbringing. Many of his family were murdered at the Nazi death camps in Poland. Ronnie Kray, of the notorious Kray twins (also of Jewish origin), had a twisted loathing of Mickey Duff and used to call him "that bastard Mickey Duff, he's a slag and I once sent him a dead rat through the post, he deserved it. I should have killed him when I had the chance.

"What they cannot control, they legalise."
Chris Lambrianiou – Former Kray gang member commenting on the government trying to control the drug abuse situation.

Reports of the Krays making £m's from within prison by selling their name and merchandising is a far-fetched story, although a romantic notion for those wishing to perpetuate the Kray legend.

Yes, it was true the Krays would sell the rights to their name being used, income was obtained this way throughout their imprisonment, there were those that would be enthralled by the Kray name and would still accept that they were the main men in London, even 25 to 30 years after they were taken off the streets the very mention of the 'Krays' would send people off in a frenzy of worry.

But the claims that the merchandise sold from the Kray web site ran into the £millions were highly exaggerated. Admittedly certain stories were true, like the one when a leather jacket with a portrait painted on it of Reggie and Ronnie Kray brought £750 was true.

Since the death of HRH Princess Margaret it might be that certain information held on file could be released linking Princess Margaret into visits she regularly made to a Kray gambling club in the 60s. Nine police files have been ordered to be kept under lock and key at the Public Records Office, eight will remain locked away for 50 years and the ninth for 30 years!

The Government ordered the files to be locked away after a constituent wished to look at them. The MP for Leyton and Wanstead, Harry Cohen, said, "These files should be made public. This dossier is historic and should not be kept hidden."

464

BANNED! THE KRAYS' SECRET ROYAL DOSSIER

EXCLUSIVE by NIGEL NELSON

A SECRET dossier on Princess Margaret by gangster Ronnie Kray is to be locked away for 50 YEARS.

The astonishing move was ordered by the Lord Chancellor's department after officials read its explosive contents.

In his memoir, Ronnie named royals and top politicians he and twin Reggie rubbed shoulders with when they terrorised London

CLUB at least twice.

A gangland insider said: "The boys were chuffed when she turned up."

Home Office minister Charles Clarke revealed that nine police files on the Krays – both now dead – have been handed over to the Public Record Office.

But eight will remain shut for 50 years and the ninth cannot be made public for 30 years.

Among police reports and witness statements is the memoir penned by Ronnie. He wrote it while serving 30 years for shooting dead rival gangster George Cornell in East End pub The Blind Beggar.

Historic

The Government admitted to Labour MP Harry Cohen that it had ordered the documents kept under lock and key after a constituent asked to see them.

Mr Cohen, MP for Leyton and Wanstead, said:

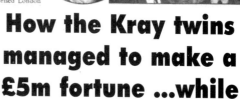

How the Kray twins managed to make a £5m fortune ...while they were in prison

Reggie and Ronnie Kray were jailed in 1969, but their name still lives on.

'Each got an average of 200 letters a week'

Ronnie's widow tells how money poured in from crooks and firms desperate to cash in on gangsters' evil past

Charlie Kray 'link to tycoon's murder'

By Chester Stern
CRIME CORRESPONDENT

GO-BETWEEN: Charlie Kray, above.

Signed by Martin Kemp
The Film - The Krays... starring the Kemp brothers

> "Crime doesn't pay, but the hours are good."
> **The Legendary Joe Pyle**

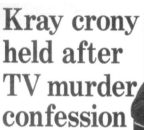

Kray crony held after TV murder confession

Frank Mitchell: 'Mad axeman'

ONE of Britain's most notorious criminals was yesterday arrested after he admitted on television that he carried out at least two murders on the orders of the Krays.

Freddie Foreman was acquitted of the murders but detectives launched a new investigation after he made his confession to millions of viewers.

Under the 'double jeopardy' rule, he cannot be tried again for the murders but he could face

By Peter Rose
Chief Crime Correspondent

land Yard detectives arrested Foreman yesterday and questioned him after studying tapes of the two documentaries. He was later bailed until July for

Freddie Foreman: He claimed he carried out killings on Krays' orde

Killer for the Kray gang escapes again

A GANGLAND hit man has escaped prosecution after admitting on television that he carried out at least two murders on the orders of the Kray brothers.

Freddie Foreman was arrested by Scotland Yard detectives following his confession to millions of viewers.

By Wayne Francis

under the 'double jeopardy rule. But he could have been charged with perjury and perverting the course of justice.

The Crown Prosecution Service, however, has now told 66-year-old Foreman that he will not face trial.

A Scotland Yard spokesman said: 'The CPS decided not to

Freddie Foreman, author of the best selling book 'Respect', was once one of Britain's most notorious criminals, being a former associate of the Krays. Somehow a TV documentary managed to illicit a confession from Freddie that he'd been involved in murder and he admitted in the documentary that he had carried out at least two murders on the orders of the Krays.

Detectives immediately launched a new investigation after he made his confession to millions of viewers. Under the 'double jeopardy' rule, he cannot be tried again for the murders.

Freddie confessed that a few months after he'd been involved in intimidating witnesses who had seen Ronnie Kray shoot dead George Cornell in the Blind Beggar pub, in Whitechapel, East London, in 1966, he took part in the killing of mad axeman Frank Mitchell. The CPS took no action over the TV confession.

Obviously such a TV confession must be taken with great caution, bearing in mind that Freddie had already been acquitted of the two murders, one of them Mitchell, in the 60s, he could not be retried for this confession. Given that Freddie had nothing to lose by this TV confession it certainly added drama!

467

Gangland

The Long Good Friday...based on Freddie Foreman

 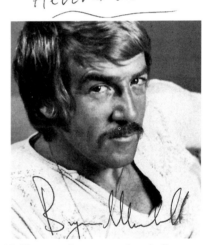

During the Old Bailey trial, in 1969, another gangland figure, Albert Donaghue, gave evidence against Freddie Foreman, the Kray twins and their brother Charlie. But the judge ruled that because Donaghue was also involved in Mitchell's escape from prison, his evidence could not he accepted without corroboration. Freddie and the Krays were acquitted.

The acclaimed film 'The Long Good Friday' is claimed to have been based on Freddie Foreman's exploits. Cockney actor Bob Hoskins portrayed the role of Freddie Foreman. Such a film, because of its realism, is now classed as one of the top ten in the list of all time great gangster movies.

http://www.freddieforeman.com

Crime Through Time

Charles Bronson - slammed by the the media

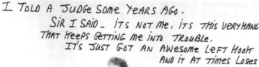

I TOLD A JUDGE SOME YEARS AGO.
SIR I SAID _ ITS NOT ME, ITS THIS VERY HAND
THAT KEEPS GETTING ME INTO TROUBLE.
ITS JUST GOT AN AWESOME LEFT HOOK
AND IT AT TIMES LOSES
CONTROL.
BUT THE OLD
BASTARD STILL
GIVE ME 20 YRS

Charles Bronson

Bronson's life term slammed

■ Above: Lifer Charles Bronson, pictured during a rare spell outside prison in 1992 with his dog Della. The strongman claimed in court if he were a dog, the RSPCA would have fought his case.
■ Inset: Crime Through Time museum owner Andy Jones says he is a friend of the

ODD COUPLE: Bronson, left, and Saira with love tattoo on her hand

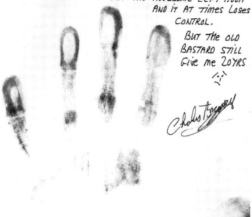

BRIDE OF PSYCHO

Saira to marry crazed Bronson ...after one visit

THIS is the woman who plans to marry Britain's most dangerous convict – after meeting him just once.

Mum-of-one Saira Rehman started writing to violent psychopath Charles Bronson, who has spent nearly 27 years in jail after seeing his photo in a newspaper.

Then the pretty Muslim divorcee arranged to visit Bronson behind bars – and fell for him straight away.

The pair now say they will name a wedding date as soon as prison chiefs give them the go-ahead.

Battered

Saira, 38, said: 'As soon as I entered the prison room something clicked between us. He kept touching my face and we were dreading ever each other.'

Lifer Bronson, 46, even introduced her to the Governor at Woodhill Prison, Bucks, as his 'future wife'.

He added: 'It was quite flattering, even though he hasn't properly proposed to me yet. When he does the answer will be yes. I'm the happiest woman on...

WRITE NUT: Bronson note to Saira's young daughter

Museum bids £2,000 for Bronson's brain

Luton Gazette - Jan 10th 2001

EXCLUSIVE by GEOFF COX

BRITAIN'S most notorious prisoner, Luton-born Charles Bronson, is offering his brain for sale.

The convict and his supporters believe people will be queuing up to own a piece of the serial hostage-taker, who has spent more than half his life behind bars.

One bid for £2,000 has already been made in writing by Andy Jones, who runs the Crime Through Time Museum in Gloucestershire.

Mr Jones, whose museum includes a display on Bronson's life and crimes, described him as a genius and a legend.

All proceeds from the brain sale will go to the notorious hardman's own charity, Bronson's Children, which is currently trying to raise enough money to search for the body of Moors

■ BRONSON, who spent the first 15 years of his life in Luton and was thrown out of two of the town's high schools, keeps in touch with events in his home town by reading the Luton News each week.

The convict is an award-winning artist and one of his inkjet works is a wedding congratulations card for local hardman Billy Schwer and his bride Nikala. He sent the card to The News-Gazette, to be forwarded to the couple, after reading our exclusive story about their marriage in Florida.

Inside was the following message

many months after his body was buried. The brain was eventually handed over and it was buried alongside Ron. Charlie would hate that it happen to him."

Mr Richards added "Charlie doesn't want to come out of prison as a frail old man near death's door. I'm sure someone would love to own the brain so that they can look into the mind of someone classified a insane.

"What a shame someone could not buy the brain of Churchill or Hitler. Imagine Charlie's brain next to the

Crime Museum won the bid for Charles' brain.

Gangland

The Godfather…I'm no monster, says Bronson

http://www.bronsonmania.com

Crime Through Time

**Welsh Bernie, photo below courtesy of the book
'The Firm' by Jocelyn Bain-Hogg**

All the best from Bernie and the infamous Welsh Connection

Dave Courtney & Bernie Davies

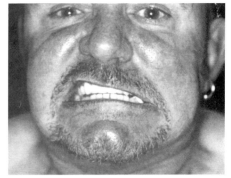

Don't mess with me...

**W
E
L
S
H

M
A
F
I
A**

> "I was the first one to put Bruce Reynolds up (after the Great Train Robbery), he lived with me above a dry cleaners."
>
> The Legendary Joe Pyle

BILLY MURRAY
as D.S. DON BEECH
FROM THAMES TV'S

BILL STAR: I'M GREEDY... BUT NOT A CROOK

I was set up says Murray

EXCLUSIVE by
GARRY BUSHELL

ANGRY telly star Billy Murray yesterday denied claims that he was a real-life crook.

Murray, who plays bent cop Don Beech in The Bill, was accused by a Sunday newspaper of dealing in hi-tech goods, knowing they had been stolen by drug addicts.

But furious Murray insisted: "I am greedy but I'm no villain — and I would never knowingly deal with drug addicts, who I consider the scum of the earth."

The star said he had been set up by the newspaper and duped by a notorious police informer with a string of convictions.

Murray, 58, said: "I'll hold my hands up to being a greedy bastard and a wheeler dealer. I'm

Murray ... 'wheeler-dealer'

take the risk of dabbling in crime and destroying my career."

Murray was secretly taped arranging to buy mini-discs, a digital camera and a hi-fi system from an ex-convict.

Yesterday he said: "The person who approached the newspaper is someone I have known for 12

Bad name ... TV star's house

told me the goods were hot, but I thought he was trying to make himself look big and didn't take him seriously."

In 1998 Murray was cleared of GBH against two drug dealers who had lured away his daughter Lizzie, who was 14 at the time. He lives in a home worth nearly

Ronnie Kray fancied me.. thank God he always called me 'the one that got away'

SAYS TV COP BILLY MURRAY

MACHO Bill TV star Billy Murray is used to female attention—but when gay gangster Ronnie Kray got the hots he suddenly felt very nervous.

The hardman East End actor, who used to work for the notorious Kray twins, recalls: "They once hired me to be a minder for one of Ronnie's boyfriends.

"I had to take this bloke out and make sure he behaved himself. Ronnie was very uptight and worried we too were kept at all times.

"I knew Ronnie was sweet on me, but he always called me 'the one that got away'—which is a bit of luck as I'm 100 per cent heterosexual.

"Mind you, that wouldn't have stopped Ronnie I reckon if he wanted something he'd take it one way or the other."

But 57-year-old Billy, currently at the centre of a blockbuster Bill plot as star detective Don Beech, admits he owes his showbiz success to the rays. After meeting them at his teens they became lifelong friends and moved him through drama school.

EXCLUSIVE

BY STEVE SMITH & LEWIS PANTHER

BILLY AND RONNIE

Kray on hols with Bill star he had hots for

Double escape ... young Billy Murray, above right, on hol with Kray — and, left, how the star of The Bill looks now

A very rare mistake by the press, okay, we all get it wrong at times, but on this occasion embarassment was caused to actor Billy Murray when he was mistakenly said to be the man to the right of Ronnie Kray, in the above cutting. The article suggested this was the young actor on holiday with Ronnie Kray. It is in fact Bobby Buckley, an old Eastend friend of Ronnie's.

See the full story on the Crime Through Time web site.

Crime Through Time

Jill Dando's killer…not?

Gangland

Barry George (Bulsara) was convicted of the murder of popular television presenter Jill Dando on the 2nd July 2001. Barry was convicted on circumstantial and forensic evidence obtained one year after the crime was committed. Here was a man unable to take the stand alone and required a helper to explain the questions and to monitor his health. This is not a man who would be capable of committing the crime he is accused of. Barry, admittedly, is a loner and quite obviouisly different to others, but could he possibly have shot Ms Dando in broad daylight in a normal suburban street and remain undetected for so long?

Jill Dando was shot at about 11.30am on Monday, 26th April1999 on the doorstep of her house at 29 Gowan Avenue, Fulham, West London, England. Shortly before her killing she was captured on CCTV in several places. There was no evidence from the videotapes of anyone following her.

Ms Dando was found lying with her head against her front door. Her car keys were in her hand and her handbag open with the strap over her arm. She was about to open her front door when attacked. Damage to the lower part of the door suggested that Ms Dando was crouching when shot. There was a small bruise on her right forearm, which was probably made by the killer grasping her arm. The killer probably forced her to the ground and held her in position for the killing. Ms Dando was killed by a single shot to the head made at very close range. The fatal bullet went into her head just behind the top of the left ear and exited above the right ear.

Various rumours circulated after the killing. Could it have been an underworld figure that Crimewatch had damaged or angered? To be convicted on the flimsiest of evidence is dangerous. See Charles Bronson's book, *'Legends Vol.1'*.

Was it a revenge attack by Serbs following Miss Dando's appearance on a programme dealing with the Nato attack on a Serb television station during the Kosovan war? Also Ms Dando, rumour has it, was trying to infiltrate the underworld. Barry George lost his appeal in 2002.

http://www.petitiononline.com/justice/petition.html

> ### "My one ambition has always been to be a good thief.
> ### The only thing I regret is that I was caught."
> #### Francis Davidson Fraser

Marilyn Wisbey is the goddaughter of Freddie Foreman, her father, Tommy, was one of the Great Train Robbers. In 1991 when Mad Frankie Fraser was going to visit Tommy Wisbey in prison, Marilyn accompanied him; they became an item for the next 10 years.

Mad Frankie was certified insane three times and has served a total of 42 years in prison. He's had more bread and water than any man alive. Received countless floggings, when they were lawful, and made numerous murder attempts on prison guards. His inability to bow to authority and his orchestration of the biggest jail riots of the 70s caused him to become a prison legend.

Dubbed the most dangerous man in Britain, by two Home Secretaries, makes him a living legend, so when his girlfriend, Marilyn, of 10 years revealed to a national Sunday newspaper (Sunday People) that they'd only ever had sex once in 10 years people thought she was the one who was mad. Particularly when she went on to reveal that she'd had numerous lovers during the time she spent with Mad Frank!

After spending a total of 42 years in prison Frank would have had to be prised from any hot blooded woman, after all crime and sex go hand in hand, maybe Marilyn had just had an off day and was feeling upset at Frank…we hope!

> ### "There's always been crime in Britain and always will be.
> ### There's always been gangsters, I'm happy to say."
> #### Mad Frankie Fraser

Gangland

Wendy Mason fell for an ex gangster

L
O
C
K

S
T
O
C
K

Signed picture of Vinnie Jones

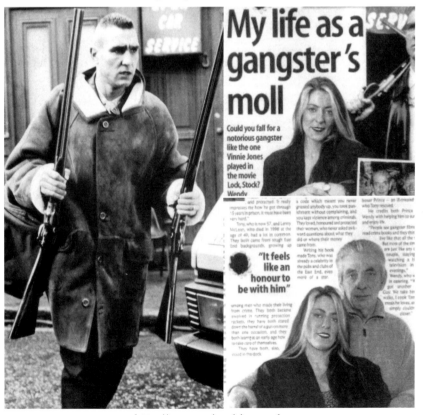

My life as a gangster's moll

Could you fall for a notorious gangster like the one Vinnie Jones played in the movie Lock, Stock? Wendy

"It feels like an honour to be with him"

Ronnie Biggs…I was a Sex Pistol for a day

Gangland

The Legendary Joe Pyle

Joe Pyle, pictured centre, wrote a book, Looking at Life, he signed all his royalties over to a hospice for babies. Featured in the photograph is Dave Courtney, left, and Joe's son, Joe Jnr., right.

http://www.joepyle.com

Foreword to
Crimes That Live On
By
James 'Le Prince of Darkness' Nicholson

Le Prince of Darkness - A Legend

During my five decades of covering crime stories I have many memories of crimes that live on. A particular crime that springs to mind is the moors murders - if only because I am the only crime-man still around who covered the story in 1965.

This meant months of tramping round the moors seeing police dig up bodies of two of the victims...10-year-old Lesley Ann Downey and 12-year-old John Kilbride. To be followed by the trial at Chester of the infamous pair, Ian Brady and Myra Hindley.

479

Crimes That Live On

Also, I am the only crime journalist still working who covered the A6 murder and was lucky enough to get the exclusive story – of James Hanratty's arrest in Blackpool...in 1963...sadly for me it was too late for the last Daily Sketch edition and I missed one of my greatest exclusives!

I went to the Bedford trial where the judge put on his black cap and sentenced Hanratty to death. The controversy still rages, was he guilty...I say, sadly for him, yes! The last person Hanratty saw in his life was a friend of mine - the hangman of the day Harry Allen... I was also a friend of his predecessor Albert Pierrepoint.

And another unique crime story under my belt is the last ever hangings. This time the hangman was my drinking buddy - Harry - who took over from Pierrepoint as the No1 hangman. That was in august 1964 - when the death sentence was carried out on Peter Anthony Allen and Gwynne Owen Evans. They murdered 53-year-old, van driver John Allen West at his Workington home.

Most serial killers, also, are included in my diary of crime - the infamous Black Panther, Donald Neilsen - and his namesake Dennis Nielsen – killed 21 between them.

Butler, Archchibald Hall who with his pal took out five people including an MP...and his wife.

Several child killers have also been part of my reporting life...I was a standby witness against David Burgess...who murdered two children at Beenham, near Reading, England.

Then I gave evidence in the classic 'Red Mini;' murder at Oxford, when three people got life! The three defendants were Raymond Sydney Cook, Valerie Newhall and Eric Jones. The victim was Cook's 40-year-old schoolteacher wife, June. Cook was in love with Newall, they arranged for Jones to stop the family's red Mini in a country lane at Nettlebed, Oxon in March 1967. Jones beat June Cook with a car jack and drove the car into a tree... faking an accident... Cook received minor injuries. I interviewed Cook before he was arrested, and what he said to me was given in evidence by me, which helped to convict them at the Oxford trial. A book written by a top Scotland Yard cop, Ian Forbes, about the incident gave me a mention, even so long ago... so what's new!!!!

More recently, I've appeared in TV reports at the Rose West trial

- she and her hubby Fred were, in my opinion, far worse than the moors' murderers.

I'm the only reporter left who met the Krays - before they went inside, and no one is around except me who covered their trials. Along with the Richardson's torture trials this is where I first saw icons: Freddie Forman, Frankie Fraser and Tony Lambrianiou.

The occasion when I met the Kray twins - before they were nicked was when the brothers held a press conference at a west end club...they wanted to protest about the newspaper stories linking them with the George Cornell murder at the Blind Beggar pub and Frank the 'Mad Axeman' Mitchell's disappearance. Their denials were reported by me in the Daily Sketch...only for me to see them standing in the dock at the Old Bailey a few months later!!! I pulled no punches when I wrote daily about the violent side of their lives...and the antics of 'the firm'.

I won their respect after writing about the dedication of their mother, Violet. I ended up visiting Reggie and Charlie Kray in prison and later saw Ronnie Kray in Broadmoor...in later years, I gave evidence for Charlie in his last trial...it did not help much! He got 12 years - and his death sentence

The Italian stallion Valerio Viccie - was shot dead on the eve of Charlie Kray's funeral...after a shoot-out in Italy with the Italian cops. I still can't work this shooting out, Valerio was sitting on multi-millions from the Knightsbridge Safety Deposit Box Robbery and did not need another heist. Yet the police say he was planning one when he was shot!! Eight times!! After covering the trial of the robbery I helped Viccie with his best selling book. Ironically, the shoot-out occurred while they were involved in a TV documentary. The TV show will hopefully include the mystery behind the Italian's death!!

Among my friends is the Great Train robber Bruce Reynolds. And I got on well with Buster Edwards and Roy James, sadly no longer with us.

Prisons most notorious prisoner and serial hostage taker Charlie Bronson rates me as a guy he has 'respect' for and he has listed me as a close friend on his website. (www.bronsonmania.com) It was Valerio Viccie who asked me to look Charlie Bronson up many years ago in Parkhurst prison. I see him in various prisons and have covered his many trials, in fact I am the only crime-man to have covered all of his major trials. He was given life for his hostage taking antics, but I hope he wins his appeal.

The prison establishment created him…and now they should look after him. He does not deserve to be caged like an animal!!! I know he has had trips to Broadmoor and was discharged sane but to keep him locked up like a mad dog is not the answer.

I have covered hundreds of major crime stories. I have even got a London bank robber to confess to me that he killed an innocent bystander outside a bank...27 years after the shooting…he was given life…but still thanks me for helping him to serve time back here in the UK!!! The man was Arthur Jackson - the interview – Los Angeles jail. The sentence - the Old Bailey…yes, I was a standby witness but he pleaded guilty, he is now in Broadmoor.

It came as a surprise to me when they gave me the tag, Le Prince. I think anyone who knows me will say that I am an ordinary working hack who enjoys crime writing and drinking Guinness.

I have really become a 'rent a mouth' in crime because none of my other crime buddies who covered those epic stories are still around.

They were old when I was young, and now I am the old guy surrounded by young top crime reporters. I have made some great friends in the world of crime...cops have always been part of my life. One of my best friends, Supt Gerald Richardson, was shot dead by an armed robber...George Sewell! And that gutted me...I got a little satisfaction later! Yes…I was at the trial and saw Sewell get 30 years!

Top lawyers and judges are also amongst my friends...as a member of the Old Bailey Court Reporters I have played golf against them. And won!!! I am also friendly with many notorious villains who have hit the headlines. These are men who don't deny what they did...tough and dangerous guys in their day. So far as I am concerned they have paid their debt to society. Some of them got 25-year sentences and they are now pensioners who just want to get on with their lives - in spite of their notoriety.

Crime Through Time

I have been accused of glamorising villains and making them into cult figures...yes suppose I can't deny this!! But their very actions before they went inside created their own cult image. There were certainly no 'Robin Hoods' among them - guys who robbed the rich to give to the poor?!

Life goes on at the Old Bailey - two serial killer rapists in the dock together - unknown in crime annals – they got life! –

And then we have his Lordship Jeffrey Archer on perjury charges!!! Yes I know him too! I was with the Daily Star when he sued for libel and won...he won £500,000. Now it is pay back time...and we will see who was right about this devious man-who would be mayor!! A friend? No! I would rather be out drinking Guinness with Bruce Reynolds, Freddie Forman, Frankie Fraser, Charlie Bronson and co...cheers.

Le Prince

Lord Jeffrey Archer with wife Mary.
He too went to battle in the High Court to clear his name and won record damages only to end up doing four years

SUGAR DADDY FOR ARCHER!

JAILED Jeffrey Archer has been befriended by a brutal cellmate–who vowed to lend him sugar whenever he wants.

The disgraced Tory peer was banged up with Christopher Mitchell, 36–serving five years for wounding with intent to cause grievous harm.

Mitchell's mum Joan, 66, said last night: "I think it's hilarious that, despite being so rich, Archer had to depend on my son, who hasn't got two pennies to rub together. But he was in good hands and Chris

ARCHER: Shamed

ARCHER LORDS IT OVER LAGS

Fury as he wears shirt like screws

DISGRACED Lord Archer has enraged fellow prisoners—by strutting around tough Belmarsh jail in a WHITE SHIRT like the officers.

One furious inmate revealed: "None of us are allowed to wear white shirts be-

483

Crimes That Live On

James 'Le Prince' Nicholson was born in Batley, Yorkshire, England; he now lives and works in London. A guy who really does make crime pay. Fleet Street hacks, cops, robbers, and even judges know him as 'the prince of darkness'. In a book by, his now dead pal, Valerio Viccie, the £60m Knightsbridge safe deposit box robber - Le Prince is described as 'Britain's most celebrated crime reporter', even his most jealous minded fleet street buddies grant him this because his career with national newspapers has lasted longer than any of them, nearly 45 years and still he goes on.

He joined the Daily Sketch in 1960 as a crime reporter and went on to work with the Daily Mail, the Daily Express and later the Daily Star. During those years he won the Reporter of the Year title, became president of the Crime Reporters Association and still is vice president.

Outside crime, he was chairman for two years of the prestigious London Press Club. Following in the footsteps of the great crime writer Edgar Wallace! And where does he get the 'prince' title? It was bestowed on him years ago by fellow journalists when he haunted murder scenes wearing a black cape on top of his well tailored, high collared black suits, and black high boots. To add to this ghostly presence, he wears dark tinted specs, black Old Bailey ties and drinks black Guinness - topped up with champagne - black velvet.

He is now the only freelance crime reporter at the Old Bailey - working for all the national media and TV - still wearing black. Behind him are some of the greatest crime stories of the last four decades...

What follows may be distressing to some readers of a weak constitution. Graphic photos used for illustration purposes contain some scenes that some people of a sensitive nature might find offensive. With this in mind the museum accepts no responsibility for potential or consequential claims resulting from alarm or distress caused herein.

12

Crimes That Live On

22nd November 1963...Killing of a President

 **A WINDOW**

 **A BULLET**

Crimes That Live On

A DEAD PRESIDENT TELLS NO LIES

JFK Assassination...was it a cover up?

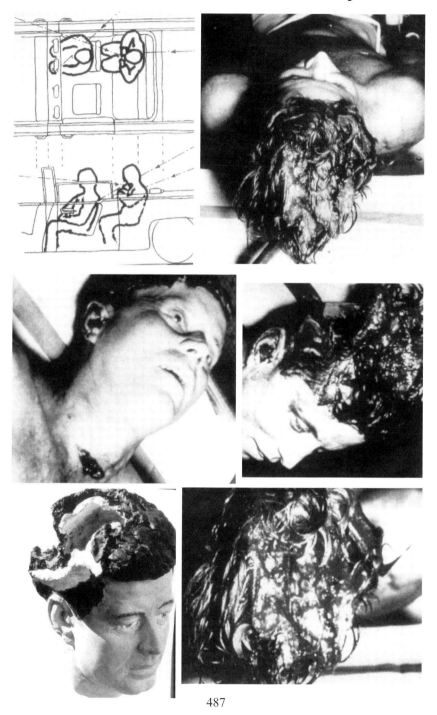

Crimes That Live On

ON THE SLAB

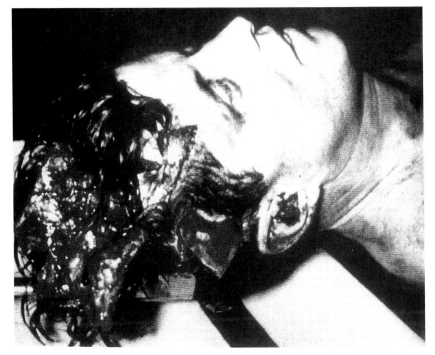

MORE QUESTIONS THAN ANSWERS!!!

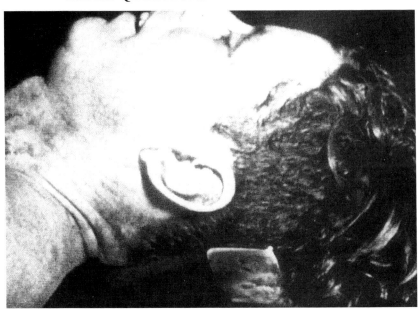

James Bulger R.I.P. Words are not enough

VIDEO NASTY . . . little James Bulger is led to his tragic death

http://www.jamesbulger.co.uk

Crimes That Live On

OJ Simpson…Every Woman's Nightmare

D I D   H E

D I D N 'T   H E

Signed Photo of OJ Simpson

Cigar dipping Clinton...yuk, never taste the same again!

'I JUST
LOVE
CIGARS'

OPEN WIDE!

From
MONICA LEWINSKY

Monica

With Best Wishes

AUTOGRAPH

To Monica – Happy Birthday! Bill Clinton
7-23-97

FIRST COUPLE BANK ON CASHING

Clintons shrug off debts of £5million

Clinton: Massive legal bill

WASHINGTON: Bill and Hillary
Clinton owe £5million more than
they are worth, according to
details of their finances
published yesterday.

worth of gifts over the last year,
mostly from rich friends in
Hollywood.
These included three golf clubs
worth £860 from Jack Nicholson
a £250 piece of animation art fr

CLINTON'S REVENGE

HE UNLEASHES IRS DOGS ON HIS EX-LOVERS

'The White

The most defining image of the 20th Century – Che Guevara

Admen face £2m bill for hijacking Guevara's image

By **Barbara Jones**

A POOR Cuban photographer who took one of the most defining pictures of the 20th Century is suing a British-based advertising agency for hijacking it to promote vodka.

Alberto Korda, 71, captured the famous shot of Marxist guerrilla Che Guevara in downtown Havana 40 years ago.

The defiant image of the bearded revolutionary has appeared on millions of posters and T-shirts, earning their makers an estimated £1 billion. It also made the beret Guevara wore a best-selling fashion accessory.

But Korda has barely seen a penny of it.

At first he didn't mind. He supported Guevara's Communist ideals and was proud

to have launched his friend and hero as a universal icon. But now he is angry that the photograph is being used in advertisements alongside the slogan 'Hot Fiery Bloody Smirnoff – the Complex-Flavoured Vodka'.

He is suing the advertising agency, Lowe Howard-Spink of Knightsbridge, for £1.9 million over the Smirnoff campaign.

At his home in Havana he said last week: 'To use the image of Che Guevara to sell vodka is a slur on his name and his memory.

'He never drank. He was not a drunk, and drink should not be associated with his immortal memory.'

Korda took the picture for a Cuban newspaper on March 5, 1960, at a rally for 200 sailors and stevedores

killed when a Belgian arms ship was blown up in Havana harbour by counter-revolutionaries.

He recalls: 'The mood was sombre, but very dramatic. The streets were lined with thousands of mourners. Che was standing in the row behind Fidel Castro on the

platform. You couldn't see him. Then, suddenly, he stepped forward to the edge of the platform.

'I was standing below. It was only a brief moment. I managed two frames and then he was gone.'

A few months later, Guevara was executed in Bolivia by

CIA-backed government troops. His hands were cut off and sent to Cuba as proof of his murder.

Korda said: 'Life may not have granted me a great fortune, but it has given me the even greater fortune of becoming a figure in the history of photography.'

SUING: Alberto Korda, left, with his daughter Norka. His picture, above, sparked a fashion (right)

492

Dr Harold Shipman...may have killed 300 or more!

The unlikeliest choice to play a serial killer

WHEN it came to finding an   By Mark Reynolds

UNLIKELY LAD

Comedy star James set to chill viewers as Dr Death

A LIKELY LAD TO PLAY THE PART!

Does crime make celebrities bigger celebrities? Without crime where would the stars of crime related TV soaps be? Crime puts money into the pockets of TV companies; it has become an industry far surpassing what anyone could have expected from 50 years ago!

Inspector Morse, Frost, Stallone movies, Schwarzenegger movies, The Bill, TV documentaries, videos, signed photos of notorious characters all make up the crimebiz dimension – crime certainly seems to pay and the public are continuously in awe of the perpetrators of crime...thus perpetuating the crime industry...don't you think?

493

Crimes That Live On

Andy Jones Meets

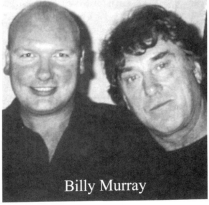

Billy Murray

Bernie Davies

Jeremy Beadle

Chris Read

Dave Ford
www.whosthethief.com

Crime Through Time

Andy Jones Meets

Joe Pyle

Charlie Richardson

Freddie Foreman

Bruce Reynolds

Dave Courtney

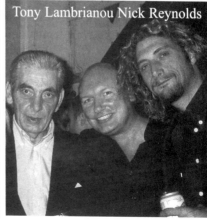

Tony Lambrianou Nick Reynolds

Nazi horrors and Fred West claims to spark furore

Black Museum goes into print

by Colin Ricketts
Staff reporter

CONTROVERSIAL museum owner Andy Jones of Newent is preparing to set the cat among the pigeons once again when he releases a book on his collection: The Black Museum - Crime Through Time.

The book may well be banned by bookshops but, if so, the authors intend to sell it on the Internet.

The cover depicts the museum logo, a graphic image of a Christ-like Hitler crucified on a swastika against a Star of David. This image is surrounded by photographs of celebrities, villains and murderers including Jamie Bulger killers, John Venables and Robert Thompson, Myra Hindley, O J Simpson, Fred West, Dr Harold Shipman and a hooded Klu Klux Klansman.

There are also pictures of Diana Princess of Wales, Marilyn Monroe and Bill Clinton.

Mr Jones also promises to shed new light on the Cromwell Street murders in Gloucester.

Police have recently been collecting statements after receiving complaints about the Hitler crucifixion logo displayed outside the Newent museum.

Mr Jones and author Stephen Richards, of Mirage Publishing, are prepared for the furore that the book's cover might cause and are planning to make it available via the Internet should they run into problems with distributors.

Promising a 'no holds barred' look at crime, scandal and notorious characters, the contents of the book are also likely to attract legal attention.

"It will contain harrowing photographs of human pain and suffering that will cause

COVER STORY: Andy Jones's book due to be published this autumn.

shock in themselves," Mr Jones says in a written statement to The Forester.

"I expect the writs to go flying," he adds, detailing some of the allegations the book will contain.

Mr Jones says he has seen video footage of the investigation into the Cromwell Street murders that he was told Gloucestershire Constabulary had sold for £100,000. His book will include the allegation that police are aware of other victims of Fred and Rosemary West and also know that others participated in their crimes.

"Fred and Rose were not the only guilty ones, that's for sure," he says.

"The police know this, but the Government was not prepared to throw any more money at the case. The suicides of Fred and John West apparently saved the Government a fortune."

Mr Jones also promises revelations

concerning the time Fred West sp Newent.

Stephen Richards, who has writt published a number of bool underworld figures and was for Charles Bronson's manager, is bemu the fuss surrounding the cover.

"It is ironic that the Imperia Museum has received £17 million fr on the strength of their hold exhibition while Andy Jones, exhibition is far better and does m highlight the plight of holocaust sur is being persecuted," he said.

Mr Richards thinks that the o caused by the sign is simply a ma misunderstanding and that anyone had the symbolism explained to would be 'on our side'. He also refer the right to free expression guarant Article 11 of the Human Rights Act.

Commenting on the possibility book being banned, he said more would be sold if it were. "We h number of means of distribution an looking at going underground with

He also confirmed that allegations book would ruffle feathers when it out. "Releasing the book with the being sued would be like hav deathwish, but the book is going t with a bang when it is released," he

Mr Jones is equally aggrieved th image has caused offence and vehen denies any Nazi sympathies.

"The sign simply shows that I through his own tyranny and hatred Jews in particular, sacrificed himsel the record I have no connection wit do I support any notorious po movements and never will.

"The museum touches on many and sensitive subject matters. It is a c this being the only way to preser collection."

Above, the furor about this Book!!! Surely a book is deemed to be part of the European Human Rights as a freedom of expression???

Racism gone mad!!!!!!!!!!!!!!!!!!!!!!

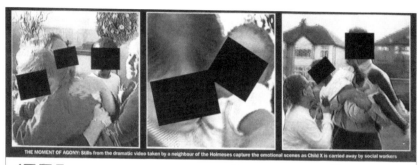

THE MOMENT OF AGONY: Stills from the dramatic video taken by a neighbour of the Holmeses capture the emotional scenes as Child X is carried away by social workers

'Wrong race' couple banned from fostering for daring to speak out

The cult TV soap 'Love Thy Neighbour' was a regular TV show in the 70s, but if broadcast today it would be banned in a world gone mad on racist issues. In short, everyone is racist...fact!

From 'Love Thy Neighbour'

Crimes That Live On

Racism is a crime; it affects many peoples' lives

Would TV soaps be allowed to broadcast this today?
Photos from 'Love Thy Neighbour,' on display in the museum.

Crime Through Time

Below, A 50-year-old black man, Lint Shaw, is hanged by an angry mob in Georgia, USA in 1936. The man was previously indicted on charges of criminally assaulting two girls...white.

Above, in 1935, two black men, Dooley Morton and Bert Moore, were lynched by an angry mob of whites. After the men were accused of attempting to sexually assault a white woman the crowd tore them from the police and hung them. The incident took place in Mississippi, USA.

Crimes That Live On

A member of the Kennedy family rode with the Ku Klux Klan!

Stetson Kennedy, although not related to JFK, was an 'undercover agent' for the Georgia Department of Law investigating Ku Klux Klan activity. To get material for prosecutions, he risked his life by joining the Klan, rising to the rank of Kleagle (Organiser), and serving on the Klan's Murder Squad.

His story is thrilling, but at the same time disturbing. The Klan claims now to have 600,000 members in the U.S. (according to Kennedy), and boasts that in time it will have America completely 'kluxed.'

If so, with its record of racial intolerance, of rape, murder, violence, and big-business blackmail, the situation is serious. The difference between Fascist brutality and Klan atrocities appears indistinguishable.

Above, an extremely rare 1920s KKK membership card, issued by Invisible Empire Knights of the Ku Klux Klan, on display in the museum.

Above, left, KKK Calling Card   **Above, right, Combat 18 Calling Card**

Crime Through Time

Oswald Mosley's Blackshirts

If, then, the difference between Fascist brutality and Klan atrocities appears indistinguishable what of the British politician who was a Conservative, Independent and a Labour MP before becoming a Fascist.

Sir Oswald Mosley rose to become leader of the British Union of Fascists, who were responsible for anti-Semitic violence in London's East End and who gave outspoken support for Hitler during the war.

WAS MOSLEY RIGHT ?  **LOOK BACK IN ANGER**

Above, signed photo of Oswald Mosley on display at museum.

Above, left, Diana, wife of Mosley, with Hitler in 1936.

Above, right, Mosley with his private army. Peak cap and uniform on display in the museum.

Crimes That Live On

Mosley in his heyday. But during the War he was interned for its duration.

The Great Blackshirt meetings in open air were outlawed, indoor meetings weren't though.

Mosley wanted Britain for the British people

Above, an authentic propaganda leaflet.

Visit Crime Through Time to see much more BUF & Blackshirts exhibit items on display, to include uniform items and associated material.

Another propaganda leaflet from the 1930s

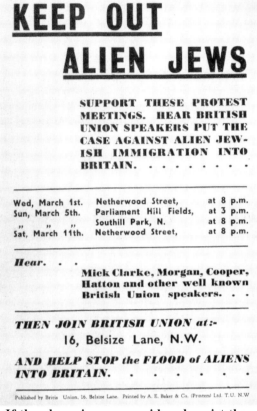

KEEP OUT
ALIEN JEWS

SUPPORT THESE PROTEST MEETINGS. HEAR BRITISH UNION SPEAKERS PUT THE CASE AGAINST ALIEN JEW-ISH IMMIGRATION INTO BRITAIN. . . . .

Wed, March 1st.	Netherwood Street,	at 8 p.m.
Sun, March 5th.	Parliament Hill Fields,	at 3 p.m.
„ „ „	Southill Park, N.	at 8 p.m.
Sat, March 11th.	Netherwood Street,	at 8 p.m.

Hear. . .

Mick Clarke, Morgan, Cooper, Hatton and other well known British Union speakers. . .

THEN JOIN BRITISH UNION at :-
16, Belsize Lane, N.W.

AND HELP STOP the FLOOD of ALIENS INTO BRITAIN. . . . . . .

Published by British Union, 16, Belsize Lane. Printed by A. E. Baker & Co. (Printers) Ltd. T.U. N.W

If the above is now considered racist then what of the 'Rivers of Blood' speech made by the late Enoch Powell?

John Enoch Powell, MBE politician, was born in Birmingham on 16th June 1912 and Died on 8th February 1998. His Rivers of Blood speech caused controversy back in April 1968 and continues to inflame many today. But he was supported in his outspoken views by many hundreds of thousands.

Now, many years on, has Britain become an easy touch for asylum seekers? With benefits given out to those seeking sanctuary in Britain it seems to have become an easy option for those running from invisible enemies. Free mobile telephones, food vouchers (which have been sold by asylum seekers for cash) and extra benefits above the norm, has this made Britain a first class stop?

The Rt. Hon.
J. ENOCH POWELL, M.B.E.
M.P. for Wolverhampton South-West

HOUSE OF COMMONS
LONDON S.W.1

30 TETTENHALL ROAD
WOLVERHAMPTON
TELEPHONE 24831

"Was Enoch Powell right or wrong??"

Signed business card from Enoch Powell

Crimes That Live On

Extracts from the Rivers of Blood speech
(Some startling predictions made in 1968)

"Like the Roman, I see the River Tiber foaming with much blood."

"A week or two ago I fell into conversation with a constituent, a middle-aged, quite ordinary working man employed in one of our nationalised industries. After a sentence or two about the weather, he suddenly said: *"If I had the money to go, I wouldn't stay in this country."* I made some deprecatory reply to the effect that even this government wouldn't last for ever; but he took no notice, and continued: *"I have three children, all of them been through grammar school and two of them married now, with family. I shan't be satisfied till I have seen them all settled overseas. In this country in 15 or 20 years' time the black man will have the whip hand over the white man."*

I can already hear the chorus of execration. How dare I say such a horrible thing? How dare I stir up trouble and inflame feelings by repeating such a conversation? The answer is that I do not have the right not to do so.

Here is a decent, ordinary fellow Englishman, who in broad daylight in my own town says to me, his Member of Parliament, that his country will not be worth living in for his children. I simply do not have the right to shrug my shoulders and think about something else. What he is saying, thousands and hundreds of thousands are saying and thinking - not throughout Great Britain, perhaps, but in the areas that are already undergoing the total transformation to which there is no parallel in a thousand years of English history.

In 15 or 20 years, on present trends, there will be in this country three and a half million Commonwealth immigrants and their descendants. That is not my figure. That is the official figure given to parliament by the spokesman of the Registrar General's Office. There is no comparable official figure for the year 2000, but it must be in the region of five to seven million, approximately one-tenth of the whole population, and approaching that of Greater London. Of course, it will not be evenly distributed from Margate to Aberystwyth and from Penzance to Aberdeen.

Whole areas, towns and parts of towns across England will be occupied by sections of the immigrant and immigrant-descended population."

"Already, by 1985 the native-born would constitute the majority. It is this fact which creates the extreme urgency of action now, of just that kind of action which is hardest for politicians to take, action where the difficulties lie in the present but the evils to be prevented or minimised lie several parliaments ahead."

"It almost passes belief that at this moment 20 or 30 additional immigrant children are arriving from overseas in Wolverhampton alone every week - and that means 15 or 20 additional families a decade or two hence. Those whom the gods wish to destroy, they first make mad. We must be mad, literally mad, as a nation to be permitting the annual inflow of some 50,000 dependants, who are for the most part the material of the future growth of the immigrant-descended population. It is like watching a nation busily engaged in heaping up its own funeral pyre."

"On the contrary, even at the present admission rate of only 5,000 a year by voucher, there is sufficient for a further 25,000 dependants per annum ad infinitum, without taking into account the huge reservoir of existing relations in this country – and I am making no allowance at all for fraudulent entry."

"Hence the urgency of implementing now the second element of the Conservative Party's policy: the encouragement of re-emigration." **(Is this comparable to Hitler's Final Solution?)**

"The Commonwealth immigrant came to Britain as a full citizen, to a country which knew no discrimination between one citizen and another, and he entered instantly into the possession of the rights of every citizen, from the vote to free treatment under the National Health Service."

"But while, to the immigrant, entry to this country was admission to privileges and opportunities eagerly sought, the impact upon the existing population was very different. For reasons which they could not comprehend, and in pursuance of a decision by default, on which they were never consulted, they found themselves made strangers in their own country."

"They found their wives unable to obtain hospital beds in

childbirth, their children unable to obtain school places, their homes and neighbourhoods changed beyond recognition, their plans and prospects for the future defeated; at work they found that employers hesitated to apply to the immigrant worker the standards of discipline and competence required of the native-born worker; they began to hear, as time went by, more and more voices which told them that they were now the unwanted. They now learn that a one way privilege is to be established by act of parliament; a law which cannot, and is not intended to, operate to protect them or redress their grievances is to be enacted to give the stranger, the disgruntled and the agent-provocateur the power to pillory them for their private actions."

"The sense of being a persecuted minority which is growing among ordinary English people in the areas of the country which are affected is something that those without direct experience can hardly imagine. I am going to allow just one of those hundreds of people to speak for me:"

"Eight years ago in a respectable street in Wolverhampton a house was sold to a negro. Now only one white (a woman old-age pensioner) lives there. This is her story. She lost her husband and both her sons in the war. So she turned her seven-roomed house, her only asset, into a boarding house. She worked hard and did well, paid off her mortgage and began to put something by for her old age. Then the immigrants moved in. With growing fear, she saw one house after another taken over. The quiet street became a place of noise and confusion. Regretfully, her white tenants moved out. The day after the last one left, she was awakened at 7am by two negroes who wanted to use her phone to contact their employer. When she refused, as she would have refused any stranger at such an hour, she was abused and feared she would have been attacked but for the chain on her door. Immigrant families have tried to rent rooms in her house, but she always refused. Her little store of money went, and after paying rates, she has less than £2 per week. She went to apply for a rate reduction and was seen by a young girl, who on hearing she had a seven-roomed house, suggested she should let part of it. When she said the only people she could get were negroes, the girl said, 'Racial prejudice won't get you anywhere in this country.' So she went home.

Crime Through Time

The telephone is her lifeline. Her family pay the bill, and help her out as best they can. Immigrants have offered to buy her house – at a price which the prospective landlord would be able to recover from his tenants in weeks, or at most a few months. She is becoming afraid to go out. Windows are broken. She finds excreta pushed through her letter box. When she goes to the shops, she is followed by children, charming, wide-grinning piccaninnies. They cannot speak English, but one word they know. 'Racialist', they chant. When the new Race Relations Bill is passed, this woman is convinced she will go to prison. And is she so wrong? I begin to wonder"

"The cloud no bigger than a man's hand, that can so rapidly overcast the sky, has been visible recently in Wolverhampton and has shown signs of spreading quickly. The words I am about to use, verbatim as they appeared in the local press on 17 February, are not mine, but those of a Labour Member of Parliament who is a minister in the present government." *"The Sikh communities' campaign to maintain customs inappropriate in Britain is much to be regretted. Working in Britain, particularly in the public services, they should be prepared to accept the terms and conditions of their employment. To claim special communal rights (or should they say rites?) leads to a dangerous fragmentation within society. This communalism is a canker; whether practised by one colour or another it is to be strongly condemned."* All credit to John Stonehouse for having had the insight to perceive that, and the courage to say it. "As I look ahead, I am filled with foreboding; like the Roman, I seem to see "the River Tiber foaming with much blood". That tragic and intractable phenomenon, which we watch with horror on the other side of the Atlantic but which there is interwoven with the history and existence of the States itself, is coming upon us here by our own volition and our own neglect. Indeed, it has all but come. In numerical terms, it will be of American proportions long before the end of the century. Only resolute and urgent action will avert it even now. Whether there will be the public will to demand and obtain that action, I do not know. All I know is that to see, and not to speak, would be the great betrayal."

Original source: the Sterling Times web site –
http://www.sterlingtimes.org/textriversofblood.htm

13

Finally

We would like to thank you for your involvement by showing an interest in the exhibits on display in the museum. By your reading this book or even taking a peek or two at the photos, including mine , I know that you will have gained something very special from it all.

Maybe some of you have found certain items have embarrassed you or for some of you they may have titillated and amused you, whichever …remember we are only human - full of frailties and weakness. Temptations are sometimes too great to resist!

The museum, as already pointed out, has no affiliation with any political organisation and does not hold any political, religious or moralistic views. We represent the human race and for that we do not apologise. Now look on the next page to see a really sexy man…well I think so!

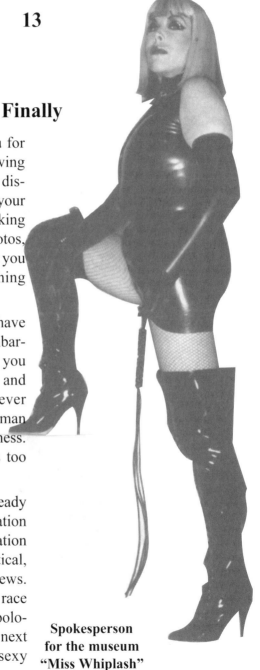

Spokesperson for the museum "Miss Whiplash"

Crime Through Time

The Right Honourable Jack Straw, MP, Minister

Signed photo as on display in the museum

Sometimes, when you're in a position of authority, your family, too, have to be ambassadors for what you do. When Jack Straw, MP, was the home secretary for the home states in the UK he suffered some embarrassing times. After all, here was a man who had to uphold the law, sadly his family, often, let him down.

The brother of Jack Straw was found guilty of an indecent assault on a 16-year-old girl. William Straw, 48, of Bramcote, in Nottingham, England, was placed on the sex offenders' register for the five years. Straw had denied the charge at Nottingham magistrates' court. But stipendiary magistrate Peter Nettle found him guilty of assaulting the girl at her home and fined him £750 and £275 costs.

William Straw, Jack Straw's son, was cautioned for supplying undercover journalists in a pub with cannabis. (When Jack Straw was home secretary he opposed the reclassification of cannabis from 'B' to the less serious 'C'. Amazing though, when David Blunkett replaced him the drug was reclassified to 'C' class?)

Finally

The Night Stalker's Curse

Some self-styled Satanists engage in criminal activities, ranging from paedophile acts and animal mutilation to murder, and their crimes conform to their self-invented ideologies. It is in this category of Satanism that most ritualistic crimes are placed; satanic ritual abuse is often mistaken for a form of sexual sadism or serial murder.

A classic example of a self-styled Satanist is Richard Ramirez, dubbed "The Night Stalker", who in 1985 terrorised Los Angeles by breaking into people's homes, raping, torturing, mutilating, and murdering his victims, and, most notably, forcing them to declare their love for Satan.

In the spring and summer of 1985, Ramirez committed over twenty attacks. In 1989, Ramirez was found guilty on 13 counts of murder and, in a famous gesture during the trial, raised his hand with a pentagram on it and said, "Hail Satan." Currently awaiting execution at San Quentin prison, he continues to be completely devoted to Satan.

Ramirez was, reportedly, led into his obsession with the occult and ritual murder through rock groups like AC/DC. A schoolmate reported that it was their song 'Night Prowler' that particularly seemed to affect Ramirez.

On the record cover for 'Highway to Hell', the album in which 'Night Prowler' appears, the singer of the song wears a pentagram around his neck. The most common of satanic symbols, it became Ramirez's calling card, appearing on the walls of his victims' homes and sometimes on the victim.

WARNING – DO NOT TOUCH THE NEXT PAGE!!!!

N
I S
G T
H A
T L
K
E
R

**13
MURDERS
SATANIST
OCCULTIST
RITUALS
666**

Ramirez and his Satanic symbol…what a show off.

Above, proof that what follows on the next page is not a stunt. Above, Ramirez, is showing off what he's had tattooed onto the palm of his left hand, a pentagram with '666' inscribed beneath it.

The item on the next page is a copy of an exhibit that is on display in the museum, not actual size, as supplied directly from Richard Ramirez, the Night Stalker.

He drew around his own hand, when viewing it you will see that to the left of his hand tracing he has written, 'Evil Hands are Happy Hands', and underneath the drawing you will see that he has, very kindly, signed it, 'Night Stalker Richard Ramirez'.

People that have placed their palm up against this drawing, over the page, have all suffered bad luck in various degrees including Richard Lunn, Webmaster of the Crime Through Time web site. After Richard, for a laugh, placed his palm on the original drawing, in the museum, he drove off in his nice shiny BMW, a few minutes later the car was written off and he was lucky to be alive.

Please don't be tempted to lay your palm against the drawing! The museum and the publisher of this book will not accept any responsibility for the consequences, you have been warned!

Finally

WARNING – DO NOT TOUCH!!!

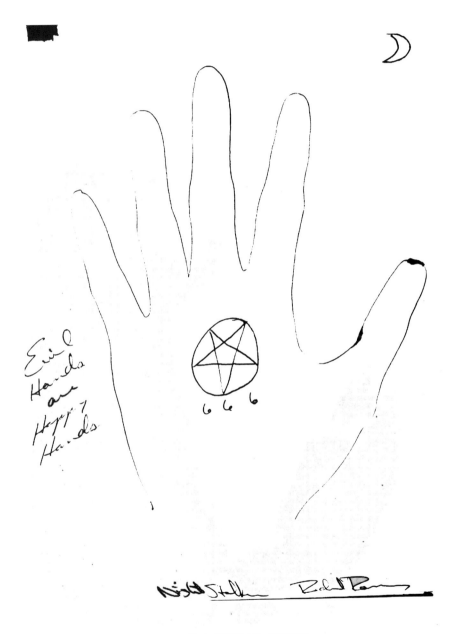

'NOT ACTUAL SIZE'
Authentic hand print sent by Richard Ramirez in his correspondence to Andy Jones of Crime Through Time.

Crime Through Time

2,800 People Murdered

"The American elites can talk about honour and creativity until the cows come home, but it's not going to be like the Iraq shooting fish in a barrel situation, like they did when they destroyed Iraq in 1991. Frankly, part of me says - even though everything since September 11 has been a nightmare - 'you know what, we deserve the problem on our hands because some things Bin Laden says are true'. One of the things he said on that last tape was that 'until we live in security, you're not going to live in security', and there is a certain amount of rightness in that. Why should Americans go on with their lives as normal, worrying about calories and hair loss, while other people are worrying about where they are going to get their next piece of bread? Why should we go on merrily with our lives while so much of the world is suffering, and suffering incidentally not with us merely as bystanders, but with us as the indirect and direct perpetrators." **Norman Finklestein**

"Israeli tanks and tracked vehicles also enter to wreak havoc in Palestine, in Jenin, Ramallah, Rafah, Beit Jala, and other Islamic areas and we hear no voices raised or moves made."
Bin Laden

$25,000,000 Reward

"I wish to declare that if America used chemical or nuclear weapons against us then we may retort with chemical and nuclear weapons. We have the weapons as a deterrent." Bin Laden

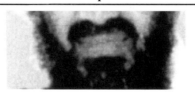

Dead or Alive!

"Hundreds of thousands of people, young and old, were killed in the farthest point on earth in Japan." Bin Laden

Finally

Some Museum Exhibits

Above, Charles Bronson's glasses & pocket watch from the Kray brothers
Right, Close up of watch inscription - note it is in Bronson's old name 'Mick.'

Left, Roy Shaw's title winning belt. Right, close up - British Heavyweight Champ.

14

Visiting The Museum

Where is it? The museum is based in Newent, Gloucestershire, England. When you approach Newent, simply follow the brown 'Crime Through Time' tourist information signs.

Car Parking? All cars and coaches can easily be accommodated in the town's main car park or at St Mary's Church car park. Disabled drivers should drive directly to the museum where direct parking will be arranged. (Must be registered disabled, displaying blue badge.) All car parking is at a convenient walking distance.

Opening Times? Open all year round. Weekends only during the winter season, excluding Christmas Day, Boxing Day and New Year's Day. Open daily from 10am to 5pm.

Special Corporate Days and Evening Visits? These can be arranged for parties of 20 or more by prior arrangement.

Are Children Allowed Entry? Children are allowed in under the supervision of adults or their guardians and must, at all times, be under strict supervision by an adult. There are warning signs advising that certain displays might not be suitable for children and therefore it is up to the child's guardian to make such a decision, thereafter the museum accepts no responsibility.

Can I Telephone or Fax The Museum? Yes, our telephone number if phoning from the UK is: 01531 – 821888. Our Fax number is: 01531 – 821238.

Disabled Facilities? Car Parking is as described above. Due to the layout of this Victorian building, access at times can be restrictive. We promise to help and assist as best we can.

Visiting The Museum

Toilet Facilities? Yes, there are toilet and washbasin facilities.

Have you a web site? www.crimethroughtime.com

Can I send an email to the museum?

andy@crimethroughtime.com

or alternatively use the link directly from the web site.

Newent is a market town and is eight miles from Gloucester, and has hot springs.

Why not spend a few days around Newent

The Shambles, Newent. A delightful museum of Victorian life, set out as a complete town of shops, cottages, and houses in a maze of cobbled streets and alleyways with even a tiny chapel and cottage garden all recreating the life and atmosphere as it would have been in Victorian times. Gift shop, teas and light lunches. The Shambles Museum, Church Street, Newent, Glos. GL18 1PP. Tel: 01531 822144 Opening Tuesday to Sunday and Bank Holiday Mondays 10am - 6.00pm. Last admission 5.00pm. Admission: Adults £3.25 Child £1.95 O.A.P. £2.85

The National Birds of Prey Centre started in 1967 as the Falconry Centre and was founded by Phillip Glasier and since then the centre has grown from a private collection of twelve birds to now being one of the largest collections in the world. Tel: (01531) 820286, Fax: (01531) 821389 Newent, Gloucestershire. GL18 1JJ Opening times: 10.30am - 5.30pm (dusk if earlier) 1st February to 30th November inclusive. Admission: Adult £4.25, Child 4-15 years £2.25 (Under 4's free) Family ticket (2+2) £11.50. Special Group Rates

Three Choirs Vineyard & Restaurant Set in 65 acres of rolling Gloucestershire is everything you need for a great family day out. Choose from self-guided tours of the winery and video, the story of wine making, vineyard walks, free wine tasting, well stocked shop and excellent restaurant. Open 7 days a week 10.00-17.00 Phone: 01531 890223.

Staying in Newent – Highly recommended by the author of this book is The George Hotel on Church Street. They do a full English breakfast and have extensive bar & restaurant menu available. En-suite available. From: single £25, double £35, family £50. Church

Street, Newent, Glos, GL18 1PO. Tel: 01531 820203. Prices quoted are correct at time of going to press.

Dymock Woods on the outskirts of Newent is well known each spring for the carpets of wild daffodils. Dymock was also the home of the Dymock Poets - Lascelles Abercrombe, Rupert Brook, John Drinkwater, Wilfred Gibson, Edward Thomas, and American poet Robert Frost. Robert Frost left America with his family in 1913 and rented a cottage near the home of the Dymock Poets. He eventually returned to America, and wrote a poem specifically for the inauguration of President Kennedy.

May Hill, three miles to the southwest of Newent lies May Hill (National Trust Land). The hill rises to over 900ft. The conifers on top of the hill were planted to commemorate the Golden Jubilee of Queen Victoria. The magnificent view from the top of May Hill stretches over Gloucestershire and extends to Bristol. On a clear day, May Hill itself can be clearly seen from over 45 miles from the north, and from Dundry 50 miles to the south, easily identifiable by the clump of trees on its summit.

Newent Golf Club, Coldharbour Lane, Newent, Gloucestershire, GL18 1DJ. Also has six twin and two family lodges available. All fitted to a very high standard. All en suites with remote control television, hairdryers and hospitality trays. Each lodge has its own entrance on to a landscaped courtyard with trellised seating areas to relax and enjoy the peace and quiet. Full breakfast is served in the clubhouse. Telephone: 01531 820478 Fax: 01531 820478.

Church Farm Guest House, Bed & Breakfast, Church Farm, Kilcot, Newent, Gloucestershire, GL18 1PD Phone: +44 (0) 1989 720255, Fax: +44 (0) 1989 720255

The Granary Farm House, Lower House Farm, Kempley, Dymock, Newent, Gloucestershire, GL18 2BS Phone: +44 (0) 1531 890301, Fax: +44 (0) 1531 890301

Tourist Information Centre can provide you with all the information you need, telephone +44 (0) 1531 822468.

www.crimethroughtime.com

Visiting The Museum

Andy Jones – Owner and Curator of the museum

"Being the founder, curator and owner of a crime museum brings with it the job of 'confidante' to a great many, so say, infamous and notorious characters and movements ("purportedly"), it can be at times a potentially dangerous industry to become involved in and with. Rather like the Canadian Mounties (Mounted Police), I always get my man, but along with the territory comes the added element of danger."

I would like to says thanks the following people for helping make the museum a success:

Very Extra Special Thanks

It is particularly with this in mind that firstly give a special thanks to my always loving, beautiful, patient and dear wife, Nicola - mother to four of my six wonderful children, Dean, Luke, Kirsty, Tasmin, Ross and Isabel.

In dealing with such great many, so say, allegedly undesirable characters, as well as the infamous and notorious, I do not even confide on such matters with my wife. In the course of my search for ever more desirable exhibits, this quest has taken me far and wide around the world, which has been, at times, difficult for Nicola to come to terms with some of my turmoil, planning battles and potentially worrying moments. The buck, as they say, stops with me. Nicola plays no part whatsoever in either the collecting side, research or otherwise. (With four children to look after, that's time consuming enough, which I thank her for.)

Very Special Thanks

To a great many friends and participants that include: Charles Bronson, Joey Pyle, Freddie Foreman, Tony Lambrianou, Charlie Richardson, Reg Kray, Roy Shaw, Bruce Reynolds, Nick Reynolds, Bill Murray, Dave Courtney (and his wife Jenny), Bernie Davies and all the lads from the Welsh Valleys, Harry Marsden and the all the chaps Up North from the legendary die hard North East of England, James Crosbie, John 'Alfie' Lodge, The Swellbellys, Kate Kray, Stewart Evans, Ronnie Biggs, Mike Biggs, Dave Ford, Paddy Hills, Terry Elcock, Johnny Melfah, Miff and Garrison Damn, Flanagan, Frankie Fraser, Rich Grayston, Mick Gallagher, Jock Fraser, PJ Maguire, Gary Mills, Tony Poole, John Pitman, Chris Read, Alan Parker, Jamie Saysall, Adam Hatch, Kenny Noye, Reece Huxford, Jan Lamb, Richard Lunn (webmaster), Paul Duncliffe, Piers Hernu of the Front magazine, James Nicholson, Martin Brunt and Sky News, Paul Bridgeman, Ray Williams, Animaland crew, Gary and Jenny Lee, Ross, Saira & Sami, Demob and all those that I am unable to mention by virtue of them still being active on the business fronts…you all know who you are!!! And to all of those that have asked to remain anonymous.

Crime Through Time

Special Thanks

To all the allegedly, so say, famous, infamous and notorious movements that have contributed in some form or other, including the KKK, Black Panther Party, National Front, Combat 18, Hells Angels, Oswald Mosley's Black Shirts/BUF and Football Hooligans, my Chinese, Indian, Black, Jewish friends and acquaintances.

A Great Big Thank you to

The Crime Through Time part-time staff of Noel, Griff, Jenny and Dean. (Glad you're in the front line to receive the public and not me??) And the many people in the beautiful town of Newent that have made me feel welcome since my arrival in August 1998.

Particular Thanks

To fellow collectors in America and here in the UK, to include in particular: Keith Beaumont, Phil Froom, Stewart Evans, Alan Parker, Arthur (America), Ken (America), Paolo (America) and all those that wish to remain anonymous...too many to mention.

Special mention to the local drinking dens in Newent town

Newent Circle Club, George Hotel, Black Dog pub and the King's Arms and The Red Lion and all those that frequent them.

Grateful Thanks

My in-laws....Mike and Eve, brothers and brother-in-law.

Without You I Wouldn't be here Thanks

My mum and dad...Ron and Margaret.

And a Final Thanks

To Steve Richards (Investigative Author) and Sharon Anderson (Artistic Director) of Mirage Publishing who kindly chose to publish and heavily participate in piecing this book together.

Kind regards and best wishes,
Andy Jones

Founder, Curator and Owner of Crime Through Time Museum

http://www.crimethroughtime.com

About The Author

P
A
N
T
O
M
I
M
E

G
A
N
G
S
T
E
R

Bad Boy Richards

The, so say, controversial figure of Stephen Richards has had regular run-ins with the law and order brigade, although mostly in bizarre circumstances!

He was arrested along with two female researchers, as a result of research he was doing into an investigative consumer book (*Public Consumer Enemy*). After he and his researchers were bailed time and time again, eventually police action was dropped. Food and drinks companies had complained when he got to too close to the truth!

Not content with arresting Richards, the police seized a computer and computer discs in the hope of finding out what research he had done into finding out the identity of a police informant turned gangland killer. (Relating to murdered northern hard man and underworld figure, Viv Graham.) Richards has written four books relating to gangland activities involving the late Mr Graham and numerous other members of the criminal fraternity. So well respected is Richards that he successfully convinced Paul 'Gazza' Gascoigne to write a foreword to one of the 'Viv' books.

Being involved in the world of criminals has had drawbacks for Richards. Twice, he has been blackmailed, once by a prominent underworld figure and once by a world champion martial arts fighter...both threatened to reveal certain aspects of Richards' background. One demanded that Richards stop writing about him in books whilst the other demanded money... thugs!!!

> **"To go to the police would lose me credibility within the underworld fraternity I deal with, day in, day out. I can't very well promote underworld figures and then when I get a few problems go running to the police."**
> **Richards on being blackmailed twice**

All the grisly details and names are expected to appear in a forthcoming book he is working on called, *Sex, Drugs and the Stamp Scam*, the hardback book is due for release in 2003.

Frozen Genius

Richards is dyslexic, he calls this the affliction of a 'frozen genius'.

> **"It's rather like being a six-fingered typist on LSD."**
> **Richards on his dyslexia**

He puts this dyslexic condition down to being forced to write with his right hand in a school system geared up for 'right-handers only', when in fact he was a natural left-hander! Now, just about ambidextrous, in everything but handwriting, he has come to terms with it. His writing style, he calls 'Puritanical' – warts and all, which means he jealously guards his mistakes as his own and says, "All mistakes have a subliminal meaning, the frozen genius within is trying to speak through the dyslexic's hand."

Aggravated at the lack of knowledge the public display about dyslexia he dispensed with proofreaders and put his work out as it was written...to the chagrin of the media and the press! Not revealing, until very recently, his condition, he hoped to be accepted for his unique writing style. Now, just about, conforming to the constraints, as he calls them, of modern grammar he has not accepted the misnomer the public have equated with dyslexia... "Being dyslexic," Richards says, "...does not mean you are an idiot!"

www.bronsonmania.com/SteveRichards.html

About The Author

WANTED . . NEW VIV

Movie-maker seeks hardman lookalike

By CAROLINE SMITH

TOP movie stars are being lined up to appear in a film about murdered North hardman Viv Graham.

Actors Pete Postlethwaite, Michael Caine and Ray Winstone are to be offered roles in the movie which will hit the big screen next year.

And unknown Tynesiders are being invited to audition for the part of ex-heavyweight boxer Viv, who was gunned down in a gangland killing in 1993.

Scriptwriter and producer Steve Richards said: "It will have to be someone who looks reasonably similar to Viv, but it doesn't have to be a 19-stone, hard-as-nails hulk.

"They don't need any acting experience but they will need to have knowledge of Viv.

"Part of the screen test will involve questions about him and they will be asked to react to how they think Viv would have done. We are looking for someone with presence . . . it could just be down to a shifty set of eyes!

"This is quite unique in that I am not going to fully write the script until we have found the central character and we can incorporate their traits."

KILLER

Viv, 34, who ran security at pubs and clubs throughout Tyneside, was shot on New Year's Eve in 1993 as he walked to

HAPPY . . . Graham show

COPS KNOW WHO KILLED VIV, CLAIMS AUTHOR

AN underworld expert has claimed that police know who murdered North hardman Viv Graham but will...

...author Steve Richards is set to name suspects.

Charity-bash publisher hits back over cash

By GUY ANDERSON
Investigative reporter
guy.anderson@nentwest-press.co.uk

A PUBLISHER who represents underworld writers has angrily denied claims that cash raised for a children's charity vanished.

Mirage publishing boss Steve Richards organised a bash at the Barnes Hotel, Sunderland, in June to publicise the biography of local professional fighter Ian Freeman.

Cash raised during the evening went towards Bronson's Children a charity set up by notorious prisoner Charles Bronson to fund a search for the body of Keith Bennett, who was murdered by Myra Hindley and Ian Brady.

But previous claims that £1,500 was raised on the night - and that the money disappeared - have been denied by Mr Richards.

The Gateshead-based publisher – who represents Bronson's Children – produced bank statements showing that £241 was deposited following the Barnes book launch.

Mr Richards said: "it is claimed that £1,500 was raised during the book launch and that is just not the case.

"In fact, I have bank statements to prove that just £241 was raised and that money was paid into the Bronson's

Children Account."

The money was raised from the 6 guests at the launch, and the proceeds world figure Dave Courtney.

On allegations that the money dis peared, Mr Richards added: "On w that night in front of 60 people, I writer money was emptied from the box and to the table on the stage. The audi ...

...led a perfect opportunity film, with the working Viv, in the brainchild of Richards, who has writ woke on Viv Graham. He the script and is the pro- d an unknown actor to he part of 18-stone heavyweight Viv. e thought picking

he approached me. I knew he would be perfect. I think he's on the stepping stones to a great future and I'm pleased we've got hold of him first. He's going to be huge."

The film is to have strong North East connections, with locations such as the Quayside and Tyne Bridge featuring strongly.

Mr Richards said: "North East films ...

Steve has already got Ray Winstone lined up for a smaller part, and says he is hoping to get Ant and Dec involved as brothers of a gangster family.

He also hinted that Michael Caine might have a cameo role, saying "I can't say what it is, but let's just say there's a Get Carter connection with this actor and he's very famous."

Another virtual unknown, Andrew Hutt, has been cast as Viv's rival, Lee Duffy. Andrew has had roles in films

lot of pressure and I'm representing the region, but I know I can do this."

Steve is hoping to attract a big name to direct the film too. He has approached North East-born Ridley Scott, famous for the Oscar-winning Gladiator, as well as local man Mike Figgis who directed blockbusters such as Leaving Las Vegas.

Other names Mike Hodges, who made Get Carter, which was also set in the Tyneside area.

Legends of his reached mythical

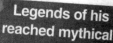

FORMER pub and club doorman Viv Graham was gunned down on New Year's Eve, 1993, in a gangland killing.

The 17-stone hardman was shot twice with a revolver as he left the Queen's Head pub in Wallsend.

crawled 30 yards before collapsing outside a newsagents.

He was found by fellow bouncer Terry Scott. At Graham's inquest, Scott said: "He was lying in the gutter facing me. As our eyes met, I knew it was serious. He kept saying 'I'm going. I'm going, as I held his head."

Police found a wad of money totalling £1,400 in his pockets.

An inquiry was launched and 60 officers took 350 statements, interviewed more than 1,000 people and visited over 500 homes. His family then offered a £100,000 reward for information leading to the arrest.

But despite this the mur...

Ram raiding: the North crime

SMASH

By MATT McKENZIE

THREE high-powered cars smash through the entrance to a shopping centre in a cloud of shattered glass.

Within seconds, a luxury sports car is driven 100 yards along the mall before ramming the front window of an electrical store.

A gang of men jump out and escape with more than £20,000 worth of equipment and within seconds they are nowhere to be seen.

This is not a scene from a Hollywood blockbuster but a description of one of the North's most infamous crimes.

And the amazing thing about this

And Finally...

Just as you thought the book was at an end, here is a little snippet to keep you going for a few minutes.

Some never before revealed information pertaining to Fred West is that he used to frequent a brothel that was once housed above the now closed 'Café Rendezvous', in Newent town, only a stone's throw away from the museum and only a couple of doors away from Newent's popular drinking den, the Circle Club. It was a known fact that Fred West had an insatiable appetite for sex.

As Fred West said, "It will all come out in time," and that is a sure fact given that Fred and Rose West could not have acted alone in what they did.

A great many people appear to have been let off the hook when Fred and his brother, John, conveniently hung themselves. No doubt the police breathed a sigh of relief and could close the investigation and stamp it as 'Finalised – case solved'. This is far from the end and given that certain other information does surface it will result in further prosecutions of those who escaped by the skin of their teeth!

Although Andy Jones knows the goings on relating to certain aspects of the Wests private life he would like to make it clear that he would not infringe on the family of Fred's sister, Gwen, who he knows quite well. Andy Jones also wishes to make it known that he would not cause any upset to the family of Fred's sister, they are well-respected people. They went through a lot of disgraceful hounding and rumour mongering at the time of the case when in fact they are a very warm and friendly family.

The next page features Jamie Theakston, radio personality; he too seems to have an insatiable appetite for sex. Dumped by his girlfriend he found solace in dungeon sex. If he'd played his cards right he could have made such publicity work for him!

And Finally...

INDEX

Index

Crime Through Time

Index

Crime Through Time

Index

Crime Through Time

Index

Books By The Author And Others

The Successful trilogy in the 'Viv' series of books starts with:

'Viv (Graham) – 'Simply the Best' **(Vol.1)** True Crime
*True Crime paperback 242 pages *Foreword by Gazza *£7.99
*ISBN No: 1–902578-00–7 *Mono Stills by Stephen Richards

New Year's Eve 1993, hard man and notorious underworld figure Viv Graham's life climaxes in a violent end. The Geordie Mafia is unfolded. Gripping catalogue of Murders, Kneecappings, Shootings, Stabbings, Glassings, Drug Dealing, Protection Rackets, Blackmailing, Robberies, Torturing and more. Feared gangland reprisals abruptly end academic views. Hitman based in Manchester - his professional opinion on the gangland assassination of Viv. Manchester v Newcastle - Super City comparisons. Riots across the North East of England, eventually dominoes throughout the UK. Graphic details of Viv's murder. The funeral visited by some of Tenerife's underworld. Viv's involvement with celebrities Tim Healy and Gazza. Gazza – "My comments on Viv." Viv - Tyneside's own 4th Emergency Service.

'Viv – and the Geordie Mafia' (Vol. 2) True Crime
*340 pages *World-wide Best Seller   *Mono stills   *RRP £9.99
*ISBN No: 1-902578-01-5 by Stephen Richards

Police arrest the author and two researchers, seizing computer & disks in the hope of catching the killers. Blackpool's Candy Rock Resort underworld revealed & explored - Drug Dealing, Kidnapping, a beach murder and the club doorman scene. Convicted Beach murderer alleges Viv was his alibi. Murders, Kneecappings, Shootings, Drug Dealing, Protection Rackets, Torturing and Scams. Liverpool's club doormen scene compared to Newcastle's. Viv's three lovers fight over insurance payouts. Insurers describe his death as 'self inflicted'. Viv's three lovers reveal intimate details, love 'em and leave 'em, not likely they became his possessions! The truth! When Reg Kray visited Newcastle, was he kicked out like they say – original 'Geordie Mafia' member reveals all? Plier's torturer Paddy Conroy claims jury-rigging helped convict him. Exclusive. Viv's mother and father interviewed. Viv's murder suspect gives an exclusive interview! Tyneside's Pubs 'n' Clubs guide.

Books By The Author And Others

'Viv (Graham) – The Final Chapter' (Vol. 3) True Crime
*288 pages *World-wide Best Seller   *16 pages Mono stills *RRP £8.99
*ISBN No: 1-902578-16-3 by Stephen Richards

The 3rd and final in the trilogy of successful true crime books that revolve around murdered hard man Viv Graham. £15m drugs swoop ends in police officers being suspended. Monarch of the underworld, Dave Courtney, exposes fake informants scam. Covers underworld activities in: Tyneside, Wearside, Teesside, Blackpool, Liverpool, Birmingham, London, Spain & more.

Featuring a full investigation into the killing of legendary Teesside hard man Lee Duffy, his life and his death, with underworld contributions.

Tyneside's club doorman turned businessman Stu Watson speaks for the very first time of the night Viv's gang wanted to kill him and of a running gun battle in a Tyneside housing estate with the Geordie Mafia.

Exclusive & Revealing interviews from the underworld and beyond: Phil Berriman, Ernie Bewick, Brian Cockerill, Paddy Conroy, Dave Courtney, Tommy & Lee Harrison, T, Harry Marsden, Terry Mitchell, Stephen Sayers, Lisa Stockell, Gary Ward, Stu Watson & more.

Chapters cover: Bent & Straight Coppers, Informants, Murders, Drug Smuggling, Gunfights, Punishment Beatings, Unsolved Murders, Blackmailing, Thugs, Muggers, Slashings, Murder Confessions, Russian Roulette, The Lancet Inquiry, Murderers Square Mile is "Evil" says author + More

Viv Graham & Lee Duffy's - Parallel Lives
*Hardback *ISBN: 1902578-20-1 *RRP £14.99 *Mono stills
Replaces the successful trilogy in the 'Viv' series of books:

'Viv (Graham) - 'Simply the Best' True Crime
'Viv - and the Geordie Mafia' (Vol. 2)
Viv (Graham) - The Final Chapter (Vol. 3)

Omnibus Limited Hardback Edition with updates.

Author: Stephen Richards
The phenomenally successful trilogy in the 'Viv' series of books are now bound in one hardback special limited abridged edition.

Books By The Author And Others

The series of books that outsold Catherine Cookson on Tyneside now has a cult following. On the instructions of the author, the paperbacks are not to be reprinted, your chance to own a unique book.

Viv Graham and Lee Duffy fiercely resented each other - their names stood for violence - both sworn enemies! Both ran parallel lives as pub and club enforcers raging their gangland turf wars with a fierce frenzy of brutality and unremitting cruelty!

Engaging each other in a vicious organised brawl would be the ultimate challenge! Warfare and combat would mean bloodshed and carnage - both men met brutal and violent deaths! Featuring updates on the £22m Freddie Knights murder trial, which led to two acquittals!

Ramraiders True Crime
*Paperback *16 Pages mono-stills *RRP was £7.99 now UK RRP £3.99
*Foreword by Freddie Foreman ISBN: 1-902578-10-4 *by Stephen Richards*

The 'Yellow Pages' ram raid gang. £100m ram raid gang escape totally undetected into Europe, the biggest and cleverest ram raid ever! Bizarre ram raids as well as the wacky and weird. Top ram raiders reveal all about the business. The ram raid phenomenon was a crime exported worldwide. Spectacular ram raids in the UK, Australia and New Zealand. Police were rendered impotent by the gang's ability to defeat them. £3.5m ram raid gang given a total of 33-years behind bars. Counter surveillance techniques, getaway routes explored, attempted murder— and more! Prison life uncovered with never before published photos smuggled out of UK prisons showing the true extent of this gang's power right under the noses of prison authorities — drink and drug parties within prison. Prison violence becomes a way of life for the gang that started a crime wave of ram raiding throughout the world — their own story.

'Birdman Opens His Mind'
*ISBN No: 1-902578-03-1. *RRP was £7.99 now £3.99 *Full of Bronson's colour hand drawn illustrations *Some Surprises & More. Hardback book.

Colour illustrated adult humour - hardback cover. Bronson's laughing all the way to the crematorium written and colour illustrated by the Poet from Hell. Get one if you can. In Charlie's own inimitable style and in his own words he will make you laugh. Don't get hooked up on the word 'poetry', 'humour' is the word - don't miss it! In limited supply, sure to become a collector's item. Edited *by Stephen Richards*

Books By The Author And Others

Charles Bronson – 'Sincerely Yours' – *Video Documentary* *Directed by Stephen Richards* *£15.99 *2¹/₂ hours ISBN: 1902578198 VHS Format

The one the UK government tried to ban. The one that Jack Straw took Steve Richards to court for. The one that got Richards a three-week prison sentence for. Exclusive footage and audio action never ever before seen or heard. Features: Joe Pyle; Snr., Lord Longford, Kenneth 'Panda' Anderson (the original Geordie Mafia), Andy Jones (owner of 'Crime Through Time Museum'), Tony Lambrianiou, Charlie's mother; Eira first time filmed interview, Loraine; Charlie's cousin, Ray Williams; long time civilian friend of 30+ years, Jan Lamb; 'The Sport' newspaper celebrity pinup, James Crosbie; Scotland's most prolific bank robber, John 'Alf' Lodge; Wales' answer to James Crosbie and that flash showbiz character Dave Courtney and 'Harley', Charlie's gangster dog. Audio of an actual prison hostage-taking situation involving Charlie! 'The Swellbellys' a contemporary punk band from Scotland perform a song for Bronson ('Caged'). Jim Dawkins, formerly 'Prison Officer Dawkins', used to guard Charlie in HM Prison Belmarsh!

See Bronson boxing in an unlicensed fight, watch a gun fall to the floor of the boxing ring out of someone's coat pocket, as one hell of a fight breaks out. A highly controversial documentary, worryingly, for the authorities. Can be ordered from any bookshop if you give them the ISBN number of 1902578198.

'Silent Scream' – The Charles Bronson Story
His own story in his own words – 'Autobiography'
*Serialised in national UK newspaper for five days. *16 pages of stills.
*ISBN: 1-902578-08-2. *RRP £15.99. *With Stephen Richards*

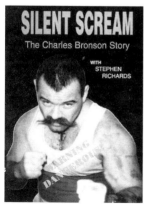

The silence has been broken with this best seller. The truth about Bronson's life and his ill treatment by the authorities in penal and mental establishments. He's had more porridge than Goldilocks and the three bears. He's taken more hostages inside of prison than any other UK prisoner. Holds many awards for his art and writing. Banned from the Guinness Book of Records - holds six world records for feats of strength and fitness. More prison rooftop protests than anyone living or dead. Violence, violence and more violence, inflicted on him by the prison service! In Bronson's own words find

Books By The Author And Others

out what makes him tick and explode. Hannibal Lecter is kids stuff compared to this real life action, full of sex and violence. Given a top review in UK's 'Front Magazine'. Bronson's story in his own words.

'PUBLIC consumer *ENEMY' Investigative Consumer 'The Amazing little A-Z Handbook of how to complain and Win!' *You, the consumer, are being ripped off *Paperback pocketbook *ISBN 1-902578-02-3 *RRP was £5.99 now £1.99 By Stephen Richards*

Police arrest author and his researchers for alleged deception after national food and drinks companies complain to the police about the amount of complaints they're receiving! Simply put it's THE complainer's bible. Don't join Internet companies who claim to complain for you, this book does it all for you, includes legal advice. Repays its RRP time and time again. A must-have for anyone whoever complains.

'LEGENDS' – By best selling authors: Charles Bronson & Stephen Richards True Crime *ISBN 1902578-11-2 *Hardback *100's of photographs *RRP £14.99   *300+ pages

Serialised in a national newspaper for four days. Banned by a national chain of bookshops but can be ordered from any Watersone's bookshop or www.amazon.co.uk. The OFFICIAL Charles Bronson guide to who's who in the underworld and beyond. Legends that Charlie feels deserve space in this A-Z guide of Criminals and those connected in some way to them. Includes a chapter from Manchester's Paul Massey. Short succinct write-ups. Bronson goes overboard in this book with a universal appeal. Nicknames leave little to the imagination: The Mummy, The Wolf Man, The Human Slug, Semtex Man, The Pie Man, The Wizard, Cannon Ball, Quasimodo, Voodoo Man, The Promoter and hundreds more – all real people. Legendary Scottish Bank Robber, James Crosbie - guest contributor for Scotland's chapter. Foreword by Joe Pyle Snr. Ireland isn't forgotten either. Icons are few Legends are many.

Books By The Author And Others

Looking at Life by the legendary Joe Pyle 'The Hood with a Heart'
*ISBN: 1-902578-09-0 *RRP was £8.99 now £3.99 *Full colour
photographs & Illustrations *Foreword by actor Ray Winstone
Edited by Stephen Richards

Take a moment to read this, please, and in doing so you'll help some terminally ill babies at the only hospice for babies in the UK. Some of the hardest men in the UK helped contribute towards this book - some of the softest hearted people you could ever wish to meet. Features inclusions by Gerry Adams the President of Sinn Fein, Sir Elton John, Sir Trevor McDonald, Richard Branson, Mohamed Al Fayed, Lulu, Roger Daltrey, Roy Shaw, Freddie Foreman, Dave Courtney, Tony Lambrianou, Charlie Richardson, Charlie Bronson, Johnny Nash, Frank Maloney and many, many more. Joe Pyle as featured on TV's 'Hard Bastards' and in Blake Publishing's 'Hard Bastards'.

'A Sting in the Tale' (Hardback)
*Only Biography authorised by STING *RRP £14.99
*ISBN: 1902578-13-9 *Mono Stills *Foreword by Sting

The only authorised Biography
Approved by Sting

An eye-wateringly funny book will guarantee to have you laughing and in stitches regardless of whether you're a Sting fan or not. Short succinct chapters show the bizarreness of what it's like to have such a world famous rock star as a friend. Written by Sting's closest friend for the past 38 years, the only book to be given Sting's blessing covering his life with the author from their schooldays right up to Sting's marriage to Trudy Styler. Serialised in News of the World, Sunday Mail's Night & Day mag book of the week, Top Review in the Independent on Sunday's Review mag, featured on Richard & Judy show, TV, Radio, Sunday Life (Belfast) - top review, Sunday Sun, Outlandos Web Site (Sting's fan club on the Web)

Books By The Author And Others

Solitary Fitness by Charles Bronson & Stephen Richards (Editor)
*ISBN: 1902578-1-20 *RRP £7.99 *See details on: www.solitaryfitness.com

Charles Bronson has served 28 years behind bars, 24 of those years have been in solitary confinement, yet in spite of this he remains supremely fit. What are the secrets to his phenomenal strength? Find out what this book can do for you and how you can become bigger, fitter and stronger when these super human strength secrets are unveiled. The mystery revealed of how his fitness is unmatched while on an extreme prison diet. Using the power and speed of his bare fist he can punch through bulletproof glass. With the might and force of his persuasively powerful legs he can kick in and bend solid steel cell doors. Prison sit-ups and press-ups champion and holder of six world records for his feats of strength. Vigorous exercise has built Bronson into a robust solitary athlete and an unbeatable force.

'Sex, Drugs & the Stamp Scam' True Crime Autobiography
*Due for release in November 2003 ISBN: 1-902578-15-5
*Mono Stills (Not for those with a weak heart) £14.99

How a gang masterminded what was said to be a multi-million pound stamp fraud right under the noses of the Post Office fraud investigators. Insignia (Royal Mail) are said to be losing £1M per day and may have to be taken over. This gang stopped the post office being privatised,it is said, on two occasions. The gang were eventually jailed, but not before they had a good run for their money!

"Nazi, Nazi, Nazi," was the ongoing chant that became louder and louder with each 'Nazi' that the children in the schoolyard were directing at a frightened looking boy seeking refuge by the locked door to the school building – England 1960's. "I'll kill you, you little bastard," the balding man said to the eight-year-old boy as he had his hands grasped around the boy's throat lifting him clear of the floor. As the boy's face turned blue and he made choking sounds he was dropped like piece of hot coal. One man's story of overcoming racial hatred, a turbulent and violent upbringing, the trauma of prison life, plots to blackmail him and his rise from the ashes of a wrecked and plundered life. A story too unbelievable to believe.

A very, very special true crime story from the man with the Golden Pen – acclaimed best selling investigative author and Underworld Expert Stephen Richards. Every word carrying part of Richards' soul, every comma and full stop bearing testament to his efforts. Full to overflowing with violence, sadness, nymphomaniacal romps, sexual fetishes so bizarre they nearly kill those taking part, lesbian romps, wife swapping, under-

Books By The Author And Others

world drug deals and ultimately the subject matter in question - 'Stamps'. A story of oppression, racism, hatred, neo-Nazis, love, deceit, crime and a soul-destroying end that will see you cry for those that could not. Hard hitting yet sensitive enough to have you share the pain of the characters within. Richards will not fail to light up your passions, fuel your anger and leave his mark in the depths of your mind for the rest of your life with this creation. Will probably be the best selling book of 2002, given the true crime content will be too unbelievable for you to believe it to be true!!!!!!!!!!!!!!!!!!!!!!!!!

All book titles and the 'Sincerely Yours' video can be ordered from any good bookstore, worldwide, by quoting the ISBN number. Don't take "NO" for an answer because they can order any of the current stock of titles in. (Not those listed under 'Future Titles' until the release date.) In the unusual case of difficulty you can order books by post directly from Book Traders (Address at the end.) or from the merchandise section of the following website **www.miragepublishing.com** (where credit cards are accepted) OR Send cheque or Postal Order (P+P free in the UK) Europe send payment drawn against UK bank or Euro Cheque or International Money order + 10% of order value for P+P. P+P for rest of the world send + 20% of order value. British Forces using BFPO address is postage free on any item. Always try your local bookstore, as we have accounts with all of the major bookstores (Waterstone's, Ottakers, HMV, Thins/Volumes, WH Smith, etc.) in the UK and our book wholesalers' export to 106 different countries. All prices are in £ Sterling.

UK PRISONERS 50% off Books only

Books By The Author And Others

Price List - Reminder

Viv (Graham) – 'Simply the Best (Vol.1)	£7.99
Viv – and the Geordie Mafia (Vol. 2)	£9.99
Viv (Graham) – The Final Chapter Vol.3	£8.99
Viv - Parallel Lives	£14.99
Ramraiders	£3.99
Birdman Opens His Mind - Charles Bronson	£3.99
Sincerely Yours (Video) Charles Bronson	£15.99 P & P add £2.00
Silent Scream (Bronson's own words)	£15.99
PUBLIC *consumer* ENEMY	£1.99
Legends	£14.99
Solitary Fitness	£7.99
Looking at Life Joe Pyle	£3.99
A Sting in the Tale	£14.99
Viv Graham Poster (A3 size – not shown in this book)	£1.99
'Bronson' Metal Pen	£1.00
'Bronson Bizarre Artwork Poster	£1.99

Make Cheques or PO Payable to BOOK TRADERS Total   £......

P+P for books/posters/pens/ is free in the UK. Europe
add 10% rest add 50%.

We <u>do not accept credit cards</u> when ordering direct.

Send your payment with order, delivery name and
address to:

BOOK TRADERS, PO Box 161, Gateshead, NE8 4WW, England

Pay by credit card on website

www.miragepublishing.com

Books can also be ordered from **www.amazon.co.uk**

**Our thanks to All the good bookshops that sell our
books particularly: Waterstone's and WH Smith**